CW01066537

The Universal Declaration of Human Rights:
A Commentary

The Universal Declaration of Human Rights: A Commentary

edited by

Asbjørn Eide, Gudmundur Alfredsson,
Göran Melander, Lars Adam Rehof and Allan Rosas,
with the collaboration of Theresa Swinehart

SCANDINAVIAN UNIVERSITY PRESS

Scandinavian University Press (Universitetsforlaget AS), 0608 Oslo 6
Distributed world-wide excluding Scandinavia by
Oxford University Press, Walton Street, Oxford OX2 6DP

London   New York   Toronto
Delhi   Bombay   Calcutta   Madras   Karachi
Kuala Lumpur   Singapore   Hong Kong   Tokyo
Nairobi   Dar es Salaam   Cape Town
Melbourne   Auckland

and associated companies in
Beirut   Berlin   Ibadan   Mexico City   Nicosia

Cover design: Ellen Larsen

© Universitetsforlaget AS 1992

British Library Cataloguing in Publication Data

Eide, Asbjørn
  Universal Declaration of Human Rights:
  Commentary
  I. Title
  323.4

ISBN 82-00-21339-0

Printed in Norway
Tangen Grafiske Senter AS, Drammen

Table of Contents

The Universal Declaration of Human Rights: How the Process Started

Jakob Th. Möller

Iceland

The history of the drafting of the Universal Declaration of Human Rights (UDHR) from the time the General Assembly, at its first session, on 11 December 1946, referred the matter to the Economic and Social Council (ECOSOC) for submission to the Commission on Human Rights (the Commission), until the proclamation of the Declaration by the General Assembly on 10 December 1948, spans only two years.[1]

At its first session (27 January to 10 February 1947) the Commission decided that the members of its Bureau (Mrs. Roosevelt, Mr. Chang and Mr. Malik), with the assistance of the Secretariat, should, as a drafting group, formulate a preliminary draft of the International Bill of Rights to be submitted to the Commission's second session. (The drafting group was also to study an Australian proposal for the establishment of an International Court of Human Rights). The Commission offered the following guidance to the drafting group: "That the Bill should be acceptable to all Members of the United Nations; that it should be short, simple, easy to understand and expressive." On 24 March

---

[1] During the San Francisco Conference the representatives of Cuba, Mexico and Panama had proposed that the Conference should adopt a Declaration on the Rights and Duties of Nations and a Declaration on the Essential Rights of Man. Time, however, did not permit the Conference to deal with the matter. The delegation of Panama, thereupon, had submitted a draft Declaration on the Rights and Duties of States and a Draft Declaration on Fundamental Human Rights and Freedoms to the first session of the General Assembly, with the request that these Draft Declarations be considered at the second part of the first session. On 31 October 1946, the General Assembly referred the first Draft Declaration to the International Law Commission (Committee on the Codification of International Law), and, on 11 December 1946, acting on the recommendations of the First and Third Committees, the General Assembly decided to refer the latter Draft Declaration to ECOSOC for submission to the Commission.

1947 the Chairman of the Commission (taking into account views expressed at the fourth session of ECOSOC that the drafting group should be enlarged) informed the President of ECOSOC that she intended to appoint a Drafting Committee consisting of representatives of the following members of the Commission: Australia, Chile, China, France, Lebanon, the Soviet Union, the United Kingdom and the United States of America. This was noted with approval by ECOSOC which, at the same time, requested the Secretariat to prepare "an outline concerning an International Bill of Rights", on the basis of which the Drafting Committee was to draw up its preliminary draft, to be submitted to the second session of the Commission. Pursuant to the resolution of the General Assembly of 11 December 1946, ECOSOC also decided to transmit to the Drafting Committee and to the Commission the draft Declaration already presented by Panama to the General Assembly, as well as any other draft declarations received from Member States.

When the Drafting Committee held its first session (9–25 June 1947) it had before it: (a) a draft outline prepared by the Secretariat (which included the rights mentioned in various national constitutions and in various suggestions for an International Bill of Human Rights); (b) a draft bill of rights proposed by the United Kingdom; and (c) various proposals made by the United States for re-wording the text contained in the Secretariat outline. The idea emerged that two documents should be prepared, one outlining a declaration of general principles, the other outlining the contents of one or more conventions flowing from these principles. A draft declaration prepared by Professor Cassin was studied, reviewed and revised, and thereafter submitted to the Commission as a working paper for a preliminary draft of an International Manifesto or Declaration on Human Rights. With certain additions, it was agreed that the UK draft bill would form the basis of a draft convention to be elaborated by the Commission on Human Rights.

From the foregoing it emerges that it only took a year and a half from the time the initial 'Draft outline of the International Bill of Human Rights' was placed before the pre-session Drafting Committee of the Commission until the final text was proclaimed by the General Assembly on 10 December 1948. Measured on this time-scale, all subsequent UN standard-setting work in the field of human rights pales. However, the drafting of the Universal Declaration went through a complex series of stages from June 1947 to December 1948. To facilitate understanding of this process, the main stages may be listed as follows, taking the Secretariat outline as the starting point.

1.	Secretariat: Draft outline of the International Bill of Human Rights	(E/CN.4/AC.1/3, Annex and Add.1)
2.	Drafting Committee, first session	E/CN.4/21, Annex F
3.	Sub-Commission on Prevention of Discrimination and Protection of Minorities (first session)	E/CN.4/52, (certain articles)
4.	Commission on Human Rights (second session), Working Group on the Declaration (in session)	E/CN.4/57
5.	Commission on Human Rights, second session	E/600
6.	Government comments	E/CN.4/85
7.	Drafting Committee, second session	E/CN.4/95, Annex A (some articles)
8.	Commission on Human Rights, third session	E/800
9.	ECOSOC, seventh session	A/625
10.	General Assembly, Third Committee	A/777
11.	Sub-Committee 4 of Third Committee	A/C.3/400 and 400/Rev.1
12.	General Assembly, third session, 183rd plenary meeting, last changes and voting on final text	GAOR, Third Session

Introduction

Asbjørn Eide and Gudmundur Alfredsson[*]

Norway and Iceland

I. Significance and Impact

The Universal Declaration of Human Rights (UDHR), despite its youth, has acquired major significance in national societies and international relations. The impact extends to the moral, political and legal spheres. The UDHR and the forces of moderation, tolerance and understanding that the text represents will probably in future history-writing be seen as one of the greatest steps forward in the process of global civilization. In several respects, the UDHR was an innovation, the full consequences of which we only gradually and still dimly recognize today.

A. The Moral Sphere

The UDHR constitutes both a moral platform requiring respect for the freedom and dignity of everyone, and a future-oriented project requiring continuous efforts at all levels to make human rights universally enjoyed in reality. The UDHR did not stop at proclaiming the rights but called also for a transformation of the social and international order in such a way that the rights established could be enjoyed in practice.

The UDHR is presented as a standard of achievement "to the end that every individual and every organ of society, keeping this Declaration constantly in mind, shall strive by teaching and education to promote respect for these rights and freedoms and by progressive measures, national and international, to secure their universal and effective recognition and observance..." The

---

[*] Mr. Alfredsson is a staff member with the United Nations Secretariat. Views expressed in this article are privately held and do not necessarily reflect the position of the Organization.

'progressive measures' should lead to the formation of a "social and international order in which these rights can be fully realized" (see also article 28, the significance of which is examined by Asbjørn Eide in his analysis of that article).

B. The Political Sphere

In the political sphere, the UDHR includes several innovations. It not only reaffirms but decisively expands the principle of non-discrimination, which had been established in the UN Charter. The expansion has been confirmed by a series of subsequent human rights instruments. The UDHR, furthermore, created a self-contained, comprehensive system of rights, and it places social, economic and cultural rights on the same level as civil and political rights. This approach, long disputed and even denied in a period of ideological divisions, has now resurfaced in solemn policy statements by the General Assembly to the effect that all human rights are indivisible and interdependent. Recent instruments, such as the Declaration on the Right to Development and the Convention on the Rights of the Child, are living proof of the validity of this view.

The UDHR, including its Preamble and all its 30 operative articles, has been and continues to serve as a source of inspiration and direction for the standard-setting and implementation activities of the United Nations in the field of human rights. This is true for the work of other intergovernmental and non-governmental organizations as well, at both international and regional levels.

There are many instances where this role of the UDHR has been concretely manifested. The text has seen repeated use during the preparation of international instruments, including the two International Covenants and other human rights treaties and declarations. This is also true for ongoing standard-setting exercises, most recently in the first draft of the Universal Declaration on the Rights of Indigenous Peoples under elaboration by the UN Working Group on Indigenous Populations.

C. The Legal Sphere

As to the legal significance of the UDHR, it is worth keeping in mind that the Declaration is a resolution of the General Assembly and not a convention subject to the usual ratification and accession requirements for treaties.

Nevertheless, the UDHR carries legal weight far beyond an ordinary resolution or even other declarations coming from the General Assembly. The role of the General Assembly in interpreting provisions of the UN Charter, references in other instruments and resolutions, statements made by the Secretary-General and by Governments in international fora, and the above-mentioned influence of the UDHR on subsequent standard-setting activities are part of this picture, especially when these instances make use of the UDHR as law or for the purpose of providing a legal framework.

Similarly, many states have incorporated or drawn on the UDHR as a model for their constitutional and other legislative acts. Both the International Court of Justice and national courts have relied on the UDHR in their decisions.

The UDHR forms the basis of implementation mechanisms at the UN level. This is the case with regard to the communications and investigative procedures in the human rights field. Notably the so-called 1503 procedure, established by a resolution of the Economic and Social Council (ECOSOC), builds on the UDHR and its provisions, with the added advantage that the procedure covers all countries because the UDHR as a resolution rather than a treaty is applicable to the whole world.

In their still infant-like investigative functions, Special Rapporteurs of the Commission on Human Rights (the Commission) have made use of the UDHR when treaty law has failed.

Finally, the UDHR has been at the forefront of the political and public debate about country performance and the striving for increased compliance with basic and fundamental rights and, not the least, gross violations of the same. Non-governmental organizations, such as Amnesty International and Article 19, frequently rely on the UDHR in their endeavours to uphold international standards.

This plentiful evidence of general and specific practice by the international community and its components has led several statesmen and scholars to conclude that the UDHR constitutes binding law as international custom in accordance with article 38 of the Statute of the International Court of Justice. It would seem that their reasoning is good and the scholarly voices may even be a source of law in their own right. Other authors have suggested that at least many of the rights spelled out in the UDHR have emerged as rules of customary law. Still other authors have come to altogether different conclusions.

The editors of this volume will not deliver judgement on this issue. It is nevertheless clear that the UDHR has fulfilled the promise of its own Preamble, namely to become "a common standard of achievement for all peoples and all nations." The yardstick may be legal, political or moral, but the fact remains that the UDHR has made a significant if not crucial contribution to subsequent developments in the field of international human rights work.

II. Roots

The UDHR represents a considerable innovation over previous international as well as national experiences, but has deep and widespread historical roots.

In European history, the roots may be traced back into antiquity, but it was during the Renaissance that the emphasis was first placed on the dignity of the individual. Merging with the rediscovery and elaboration of Roman law that had taken place at the earliest universities during the late medieval period and with intellectual controversies over legitimate systems of governance sparked off by authors like Machiavelli, the newfound emphasis on the dignity of the individual animated the discussion of natural rights in the 17th century. It was further conceptualized within the framework of the theory of social contract. Authors like Johannes Althusius, John Locke, Jean-Jacques Rousseau, Thomas Paine and Thomas Jefferson provided significant contributions to the debate about the relationship between the individual and the authority. It found expressions in documents like the English Bill of Rights in 1689, the American Declaration of Independence in 1776, and the French Declaration on the Rights of Man and the Citizen of 1789.

A. The Human Struggle

The real-life background to these theories and declarations were long periods of human struggle for freedom and dignity, often met with severe repression causing extensive suffering. Sometimes it also led to widespread violence in the name of freedom and justice. For centuries, the evolution of democracy had its ebbs and flows in Europe. New theories replaced that of the social contract. Historicism, utilitarianism, Marxism and positivism all tended in the 19th century to reduce the significance of the revolutionary ideals of human rights of the 18th century. Theories of transition stages emerged, according to which authoritarian or totalitarian rule could be justified and even be desirable during certain stages, in order to lay the ground for a more comprehensive freedom later. Traces of this thinking can still be heard today, albeit in different contexts. In the name of such theories, human rights are again extensively and cruelly violated. Societies formed by descendants of European settlers abroad (in North America, Latin America, Australia and New Zealand) took part, in their respective and unilateral ways, in this process.

The roots of the UDHR go beyond the West. Many cultures and religions have contained principles inherent in the human rights debate as demonstrated by studies undertaken by UNESCO. Certainly, all the great religions have elements which point in the direction of human rights. But all religions including Christianity have also contained principles which could not easily be made compatible with the broadening concepts of human rights, and what is more: in the name of religions, human rights have been extensively violated in all parts of the world at various times. Cultural practices from around the globe have likewise steered in both directions: respect for and denial of dignity and human treatment.

Respect for the dignity of the individual came to the test whenever the individual was opposed to the will of the ruler, or to the prescriptions of the religion, or to the mores of the community. In such cases, the dignity of the individual was precarious in many places of the world, and it still is.

European settlers and their descendants abroad very often did not extend their concern with the dignity of the individual to the members of the peoples and the peoples themselves whom they met in the territories they colonized. Racial discrimination, marginalization, domination and in some cases outright extermination followed in the footsteps of many of the European settlers.

Other Europeans, both at home and in the new territories of settlement, and an increasing number of individuals and groups among the colonized peoples, absorbed the human rights ideas and started to make use of them in the struggle for liberation and took up the struggle against these policies and practices of violation.

B. The 1940s and World War II

The immediate background for the UDHR were the experiences in the 1940s and during World War II. There was an intensification of repression and brutality which had not been experienced for a long time; Mussolini's Fascist government of Italy, the Spanish civil war and the Franco regime, Japanese militarism and brutal occupation policies, and above all the Nazi expansion and extermination practices under Adolph Hitler, coinciding with Stalin's reign of terror in the Soviet Union, shocked the conscience of human beings worldwide, and laid the ground for a broad consensus that a new humanistic legal order would have to be established.

The most significant formulation of this vision of a new international legal order was the Message to the US Congress by Franklin D. Roosevelt in January 1941, in which he spoke of the Four Freedoms. Freedom of expression, freedom of faith, freedom from want and freedom from fear — these are what President Roosevelt saw as the aims of the future world order to be established when the nightmare was over. On this basis, planning for the United Nations was started, and his thoughts about the Four Freedoms sparked an activity throughout the world to formulate the standards by which human beings should behave towards each other in future years.

When the Charter was adopted at San Francisco in the spring of 1945, many states and non-governmental organizations pressed for the inclusion of a Bill of Rights in the Charter. While this was not adopted in San Francisco, it was agreed to establish a Commission on Human Rights, which was to draft and present to the General Assembly an International Bill of Human Rights. This Commission convened in January 1947, and completed its work by the summer of 1948. Its sources of inspiration were a number of drafts already made by non-governmental groups and by States, including comprehensive drafts by the American Law Institute and by the Organization of American States. Other drafts were presented by individuals, including Professor Hersch Lauterpacht on behalf of the International Law Association, and by the trade unions, such as the American Federation of Labor.

C. The United Nations

At the United Nations, the first preparations were made in the Secretariat, namely the Division of Human Rights, then led by John

Humphrey, a Canadian professor of law. He was ably assisted by Egon Schwelb and other members of the Secretariat. Drawing on the drafts already mentioned, and on constitutions assembled from countries all over the world, they presented a comprehensive draft to the Commission. Chairing that body was Eleanor Roosevelt, carrying with her the Roosevelt visions of a New Deal, and of the Four Freedoms. She played a leading and a mediating role in the Commission. Two competing influences were already at work within the US delegation; the liberal/social tradition of the Roosevelt period, and the conservative, isolationist tradition were struggling for influence. Thus, Eleanor Roosevelt had to mediate not only the Commission, but also her own delegation.

The other prominent and influential participants came from all parts of the world. One of them was René Cassin, who was an eminent draftsman with a deep social commitment. He was able to draw on the long-standing tradition of human rights in French history, and his own social commitment made him a strong supporter of social and economic rights. The other main participants were Mr. P.C. Chang, former professor at Nanking (China); Mr. Hernán Santa Cruz, a lawyer from Chile; Mr. Charles Malik, professor of philosophy in Lebanon; Mr. Omar Loufti (Egypt); Ambassador Mrs. Hausa Mehta (India); General Carlos P. Romulo (the Philippines); Mr. Bogomolov (Soviet Union) and Mr. Ribuikar (Yugoslavia).

D. A Western Approach?

It is often argued that the UDHR is predominantly 'Western' (or 'Northern') in approach. There is some truth to it, but it is frequently exaggerated. As seen from the names above, participants came from all parts of the world. Admittedly, there was only one participant from the African continent (Egypt). Indigenous peoples and minorities had no representation during the drafting and adoption stages. While this may be true, today the broad wording of the Declaration and its general principles together with subsequent standard-setting and implementation activities reduce the value of this statement to history.

III. Contemporary Appraisal

At the time of writing, the UDHR has existed for over 40 years. At no other time in history has the appeal for human rights had a stronger political impact. The dramatic changes in Europe have been promoted under the banner of human rights. Ideological divisions between East and West on priorities and interpretation have almost disappeared. The reluctance that had been expressed at the time of adoption in 1948 by the Soviet Union and other socialist countries, a reluctance which had then led to an abstention in the vote on the UDHR was entirely eliminated in 1988.

The decolonization efforts of the United Nations reached a certain culmination in the election organized for Namibia. Fundamental changes are imminent in South Africa. In other parts of the world, the United Nations has supervised elections and referenda. All of these activities have a significant human rights component which is respect for the will of the people and the freedoms of expression and association, only to take examples from the UDHR. In two recent instances, in El Salvador and Campuchea, agreements relating to cease-fire and elections have been concluded or are being negotiated and these agreements foresee a specific human rights role in the process of national reconstruction to be undertaken by the United Nations.

A. A Universal Consensus?

These remarks do not mean that there is universal consensus about human rights. There are still disagreements and conflicts on various points and many instruments, including the UDHR and rights and duties contained therein, are subject to violations by a large number of governments. There are indications to the effect that previous tensions between East and West are being replaced by increasing differences between North and South. These differences, to the degree they are substantive in nature rather than transparent methods for holding on to power and privileges gained by means of repression, relate to priority-setting for human rights in general when compared with other elements needed for progress and development. Differences also exist as to the emphasis on methods and practicalities of implementation.

In this debate, the UDHR has a special place because of its approach to and balancing of civil, cultural, economic, political and social rights, together with its references to duties and an international order for the realization of the rights. The Declaration, because of the cleverness and foresight of the drafters, continues to be a classic instrument and a possible bridge, currently and in the future, between different points of view.

B. *The Adoption of the Universal Declaration of Human Rights*

The UDHR was adopted by the General Assembly on 10 December 1948. The date is well known. It has subsequently been proclaimed as the Human Rights Day of the United Nations and it is annually celebrated as such.

It is less well known that the resolution by which the Declaration was adopted, resolution 217 (III) from the Assembly's third session, was divided into five parts and it is part A which contains the text of the UDHR.

Part B of the resolution is entitled 'Right of Petition'. It spells out that the right of petition is an essential human right, as is recognized in the constitutions of a great number of countries; it refers to a draft article on petitions for insertion into the Declaration (in document A/C.3/306) and amendments submitted thereto; it decides not to take action on the matter at the third session; and entrusts the Commission to examine the problem of petitions when studying the Covenants on human rights and measures of implementation, so as to enable the Assembly to consider further action at its next regular session. It took a little longer, but nowadays the UN human rights programme offers a number of treaty-based and resolution-mandated communication or complaint procedures.

Part C of resolution 217 is entitled 'Fate of Minorities'. It begins with the observation that "the United Nations cannot remain indifferent to the fate of minorities"; finds it difficult to adopt a uniform solution of this complex and delicate question which has special aspects in each state in which it arises; decides not to include a specific provision on minorities in the text of the Declaration; and refers the relevant proposals (in document A/C.3/307/Rev.2) to the Commission and the Sub-Commission for a thorough study of the problem and later action.

The Charter, the UDHR and many other subsequent instruments prohibit discrimination on a number of grounds, including those most likely to benefit persons belonging to minorities. Likewise, several instruments provide for minority rights by means of special rights or preferential treatment as necessary tools for achieving equality, including the International Covenant on Civil and Political

Rights, the Convention on the Prevention and Punishment of the Crime of Genocide, the International Convention on the Elimination of All Forms of Racial Discrimination, the Convention on the Rights of the Child, the UNESCO Convention against Discrimination in Education, the UNESCO Declaration on Race and Racial Prejudice, and the International Labour Organisation Conventions on Indigenous and Tribal Peoples in Independent Countries (nos. 107 and 169). Most of these instruments focus on individual rights while others recognize the group, or at least a group element, as a beneficiary.

Notwithstanding attempts and good intentions, there is still no human rights instrument dealing solely and comprehensively with minorities. The Commission has for the last 14 years been preparing a draft declaration on the rights of persons belonging to national, ethnic, religious and linguistic minorities; a first reading was completed by a working group of the Commission in 1990 and this group will meet twice in 1991 in order to try to finish the second reading, but the text as it currently stands does not offer extensive protection and it may even fall short of existing standards. In the meantime, the studies multiply and the problems remain.

Part D of the resolution carries the title 'Publicity to be Given to the Universal Declaration of Human Rights'. It calls the adoption of the UDHR a historic act destined to consolidate world peace through a contribution "towards the liberation of individuals from the unjustified oppression and constraint to which they are too often subjected", and recommends, in three operative paragraphs, to governments, the UN Secretary-General, the specialized agencies and non-governmental organizations that they disseminate the text as widely as possible among all peoples throughout the world. In the case of governments, the resolution calls on them to use every means within their power to this end and thus show their adherence to article 56 of the Charter. The Secretary-General is requested to publish and distribute the text in all languages possible and not only in the official languages of the United Nations.

Much work has been done over the years to achieve this goal, but it can be safely said that the task is not fully accomplished. The resolution states that the UDHR is to be displayed, read and expounded in schools and educational institutions everywhere and this is unfortunately not yet the case. Furthermore, the UDHR is only available in some 200 languages, which falls far short of all languages possible. For these reasons, the current publicizing and publication effort of the UN Secretariat under the leadership of the Under-Secretary-General for Human Rights, Jan Mårtenson, is particularly welcome. Part E of resolution 217 is entitled 'Preparation of a Draft Covenant on Human Rights and Draft Measures of Implementation'. It goes on to observe that the plan of work of the Commission provides for an International Bill of Human Rights which is to include a Declaration, a Covenant and measures of implementation, and assigns the Commission to continue the drafting on a priority basis. It took another 18 years before the Assembly adopted not one but two Covenants and an Optional Protocol for one of them, and altogether 28 years before these treaties entered into force. It is better late than never and it is still, after all, a short time in a historical context.

IV. This Study, Its Approach and Methods

This study of the UDHR was undertaken on the occasion of the 40th anniversary of the Declaration. In addition to this symbolic timing, it was felt that there was need for a comprehensive treatment of the rights and duties contained in the UDHR in the light of its history, the intentions of the drafters, and subsequent standard-setting and implementation activities which have grown out of its existence.

The authors of the study are all from the five Nordic countries: Denmark, Finland, Iceland, Norway and Sweden. As evidenced by their short biographies published elsewhere in this book, they have all been active, albeit to varying degrees, in human rights work with universities, research institutes, non-governmental organizations, international organizations, and governments. The editors also come from these same countries and they work together as the Nordic consultative committee for the Norwegian human rights journal *Mennesker & Rettigheter*.

Editorial policies and messages to the authors foresaw that they should cover, one author for each article of the UDHR:

- The historical background of the UDHR, that is, where the ideas came from and where and in what context they had previously been promulgated;
- The history of the drafting and adoption at the United Nations, that is the *travaux préparatoires*, including the intention of the drafters and other indications from the preparatory stages;
- Subsequent normative developments at national, regional and international levels;

- The follow-up measures undertaken with regard to country performance and compliance with the UDHR and instruments derived from or related to it; and
- The positions and performance of the Nordic countries in this same context.

Most of the authors have by and large followed these guidelines, but any differences in treatment and approach are due to the fact that each author has been free to write without subsequent editorial interference or coordination.

It is our hope and expectation that the study will serve not only as a monument to the UDHR but also as a contribution to increased awareness and understanding of its text in particular and human rights in general, as well as encouragement to our readers to the same end.

The Preamble of the Universal Declaration of Human Rights and the UN Human Rights Programme

Jan Mårtenson

Sweden

Few documents have marked their time and the struggle for human dignity as has the Universal Declaration of Human Rights (UDHR). This became apparent soon after its adoption and has been increasingly evident ever since. The UDHR marked its time as a statement of the ultimate value of the human person in refutation of the Fascist and Nazi theories, which lay at the basis of so many barbarous acts, as a justification for the suffering and sacrifices that went into the struggle against those regimes and as a programme of action to prevent a renewal of the horrors still all too present in the minds of the UDHR drafters. The UDHR in its succeeding years and with increasing force inspired, guided, and directed national and international energies towards the achievement of a worldwide awareness of the value of the human person, as well as national and international standards and machinery to protect human rights; these have far outstripped the vision of many at the time of the UDHR proclamation. Today, the UDHR poses the challenge of its unfinished revolution — the revolution of placing the human person squarely at the centre of national and international values. While achieved in theory, this recognition of human dignity still awaits being effectively made an essential element in international and national deliberations. The UDHR still awaits real means being placed at its disposal as they are placed at the disposal of other important principles of contemporary international society: for example, respect for the sovereignty and territorial integrity of States.

Human dignity, while the most revolutionary of the concepts, is not the invention or creation of any one society, culture, philosophy, or religious approach to life. It is certainly not a 20th century invention. Rather, the imperative of respect for the dignity of the human person is visible in the traces of civilization going back to the dawn of recorded history. The quest for a definition of the essential dignity of the human person and ways of ensuring protection for that dignity can be seen throughout the story of humankind.

The struggle for the protection of human rights before 1945 was carried out largely on the national level and reflected in such historic documents as the Magna Carta, the American Declaration of Independence and Bill of Rights, the French Declaration of the Rights of Man and of Citizens, and more recently, the 1919 Mexican Constitution. With the establishment of the United Nations, the search for ways to protect human dignity was clearly placed on the international level.

One of the most sacred trusts placed in the hands of the new world organization in 1945 by 'The Peoples of the United Nations' was the promotion of respect for human rights and fundamental freedoms for all without distinction as to race, sex, language or religion. Unlike the Covenant of the League of Nations, human rights were woven as an important, indeed a guiding, thread throughout the fabric of the UN Charter. The Charter's Preamble and article 1 contain explicit references to human rights, "while the Charter also charged specifically the General Assembly and the Economic and Social Council with promoting respect for human rights and gave a similar mandate to the trusteeship system." Although the San Francisco Conference decided not to include a declaration of human rights in the Charter itself, it did provide in that document for the establishment of the Commission on Human Rights (the Commission), which had as its first task the drafting of the International Bill of Human Rights.

The commitment to human rights is not an isolated element in the Charter. Rather, it forms an integral part of the purposes of the United Nations in preserving international peace and security, promoting economic and social development and ensuring the rule of law. The prescience of the Charter's drafters is fully borne out by today's world. We have come to understand ever more clearly that international peace and security must be founded on respect for human rights; that social and economic development are viable only in a context in which human rights are respected; and that — on the positive side — respect for human rights has an important contribution to make to the promotion of peace and to sustainable economic and social development.

Preambles are often thought of as of secondary importance and in approaching a treaty or other international instrument we tend to skip over, or at most read lightly, the preamble and pass on to the more concrete parts of the text. The Preamble of the UDHR, however, merits attention and reflection. This may be because in drafting the Declaration, the Preamble was dealt with at the end of the various sessions and it thereby had instilled into it the essence of the drafters' substantive reflections, their views of the world in which the Universal Declaration was to be placed and their vision of the programme for the future.

The Preamble can be divided into three parts. The first three paragraphs focus on human rights and dignity and the consequences for the world of violations; paragraphs four through seven deal with the international dimensions of human rights and the need for standards; and the final paragraph, the Preamble's third part, describes the nature of the UDHR, and the future action to be based on its provisions.

The first part of the Preamble reflects in a few words the fundamental dialogue of the World War II years. It first states unequivocally that the foundation of freedom, justice and peace in the world is the recognition of the inherent dignity and the equal and inalienable rights of all members of the human family. Secondly, the UDHR, referring to World War II and the atrocities carried out during the War, states that the barbarous acts that had outraged the conscience of mankind were caused by disregard and contempt for human rights and that the contrary situation, a world of the four freedoms — of speech and belief, from fear and want — is the highest objective of the common people. Thirdly, the Assembly tells us that it is essential that human rights be protected by the rule of law to avoid tyranny and oppression and man's recourse to rebellion as a last resort.

In its second part the Preamble deals with human rights on the international level, beginning in the fourth paragraph with a recognition of the importance of promoting the development of friendly relations between nations. This paragraph serves as a bridge between violations — which engender tensions between nations — and the work of the United Nations in furthering peace and human rights, dealt with in the following paragraphs. In the next paragraph (five), reference is made to the wide-ranging objectives of the Charter concerning human rights and the dignity and worth of the human person, the equal rights of men and women and the undertaking to promote social progress and better standards of life in larger freedom. Here we hear the echo of the Four Freedoms from the second paragraph and find a reaffirmation of the UN commitment to protect all the rights of the human person, both those touching spiritual and physical integrity and those relating to social progress, better standards of life and freedom from want. The following paragraph (six) reminds us of the pledge of Member States to achieve — in co-operation with the United Nations — the promotion of universal respect for and observance of human rights and fundamental freedoms. The Preamble's argument thus closes in the penultimate paragraph, which connects the rights of the individual, so fundamental to achieving the aspirations of human kind, with the work of the United Nations, by stating that a common understanding of what is meant by human rights is of the greatest importance in enabling Member States to realize fully their pledge.

The third part of the Preamble — its last paragraph — tells us that the UDHR is a common standard of achievement — for all peoples and all nations — and that it is intended to serve as the basis of action by every individual and every organ of society — to promote universal and effective recognition and observance of human rights. These two objectives — the promotion of respect for human rights, on the one hand, the securing of their universal and effective recognition and observance on the other — are to be achieved each by its own means. Teaching and education are set out as the means to promote respect, and progressive measures, both nationally and internationally, are to be used to secure recognition and observance.

The argument of the UDHR is as true and self-evident today as it was for those just escaping from the horrors of World War II. Respect for human rights is the basis of freedom, peace and justice and human kind still yearns for a world free from fear and want and one of freedom of belief and speech. On the other hand, we see a periodic if not a continuous demonstration that violations of human rights lead to barbarous acts; force people to rebel against tyranny and oppression; and endanger friendly relations between nations. Finally, the role of the United Nations in promoting respect for human rights based on the UDHR common understanding of human rights is more important today than ever in the past.

The spirit and philosophy of the UDHR is focused on the individual, the rights necessary to the inherent dignity of the individual alone, and on her or his relation to others and society. It is not exclusive of one group or another but aims at the protection of the human rights of every person. Further, it is clearly an inter-state document, in fact States are mentioned rather infrequently. This realization of the fundamentally supra-national or one could say pre-national nature of the Declaration led to the change of its title from 'International' to 'Universal' Declaration by the General Assembly. Its universality has since been so clearly demonstrated that we have come to admire the collective wisdom and sensitivities of its authors. In the more than 40 years since its adoption, the UDHR has shown itself to be truly universal, as the peoples of newly liberated independent countries have found in it a reflection of their deepest aspirations. The UDHR has inspired numerous other UN declarations and treaties as well as regional systems for the protection of human rights; it has served as the foundation for numerous constitutions and national laws; and it has been the standard applied by the UN human rights bodies when investigating allegations of violations of human rights. Today, the UDHR is cited more widely and frequently than ever and it continues to be the starting point and touchstone for new human rights activities by the United Nations.

The universality and continuing relevance of the UDHR in a vastly changed world is not due to its legal style or precision, nor to the expertise of its authors. Rather, the UDHR is relevant today because it reflects profound truths about human nature and the requirements of human dignity. The physical existence of each individual is protected by the proclamation of the right to life, to food, to housing, to health, to medical care and necessary social services, to liberty and security of person, to freedom from slavery and torture and from arbitrary arrest, among other rights. The intellectual and spiritual dimensions of the human person are proclaimed through the right to freedom of thought, conscience and religion, freedom of opinion and expression, the right to education and to take part in the cultural life of the community. A further fundamental dimension of the human person that is protected by the UDHR is the right to participate in decisions affecting the community in which we live. We have come to learn of the capital importance of this right to the whole human endeavour. Thus the UDHR lays down the right to freedom of assembly and association and the right to take part in government, *inter alia*, through periodic and genuine elections based on universal and equal suffrage.

One requirement underlines each sentence, each right in the UDHR, and that is the equal dignity and rights of each member of the human community. Everyone is entitled to the rights proclaimed by the Universal Declaration "without distinction of any kind, such as race, colour, sex, language, religion, political or other opinion, national or social origin, property, birth or other states." Finally, but today not least in importance, the drafters of the Universal Declaration placed the rights announced therein squarely in the international context by proclaiming that "everyone is entitled to a social and international order in which the rights and freedoms set forth in this Declaration can be fully realized."

There is abundant literature analysing the binding or non-binding nature of the UDHR in international law, trying in fact to answer the question of what it did mean and what it does mean now to be "a common standard of achievement." Whatever the situation at the time it was adopted, it would be difficult today to identify an article of the UDHR which States would not be bound to observe. Indirectly, of course, the numerous international human rights instruments, which the UDHR gave rise to, have made the Declaration's rights binding on the respective States Parties. But we must not forget that the complex and extensive machinery for monitoring human rights violations established within the United Nations, be they working groups, special rapporteurs, or complaints procedures, often criticize government conduct based on the UDHR and few if any governments have the temerity to say the Declaration does not apply. Further, failure to live up to the standards of the UDHR can have very definite negative consequences for States to the extent that multilateral and bilateral relations, for example in the economic and political spheres, are increasingly affected by human rights observance or violations.

The last paragraph of the Preamble of the UDHR clearly sets out the road to be followed by the United Nations in its efforts to give meaning to the Declaration's provisions. Education and teaching on the one hand, and progressive measures on the other, together with the establishment of international standards, make up the three pillars of UN action in human rights: standard-setting, implementation, and education and information.

It is worthwhile to reflect on the success of the international community in pursuing these three lines of development in over 40 years since the UDHR was adopted. We must remember that in 1948 the Universal Declaration was the only human rights standard of universal dimension, and there was no machinery to deal with complaints from individuals or groups that their human rights were being violated. In the period since then, impressive progress has been made both in laying down international standards and in setting up international machinery to deal with complaints.

Beginning with the adoption of the UDHR, the United Nations has put into place a true international code of human rights, consisting of the Declaration, the two International Covenants on

Human Rights[1] (ratified by over 90 countries), and numerous other instruments setting detailed human rights standards in areas such as racial discrimination, equality of women, treatment of detainees, and prevention of torture. Most recently the Assembly has adopted treaties on the rights of the child, the rights of migrant workers, the abolition of the death penalty and basic guidelines on computerized personal files.[2] The UDHR has also had its impact on regional systems for the protection of human rights in Africa, America and Europe, which have developed their own standards and implementation machinery.

Undeniably, the very existence of these standards has a salutary effect on the enjoyment of human rights throughout the world. Many modern constitutions reflect the basic norms of the UDHR and many countries have introduced into internal legislation the more detailed provisions of international human rights treaties, thus affording to the people of those countries the legal bases for claiming respect for their rights through national remedies. The Convention on the Rights of the Child is a striking example here; even before it had been adopted by the General Assembly, several States had carried out revisions of their national law based on the provisions of the draft Convention which thus, even before its official birth, reinforced respect for the rights of many millions of children. Even when not incorporated into national law, international human rights standards have proved themselves to be powerful tools to advocacy groups seeking improved respect for human rights.

Not only do we have an international code of standards protecting human rights, but the United Nations has also developed a wide range of procedures charged with overseeing respect for those standards. First, we have the examination of reports from States Parties by committees of independent experts who discuss with government representatives — often at the ministerial level — respect for civil and political rights, economic, social and cultural rights, the elimination of racial discrimination, equality of women,

[1] International Covenant on Civil and Political Rights (CCPR) (1966); International Covenant on Economic, Social and Cultural Rights (CESCR) (1966).
[2] Convention on the Rights of the Child; International Convention on the Protection of the Rights of all Migrant Workers and Members of their Families (Resolution 45–158, adopted 18 December 1990); Second Optional Protocol to the CCPR, aiming at the abolition of the death penalty; Guidelines for the Regulation of Computerized Personal Data Files (Resolution 45–95, adopted 14 December 1990), respectively.

and the prohibition of torture. This will be expanded in the near future to respect for the rights of the child. These examinations are searching and critical and it is not unusual for States to report modifications in practices or law as a result of questions raised by committee members. Two committees are empowered to deal with individual complaints and, here again, committee decisions on such complaints can result in basic changes in national law and practices.

Three other methods of implementing UN human rights norms have evolved over the years. First, the consideration by the Commission, through special rapporteurs or working groups, of individual reports of particularly serious violations of human rights, such as arbitrary or summary executions, torture or disappearances. Under these procedures the practice of sending urgent action cables has been developed. Numerous telegrams are sent to governments in response to allegations of these violations of the physical integrity of individuals. In 1990 alone, over 1,000 particularly urgent cases were transmitted to governments by telegram and many more were sent by letter. The results of these initiatives and the responses of the governments are contained in public reports debated in the Commission.

A second method is to be found in the study by the Commission and the General Assembly of the human rights situation in specific countries or territories. For example, today we can mention such situations as those in South Africa, the occupied territories in the Middle East, Afghanistan, Cuba, El Salvador, Iran, Iraq, Romania and Kuwait under Iraqi occupation.

Thirdly, we can refer to the consideration by human rights organs of petitions from individuals and organizations which allege serious, widespread and systematic violations of human rights. In 1990, well over 120,000 such petitions or appeals were processed; governments were asked to comment and the cases were prepared for review by the competent bodies that seek to identify serious situations meriting further UN intervention.

The United Nations, in its standard-setting and international implementation of human rights, has certainly had a significant impact on the way people live throughout the world. National legislative norms in human rights have been raised for millions of people and the United Nations has helped to place in their hands recourse procedures enabling them to protect their own human rights. UN interventions in particular cases have saved individual lives, prevented torture and resulted in the reappearance of disappeared persons. Patterns of such violations have been curbed through the spotlight of UN attention, and the same attention has contributed to the favourable evolution of situations in specific countries, including the restoration of democratic government.

Great strides have been made in drafting universally accepted international standards and in developing international implementation mechanisms. Important as international standard-setting and implementation are, however, it is on the national and local levels that human rights are in the final analysis enjoyed. Thus, over the past few years there has been a marked expansion of the human rights programme aimed at fostering conditions on the national level propitious to the enjoyment of human rights. We have accordingly been focusing on national implementation through advisory services and information and education, in order to help people on the national and local levels to enjoy respect for basic human rights in their day-to-day lives and to have the political, judicial and other institutions necessary to protect those rights.

This, in sum, is our overriding objective and we thus highlight in our programmes the importance of the UDHR and seek to spread the human rights message throughout all regions and all communities. We are striving to be in a position to respond effectively and efficiently to the growing need for information coming from governments, groups and individuals throughout the world. We have witnessed the undeniable relationship between the growing awareness of human rights and the growing number of treaty ratifications, requests and actions in this field. Our objective is the creation of a truly universal culture of human rights.

The UN Programme of Advisory Services and Technical Assistance in the Field of Human Rights over the last few years has been invigorated with an action-oriented approach that has resulted in a significant widening of the programme's activities. This programme, supported by the UN Voluntary Fund for Advisory Services and Technical Assistance in Human Rights, together with the information activities of the World Public Information Campaign for Human Rights, form the core of our activities in this area. These activities, and especially the Advisory Services Programme, are complementary to existing monitoring and investigating procedures. We are careful to ensure that assistance activities never provide an excuse for not investigating or examining reports of human rights violations; in fact it is not unusual for countries subject to examination in the Commission to also receive technical assistance.

Priority in our programme goes to building and strengthening national and regional institutions for human rights. Two teams of experts were dispatched in 1990 and 1991 to two countries (Romania and Albania) to advise on the technical and legal aspects of organizing free and fair elections. In 1990 the services of experts were provided in eight countries through technical co-operation projects financed under the Voluntary Fund, as well as to the African Commission for Human and People's Rights of the Organization of African Unity. As one example, a week of briefings from high-level experts on the subject of the protection of human rights through constitutional law was organized for Romanian parliamentarians charged with the drafting of that country's new constitution. Experts under this same programme visited Romania and discussed human rights aspects of constitutional law with the full committee of Parliament charged with the drafting of the constitution, as well as with the Human Rights Commission of the lower House of Parliament, the Minister of Justice and the President of the Supreme Court.

Also as part of the technical assistance programme, the Centre for Human Rights has organized, over the past two years, some 25 seminars, training courses and workshops, in all parts of the world, including those held in Asunción, Geneva, Kiev, Moscow, Lisbon, Manila, Montevideo, Ottawa, Lomé, Sofia, and New Delhi. They dealt mainly with the administration of justice and human rights and in the process, over 2,500 administrators of justice have actively participated in those activities. A National Workshop on the Rights of the Child was organized in New Delhi in December 1990. Projects are now being prepared in order to provide assistance for the establishment of human rights institutes in several countries, in particular, in Eastern Europe.

In December 1988, the General Assembly launched the World Public Information Campaign for Human Rights, which has greatly enhanced UN action for the promotion of information/education on human rights. The priority attached to this aspect of the human rights programme — namely information and education — has been magnified by the growing relations with the wider human rights community made up of Member States, non-governmental organizations, academic and research institutions, the media, and international and regional institutions with whom the Centre for Human Rights has tried consistently to expand its co-operation. The activities for the promotion of human rights and fundamental freedoms within the framework of the Campaign have been grouped into five major areas: a) preparation and dissemination of printed public information and reference materials; b) workshops, seminars and training courses; c) fellowships and internships; d) special human rights observances; and e) coverage and promotion activities. The basic aim of this Campaign of information is the promotion of a universal culture of human rights.

The Centre for Human Rights has continued its programme of information materials begun in 1988, in connection with the 40th Anniversary of the UDHR. Sixteen Fact Sheets have been issued, the latest covering the *Rights of the Child* and *Summary and Arbitrary Executions*. The demand for such publications is rapidly growing and more and more organizations and institutions have translated and reproduced these publications into non-official languages. In addition, three issues of the *Human Rights Newsletter* have already appeared in 1990 and a fourth is in the process of being published.

These meetings, organized within the Programme of Advisory Services and Technical Assistance — despite their technical nature — have also been utilized to spread information and increase awareness of the objectives of the World Public Information Campaign for Human Rights, thus helping us move a step closer to the long-term goal of establishing a universal culture of human rights. Throughout 1990 the Centre has to this end also co-operated in the organization of, or actively participated in, some 70 workshops, seminars and meetings organized by academic and research institutions and non-governmental organizations in almost all parts of the world. In particular, the Centre also co-sponsored the NGO World Congress on Human Rights held in December in New Delhi, which decided to forward its final Act to the Preparatory Committee of the United Nations World Conference on Human Rights to be held in 1993.

The momentous changes in international relations over the last few years, the growing prominence of human rights and the establishment of democratic governments in many parts of the world made the time ripe for the international community to take stock of the achievements in the field of human rights and of the evolution that has taken place in this field since the International Conference on Human Rights held in Tehran in 1968. Thus, in 1989, the General Assembly began considering the holding of a World Conference on Human Rights for that purpose, and in 1990, the General Assembly decided to convene such a conference for 1993.

The objectives of the Conference, broadly speaking are to review and assess the progress made in human rights since the adoption of the UDHR; to identify obstacles to progress and how they may be overcome; to examine ways to improve the implementation of human rights; and to make concrete recommendations for improving the effectiveness of UN activities and mechanisms and for the resources needed to that end. An important element is the examination of the relationship between development and the enjoyment of all human rights and creating the conditions necessary to the enjoyment of all human rights.

Finally, on 16 November 1990, as part of the World Public Information Campaign for Human Rights, the second series of Human Rights Stamps depicting articles 7–12 of the UDHR, were issued in Geneva, New York and Vienna. The depiction of the other articles will follow. This is a major contribution of the UN Postal Administration in the spreading of the human rights message and in making better known the principles of that historic document.

The contribution of non-governmental organizations is of high importance to the success of our activities of promoting respect for human rights and human rights education. In this regard, consultations with non-governmental organizations have been held on activities within the framework of the World Campaign in both Geneva and New York, with participants representing several hundred human rights organizations. New co-operative endeavours in the area of promotional activities and technical assistance are being carried out or explored with the International Committee of the Red Cross and the League of the Red Cross and Red Crescent Societies, as well as with non-governmental organizations such as Amnesty International, the International Commission of Jurists, the International Human Rights Law Group, to mention but a few.

The UDHR has, to a great extent, fulfilled the promise held out in 1948. But, as with all living human rights documents, it poses its own particular challenge today, and that is, to echo the Preamble, to ensure that every individual and organ of society — including the highest instances of the State and the international community — promote respect for human rights by teaching and education, and that they take the progressive action necessary on the national and international levels to secure universal and effective recognition and observance of human rights.

We must not loose sight of the relevance of the UDHR call for action. The world has, over the last two or three years, undergone a significant and fundamental change. Sterile ideological tensions have, in large measure, been replaced by renewed commitments to multilateral diplomacy and, although periods of crisis are still a fact of international life, we do stand on the threshold of what might well be a new era of international relations. Human rights and democratic government are at the basis of these changes, and if we successfully incorporate the precepts of the UDHR into our future work we may go a long way in satisfying the basic human right laid down in article 28 of the Declaration, that is, the right of everyone "to a social and international order in which the rights and freedoms set forth in this Declaration can be fully realized."

Article 1

A New Beginning

Tore Lindholm

Norway

All human beings are born free and equal in dignity and rights.
They are endowed with reason and conscience and should act
towards one another in the spirit of brotherhood.

I. Introduction

Are these words "solemn affirmations lacking in sense"?[1] Are they
'out-dated'?[2] According to John Humphrey, former Director of the
Division of Human Rights, UN Secretariat (1946–1966), it is a
"fact that at least part of this statement is of questionable truth, it is
purely hortatory and it adds nothing to the authority of the
Universal Declaration [Universal Declaration of Human Rights]"
(UDHR). With hindsight, Humphrey, himself no doubt an unflinch-
ing defender of modern human rights, also thinks that article 1 —
being "philosophical assertions which [do] not enunciate justiciable
rights" ..... "weaken the case for saying that...the Declaration...is
now part of positive customary law and therefore binding on all
states."[3]

Such attitudes, even among friends, add urgency to the
substantive purpose of the present contribution. I want to conclude,
in section III.A, that article 1 is an innovation, and a much needed

---

[1] Alexander Bogomolov, Soviet representative to the UN Commission on Human
Rights (the Commission) in 1947, and delegate to the Third Committee (Verdoodt
1964, p. 79, Humphrey 1984, p. 44).

[2] Adolf Hoffmeister, Czechoslovakian delegate to the Third Committee of the
General Assembly in 1948. (Cassin 1951, p. 286).

[3] Humphrey 1984, p. 44.

improvement, compared to its relevant predecessor texts; in section III.B, that its practical significance may be considerable; and in section III.C, that its validity, as a normative doctrine at the basis of human rights, should be beyond reasonable dispute.

In section II, I deal with the drafting history of article 1, focusing on the protracted, and at times heated, discussions of whether the projected declaration should address the foundations of human rights at all, and in that case, where, and how?

II. A Place for Foundations?

A. Article 1 from the Drafting Committee of the Commission on Human Rights to the Third Committee of the General Assembly

a. The First Proposals for Article 1

As pointed out in the introductory chapter, the first outline of a UDHR specifically proposed for the Commission on Human Rights (the Commission) was prepared by the Secretariat, penned mainly by John Humphrey.

"I was no Thomas Jefferson," Humphrey reports. Hence, perhaps, his "draft carefully avoided any philosophical assertions which did not enunciate justiciable rights...." On this question he seems to have been in line with the various models mentioned. To Humphrey, the professor and expert on international law, philosophical statements were not appropriate for the declaration; and "if they have any place in the instrument it is in the preamble."[4] Thus, whatever the outcome of the priority struggle for father- and motherhood to other parts of UDHR, its article 1 cannot be attributed to Humphrey.[5]

The Commission established an eight member Drafting Committee chaired by Eleanor Roosevelt. Meeting at Lake Success in June 1947, the committee, after five days of preliminary discussions, set up a small working group of three: René Cassin (France), Charles Malik (Lebanon), and Geoffrey Wilson (United Kingdom). The working group requested René Cassin to prepare,

---

[4] Humphrey 1984, p. 44; see also p. 66.
[5] See Eide, forthcoming, 1991. Incidentally, we do not at present know the contribution of Emile Giraud, who assisted first Humphrey and then Cassin in preparing their respective 'first' drafts of the UDHR.

on the basis of the secretariat outline and the preceding discussions, a new draft of 'The International Declaration of Human Rights'. Cassin's draft, presented to the group on Monday 16 June, began with "a preamble and a general section which were altogether new."[6] The only enduring part of Cassin's novel proposals was in fact the primordial version of article 1, later to be adopted. It read:

> All men, being members of one family are free, possess equal dignity and rights, and shall regard each other as brothers.[7]

This text was revised by the working group during two meetings on 16 June, with the following outcome (additions in italics):

> All men *are brothers*. Being *endowed with reason*, members of one family, they are free and possess equal dignity and rights.[8]

After another two days of discussions, the Drafting Committee asked Cassin to prepare a second draft of the whole declaration, which brought no change in article 1.[9] But it was further revised by the Drafting Committee, and at the end of its first session it submitted to the Commission a 'working paper for a preliminary draft of an International Manifesto or Declaration of Human Rights'. Article 1 now read (new additions in italics):

> All men are brothers. Being endowed with reason *and conscience*, they are members of one family. They are free, and possess equal dignity and rights.[10]

While the insertion, in Cassin's first draft, of 'endowed with reason' was due to Malik (Lebanon), the addition of 'and conscience' is a (admittedly Westernized!) rendition of a Chinese notion, as proposed by Chinese Commission member Chang. A literal translation of the Chinese word 'run' would be 'two-man-mindedness', or, in ordinary English terms 'consciousness of his fellow men' or 'sympathy'. Prompted by Chang's proposal, Cassin

---

[6] "précédé d'un Préambule et d'une partie générale entièrement neufs" (Cassin 1951, p. 274). See also the introductory chapter to this volume for further details.
[7] United Nations 1949, p. 495; French text in Verdoodt 1964, p. 78; it begins with "Les êtres humains, tous membres da la même famille...."
[8] E/CN.4/AC.1/W.1, p. 2; Humphrey 1984, p. 44. Incidentally, as regards the novel first sentence, I have discovered no references to the last movement of Beethoven's Ninth Symphony.
[9] E/CN.4/AC.1/W.2/Rev.2.
[10] E/CN.4/21, p. 73.

explained that his text alluded to the three fundamental questions of liberty, equality and fraternity.[11]

It seems, however, that it was Malik who, in a critical evaluation of the Preamble of the Secretariat Outline, proposed that its "basic woof" should be the notion of "the dignity of man"[12] — a crucially important idea which Cassin in turn had imported into his very first proposal for article 1.[13]

The drafts mentioned so far are from the first session of the Drafting Committee, 9–25 June 1947. The next stage was the second session of the Commission held in Geneva 2–17 December 1947, where a six-member Working Group on the projected Declaration, chaired by Mrs. Roosevelt and with Cassin as rapporteur was set up. This group held nine meetings.[14] In Geneva the Working Group adopted, by a vote of 3:2, a proposal by Cassin and the Philippine delegate, General Carlos P. Romulo, which the full Commission in turn accepted by a 12:0 vote, with 5 abstentions:

> All men are *born* free and equal in dignity and rights. They are endowed *by nature* with reason and conscience, and *should act towards one another like brothers.*[15]

It was Romulo who, at this stage, suggested that the reference to the unity of the human family, being "illogical", should be dropped. The addition of the locutions 'born' and 'by nature' (italics above) seems to be due to Cassin and Romulo acting as a team.[16] Amado (Panama) found "All men are brothers" to be "religious and philosophic" and thus unfit to "express in a sufficiently original manner" the basic principles of the new declaration. Bogomolov (Soviet Union) found the sentence excessively abstract, adding that

[11] E/CN.4/AC.1/SR.8, p. 2. At an earlier meeting Cassin had suggested, as a comment to the Secretariat Outline, that the UDHR should incorporate the following fundamental principles: 1) the unity of the human race or family; 2) the idea that every human being had a right to be treated like every other human being; and 3) the concept of solidarity or fraternity among men (E/CN.4/AC.1/SR.2, p. 2).
[12] E/CN.4/AC.1/SR. 2, p. 4.
[13] The originator of UN official concern with human dignity, as expressed in the first article of the Preamble to the Charter, was Smuts (South Africa).
[14] Article 1 is dealt with in its report (E/CN.4/57, p. 5) and summary records (E/CN.4/AC.2/SR.2, pp. 4–7 and SR.9, pp. 21–22).
[15] E/600; E/CN.4/SR.34, pp. 4–6.
[16] E/CN.4/AC.2/SR.2 and 9.

"it would be less abstract to speak about a duty of brotherhood."[17] These objections were taken care of by the Cassin-Romulo proposal, which also picked up a notable reversal of sequence proposed by Mrs. Roosevelt, thus placing '...born free and equal...' at the beginning, and the phrase 'should act ...', indicating the duty of brotherhood, at the end of the article.[18]

The Working Group did not follow the advice of Ms. Bodil Begtrup (Denmark), who participated in her capacity of chairperson of the Commission on the Status of Women. She suggested that 'men' be replaced by 'human beings', a view supported, in the full Commission, by Mrs. Hansa Mehta (India). The outcome, for the time being, was the meagre adoption of a footnote "to the effect that the word 'men', as used [in the declaration], referred to all human beings."[19]

At the Working Group's last Geneva meeting, Bogomolov (Soviet Union) complained that the proposed article 1 was "devoid of meaning", and "that it would be an act of hypocrisy to place such a text at the beginning of the draft Declaration." It would, he thought, be "harmful to the Declaration of Human Rights, which should be immediately applicable." He also "felt such wording could not even be included in the preamble, since it would have a pompous and ridiculous effect." Bogomolov asked for the deletion of the article, but, as reported, by a narrow margin the Cassin-Romulo proposal was adopted and forwarded to, and unanimously accepted by, the full Commission.[20]

Bogomolov was not alone in protesting against the "abstract philosophical or religious notions" of article 1. Many members of the Commission seem to have been alert to various dangers involved in introducing philosophical, religious or ideologically 'deep' principles of human rights into the human rights instruments of the United Nations, and even into their own deliberations. One difficulty, of course, was the inevitably controversial nature of such principles to a forum which was supposed to be responsive to the entire world. A remarkable incident during the Geneva session may elucidate this issue.

---

[17] SR.2 pp. 4–5.
[18] SR.9 p. 21.
[19] E/CN.4/AC.2/SR.2, p. 4; E/CN.4/SR.34 pp. 5–6.
[20] E/CN.4/SR.9, pp. 21–22.

b. The Intervention by UNESCO

UNESCO, under its Director, Julian Huxley, had during 1947 carried out a theoretical inquiry into the foundations of a universal declaration of human rights, drawing on a large number of individual philosophers, social scientists, jurists and writers from UNESCO Member States; 150 persons were addressed, and about 70 replies were received, by UNESCO. In late summer 1947 the resulting report[21] was forwarded to the Commission, in the hope that it "would help to clarify its discussion and to explore the ground for a constructive agreement."[22] UNESCO later wanted to publish most of this material in order to aid "growth of public interest in the philosophical problem of human rights."[23]

The reception, in the Commission, was less than cordial. Mr. Dehousse (Belgium) found UNESCO's uninvited preparation of "this report...a very dangerous precedent. He proposed that, to show the Commission's disapproval, the UNESCO report should not be reproduced [for distribution to all members of the United Nations]

[21] Finally published as UNESCO (ed.) 1949. When submitted the report bore the title *The Bases of an International Bill of Human Rights. Report submitted by the UNESCO Committee on the Philosophical Principles of Human Rights to the Human Rights Commission of the United Nations.* It included a 13-page statement of "UNESCO's conclusions", drawn from answers to its long and detailed questionnaire, distributed to respondents in March 1947. This conclusion, called *The Grounds of an International Declaration of Human Rights*, was prepared in Paris, July 1947, and signed by Edward H. Carr (British diplomat and professor of international politics), Richard P. McKeon (American philosopher), Pierre Auger (French atomic physicist and UNESCO official), Georges Friedmann, Harold J. Laski (British political scientist and Labour politician), Chung-Shu Lo (Chinese philosopher), and Luc Somerhausen (Belgian civil servant and publicist). "All rights derive," it says, "on the one hand, from the nature of man as such and, on the other, since man depends on man, from the stage of development achieved by the social and political groups in which he participates." A modern declaration of human rights must recognize that civil and political, as well as economic and social rights, "belong to all men everywhere without discrimination of race, sex, language or religion" ..."not only because there are no fundamental differences among men, but also because the great society and community of all men has become a real and effective power, and the interdependent nature of that community is beginning at last to be recognised." The paper goes on "to draw a list of fundamental rights on which", the authors are convinced, "all men are agreed." (UNESCO 1949, pp. 268, 267).

[22] UNESCO 1949, p. 8.

[23] E/CN.4/78, p. 3.

but should be distributed to the members of the Commission only."[24] This proposal was adopted by 8:4 with 1 abstention, in spite of the Secretariat's "opinion that, under the terms of agreement between UNESCO and the United Nations, the document ought to be published."[25]

Why this negative attitude? One reason may have been territorial rivalry: "...UNESCO's action was most regrettable," Dehousse said, and he went on: "The Review *Syntèses*, published in Brussels, has devoted a special number to the Bill of Human Rights prepared by UNESCO. In all its articles the Human Rights Commission of the United Nations was not mentioned once."[26] At a somewhat deeper level the concern of the majority of the Commission members may have been the undeniably controversial nature of the contents of the UNESCO Report as a whole, eloquently spelled out in Maritain's 'Introduction':

> This book then is devoted to the rational interpretation and justification of those rights of the individual which society must respect and which is desirable for our age to strive to enumerate more fully. Many schools of thought are represented, each of which brings to the whole its particular view and justification of individual rights, leaning in various degrees towards the classical, or the revolutionary, interpretation: it is not the first time that expert witnesses have quarrelled among themselves. The paradox is that such rational justifications are at once indispensable, and yet powerless to bring about agreement between minds. They are indispensable because each one of us believes instinctively in the truth, and will only assent to what he himself has recognised as true and based on reason. They are powerless to bring about a harmony of minds because they are fundamentally different, even antagonistic....The very diversity of the interpretations and justifications put forward in the essays in this book is in itself an important object lesson for the reader....Is there anything surprising in systems antagonistic in theory converging in their practical conclusions?[27]

Maritain goes on to explain why he, on such a pluralist platform, finds expert witnesses quarrelling among themselves to be, nevertheless, indispensable.

But most members of the Commission felt, so it seems, that they

[24] E/CN.4/SR.26, pp. 16–17, see also p. 10–11.

[25] Ibid., p. 14.

[26] Ibid., p. 12; my italics.

[27] UNESCO 1949, pp. 9 and 12.

could do without the initiative taken by UNESCO. UNESCO's permanent representative with the Commission, Mr. J.L. Havet, in a letter to its chairperson ten days later, tried to make amends:

> UNESCO's work in the field of philosophy consists mainly in trying to bring about a better understanding among men belonging to different cultures and professing different ideologies. Under this programme, the General Conference of November 1946 decided that the first centre of interest would be the difficult problem of the philosophical bases of human rights.
>
> Of course, a purely philosophical enquiry into the basis of human rights is very different from the task of drafting an International Declaration or Convention. However, certain of the fundamental difficulties, which it was essential to solve for the purpose of drafting such texts, sprang from the clash of opposing ideological viewpoints. It was therefore decided that UNESCO's work should be carried out in collaboration with the United Nations Commission on Human Rights and that the conclusions it reached should be respectfully communicated to the Commission, in the conviction that this clarification of opposing ideologies and this attempt at a constructive synthesis could be used by the delegates to reach an agreement, without their being bound by them in any way.[28]

The significance of UNESCO's effort for the drafting of the UDHR, though hard to estimate, may have been considerable.[29]

c. Other Contributions

Next, in the processing of article 1, came two amendments proposed in January 1948 by the Commission on the Status of Women and supported by the Economic and Social Council (ECOSOC) in March. Responding to this at its third session (Lake Success 24 May to 18 June 1948) the Commission now accepted the substance of the earlier proposals by Begtrup and Mehta; the terms 'men' and 'like brothers' were replaced by the terms 'human

---

[28] E/CN.4/78, p. 1.

[29] In the discussions of the Third Committee of the General Assembly it was approvingly referred to by Malik, who was Chairman, and the French delegate, Grumbach, arguing for deletion of 'God' and 'Nature' from article 1, elaborated on Maritain's 'Introduction', quoted above. (Official Records of the Third Session of the General Assembly Part I (3. Committee), pp. 42 and 117.)

beings' and 'in a spirit of brotherhood' respectively. Inserting the term 'sisters' was contemplated but not deemed necessary to avoid gender discrimination.[30] This revision was the beginning of a thorough reexamination, article by article, of the entire draft declaration prepared in Geneva. But prior to the Commission's third session two other developments had taken place. During the three preceding weeks (May 1948) the Drafting Committee had once more reviewed the text, but without getting around to the Preamble and articles 1–3. However, in its report to the Commission it also included a drastically shortened draft declaration in ten articles submitted by the representative of China, in which all of article 1's contents were deleted.[31]

d. The Voices of Governments

In the first months of 1948, governments had been invited to comment on the Draft Declaration. As for article 1 these comments were few, but worth mentioning.[32]

Brazil held that of article 1 "[o]nly...the statement that all men 'should act towards one another like brothers', might be retained... since it involves a duty...The remainder of Article 1 has a certain philosophical and mystical character. Unfortunately, it is not exactly true that all men are endowed by nature with reason and conscience." (Add. 2, p. 2) — This sceptical note contrasts sharply with the Brazilian proposal, few months later, to insert a reference to 'God' in article 1!

South Africa wrote: "It is of the greatest importance, therefore, that [the Draft Declaration] should not be passed in a form so completely unacceptable" since it "embraces much more than ... that minimum of rights and freedoms which the conscience of the world feels to be essential, if life is not to be made intolerable, at the whim of an unscrupulous Government." Among the excesses, in their eyes, was article 1, which does not "purport, expressly or by implication, to define any right or freedom at all." (Add. 4, pp. 25 and 24).

France now proposed a much revised version of article 1: "All

---

[30] For details see: E/CN.6/SR.28, pp. 5–6; E/CN.4/SR.50, pp. 9–13.

[31] E/CN.4/95, pp. 14–15.

[32] E/CN.4/82, with a number of 'Additions' referred to in the subsequent few paragraphs.

members of the human family are born free and equal in dignity
and rights. They remain so by virtue of the laws.[33] They are one
brotherhood. Each is responsible for the life, liberty and dignity of
all." (Add. 8, p. 2).

The United Kingdom approved of amendments to article 1
recommended by ECOSOC on 3 March 1948: 'All people are
born', etc., until 'should act towards one another in the spirit of
brotherhood'. There is no indication that ECOSOC intended to refer
also to collectives. However, the United Kingdom preferred
'persons' in lieu of 'people'. (Add. 9, p. 3).[34]

New Zealand wrote: "The declaration should, however, state the
philosophical basis of human rights and fundamental freedoms...."
(Add. 12, p. 4). And as for article 1 their proposal was:

1. All men are born free, equal in dignity and rights as human
   beings endowed with reason and conscience, and bound in
   duty to one another as brothers.
2. All men are members of communities and as such have the
   duty to respect the rights of their fellow men equally with their
   own.
3. The just claims of the State, which all men are under the duty
   to accept, must not prejudice the respect of man's right to
   freedom and to equality before the law and the safeguard of
   human rights, which are primary and abiding conditions of all
   just government. (Add. 12, p. 24).

The proposed article 1, paragraphs 2 and 3, are reflected in articles
29 and 30 of the final declaration, and 1(3) was 'prophetic' of later
developments in inter-State relations, making recognition and
protection of human rights a condition for the international
legitimacy of States and their governments.

[33] During the third session of the Commission the sentence "They remain so..." was
deleted from the French draft, on the suggestion of Mr. Loufti (Egypt) and with the
consent of Cassin, before the draft was rejected by 7:5, with 3 abstentions
(E/CN.4/SR.50, p. 14).
[34] In the Drafting Committee the expression 'human beings', first suggested by
Begtrup, was chosen. One consideration was ease of translation into French and
Russian.

e. The Final Proposal by the Commission on Human Rights

Early during the third session, India and the United Kingdom introduced a series of additional amendments. As regards article 1 the changes did not go beyond introducing gender-neutral language.[35] This was by now uncontroversial. But Chang (China) added a further amendment, proposing that the sentence 'They are endowed by nature with reason and conscience' — in part due to his own suggestion at an earlier stage — should be deleted, since its "import...was controversial and its deletion would clarify and shorten the text."[36] Chang was vehemently, and eloquently, opposed by Malik, who deplored "the proposal to delete 'nature, conscience and reason'" and insisted that "[t]he first Article...should state those characteristics of human beings which distinguished them from animals, that is reason and conscience" (p. 13) — incidentally a view to which Chang reverted, later on. Now Malik received unexpected support from Pavlov (Soviet Union) who thought a solution could be found in the formula:

> 'They are endowed with reason and conscience', without mentioning the agent,[37] with respect to which legitimate doubts had been expressed.

Pavlov's diplomatic formula fitted Malik's argument but was not yet turned into a formal proposal. Pavlov would, he said, abstain from voting on article 1 since it appeared wholly misleading "in the light of present realities." Thereafter the proposed deletion of 'nature, reason and conscience' was defeated by 6:5, with 6 abstentions. By this route the draft article 1 in the Report of the Commission to ECOSOC read:

> All *human beings* are born free and equal in dignity and rights. They are endowed by nature with reason and conscience and should act towards one another *in a spirit of brotherhood.* (E/800)

---

[35] E/CN.4/99, p. 1.

[36] E/CN.4/SR.50, p. 11.

[37] Ibid., p. 14. To Pavlov the 'agent' seems to refers to nature in her capacity of endowing or bestowing human beings with reason and conscience, thus construing the draft text on the model of the American Declaration of Independence: '...endowed by their Creator with certain unalienable rights....' But this is a misreading of the phrase in question. The intended meaning is not *natura naturans*: an endowing agent (cpr. 'Creator'), but *natura naturata*: the essential endowment of human beings (viz. 'reason and conscience').

ECOSOC decided, because of pressure of business, to deal with the draft declaration only in plenary session. After two days of deliberations, 25–26 August, it transmitted the draft 'International Declaration of Human Rights', as prepared by the Commission, to the General Assembly, where it was referred to its Third Committee.

B. Article 1 before the Third Committee of the General Assembly

The 88th through 179th meetings of the Third Committee, from 30 September–8 December 1948, with delegations from all 58 UN Member States participating, were devoted to a thorough review of the entire draft declaration. Article 1 received more time and attention than almost any other — six full meetings of at times heated discussion and frequent mention in the general debate.[38] The main points were the following.

a. Transfer of Article 1 to the Preamble?

The fundamental importance of the content of article 1 was recognized, it seems, by the vast majority of delegates. It was variously named 'keystone', 'cornerstone' and 'credo' of the whole declaration; 'principles', 'basis', 'foundation' and 'framework' of the rights enumerated in its various articles.

Yet many delegates wanted it transferred to the Preamble. To most adherents of transfer this was no denigration of the contents of article 1. Cisneros (Cuba) early in the general debate pointed out that

> article 1 of the draft was a statement of fact and not a statement of a right and that, owing to its importance, it would be better to insert it in a special preamble (p. 38).

Bauer (Guatemala) followed suit. Being "general principles" and "the fundamental statement of fact" in the declaration its article 1

---

[38] The Summary Record of the meetings devoted to article 1 takes up 36 of the 901 pages of *Official Records of the Third Session of the General Assembly Part I* (pp. 90–126) — annexes and a number of additional references to article 1 not included; hereafter referred to simply by page numbers in the text. The UN abbreviation for this source is GAOR C.3.

should be moved to the Preamble (pp. 67 and 96). Beaufort (the Netherlands) argued for transfer to the Preamble saying that

> [t]he function of the preamble was to furnish a basis upon which the whole structure of the declaration could be erected. It was, consequently, the logical place for the insertion of fundamental principles which would justify the existence of that international instrument (p. 104).

The delegates from Venezuela, New Zealand and Uruguay argued in a similar vein. The case for transfer was not, perhaps, strengthened by South African support. South Africa's Te Water withdrew his earlier proposal of a much weakened version of article 1 (see below), a proposal which had aroused the indignation of Dedijer (Yugoslavia). Te Water now agreed "that the substance of article 1 should be incorporated in the Preamble" (p. 96). This move by South Africa, may, in effect, have strengthened the case for retention.

Carton de Wiart (Belgium) was the first to speak against transfer, saying that "[a]rticle 1 was important as a first article of a solemn document, since it affirmed a principle which in some measure summed up the articles that followed" (p. 96).

Chang (China) now "felt that article 1 of the declaration should remain where it was, and that the two sentences which made up that article should not be separated. A happy balance was struck by the broad statement of rights in the first sentence and the implication of duties in the second. Should article 1 be taken out of the body of the declaration, it would not claim as much of the reader's attention as it deserved to do...." (p. 98).

But some were less acknowledging. Article 1, Panama's Alfaro said, failed to give a clear definition of the right to equality and individual freedom, which were enumerated in other articles. Thus its first part "should simply be deleted" (p. 90), and its second part be transferred to the Preamble. Transfer of the second sentence now to draft article 27 (on duties — in the final text article 29), was proposed by Rozakis (Greece), in order not to weaken the effect of the first sentence (p. 98)!

Arguments for undiluted retention prevailed. In answer to Beaufort (the Netherlands), Frede Castberg (Norway) "pointed out that in the interpretation of texts in international law ...[t]he provisions of the articles had, no doubt, greater weight [than the Preamble], being as they were, definite pledges." He praised "the equilibrium of the structure so carefully planned by the Commission on Human Rights" and concluded that article 1 should remain were it was (p. 104).

Castberg was alluding, it appears, to the above statement by Chang. Other adherents of retention were Watt (Australia) (p. 103), Matienzo (Bolivia) (p. 103), de Alba (Mexico) (p. 105), and most notably Cassin who "felt strongly that if article 1 were transferred to the Preamble, the whole conception of the declaration would be upset thereby...." And the principles it contained needed repetition, Cassin argued:

> Within the preceding ten years, millions of men had lost their lives precisely because those principles had been ruthlessly flouted. Barbarism, which men had thought safely buried, had risen once more to stalk the world. It was essential that the United Nations should again proclaim to mankind those principles which had come so close to extinction and should explicitly refute the abominable doctrine of Fascism (p. 99). ...He reminded the Committee of the serious responsibility it would incur if it hesitated to formulate in article 1...principles which might meet with general agreement, despite all differences of doctrine. It was a declaration of vital importance. If it were set out in a long preamble, public opinion would say that the United Nations General Assembly had been afraid to proclaim its ideals (p. 106).

The vote, taken by roll-call, showed the following in favour of removing the content of article 1 to the Preamble: Panama, Union of South Africa, Venezuela, Guatemala, the Netherlands, New Zealand. Twenty-six countries were opposed (among them Cuba, thus voting against its own proposal), and ten countries abstained (among them the socialist countries). Thus, the proposal for transfer was rejected.

As far as the Third Committee of the General Assembly was concerned, the issues addressed in draft article 1 were hereby declared to be of pivotal importance for the entire declaration, and their weight underlined, by covering them in its first article proper.

But the substantive questions were still open, and to some of these we now turn. What were to be the foundations of human rights as proclaimed by the United Nations?

b. Exit God, Nature and Human Nature:
Debating the Sources of Human Rights

As suggested above, the locution 'endowed by nature with....', in the draft article, was not intended to imply (nor to exclude) that human beings were endowed with reason and conscience by some entity beyond themselves. The English text would be clearer, Third Committee Chairman Malik explained, if it read: "They are by nature endowed with...." (p. 97). This interpretation is unequivocally borne out by Lebanon's Azkoul (p. 119) who, as if to make his point, affirmed that he would have preferred reference both to human nature (man's essential characteristics) and to God (the endowing agent).

Brazil's de Athayde had raised the question of origins by proposing the following amendment of the second sentence:

> Created in the image and likeness of God, they are endowed with reason and conscience, and should act towards one another in a spirit of brotherhood (p. 55).

De Athayde assured "that he did not wish to start a discussion on religious or philosophical matters but...simply intended to express the religious sentiments of the Brazilian people, sentiments which were, moreover, shared by the peoples of countries represented on the Third Committee." He felt sure that his amendment "would be welcomed by an overwhelming majority of peoples if the world" (p. 91).

Support came from the delegates of Argentina (p. 109), Columbia (p. 112), and Bolivia (p. 113), all of whom interpreted the reference to God in an exceedingly broad manner. To no avail: it was rejected by other Latin American countries, such as Ecuador and Uruguay, whose delegates argued "that the Committee should distinguish between the divine and the human, and should refrain from placing the divine on the political plane by introducing it into the declaration [which was] intended for people of all faiths." Furthermore, "[n]o reference to a godhead should be made in a United Nations document, for the philosophy on which the United Nations was based should be universal" (pp. 100 and 101).

Belgium's de Wiart took the Brazilian proposal to be triggered by the locution 'endowed by nature with reason and conscience', a reaction which showed that "[t]hose words might be ambiguous and lead to long philosophical arguments and...amendments...of a particularly delicate character" "...[B]y deleting the words 'by nature', which were unnecessary,...the resultant wording would find general acceptance", he hoped — thus in fact following an earlier suggestion by Pavlov (Soviet Union) (pp. 96–97).

Chang (China) agreed, saying that this "measure would obviate any theological question, which could not and should not be raised in a declaration designed to be universally applicable." And he added the following weighty considerations:

> While the declaration would no doubt be accepted by a majority of
> Member States, in the field of human rights popular majority should not
> be forgotten. The Chinese representative recalled that the population of
> his country comprised a large segment of humanity. That population had
> ideals and traditions different from that of the Christian West. Those
> ideals included good manners, decorum, propriety and consideration for
> others. Yet, although Chinese culture attached the greatest importance
> to manners as a part of ethics, the Chinese representative would refrain
> from proposing that mention of them should be made in the declaration.
> He hoped that his colleagues would show equal consideration and
> withdraw some of the amendments to article 1 which raised
> metaphysical problems. For Western civilization, too, the time for
> religious intolerance was over (p. 98).

Later on Chang urged that 'by nature' be deleted in order to
facilitate that Brazil "withdraw its amendment and so spare the
Committee the task of deciding by vote on a principle which was in
fact beyond the capacity of human judgement" (p. 114).

Grumbach (France) followed suit, referring to Maritain's
argument as presented in the 'Introduction' to the previously
mentioned study by UNESCO:[39]

> ...such controversial issues should be avoided. The Committee's
> essential aim was to reach agreement on fundamental principles which
> could be put into practice. That attitude would be endorsed by believers
> and non-believers alike. The great Catholic, Jacques Maritain, had stated
> in relation to that very question that the nations should try to reach
> agreement on a declaration of human rights, but that it was useless to try
> to reach agreement on the origins of those rights. It had been that
> agreement on practical fundamental rights which had kept the leaders of
> his country strong and united during the terrible years of the occupation
> (p. 117).

In the end the representative of Brazil gave in, withdrew the
proposed theological amendment and hinted that the issue would be
raised again, when dealing with the Preamble (p. 117).

Many delegates seemed to grasp that the locution 'by nature' in
the draft was not intended to refer to the originating source of
human rights, but rather to state that reason and conscience were
essential attributes of Human Nature. Nevertheless it was dropped.

---

[39] See note 21 and the text to note 27 above.

After Brazil's withdrawal, the Belgian proposal to delete the words 'by nature' was adopted by 29:4, with 9 abstentions. And at the beginning of the following meeting a Lebanese proposal to insert the words 'by their nature' after the words 'are endowed' was, similarly, rejected by 16:6, with 8 abstentions (p. 125).

Why, then, was the expression 'by nature' deleted from article 1? Hardly just to appease the adherents of 'God', although at least one delegate, Chile's Santa Cruz, insisted that "[s]ince the Brazilian amendment had been withdrawn...the words 'by nature' should certainly be deleted ... and no mention should be made of the origin of man's reason and conscience" (p. 120). The dominating rationale was argued by de Wieart and Chang; they wanted to drop 'by nature' so as to avoid interminable, and specifically Western, debates about either God or Nature or Human Nature.

Thus, it is plausible to conclude that the Third Committee of the General Assembly wanted article 1, which it held to be the foundation and cornerstone of the entire declaration, to neither assert nor to imply that the system of human rights is based on any conception of Human Nature, or of Nature, or of God.

What was then to be the basis of human rights — according to article 1?

c. 'Born Free and Equal in Dignity'?

We have seen that the first sentence of draft article 1 was repeatedly said to be a fundamental statement of fact (pp. 38, 67, 96) — and, some added, for that reason ought to be transferred or deleted.

Dissatisfaction with the locution 'are born free...' was voiced by several delegates. Lebanon proposed that 'born' be dropped, so as to avoid the implication that though born free and equal, people might later on lose their freedom and equality. Support came from China (this time weary of the draft text's reminiscence of Rousseau), from Iraq (arguing for 'should be free and equal...' so as to express rights rather than a fact), from Ecuador (arguing for 'have the right from birth to be free and equal...'), and from Venezuela (so as to avoid the implication that equality existed only at birth — and not from the conception of a human being until its "development had been completed" (p. 111). Chile, very late in the debate, moved that the words 'and remain' be inserted (p. 124).

Pavlov (Soviet Union) held the theory that all men were born free and equal to be a somewhat shaky basis for the declaration. It is a fact, he held, that equality of rights before the law is "determined not by the fact of birth but by the social structure of the state. Thus it was obvious that in the days of feudalism men had not been born free and equal" (p. 110).

To this Moreno (Columbia) retorted that the philosophical basis of the phrase 'all human beings are free and equal' was fragile, not least because a "certain materialistic school of thought considered man only as the material expression of evolution and denied that his rights were inherent" (p. 111). In a similar vein, Pavlov was taken to task by Bolivia's Matienzo, who supported the draft text by stating: "Men were born free and equal before the law and before God and the consciousness of their freedom and equality was the determining factor in building their social structure" (p. 113).

Cassin had been the first to stand up for the words 'are born free...'. They "proclaimed the right of human beings to freedom and equality, a right which was theirs from birth"... "although they might later lose those attributes" (p. 99). France's Grumbach elaborated:

> All representatives agreed that inequality did, in fact, exist, but the statement 'All human beings are born free and equal...' meant that the right to freedom and equality was inherent from the moment of birth (p. 116).

Grumbach was seconded by Egypt's Bagdadi and by Kayaky of Syria, who "felt that the word 'born' should be retained as it would exclude the idea of hereditary slavery" (p. 118).

Thus, presumably, the so-called 'fundamental fact' in question is a normative, not a factual, foundation of universal human rights, enunciating freedom and equal dignity as what is due to every human being — whether or not it is in fact accorded to them. The debate on this question was not very lucid. Nevertheless the locution 'are born' (etc.) was interpreted by most speakers, it appears, to indicate the pre-positive and normative status of freedom and equal dignity, while 'freedom' and 'dignity' were left unexplained (pp. 110–124).

By a series of votes, toward the end of the 99th meeting, 11 October, the substitution of 'are born' by 'should be' and the deletion of 'born' were rejected, as was the expansion of 'are born' to 'are born and remain' — all with comfortable majorities, and it seems, in the latter two cases also with the feeling that little was at stake between the rivaling proposals.

Other proposals were rejected or withdrawn. At its 100th meeting the Third Committee first dispensed with Lebanon's proposed reintroduction of 'by [their] nature', and then with New Zealand's proposed abbreviation of the entire draft article, sharpening its reference to duty: "All human beings are born free and equal in dignity and rights, endowed with reason and conscience and bound in duty to one another as brothers" (rejected by 14:9, with 8 abstentions).

The most far-reaching proposals never came to a vote. De Alba (Mexico) proposed that "the rights of sustenance, health, education and work" should be included in article 1 (p. 91), but later agreed to withdraw the proposal (p. 122).

Te Water (South Africa) had proposed, and then withdrawn, a much watered-down version of article 1: "All human beings are born free and equal in fundamental rights and freedoms" — with the argument that the draft "article's reference to equality of rights was an enunciation of the principle of equality in respect of all rights, personal, social, economic and political, whether or not these rights were fundamental" (p. 92). Referring to the differing legal, social, economic and political systems in the modern world and the actual conditions in different countries, Te Water insisted that the scope of equality should be limited to "fundamental human rights" (p. 92). Earlier South Africa's Louw had been equally succinct as to what constituted fundamental rights of universal applicability and worldwide recognition; not the right to participate in government or to free choice of residence, not any economic right, he claimed, but "only such generally recognized fundamental rights as freedom of religion and speech, the liberty of the person, the inviolability of person and property, and free access to courts of impartial justice. It was not, after all, the function of the Committee to codify a whole philosophy of life." Unqualified equality in respect of dignity and rights would, Louw said, destroy the whole basis of the multiracial structure of South Africa (pp. 39–40).

Only Baroody (Saudi Arabia) had proposed a still weaker version of article 1, dropping from it any reference to rights and then deducing duties of brotherhood from ultimate aspirations: "Equality and freedom being the ultimate human goals, all men should act toward one another in a spirit of brotherhood" (p. 122). While South Africa provoked indignation, which may well have contributed to the retention of article 1, the proposal by Saudi Arabia did not even provoke a comment.[40]

---

[40] The Saudi Arabian proposal might be seen as a 'secularized' Islamic approach, placing duties at the forefront of the declaration. However, other Islamic countries, notably Pakistan, Syria and Egypt, voiced no similar concern and did not support

C. The Foundations of Modern, Globally Recognized Human Rights: Moral Principles and Sociohistorical Circumstances in Conjunction?

Returning to the question of the foundation of human rights, we may conclude as follows. The normative justification of universal human rights is, according to article 1, the principle that every human being is entitled to freedom and to equal dignity. But article 1 does not answer the further questions, why such an entitlement to freedom and equal dignity helps prescribe a system of inalienable and universal human rights — as spelled out in the rest of the declaration.

We have seen that the official answer takes recourse neither to God, nor Nature, nor Human Nature — although none of these are outlawed, and each of them welcomed, as it were, as optional rationales of human rights. Certainly, the second sentence of article 1 posits Reason and Conscience as foundations, but of what? Obviously of human duties but hardly of human rights: at least it is not clear, from article 1, what job, if any, Reason and Conscience are meant to do in justifying human rights. Are they meant to be those characteristics by virtue of which (most, but not all) humans are entitled to dignity and/or rights?[41] If yes, this is still not, I think, the intended doctrine of justification for human rights in the UDHR.

Drawing now also on the text of, and the discussions devoted to, the Preamble, the following scheme of justification for the system of international human rights may be reconstructed. Article 1 provides the crucial, but open-ended, normative justificatory principle; all human beings are born free and equal in dignity. The additional essential piece of justification, drawn from the

Saudi Arabia on this score. Incidentally, early in the general debate, Baroody had "called attention to the fact that the declaration was based largely on Western patterns of culture, which were frequently at variance with the patterns of culture of Eastern States. That did not mean however, that the declaration went counter to the latter, even if it did not conform to them" (p. 49).

This comment indicates a rare understanding of the distinction between cultural conformity and cultural compatibility. Though not conforming to non-Western cultural patterns, the draft declaration might nevertheless be compatible with those patterns of culture. But, as we know, Saudi Arabia did not, at the time, support the global implementation of human rights.

[41] See Wetlesen 1990.

Preamble, is sociological and historical; it proceeds from an empirically informed interpretation of the circumstances of world society, in the aftermath of World War II. Briefly and pointedly: recent horrors as well as challenges, threats and prospects harboured by the world situation, are seen to be such that a worldwide consensus and an internationally negotiated implementation programme, on universally applicable human rights, are required to secure freedom and equal dignity for "all members of the human family", now and in the foreseeable future. (See the preceding chapter on the Preamble.)

Interpreted in its proper context, article 1 is not a traditional Western natural rights foundation for a system of human rights to be implemented globally. It provides the thin, but crucially important normative basis, on which representatives of several cultures could reach agreement. But, as I have just argued, this commitment to inherent freedom and equal dignity is a part of a more complex, more realistic, and more 'open-minded' scheme of justification of human rights, which relies equally on an interpretation of historically evolving societal circumstances.

III. Appraisal

I started out quoting harsh criticisms of article 1, by friends of human rights. It is time to settle accounts.

A. *Improvements over Predecessors*

Let us start with a swift and sweeping comparison with classic Western predecessors. The admirable and pioneering declaration of rights made by the representatives of the good people of Virginia (12 June 1776) is squarely based on natural rights and contract theory. It declares:

> 1. That all men are by nature equally free and independent, and have certain inherent rights, of which, when they enter into a state of society, they cannot, by any compact, divest or deprive their posterity....

The United States Declaration of Independence says: "We hold these truths to be self-evident, that all men are created equal, that they are endowed by their Creator with certain unalienable Rights...." thus adding self-evidence and Divinity to the foundational resources, and foundational burdens.

And as to foundations, the French Declaration des Droits de L'Homme et du Citoyen (1789) makes do without self-evidence or contract theory, but it "recognizes and proclaims, in the presence and under the auspices of the Supreme Being" a structure of "natural, inalienable, and sacred rights of man."

I do not want to deny that article 1 of the UDHR is, in part, cast in the language of its classic natural rights predecessors. But this fact does not by itself decide the question of justificatory approach. And I have demonstrated in section II that justificatory approaches along the classic lines, that is to say, by appeals to Divinity, Nature, Reason, or self-evidence, were rejected by the fathers and mothers of international human rights.

B. Practical Potential?

The practical potential and relevance of article 1, as interpreted above, in the struggle for global implementation of human rights norms may not appear striking to the hard-headed legal specialists. After all, as John Humphrey complained, it contains "philosophical assertions which [do] not enunciate justiciable rights." And Humphrey is not alone among jurists.[42]

I cannot point to political struggles or legal cases where article 1, directly and by itself, has been decisive for the outcome. But neither, considering its nature as a normative foundation of the whole edifice, is any direct efficacy to be expected. And detractors may still be proved wrong about the more direct practical relevance of article 1. In the years to come the intellectual, moral and ideological battles on human rights issues may well, to a significant extent, turn on their cross-cultural intelligibility and justifiability. The open-ended combination of moral and sociohistorical rationales for human rights, provided by article 1 in conjunction with the preamble, is likely, I would argue, to enhance the cross-cultural prospects of human rights. The reason is simple; compared to natural rights and other mainstream Western approaches, the UDHR is from the outset prone to be sensitive to differing social circumstances and it may be acceptable from the perspectives of otherwise rivalling cultural, religious and political traditions. It epitomizes a pluralism as to justification which is minimally exclusive, and yet far from spineless. Any tradition, as long as it

[42] See Introduction to this chapter.

honours inherent freedom and equal human dignity and facilitates an appreciation of the pertinent aspects of the modern world order, can be brought, I submit, to support universal human rights. On the other hand, we must add, each tradition will have its problems and resistance points confronted with the full range of international human rights standards.

C. A Reasonable Claim to Validity?

But none of this is of much avail, if the interpretation offered of the foundations of human rights according to article 1 is mistaken. And it does challenge what has become a widespread view of the philosophy of the UDHR, due to Donnelly, Morsink and others.[43]

Donnelly and Morsink are no doubt right to claim that, according to the international founding fathers and mothers of human rights, these are "logically antecedent to the rights spelled out in various systems of positive law" and "are seen as inherent and inalienable, and thus as held independent of the state."[44] Thus the philosophy of the UDHR contradicts the view that only positive rights are normatively binding and the view that human rights derive solely from man's legal and political status in society; straightforward 'positivism' in legal philosophy is out. So is, it seems, the 'Marxist' position voiced by the delegates of the Soviet Union to the Third Committee. Bogomolov made it clear that "[t]he USSR delegation ... did not recognize the principle that a man possessed individual rights independently of his status as a citizen of a given State" (p. 775).

On the other hand, as we have seen above, the international founders also excluded from the instrument the specifically natural law doctrines that human beings have human rights solely on the basis of their human nature or in virtue of Nature's endowment.

Defenders of the natural rights interpretation of UDHR may retort that any moral or legal doctrine of pre-State or prepositively valid human rights is a natural rights doctrine, by definition. While this is perhaps not myopic cultural chauvinism, it is a much watered down version of the genuine thing, according to which natural

---

[43] See Donnelly 1982a and 1982b; Morsink 1984. Here I can only assert that much of the criticism of human rights based on cultural relativism depends on similar conceptions of human rights. See Lindholm 1990.

[44] Morsink 1984, pp. 333–334.

rights may be seen to be conclusions of an argument, the premises of which propound pertinent aspects of God, Nature, Reason or Human Nature.[45]

By comparison, article 1 provides, when interpreted in its proper context, in substance a new beginning of universal human rights — less metaphysical and more political than its Western predecessors of 200 years ago (though I would not minimize the political interests served by sticking to natural rights). It is an improvement over its predecessors by making human rights sensitive to the irreducible plurality of political and cultural commitments in the modern world, while inviting adherents of all normative traditions, natural rights theorists included, to join in the elaboration of universal human rights.

But the main, and final, point is this. There is no justificatory scheme for a globally binding system of human rights which, as a matter of political and philosophical principle, is more sound than the mixed approach we have reconstructed from the beginnings of the Universal Declaration of Human Rights. Or so I would like us to think.

[45] I hold Donnelly's view to be a 'watered down' version of the natural rights doctrine because he seems to conflate holding 'human nature' to be a sufficient ground, and holding 'human nature' to be a sufficient criterion, of human rights entitlements, and then to define a natural rights approach in terms of the latter, weak, version. The former, strong, version obviously excludes interpretations of historically changing societal conditions from being an essential part of the rationale of human rights. Further, it is insensitive to the structural and cultural circumstances of human rights; it seems to be oblivious to moral and other costs of implementing human rights; and it is probably parochially Western beyond rescue — while universal human rights need to be, and may in fact be, legitimized from most non-Western normative perspectives as well. I discuss implications of these controversies about the grounds of human rights more thoroughly in Lindholm 1990 and Lindholm 1991.

References

Cassin, René, *La Declaration Universelle et la mise en oeuvre des droits de l'homme*, Paris: Recueil des cours (II), Akadémie d'Droit International, no. 31, 1951.

Donnelly, Jack, "Human Rights and Human Dignity: an Analytic Critique of Non-Western Conceptions of Human Rights", *American Political Science Review* 76, 1982a.

Donnelly, Jack, "Human Rights as Natural Rights", *Human Rights Quarterly* 4, 1982b.

Eide, Asbjørn, *Making Human Rights Universal*, Oslo: Norwegian Institute of Human Rights Publications, forthcoming.

Humphrey, John, *Human Rights and the United Nations: A Great Adventure*, Dobbs Ferry: Transnational Publishers, 1984.

Lindholm, Tore, *The Cross-Cultural Legitimacy of Human Rights: Prospects for Research*, Oslo: Norwegian Institute of Human Rights Publications no. 3, 1990. Revised version in An-Na'im (ed.), *Human Rights in Cross-Cultural Perspectives*, Philadelphia: University of Pennsylvania Press, 1991.

Lindholm, Tore, "Minority Protection and Human Rights: the Tension Between Individual and Collective Rights", (Unpublished).

Morsink, Johannes, "The Philosophy of the Universal Declaration", *Human Rights Quarterly* 6, 1984.

UNESCO (ed.), *Human Rights. Comments and Interpretations. With an Introduction by Jacques Maritain*, London and New York: Alan Wingate, 1949.

Verdoodt, Albert, *Naissance et Signification de Déclaration Universelle des Droits de l'Homme*, Société d'Etudes Morales, Sociales et Juridiques, Louvain-Paris: Editions Nauwelaerts, 1964.

Wetlesen, Jon, "Inherent Dignity as a Ground for Human Rights", in Maihofer and Sprenger (eds.), *Revolution and Human Rights. Proceedings of the 14th IVR World Congress in Edinburgh, August 1989*, Stuttgart: Franz Steiner Verlag, 1990.

United Nations Documents: E/CN.4/21; 57; 78; 82 (with several Additions); 95; 99; E/CN.4/SR.9; SR.26; SR.34; SR.50; E/CN.4/AC.1/W.1; E/CN.4/AC.1/W.2/Rev.2; E/CN.4/AC.1/SR.2; SR.8; SR.9; SR.34; E/CN.4/AC.2/SR.2; SR.9; E/CN.6/SR.28; E/600; E/800

United Nations, *Yearbook on Human Rights for 1947*, Lake Success, New York: The United Nations, 1949.

United Nations, *Official Records of the Third Session of the General Assembly Part I (3. Committee)* (GAOR C.3), Lake Success, New York: United Nations, 1948.

Article 2

Sigrun Skogly

Norway

1. Everyone is entitled to all the rights and freedoms set forth in this Declaration, without distinction of any kind, such as race, colour, sex, language, religion, political or other opinion, national or social origin, property, birth or other status.
2. Furthermore, no distinction shall be made on the basis of political, jurisdiction, or international status of the country or territory to which a person belongs, whether it be independent, trust, non-self-governing or under any other limitation of sovereignty.

I. Introduction

The principle of equality, which is reflected in non-discrimination clauses throughout the body of human rights law, is based on a belief that differential treatment due to the special features of a person or the group of people he or she belongs to, is not in accordance with the principles of this set of rules.

Non-discrimination clauses can be general or specific to individual rights, and are seen by some as the single most important provision of international human rights law. The UN Charter and the International Bill of Human Rights devote more attention to preventing discrimination than to any other single category of human rights.[1]

In the Universal Declaration of Human Rights (UDHR), the general non-discrimination clause has been given the central position of article 2, and has been interpreted to be — together with the Preamble and article 1 — part of the general principles of

---

[1] Greenberg 1984, p. 309.

human rights and the basis of the Declaration.[2]

Article 2 contains the general protection against discrimination, while other provisions prohibit discrimination in specific situations.[3]

II. Historical Development

The principle of equality has a long history in the national law of some countries, beginning with the emergence of natural rights in the 17th century. It did not enter the general international level, however, until the adoption of the UN Charter in 1945.

Unsuccessful efforts to include the principle of equality had already been made when drafting the Covenant of the League of Nations, where several proposals for equality or non-discrimination were put forward.[4] However, none were adopted, and the prohibition of discrimination against national minorities was dealt with only in individual treaties with some States.[5] The omission of a general minority clause in the Covenant in favour of a specific provision in the territorial treaties applying only to certain States[6] was later to cause much bitterness and sense of injustice regarding the obligations towards minorities, as many other States with minority populations were not bound by similar provisions.[7]

These treaties, which consequently only applied to a few states, dealt with non-discrimination only in matters concerning minorities. The general provisions in the so-called Minorities Treaties related to "all...inhabitants" and granted them full protection of life and liberty and recognized that they were entitled to the free exercise, either public or private, of all creeds, religions or beliefs, the practices of which were not inconsistent with public order or public morals. However, these provisions did not give any

---

[2] Verdoodt 1964, p. 94.

[3] See, for example, articles 4, 7, 10, 16, 18, 21, 23 and 26.

[4] Azcarate 1945, p. 92.

[5] Zimmern 1939, p. 241.

[6] Such treaties with minority treatment guarantees were signed between "the Victorious Principal Allied and Associated Powers" and Poland, Czechoslovakia, the Serb-Croat-Slovene State (Yugoslavia), Romania, Greece, Austria, Bulgaria, Hungary and Turkey....Similar obligations were assumed by Albania, Estonia, Latvia, Lithuania and Iraq upon their admission to the League of Nations. See McDougal *et al.* 1975, p. 1054.

[7] McKean 1983, p. 15.

guarantees to others than those belonging to a minority race, language or religion, as the provisions of the Minorities Treaties were guaranteed by the League of Nations only in so far as they affected members of such a minority.[8]

Notwithstanding these ideas, a general protection by the Covenant of the League of Nations was not granted, and the Minorities Treaties were severely limited in their scope. However, we can still appreciate that the idea of equality of treatment and non-discrimination had been dealt with at a fairly early stage, and scholars were analysing the issue long before the coming into being of the United Nations and its Charter, and subsequent declarations and conventions.

It was, however, by the adoption of the UN Charter in 1945 that non-discrimination clauses applying to every individual became part of written and recognized international law. In the Preamble of the Charter, the first indications of the equality standard of the human rights provisions of this instrument are to be found.[9] And throughout the Charter the principle of non-discrimination is quoted several times[10] — in fact it is the only specification of the content of human rights to be found in the Charter.

III. Developments between 1945 and 1948

Keeping the atrocities committed by the Nazis and World War II in mind, it is hardly surprising that the non-discrimination clauses obtained a central position both in the UN Charter and later in the UDHR.

Following the adoption of the UN Charter and the establishment of the Commission on Human Rights (the Commission), the drafting of the Bill of Rights was initiated. The Commission set up a Drafting Committee, to which the Secretariat's first proposal of a draft declaration was presented,[11] wherein a general non-

---

[8] Azcarate 1945, p. 58.
[9] The Preamble states that "... the equal rights of men and women and of nations large and small...."
[10] The most important provisions of the Charter concerning non-discrimination are articles 1(3), 13(lb), 55(c) and 76(c) and (d).
[11] UN doc. E/CN.4/AC.1/3.

discrimination clause was included.[12]

The Drafting Committee established a working group composed of three representatives. In its draft, the principle of non-discrimination was included only in the Preamble,[13] not in any of the substantive articles.[14] The difference from the draft presented by the Secretariat was explained by Mr. Cassin. He stated that the drafts put forward by the working group contained a Preamble which spelled out the principles, and that non-discrimination should be included among the general principles.[15]

In the final draft from the Drafting Committee, a general non-discrimination clause was again included in the substantive part of the Declaration.[16] During the discussions in the Drafting Committee, the Commission and the Third Committee of the General Assembly, these aspects were among the major topics of concern.

A. Grounds for Discrimination

The debates on the list of grounds for discrimination created several controversies. At the early stages of discussion, some delegations[17] claimed that the list of grounds for discrimination should remain the same as those in the UN Charter.[18] During the drafting process, this view was abandoned, and the inclusion of more grounds for discrimination was accepted.

During the debates in the Sub-Commission on Prevention of

---

[12] Ibid., article 45: "No one shall suffer any discrimination whatsoever because of race, sex, language, religion or political creed. There shall be full equality before the law in the enjoyment of the rights enunciated in this Bill of Rights."

[13] This section of the Preamble reads "that it is one of the purposes of the United Nations to achieve international co-operation in promoting and encouraging respect for human rights and fundamental freedoms for all without distinction as to race, sex, language or religion." See UN doc. E/CN.1/1/W.1, p. 1.

[14] UN doc. E/CN.4/AC.1/SR.7.

[15] Ibid., p. 2.

[16] The text that was sent to the Commission and the Third Committee for adoption was only slightly altered later, and reads as follows: "Everyone is entitled to all the rights and freedoms set forth in this Declaration, without distinction of any kind, such as race, sex, language, religion or other opinion, property, status, or national or social origin." UN doc. E/CN.4/52.

[17] I.e., the delegation of the United States.

[18] Notably: race, sex, language or religion. UN Charter, article 1(3).

Discrimination and the Protection of Minorities,[19] the Indian member wanted to include 'colour' in addition to 'race', as he felt that discrimination on the basis of colour was not identical to that of race. However, several members of the Sub-Commission opposed this, as they saw the notion of race to cover colour. Other members[20] claimed that by including this there, it was implying that in other international instruments in which only race was mentioned (i.e., the UN Charter) colour was excluded. A compromise was reached by including a footnote to the effect that colour was covered by the term race.[21] During later deliberations, this was changed to include colour in parenthesis after race, and in the final version, colour is included on equal footing with other grounds for discrimination.

Another area of discussion was whether to include 'political opinion'. The Soviet Union's member of the Sub-Commission opposed this at an early stage, as he saw some political opinions to "tolerate not only the advocacy of racial or national hatred, but also actions arising therefrom."[22] Equal rights could not be granted to those who professed such opinions.[23] However, from other members, there was strong advocacy for including this provision, for example, the Indian member. His proposal was that political opinions should have the same protection as religious opinions. The French member proposed to go back to the proposal that the working group had presented to the Drafting Committee, where 'opinion' had been used in general. (This had been removed at the request of the United States because they wanted to remain with the Charter's listing of discrimination grounds.)[24] On the initiative of the Australian member, a compromise was reached with the words "political or other opinion."[25]

The final major area of controversy relates to the notions of 'status', 'property' and 'birth'. When 'property' was included, the Soviet delegation to the Commission wanted to add 'social status' after 'property'.[26] This refers to the Russian word 'soslovie', which has no direct translation into English, but which refers to

---

[19] An expert organ set up by the Commission; hereinafter: the Sub-Commission.
[20] I.e., Roy (Haiti).
[21] UN doc. E/CN.4/Sub.2/SR.4, pp. 2–5.
[22] UN doc. E/CN.4/SR.35.
[23] Ibid.
[24] UN doc. E/CN.4/21, p. 59.
[25] UN doc. E/CN.4/Sub.2/SR.4, pp. 6–7
[26] UN doc. E/CN.4/52.

privileges of feudal classes, normally determined more by birth than by property.[27] The United Kingdom wanted to delete 'property' altogether, and only keep 'status' as that would cover everything. The Soviet Union opposed this and wanted to retain 'property' as "rich and poor should have the same rights."[28] China proposed a compromise which was accepted: namely, to include 'or other' between 'property' and 'status'. However, during the debates in the General Assembly's Third Committee, the Soviet Union wanted to include 'class' to cover the concept of 'soslovie'.[29] This was rejected by the US delegation as 'or other' had been included to cover this term. After referring the question to an editing committee consisting of Cassin (France), Mrs. Roosevelt (USA) and Mr. Pavlov (Soviet Union), the final agreement was to include 'birth' after property, so that the final passage reads "property, birth or other status."

Related to these grounds for discrimination listed in the article is an important point made by the Sub-Commission. They changed one of the passages in the proposed article from "without distinction as to race..." to "without distinction of any kind, such as race ... etc." This was done to indicate that the enumeration was not exhaustive.[30]

B. Link between Article 2 and Article 7

Another major area of discussion concerned the link between the general discrimination article and the "equality before the law" article.[31] During the deliberations in the Third Committee, the Cuban representative suggested a merger of article 2 and article 6 (presently article 7). The reason for this proposal was that "by grouping them in a single article, by avoiding useless repetition, the Declaration was lent both greater force and greater consciousness, qualities that were indispensable in any legal text."[32] This proposal was opposed by the Chinese delegate as article 2 "did ... aim at

---

[27] UN doc. E/CN.4/SR.52.

[28] UN doc. E/CN.4/52.

[29] Summary Records Third Committee of the General Assembly, 1948, pp. 126–142.

[30] UN doc. E/CN.4/52.

[31] Article 7 of the UDHR.

[32] UN General Assembly, Third Committee, Summary Records of Meetings, 21 September – 8 December 1948, p. 130.

ensuring that everyone, without distinction of any kind, should enjoy all the rights and freedoms set forth in the Declaration", while article 6 "aimed at translating that principle into a practical reality by granting everyone protection of the law against discrimination in violation of that Declaration."[33] Cassin expressed his agreement with the Chinese and said that article 2 "set forth the principle of non-discrimination, whereas, in [article 6] the individual was ensured the protection against discrimination within his own country. Those two ideas were very similar, but ... not absolutely identical."[34] The Cuban proposal was withdrawn and the final text includes both articles.

IV. Codification in International Law

A. The Two International Covenants on Human Rights

The two international covenants on human rights[35] both contain general and specific non-discrimination clauses.[36] The articles are remarkably similar. However, compared with the UDHR, the general non-discrimination clauses are 'not so general'; they only refer to discrimination insofar as the guaranteed rights are concerned. One difference worth mentioning, however, is that the CCPR kept the term 'distinction' rather than changing it to 'discrimination', which was done in the CESCR. Delegates in the Third Committee preferred 'distinction' because 1) the Charter and the UDHR both employed it; 2) 'discrimination' would introduce a different shade of meaning, implying action; and 3) 'distinction' would permit no differentiation of any kind, whereas 'discrimination' had acquired a separate shade of meaning.[37]

Special attention should be given to article 26 of the CCPR which has been interpreted by the Committee to mean that the right to equal protection under the law obliges the legislator not to

---

[33] Ibid.

[34] Ibid.

[35] The International Covenant on Economic, Social and Cultural Rights (CESCR), adopted by the General Assembly 16 December 1966, entered into force on 3 January 1976. The International Covenant on Civil and Political Rights (CCPR), adopted by the General Assembly 16 December 1966, entered into force on 23 March 1976.

[36] The CESCR, article 2(2) and the CCPR, article 2(1).

[37] McKean 1983, p. 149. But see Bossuyt 1976, pp. 7–27 regarding the language chosen.

discriminate in any form in any law. Article 4(1) of the CCPR, which allows limited derogation in times of "public emergency which threatens the life of the nation", contains a non-discrimination clause. It is worth noticing here that the article uses the term 'discrimination', which was adopted by the Third Committee, without any discussion,[38] and that the list of non-discrimination grounds only consists of race, colour, sex, language, religion and social origin. The CESCR does not contain any general derogation clauses.

B. Regional Human Rights Conventions

The European Convention for the Protection of Human Rights and Fundamental Freedoms[39] (ECHR) and the American Convention on Human Rights[40] (ACHR) contain similar non-discrimination clauses. Article 14 of the ECHR restricts itself to a prohibition of discrimination in regard to the "rights and freedoms set forth in this Convention." Among the prohibited grounds is also the 'association with a national minority'.

The ACHR contains a similar provision in its article 1, but adds 'economic' to the word status and thus limits this category of non-discrimination grounds. It does not contain the specification of 'association with a national minority', as the ECHR does.

In the most recent regional instrument — The African Charter on Human and Peoples' Rights[41] (African Charter) — there are four articles dealing with non-discrimination. Article 2 of the Charter is similar to the general non-discrimination clauses of other instruments, with only minor differences as to the listing of grounds.[42] Special to the African Charter is article 19, which

[38] McKean, ibid., p. 150.
[39] The European Convention on Human Rights was signed in Rome, 4 November 1950 and entered into force on 3 September 1953.
[40] The American Convention on Human Rights was signed in San José on 22 November 1969 and became the tool of the Inter-American Commission on Human Rights, which had been in existence since 1960.
[41] The African Charter on Human and Peoples' Rights was signed in Nairobi in 1981, and entered into force on 31 October 1986.
[42] Article 2 states: "Every individual shall be entitled to the enjoyment of the rights and freedoms recognized and guaranteed in the present Charter without distinction of any kind such as race, ethnic group, colour, sex, language, religion, political or any other opinion, national or social origins, fortune, birth or other status."

relates to the equal treatment of all peoples.[43]

C. The Convention on the Elimination of All Forms of Racial Discrimination[44]

One of the first major conventions to codify in more detail the specific content of one of the non-discrimination clauses contained in the UDHR, is the Convention on the Elimination on All Forms of Racial Discrimination (Convention against Racial Discrimination).

As has been shown above, the UDHR and the subsequent conventions and covenants have all included race as a prohibited ground for discrimination in their general discrimination clauses. The Convention against Racial Discrimination defines what is considered to constitute racial discrimination,[45] and spells out the obligations undertaken by the Parties to the Convention in particular detail.[46] The discrimination prohibited in the Convention against Racial Discrimination is not restricted to the rights contained in the UDHR, but includes rights in the "political, economic, social, cultural or any other field of public life."[47]

The provision in the Convention against Racial Discrimination that has been most controversial, especially for certain Western countries, is article 4, which demands that "all dissemination of ideas based on racial superiority or hatred, incitement to racial discrimination, as well as all acts of violence or incitement to such acts against any race or group of persons of another colour or ethnic origin...." shall be punishable by law.[48] This article also demands that States Parties "shall declare illegal and prohibit organizations,

---

[43] Article 19 of the African Charter reads: "All peoples shall be equal; they shall enjoy the same respect and shall have the same rights. Nothing shall justify the domination of a people by another."

[44] This Convention was adopted by the General Assembly of the United Nations on 21 December 1965, and entered into force 4 January 1969.

[45] Article 1 defines racial discrimination as: "... any distinction, exclusion, restriction or preference based on race, colour, descent, or national or ethnic origin which has the purpose or effect of nullifying or impairing the recognition, enjoyment or exercise, on an equal footing, of human rights and fundamental freedoms in the political, economic, social, cultural or any other field of public life."

[46] Article 2.

[47] McKean 1983, p. 156.

[48] Article 4(a).

and also organized and all other propaganda activities, which
promote and incite racial discrimination, and shall recognize
participation in such organizations or activities as an offence
punishable by law."[49] Some states have seen this provision as a
limitation on the right to freedom of speech and expression, to an
extent that is contrary to their constitutions. Consequently, some
countries have filed reservations to this specific provision, while
other countries have not ratified the Convention against Racial
Discrimination at all.[50]

In spite of the reluctance of a few countries in accepting this
particular provision, this Convention is one of the human rights
conventions with the most ratifications.[51] To implement the
Convention against Racial Discrimination, a Committee on the
Elimination of Racial Discrimination (CERD) has been
established.[52] The Committee receives and considers reports from
the States Parties on "legislative, judicial, administrative or other
measures which they have adopted and which give effect to the
provisions of the Convention";[53] it may receive a complaint from
one State Party on other States Parties' compliance with their
obligations;[54] and it may receive individual complaints.[55]

[49] Article 4(b).
[50] The United States has not ratified the Convention, nor has it ratified the major
human rights conventions. When the United States signed the Convention on the
Elimination of All Forms of Racial Discrimination in 1966, it filed a reservation to
the effect that "... nothing in the Convention shall be deemed to require or to
authorize legislation or other action by the United States of America incompatible
with the provision of the Constitution of the United States of America." This
reservation was specifically related to the first Amendment of the US Constitution
which guarantees the right of free speech. See Schwelb 1979, p. 139.
[51] As of 1 January 1989, 127 States have ratified the Convention on the Elimination
of All Forms of Racial Discrimination.
[52] Article 8.
[53] Article 9(1).
[54] Article 11(1).
[55] Article 14(1). This procedure is, however, optional for the ratifying States, and it
needed ten States' declarations that they accept CERD's competence to deal with
individual complaints, before entering into force, which occurred on 3 December
1982.

D. The Declaration[56] and Convention on the Elimination of Discrimination against Women[57]

After the adoption and entering into force of the Convention on the Political Rights of Women,[58] the next step in preventing discrimination against women was the adoption of the Declaration on the Elimination of Discrimination against Women, in 1967. This Declaration does not define discrimination, as article 1 merely states: "Discrimination against women, denying or limiting as it does their equal rights with men, is fundamentally unjust and constitutes an offence against human dignity." In the substantive section, the Declaration includes articles that relate to the elimination of discriminatory laws, customs, regulations and practices; on educating public opinion; the right to equal suffrage; equal rights with regard to nationality; equal rights in the field of civil law; discrimination in penal codes; traffic in women and prostitution; equal rights with regard to education; and equal rights in economic and social life.[59]

Following the adoption of the Declaration, the issue of women's rights was the subject of frequent discussion both in international and non-governmental organizations. The United Nations declared 1975 the International Year for Women, and 1975–1985 the International Decade for Women. The Commission on the Status of Women held the view that an international convention was needed, containing measures for implementation similar to those of the Convention against Racial Discrimination.[60] In 1979 the General Assembly adopted the Convention on the Elimination of All Forms of Discrimination against Women. Article 1 contains a definition of discrimination based on that found in the Convention against Racial Discrimination.[61] This Convention has been seen to be

---

[56] Adopted by the General Assembly in 1967.

[57] Convention adopted by the General Assembly on 18 December 1979 and entered into force in 1980.

[58] Adopted by the General Assembly in 1952, and entered into force on 7 July 1954.

[59] Articles 2–10 of the Declaration.

[60] McKean 1983, p. 189.

[61] Article 1(1) reads: "For the purpose of the present Convention, the term 'discrimination' against women shall mean any distinction, exclusion or restriction made on the basis of sex which has the effect or purpose of impairing or nullifying the recognition, enjoyment or exercise by women, irrespective of their marital status, on a basis of equality of men and women, human rights and fundamental freedoms in the political, economic, social, cultural or any other field of public life."

promotional and programmatic; it does not impose immediately
binding legal obligations but does require parties to take "all
appropriate measures."[62] The only implementation machinery the
Convention established is a committee to review reports submitted
by the States Parties on the "legislative, judicial, administrative or
other measures which they have adopted to give effect to the
provisions of the present Convention and on the progress made in
this respect...."[63] It does not contain any provisions for inter-State
or individual complaints procedures.

E. Religious Intolerance

The last specific area of discrimination to be dealt with in this
chapter is the field of discrimination on the grounds of religion, or
religious intolerance as it is more commonly referred to.

In 1967, a Draft Convention on the Elimination of All Forms of
Religious Intolerance (the Draft Convention), prepared by the
Human Rights Commission and the Social Committee of the
Economic and Social Council (ECOSOC) was transmitted to the
General Assembly. However, no convention has been adopted.[64]
In 1981, the General Assembly adopted the Declaration on the
Elimination of All Forms of Religious Intolerance and
Discrimination Based on Religious Belief (the Declaration),[65] and
in 1986 the Commission appointed a Special Rapporteur to report
on compliance with the standards as laid down in the
Declaration.[66]

The Draft Convention contained in article 1(a) a clarification of
the term 'religious belief' to include theistic, non-theistic and
atheistic beliefs. Though the Declaration does not include any
definition of religion or belief, the *travaux préparatoires* reveal a
general agreement to the use of the same definition as in the Draft
Convention.[67]

In contrast to the Convention against Racial Discrimination and
the Convention on the Elimination of All Forms of Discrimination

---

[62] McKean 1983, p. 193.
[63] Article 18(1).
[64] Brownlie 1981, p. 111.
[65] Sullivan 1988, p. 487.
[66] Ibid., p. 489. Also Commission Resolution 1986/20.
[67] Ibid., p. 491.

against Women, the Draft Convention did not provide for any implementation machinery. The fact that the only specification of the content of religious discrimination is done through a declaration, and that the only supervisory body to deal with this issue is a Special Rapporteur under the Commission, indicates that the protection of these rights is weaker than that found in the other fields of discrimination we have been addressing. The Commission is presently discussing whether or not to start drafting a convention.

V. Implementation of the Provision in the Nordic Countries: a Special Emphasis on Norway

This section will briefly deal with how the Nordic countries, and in particular Norway, have dealt with the issue of non-discrimination in their national settings. The limited scope of the article only allows for concentration on two issues: racial discrimination and discrimination against women.

All the Nordic countries are parties to the Convention against Racial Discrimination, but how the obligations have been implemented varies from country to country. Worth mentioning here is the Swedish appointment of an Ombudsman against Ethnic Discrimination.[68]

In Norway, racial discrimination was not an important issue at the time of the ratification of the Convention. Norway was still a fairly homogeneous society, with few problems of racial tension and it was felt that the Norwegian Penal Code already contained a sufficient provision to fulfill its obligations even under article 4 of the Convention against Racial Discrimination.[69]

After the change in the immigration patterns in the 1970s and 1980s, and the more frequent frictions between groups of the Norwegian and immigrant populations, it has been proved that this

---

[68] The Ombudsman Against Ethnic Discrimination was appointed in accordance with the Act Against Ethnic Discrimination which came into force in Sweden on 1 July 1987. Among the main tasks of the Ombudsman: to consider individual complaints; to keep a dialogue with the authorities, trade unions, employers' unions, etc.; to participate in the public debate; and to advise on new legislation.

[69] Article 135(1) in the Norwegian Penal Code makes it punishable by law for anyone to express or in other ways publicly disseminate, threaten or expose hatred, persecution or degradation of any person or group of persons, on the basis of their religious beliefs, race, colours or national or ethnic origin. (Unofficial translation by the author.)

provision does in fact prohibit racist activities. In 1981, the Supreme Court ruled that organized dissemination of propaganda for racial hatred was prohibited and should be punished.[70] When dealing with these questions and incidents of racial tension, the courts have, however, been very cautious about the possible limitations this provision may inflict on the freedom of speech, and have thus interpreted narrowly the relevant provisions in the penal code.[71]

Concerning the elimination of discrimination against women and equal treatment of both sexes, several initiatives have been taken by the authorities, in the 1970s and 1980s, both through legislation and through administrative measures.

In 1972, a Council for Equality was established. Its mandate is to give advice to public authorities on matters relating to equality, to be a link between the authorities and non-governmental organizations, to carry out research on the actual status of equality and to disseminate information about questions related to equality to the general public.

After intense work by the non-governmental organizations, the Council for Equality and pressure from female parliamentarians and the administration, an Act on Equality Between the Sexes was passed in 1978, and entered into force in 1979.[72] This act shall promote equality between the sexes, and especially improve women's situation.[73] The Act deals primarily with equal opportunities concerning employment,[74] education,[75] and cultural activities and professional development.[76] In 1981, one article concerning representation in all public committees[77] was added to the Act.

The Act also contains a set of implementation procedures, including the establishment of an Ombud[78] for Equality Between the Sexes, and a Committee to which complaints about the

---

[70] See *Norsk Retstidende* 1981, p. 1305.
[71] Ibid.
[72] Lov av 9. juni 1978, no. 45 Om likestilling mellom kjønnene.
[73] Article 1 of the Act.
[74] Articles 4 and 5.
[75] Articles 6 and 7.
[76] Article 8.
[77] Article 21 states that "in all (such) committees, both sexes shall be represented, and in committees consisting of four or more members, each sex shall be represented by at least two members." (Author's translation.)
[78] 'Ombud' viz. the new term for 'Ombudsman'.

implementation of the Act can be sent.[79]

In addition to these three bodies established by the Government, there are similar institutions in all local administrations throughout the country. The mandate for these institutions is partly to supervise the local government and local administration, and partly to receive complaints about breaches of the Act on Equality in the local communities.

VI. Concluding Remarks

Article 2 of the UDHR is derived from one of the most fundamental principles in international human rights law, the principle of equality. The prohibition of discrimination applies to all other human rights.

In article 2, the general non-discrimination principle is related to the rights enshrined in the UDHR. This has also been the trend in the other general human rights treaties that have been examined, with the exception of the CCPR article 26, which goes beyond this limitation. The Convention on the Elimination of All Forms of Racial Discrimination and the Convention on the Elimination of Discrimination against Women go still further and prohibit discrimination in all circumstances where it is based on race or on sex, respectively.

Still, even if it is one of the more basic principles of international human rights law, full respect for this principle seems to be far away. Discrimination against minorities, against people on the grounds of race, against women, against religious minorities and against poor people, is far too frequent in the world today. The resurgence of racist movements in the industrialized world, and the very fact that a system of apartheid is only now slowly beginning to weaken, more than 40 years after the UDHR was adopted, is hardly encouraging.

On the other hand, the very fact that the UDHR, and in particular its article 2, has been the model for several initiatives in human rights law, both when codifying and implementing, shows that there is hope and that with continued patience and work, these elements of behaviour in violation of human rights law may eventually be features of the past.

---

[79] Article 10.

References

Azcarate, P. de, *League of Nations and National Minorities*, Washington: Carnegie Endowment for International Peace, 1945.

Bossuyt, Mark, *L'Interdiction de la Discrimination dans le Droit International des Droits de l'Homme,* Bruxelles: Bruylant, 1976.

Brownlie, Ian (ed.), *Basic Documents on Human Rights*, Second Edition, Oxford: Clarendon Press, 1981.

Greenberg, Jack, "Race, Sex and Religious Discrimination", in Theodor Meron (ed.), *Human Rights in International Law: Legal and Policy Issues*, Oxford: Clarendon Press, 1984.

Lillich, Richard and Frank Newman, *International Human Rights: Problems of Law and Policy*, Law School Case Book Series, Boston: Little & Brown, 1979.

Lov av 9. juni 1978, no. 45 Om likestilling mellom kjønnene.

McDougal, Myres, Harold Lasswell and Lung-chu Chen, "The Protection and Respect of Human Rights: Freedom of Choice and World Public Order", *American University Law Review* 24, 1975, p. 1054.

McKean, Warwick, *Equality and Discrimination under International Law*, Oxford: Clarendon Press, 1983.

Norsk Retstidende 1981.

Schwelb, Egon, "The International Obligations of Parties to the Convention: the United States and the United Nations Treaty on Racial Discrimination", in Richard Lillich and Frank Newman (eds.), *International Human Rights: Problems of Law and Policy*, Law School Case Book Series, Boston: Little & Brown, 1979.

Sullivan, Donna J., "Advancing the Freedom of Religion or Belief Through the UN Declaration on the Elimination of Religious Intolerance and Discrimination", *American Journal of International Law*, 82, no. 3, July 1988.

United Nations Documents: E/CN.1/1/W.1.; E/CN.4/AC.1/SR.7; E/CN.4/Sub.2/SR.4; E/CN.4/SR.35; E/CN.4/21; E/CN./52; E/CN.4/SR.52; E/CN.4/AC.1/3; E/CN.4/52.

United Nations, *Summary Records Third Committee of the General Assembly*, 1948.

United Nations, *UN General Assembly, Third Committee, Summary Records of Meetings*, 21 September–8 December 1948.

Verdoodt, Albert, *Naissance et Signification de la Déclaration Universelle des Droits de l'Homme*, Société d'Etude Morales, Sociales et Juridiques, Louvain-Paris: Editions Nauwelaerts, 1964.

Zimmern, Alfred Eckhart, *The League of Nations and the Rule of Law 1918–1935*, New York: Russel & Russel, 1939.

Article 3

Lars Adam Rehof

Denmark

Everyone has the right to life, liberty and security of person.

I. Protection of Life

In the Universal Declaration on Human Rights (UDHR) article 3, it is stated that each individual has a right to life and to freedom and security of the person. This article should be seen in the context of UDHR article 5, which states that no one shall be subjected to torture or to cruel, inhuman or degrading treatment or punishment, and UDHR article 9, which states that no one shall be the subject of arbitrary arrest, detention or exile.

Article 3 of the UDHR comprises three different rights, namely, the right to life in a biological (*inter alia*, the ability to survive),[1] and a wider (human) sense, the right to personal freedom, for instance the right to move about, and the right of personal security, i.e., the right of being protected against certain intensive interferences from the State or from non-State actors (integrity rights).

These different rights have all been elaborated on and codified in subsequent binding conventions, such as the International Covenant on Civil and Political Rights (CCPR) and the UN Convention against Torture and Other Inhumane or Degrading Treatment or Punishment. In this connection the emphasis will be put on the right to life, questions of protection and preservation of human life, and the question of the degree of State responsibility for upholding and safeguarding these rights.

---

[1] See as an example of this the Special Rapporteur's (Asbjørn Eide) report on the *Right to Adequate Food*, UN doc. E/CN.4/Sub.2/1987/23. See also Eide 1989, p. 35.

Lars Adam Rehof

A. Article 3 in the Context of the UDHR as a Whole

The Chinese representative in the Third Committee of the 1948 UN
General Assembly, Mr. Chang, proposed a conceptual framework
in which the initial three articles:

> expressed the three main ideas of eighteenth century philosophy; article
> 1 expressed the idea of fraternity, article 2 that of equality, and article
> 3 that of liberty.... The idea of liberty was then analysed and applied to
> the human being in article 3. Article 3 set forth a basic principle, which
> was then defined and clarified in the nine following articles [articles
> 4–11].... In that series of articles the idea of liberty was gradually and
> progressively enlarged; it was applied first to the individual, then to the
> family, and finally to the country. That series of articles therefore served
> to develop and clarify the idea of liberty.[2]

The Lebanese representative, Mr. Azkoul, later returned to the
remarks made by the Chinese representative and added some
important considerations, pointing out that

> since the eighteenth century, however, the idea of freedom had become
> much broader. The theoretical idea of liberty had evolved into the
> guarantee of certain rights and, in particular, of social rights. In modern
> times, the fundamental right was the right of the individual fully to
> develop his personality, which implied the right to all the factors
> essential to that development.[3]

The idea of a provision guaranteeing the right to develop one's
personality is a concept of current interest, which is reflected in the
German (Bonn) Constitution, article 2 (freie Entfaltung der
Persönlichkeit)[4], and has perhaps also, in a small way, influenced
the World Health Organization definition of mental and physical
health as part of the concept of "health for all by the year 2000."

---

[2] Official Records, UN General Assembly (hereafter Official Records) 1948, p. 154.

[3] Official Records, p. 168. A proposal to amend UDHR article 3 by introducing, after
the words 'security of the person', the words 'and to economic, social and other
conditions necessary to the full development of the human personality' was rejected
by the Third Committee with a narrow margin of 21 votes to 20.

[4] The full wording of the provision is as follows: article 2 — "(1) Jeder hat das
Recht auf die freie Entfaltung seiner Persönlichkeit, soweit er nicht die Rechte
anderer verletzt und nicht gegen die verfassungsmässige Ordnung oder das
Sittengesetz verstösst. (2) Jeder hat das Recht auf Leben und körperliche Un-
versehrtheit. Die Freiheit der Person ist unverletzlich. In diese Rechte darf nur auf
Grund eines Gesetzes eingegriffen werden."

II. *Travaux Préparatoires*

A. *Rights/Duty Structure of the Provisions*

A general topic at the negotiations in the Third Committee, which also affected the deliberations of other provisions, was the Soviet contention that the UDHR should necessarily include a reference to duties of States. The Soviet delegate, Mr. Pavlov, furthermore stated that "if all mention of the rights of States were omitted, it would be impossible to include in the declaration any reference to the duties of individual citizens."[5]

This was an expression of a fundamentally different view on human rights than the view presented by most (albeit predominantly Western) States. The view, which is perhaps now, at least to a certain extent, abandoned by the Soviet government, was that human rights were not only a question of rights but also of duties of citizens. This view, thereby, ran counter to the neoclassic human rights ideology according to which human rights (i.e., predominantly civil and political rights) were, and still to a large extent are, seen as inherent rights of citizens against the (abuse of) powers of the State.[6] According to the latter view, it is not a question of the individual owing allegiance to the State, but of the State, as a matter of natural justice, respecting the rights of its citizens as — and precisely because they are *eo ipso* — free citizens and human beings.

The wording of the UDHR article 3, as it stands, is an example of those provisions in the Declaration that describe the legal position of the individual as a reflex effect of a State obligation not to interfere with the integrity of the individual.

B. *As from the Moment of Conception — Protection of Unborn Life*

In connection with the negotiations on UDHR article 3,[7] the representative from Chile proposed that the clause should be amended so that it stipulated that the right to life should be protected as from the moment of conception and that it should

---

[5] Official Records, p. 82.

[6] Not only actions *ultra vires* but also unreasonable and unjust actions.

[7] Originally article 4 of the Commission on Human Rights' (the Commission) draft universal declaration as contained in UN doc. A/777.

include the right to life for people suffering from incurable diseases, for psychiatric patients, and foreigners. It should also comprise a right to subsistence for those who could not support themselves. Furthermore it was suggested that the right to life could not be denied to anyone but those people who were sentenced to death in keeping with national legislation. The UN Secretariat also proposed a phrasing according to which the right to life could not be refused to anyone except for those who were the subjects of a lawful death sentence.[8]

Contrary to this, the Danish representative stated, in a rather formal argument, that the suggestion that article 3 should include a clause protecting the fetus from the moment of conception was unacceptable because the legislation in many countries included the possibility of provoked abortions.[9]

Verdoodt concludes[10] that the interpretation of article 3 leaves a certain amount of doubt as to the legality of (all) provoked abortions and that it is not settled when exactly the protection starts. He also mentions that no explicit stand has been taken against the use of euthanasia of incurable persons and psychiatric patients nor against the use of the death penalty, nor any explicit obligation on the part of the State to protect its citizens against criminals. Some of these questions have subsequently been receiving considerable attention in human rights case law.

C. The Question of Abolition of the Death Penalty

One of the major issues during the negotiations was the question of the death penalty. A Soviet proposal[11] to include the abolition of the death penalty in peacetime raised controversy. This proposal, which may have been made for tactical reasons only, placed some of the Western delegations in a difficult situation in as much as they could not, for domestic political reasons, support a general prohibition. On the other hand, they found it difficult to argue against the Soviet proposal, which had the advantage of being a logical extension of the right to life. The Soviet proposal was, in the

[8] Verdoodt 1964, pp. 95–96.
[9] UN doc. E/CN. 4/AC.2/SR.3.
[10] Verdoodt 1964, p. 100.
[11] UN doc. A/C.3/265.

end, turned down by a majority vote by roll-call (rejected by 21:9).[12] One reason why one may assume that the Soviet proposal was made for partly tactical reasons is the fact that the death penalty was extensively used in the Soviet Union at the time and in subsequent years; another was, of course, the general atmosphere of animosity and confrontation between East and West (the Cold War) which influenced large parts of the negotiations.

This historical background does not, however, detract from the fact that the question of the death penalty is still a highly contentious issue, not the least in the United States, viz. Amnesty International's campaign against the death penalty in the United States and the apparent discrimination between black and white convicts in the rate of executions.

D. The Question of a Wider Protection of the 'Integrity' of the Individual

Another major issue in the negotiations was a Cuban proposal[13] to include the protection of 'integrity' (especially in a physical sense) in article 3. Some delegations argued that this concept was already covered by the wording 'security of the person'. The proposal was turned down by majority vote by roll-call (19:17).[14] A subsequent Belgian amendment,[15] supported by Uruguay, proposed a wording according to which: "Everyone has the right to life, liberty and respect for the physical and moral integrity of his person." This amendment was rejected by 21:12.[16] Mrs. Roosevelt, speaking as chairperson of the Commission, however, stated that "the words 'security of the person' had been chosen after lengthy discussion because they were more comprehensive than any other expression. The French representative had especially noted that they included the idea of physical integrity and that they seemed to cover most comprehensively various views expressed in the Commission."[17] In the end, the final wording of article 3 was adopted by 36:0, with 12 abstentions (mainly the Soviet Union and, at that time, dependent States).

[12] Official Records, p. 185.
[13] UN doc. A/C.3/224.
[14] Official Records, pp. 187–188.
[15] UN doc. A/C.3/282.
[16] Official Records, p. 189.
[17] Official Records, pp. 189–190.

III. Contemporary Legal Questions

A. The Right to Life

The question of the right to life extends to a number of different legal questions covering the period from the production of human germ cells to the phase where one is faced with a corpse. All phases of individual human life is in principle encompassed by this provision. In practice certain border situations concerning the beginning of life, conception, and the causation and process of dying, for example, in connection with the death penalty, but also euthanasia, brain-death criteria, medical treatment, and experimentation (extending to research in a wider sense) on live and brain dead human beings and human corpses have given rise to controversial legal issues and, in some instances, case law.

B. Provoked Abortion

The most recent question in the case law has been whether these provisions also give basis to protection of life before birth, for example, protection and the possible human rights of embryos and fetuses. Evidently this is not solved in the UDHR, nor is it verbatim enshrined in existing legally binding human rights conventions. Only the American Convention on Human Rights (ACHR) deals explicitly with the question of protection as from the moment of conception (article 4(1)). But even there it is not a question of any absolute protection. The recent coming into force of the UN Convention on the Rights of the Child has not changed this situation as far as provoked abortion is concerned.[18]

CCPR article 6(1) states — in contradiction to the European Convention on Human Rights (ECHR) article 2 — that every human being has an 'inherent' right to life, i.e., a right that is not given or granted by the State, but which is an integrated quality of being a human person and which, as a consequence, cannot be withdrawn by State authorities. This also means that this right, albeit somewhat vague in certain respects, exists whether or not it is recognized in domestic legislation. By virtue of CCPR article 6(1), the State has an obligation to adopt a legal system of

[18] UN doc. E/CN.4/1989/48, paras. 32–47 and paras. 76–77. See also Alston 1990, p. 156.

protection of the individual, including the adoption of an act of parliament — or a regulation of similar legal quality — concerning penal law. In comparison with the ECHR article 2 in which the term 'intentionally' is employed, the CCPR article 6(1) prohibits the 'arbitrary' deprivation of life.[19]

In recent years one of the most controversial questions has been whether human embryos/fetuses are bearers of rights and/or whether these entities should be accorded special protection.[20] A possible right to life for the human fetus will immediately complicate the question of provoked abortions, which entail a termination of life in the individual fetus. In connection with the negotiations on the phrasing of the CCPR article 6(1), a draft was discussed in 1950 at the sixth session of the Commission and in 1957 in the Third Committee of the General Assembly according to which human life should be protected "from the moment of conception." This wording, however, was not adopted. Against this background it must be deemed to be unsolved whether a fetus is in fact protected, wholly or in part, by the provisions of the CCPR. If the fetus is protected, this necessarily raises the question of the admissibility of consent by proxy, for example, from the biological parents, to the inclusion of a fetus in medical research.

In the ACHR article 4, it is provided that "every person has the right to have his [sic] life respected. This right shall be protected by law and in general, from the moment of conception. No one shall

---

[19] This is probably an example of the CCPR setting a lower standard than the ECHR, at least when judged from the wording of the provisions. The legal term arbitrary comprises different requirements; first it is a requirement concerning legal procedure (due process of law); secondly it is a requirement concerning the quality of the enabling clause (specific norm adopted by the legislature on a level equivalent to an act of parliament); and lastly it is a requirement of proportionality (the principle of a goal oriented but least intensive interference). See also UN doc. A/2929, Chapter II, para. 15, and Chapter IV, paras. 3, 31 and 102.

[20] Most would agree that there is a need for increased legal protection of early human development. The exact extent of this protection is, however, highly controversial. It is important to note that the concept of 'protection' differs, perhaps fundamentally, from the concept of rights. Some argue that, if embryos/fetuses are accorded 'individual' (human) rights, this will create some unsurmountable problems in respect of the legal rights of the (biological) mother. This is not necessarily true. Questions of human rights very often involve, as the most critical part, an assessment of conflicting rights. This is, so to speak, a very common and natural situation.

be arbitrarily deprived of his life",[21] and in paragraph 5 there is a provision according to which "capital punishment shall not be imposed upon persons who, at the time the crime was committed were under 18 years of age or over 70 years of age; nor shall it be applied to pregnant women."

One case (the so-called 'Baby-boy' case)[22] was referred to the Inter-American Human Rights Commission. The question was whether the United States was in violation of the American Declaration of the Rights and Duties of Man and the ACHR by not punishing a medical doctor for having performed a provoked abortion in 1973. The majority of the Commission found that the wording of article 4(1) of the ACHR according to which the protection 'in general' starts at the moment of conception represented a compromise between pro- and anti-abortionist movements at the time of the negotiation of the convention. During the negotiations on the wording of article 4, both the United States and Brazil had clearly expressed the view that they interpreted the expression 'in general' in such a way that it opened a possibility for the participating States in their legislations to include "the most diverse cases of abortion." Secondly, these two States emphasized that the last sentence in article 4 should be seen primarily as a protection against the arbitrary deprivation of life. A provoked abortion may consequently only amount to an infringement of article 4 in very rare cases.

Also within the human rights framework in the Council of Europe the question of abortion and protection/rights of fetuses has been the object of investigation. Several complaints have been lodged with the European Commission of Human Rights and a number of these have been dismissed. In the case Brüggemann and Scheuten *v.* FRG[23] the question was raised whether provoked abortion amounted to a violation of the right to family life in ECHR article 8. The European Commission examined whether the regulation of provoked abortion was justified as an intervention in private life and concluded that "pregnancy can not be said to pertain uniquely to the sphere of private life. Whenever a woman is pregnant her

---

[21] The need for gender-neutral language in provisions such as these is, from a present day view, very conspicuous. In Canada this has led to the use of the expression 'droit des personnes' instead of 'droit de l'homme', and rightly so.

[22] Case 2141, Res. no. 23/81 of 6 March 1981. See also *Human Rights Law Journal* 1981, p. 309.

[23] Complaint no. 6959/75 DR 10, p. 100.

private life becomes closely connected with the developing fetus."

As will be noted, the European Commission evaded — and possibly, after many discussions, deliberately so — the question of whether the fetus should generally be regarded as life in the sense of ECHR article 2. Not every regulation of (i.e., restriction on) the access to discontinuation of pregnancy is necessarily a violation of the respect for the private life of the mother. The European Commission also looked at the national legislations and it stated that provoked abortion was generally allowed in most of the member countries within a certain time period. Against this background the European Commission found that no violation of private life in the sense of the ECHR had taken place.

In another case, Petrus *v.* UK,[24] the question was what meaning should be accorded to the word 'life' in article 2. The European Commission found that article 2 could either be interpreted as not covering the fetus, or as a recognition of a right to life for the fetus with certain exceptions, or as a recognition of an absolute right to life for the fetus. The Commission, beforehand, excluded the last possibility in as much as that would mean that a higher priority would be given to the fetus than to the (primarily biological) mother, which in turn would nullify any form of provoked abortion even in the cases where the mother's life was at peril. No provision in the ECHR can be found which limits the mother's right to life and this solution would consequently violate the ECHR. The European Commission remarked that, at the time of signing the ECHR, all Member States had made provisions for a certain access to provoked abortion, at least when it was necessary in order to save the life of the mother.

In this situation the European Commission did unfortunately not find it necessary to take a stand on the last two remaining possibilities of interpretation. It can be concluded that, according to the practice of the European Commission, there is no absolute prohibition against provoked abortion. It can also be concluded that the fetus has a certain legal protection, and that this protection — apart from the situation of provoked abortion — may be more or less absolute in other relations, for example, medical research.

---

[24] Complaint no. 8416/78 DR 19, p. 244.

C. Experimentation on Human Embryos
and Human Genetic Material

In the last two or three years the question of regulation of human biological reproduction and the question of legitimacy of medical experimentation and research in a wider sense on fetuses (for example, research on computerized data compiled on the basis of information extracted from fetuses), on human genetic material, including research on human sperm and egg cells, has attracted increased attention, particularly within the Council of Europe. Deliberations as to the solution of these problems and the elaboration of guidelines have been given high priority. The Committee of Ministers in conjunction with the legal directorate of the Council of Europe established a working group (CAHBI), which has produced some draft guidelines on human reproduction and other questions concerning legal protection of human sperm cells, eggs, fertilized eggs, and fetuses.[25] The Working Group is now discussing a draft framework bio-technology convention.

D. The Death Penalty

In CCPR article 6(2), it is required that the death penalty should be abolished as far as possible. Furthermore, it is, somewhat superfluously, stated in paragraphs 2 and 3 that use of the death penalty should not be made in contravention of the UN Convention on the Prevention and Punishment of the Crime of Genocide (1948). Paragraphs 2 and 6 of the said provision can be said to build on the supposition that a State Party that has done away with the death penalty cannot again reintroduce the death penalty. According to paragraph 5, persons who at the time of commission were under the age of 18 years cannot be sentenced to death, and passed death verdicts cannot be served on pregnant women.[26] In general, the death penalty can only be used in connection with the most grave

---

[25] The draft proposals are published in a report titled 'Human Artificial Pro-creation', Council of Europe, Strasbourg 1989.

[26] This, in turn, led to a discussion whether the protection of pregnant women against the death penalty was of a permanent or a temporary nature, i.e., did the protection only cover the actual period of pregnancy or did it mean that the woman was permanently exempted because of her being pregnant at the time. It has been argued that the latter interpretation should be preferred in as much as the relationship between mother and child calls for permanent protection of the mother.

offences.

According to article 6(2), appeal has suspensive effect on the execution of a death verdict handed down in a lower instance. In accordance with paragraph 4, the State should provide the necessary enabling clauses in its legislation in order to make sure that the convict (the person condemned to death) may petition for amnesty or a permutation of the penalty notwithstanding the seriousness of the case.

It is stated in article 4(2) that no derogation can take place from article 6. A less restrictive wording can be found in the analogous provision in ECHR article 15(2).

With the adoption of the Second Optional Protocol to the CCPR, the States Parties according to article 1(1), are obliged to refrain from executions, and according to paragraph 2 the States Parties should by all possible means, including legislation, abolish the death penalty. A reservation concerning access to derogation from the prohibition against the death penalty in a war situation can only be taken at the time of ratification and not later. As for those countries which have ratified the Additional Protocol No. 6 to the ECHR, the question is already solved to a large degree. According to this Additional Protocol, article 1, any enabling clause in national legislation that makes it possible to pass a death verdict in time of peace and execute previously accorded death sentences shall be repealed.

CCPR article 2, read in conjunction with article 6, leads to the conclusion that no discrimination between different groups in connection with the passing or serving of the death penalty may take place. The execution of a death sentence will not, as a starting point, amount to torture, inhuman or degrading treatment or punishment. It may be said, however, that an execution that is of an especially lengthy, painful or unusual character may amount to a violation of ECHR article 3 and CCPR article 7.

It should also be added that in several conventions on extradition, for example, the European Convention on Extradition (ETS 24 amended by ETS 86) article 11, a State may refuse to extradite a person if the offence on the basis of which the extradition is sought can lead to a death penalty in accordance with the State legislation.

E. Use of (Lethal) Force by State Agents

The use of force as part of police enforcement is not dealt with in detail either in the UDHR or in the CCPR.[27] In the ECHR, article 2(2), *litra* a–c, an exhaustive enumeration of reasons for the use of lethal force is given. The reasons include self-defence, the execution of a lawful arrest or to impede a lawfully detained person from absconding, or a lawful action to fight violent riots. At the same time it is required that the lawful means fulfil — in respect of other provisions in the ECHR — a more restrictive requirement of proportionality ('absolutely necessary'). This requirement of proportionality may, *inter alia*, mean that general use of firearms cannot be made unless the suspected offender or the detainee him- or herself makes use of firearms or in any other way puts the life of the police officer at peril. It is not in keeping with the convention to shoot to kill in general. The use of firearms should only be made in order to prevent flight or to carry out an arrest, for example, shooting at the legs or other means to stop the pursued person.

F. The Question of Positive Obligations

A recent question is to what degree the State has an obligation to take positive measures to protect the life of its citizens. In a case before the European Commission of Human Rights[28] it was stated that ECHR article 2 does not include a requirement to put bodyguards at the disposal of persons who, more or less well founded, believe their lives threatened by illegal organizations. In another case a voluntary vaccination of children, which had the unfortunate consequence that many of the children died, could not lead to responsibility on the part of the UK as the measure had been utilized in order to protect children against certain diseases.[29] In the International Covenant on Economic, Social and Cultural Rights (CESCR), article 12(2) *litra* a, it is stated that the contracting States shall take steps to eradicate child mortality.

---

[27] See, however, *UN Human Rights Committee's General Comment* 6/16, and UN GA Res. 34/169 on a Code of Conduct for Law Enforcement Officials. In 1990 a specialized conference of the UN adopted a new set of Basic Principles on the Use of Force and Firearms by Law Enforcement Officials.
[28] X *v*. Ireland, case no. 6040/73 CD 44, p. 121.
[29] X *v*. UK, case no. 7154/75 DR 14, p. 31.

IV. Concluding Remarks

It is striking how up-to-date many of the discussions in the Human Rights Commission and in the General Assembly's Third Committee still seem to be. This is, no doubt, partly due to the fact that in some areas not much has happened since 1947/48 if one looks at standard-setting and implementation. Regional case law has been able to mend some of the most acute problems, but much work remains to be done. Another reason may be that many of the problems the delegates of that time grappled with are to a certain extent eternal questions. Questions of life and death — as they are posed now by developments in modern medical technology — are not met by easy answers. This, however, should not induce us to diminish our efforts to find contemporary solutions in international human rights law. There is a need for legal protection of early human life, including human genetic material and the early stages of individual human life (embryos/ fetuses).

References

Alston, Philip, "The Unborn Child and Abortion Under the Draft Convention on the Rights of the Child, *Human Rights Quarterly* 12, no. 1, 1990.

Eide, Asbjørn, *The New International Economic Order and the Promotion of Human Rights, Report on the Right to Adequate Food as a Human Right*, E/CN.4/Sub.2/1987/23.

Eide, Asbjørn, "Realization of Social and Economic Rights and the Minimum Threshold Approach", *Human Rights Law Journal* 10, 1989.

Human Rights Law Journal, 1981

United Nations Documents: A/777; E/CN.4/AC.2/SR.3; A/C.3/265; A/C.3/224; A/C.3/282; E/CN.4/1989/48; A/2929.

United Nations, *UN General Assembly, Third Committee, Third Session, first Part, Official Records*, 1948.

United Nations, *UN Human Rights Committee's General Comment 6/16*.

Verdoodt, Albert, *Naissance et Signification de la Déclaration Universelle des Droits de l'Homme*, Société d'Etudes Morales, Sociales et Juridiques, Louvain-Paris: Editions Nauwelaerts, 1964.

Article 4

Nina Lassen

Denmark

No one shall be held in slavery or servitude; slavery and the slave trade shall be prohibited in all their forms.

I.   Introduction

Freedom from slavery was one of the first, if not the first, human right to become subject matter of international law. Unlike the case for most human rights, anti-slavery standards enjoyed recognition in and regulation by international instruments long before the establishment of either the League of Nations or the United Nations. Nevertheless, despite this long-term prohibition, slavery has not been abolished. It was alive at the time of the adoption of the Universal Declaration of Human Rights (UDHR), and it still is a worldwide phenomenon.

Reports and information provided primarily by non-governmental organizations, but also by intergovernmental organizations and governments, show that practices of new and sometimes disguised forms of slavery are increasing rather than decreasing, with the number of victims running into the hundreds of millions in all parts of the world. Whereas the traditional forms of chattel slavery may have disappeared, the most widespread forms tend now to be debt bondage, exploitation of the prostitution of others including the traffic in persons for this purpose, exploitation of child labour, and the sale and prostitution of children. Other forms include the slavery-like exploitation of domestic help, forced labour and servile forms of marriage. Manifestations of apartheid and colonialism have also been classified as practices similar to slavery.

Provisions devoted to the abolition of slavery date back all the way to the beginning of the 19th century. The first multilateral treaty to condemn the slave trade was the 1814 Peace Treaty of Paris, followed by the 1815 Second Treaty of Paris, the 1815

Declaration and the Final Act of the Congress of Vienna, and the 1822 Declaration of Verona. These instruments embodied the general principle that slave trade is repugnant to justice and humanity and called on the community of nations to prohibit slave trade and on signatory States to take separate action against it. Although calling for 'prompt suppression', the efficacy of these provisions was weakened by the lack of specific deadlines and means of enforcement, and by references to the interests, habits and even the prejudices of their citizens.

The 19th century saw the gradual banning of slave-holding by Britain (1833), France (1848), Portugal (1858), the Netherlands (1863), the United States (1865), Spain in Cuba (1870) and Brazil (1871), but the Indian Ocean slave trade bringing Africans to the Near and Middle East began to expand, and local markets in Africa remained open. Several bilateral treaties concluded with regard to the suppression of the slave trade did not prove very successful.

Another important step at the international level was the adoption of the General Act of Berlin of 1885. This instrument affirmed that "trading in slaves is forbidden in conformity with the principles of international law." It led to the conclusion of the 1890 General Act of the Brussels Conference relative to the African slave trade, which provided strong economic, military and legal measures to stop the slave trade and created the first international organizations with an active role in this field, namely an International Maritime Office at Zanzibar and an International Bureau at Brussels. Pursuant to the Brussels Conference, slave trading between Africa and Asia was largely brought to an end and many more nations abolished slavery during the period up to the outbreak of World War I. By the 1919 Convention of St. Germain-en-Laye, the Parties endeavoured in their exercise of sovereign rights or authority in African territories to secure the complete suppression of the slave trade in all its forms on land and sea.

These international undertakings culminated in the adoption by the League of Nations of the Slavery Convention in 1926, which had initially been recommended by the Temporary Slavery Commission established by the League in 1924. The Convention entered into force in March 1927 and requires the States Parties, which currently number about 70, to prevent and suppress the slave trade and to bring about, progressively and as soon as possible, the complete abolition of slavery in all its forms in any territory subject to their jurisdiction.

The 1926 Slavery Convention defines the term slavery as "the status or condition of a person over whom any or all of the powers attaching to the right of ownership are exercised." Slave trade is defined as including "all acts involved in the capture, acquisition or disposal of a person with intent to reduce him to slavery; all acts involved in the acquisition of a slave with a view to selling or exchanging him; all acts of disposal by sale or exchange of a slave acquired with a view to being sold or exchanged, and, in general, every act of trade or transport in slaves." Subsequent instruments have generally followed the same lines.

II. The Drafting Debates

There was never any question that anti-slavery standards should be reiterated in the UDHR. The Drafting Committee on an International Bill of Human Rights at its very first session in 1947, recommended to the Commission on Human Rights (the Commission) that the UDHR should contain an article providing that "Slavery, in all its forms, being inconsistent with the dignity of man, shall be prohibited by law."[1] This wording was adopted by the Commission at its 1947 session[2] and, although it was subject to several amendments and extensive discussion in the relevant drafting organs before achieving its final version, it is clear from the records that article 4 of the UDHR as adopted met with no major disagreement as to substance and scope.

The drafting debate illustrates the contents of the article quite well. When it was recommended, for example, to substitute the wording 'shall be prohibited' with 'is prohibited', it was rejected by the Commission after extensive debates and the word 'shall' remained in the final text.[3]

While it was understood from the beginning that servitude should be covered by the article, the question was raised whether it was

---

[1] Report of the first session of the Drafting Committee of the Commission on Human Rights, UN doc. E/CN.4/21, 1947.

[2] Report of the second session of the Commission on Human Rights, UN doc. E/600, 1947.

[3] See, for example, the report of the first session of the Drafting Committee of the Commission on Human Rights, E/CN.4/21, 1947; the report of the second session of the Commission on Human Rights, UN doc. E/600, 1947; the report of the Drafting Committee of the Commission on Human Rights, UN doc. E/CN.4/95, 1948; and the report of the third session of the Commission on Human Rights, UN doc. E/800, 1948.

really necessary to refer to it expressly in the UDHR. Agreeing upon an inclusion, the Commission in 1948 recommended that paragraph 1 of the article should establish that "No one shall be held in slavery or involuntary servitude."[4] The question whether 'involuntary' should thus qualify servitude prompted debates on the right to work and on the protection of human beings against their own weaknesses. The question was further debated at length in the Third Committee of the General Assembly but finally rejected. Arguments in favour of deletion were based on the opinion that the word might provide an escape clause as slave owners would try to evade it by saying that their slaves had entered into servitude voluntarily; that servitude should be abolished whether voluntary or not as it should not be possible for any person to contract him- or herself into bondage; and that linguistic considerations spoke for the same conclusion.[5]

It was clear from the beginning that the drafting organs considered systems of forced, compulsory or 'corrective' labour to be new and emerging forms of slavery or servitude, and it was therefore assumed that they were included among the institutions and practices prohibited by the article without explicit mentioning.[6]

Furthermore, in comments on article 4, it was explained that 'slavery' was meant to cover traffic in women and children.[7]

Omissions tell a story too. It was discussed whether to include references to national laws and punishment.[8] Proposals were also made to merge the slavery article with the provisions concerning

[4] Report of the third session of the Commission on Human Rights, UN doc. E/800, 1948.

[5] Report of the Third Committee of the third session of the General Assembly, UN doc. A/777, 1948; and summary records A/C.3/SR. 109 and 110.

[6] See, for example, summary records of the Working Group on the Declaration of the second session of the Commission on Human Rights, UN doc. E/CN.4/AC.3/SR.7, 1947; and of the third session of the Commission on Human Rights, E/CN.4/SR.37 and 53, 1948.

[7] Report of the Working Group on the Declaration of the second session of the Commission on Human Rights, UN doc. E/CN.4/57, 1947; and summary records of the Third Committee of the third session of the General Assembly, UN docs. A/C.3/SR. 109 and 110, 1948.

[8] Summary records of the second session of the Drafting Committee of the Commission on Human Rights, UN doc. E/CN.4/AC.1/SR.36, 1948; third session of the Commission on Human Rights, UN doc. E/CN.4/SR.53, 1948; and of the Third Committee of the third session of the General Assembly, UN doc. A/C.3/SR.109 and 110, 1948.

torture and cruel, inhuman or degrading treatment or punishment.[9] It was even suggested to delete article 4 as superfluous and because it was a mere repetition of the language: "All human beings are born free and equal" and "Everyone has the right to ... liberty."[10]

As adopted, article 4 of the UDHR proclaims: "No one shall be held in slavery or servitude; slavery and the slave trade shall be prohibited in all their forms." This article is closely related to articles 6 and 7 of the Universal Declaration which provide that everyone has the right to recognition and equality before the law.

III. The Further Elaboration of Anti-Slavery Standards

Subsequent to the adoption of the UDHR, anti-slavery standards have seen also further elaboration in the International Covenant on Civil and Political Rights (CCPR), in other international instruments and in international practice.

A. The Convention for the Suppression of the Traffic in Persons and of the Exploitation of the Prostitution of Others

In 1949, the Convention for the Suppression of the Traffic in Persons and of the Exploitation of the Prostitution of Others was adopted by the General Assembly (resolution 317 (IV) of 2 December 1949). It lays down repressive measures against persons who procure, entice or lead away another person for purposes of prostitution and to gratify the passions of others, or exploit the prostitution of another person. It has provisions concerning people who are involved in the management of brothels, or knowingly let or rent places for the prostitution of others. The Parties to the Convention also undertake to find measures to check the international traffic in persons of either sex for the purpose of prostitution as well as for the rehabilitation of its victims. The 1949 Convention does not use the word slavery in this connection, but the view that exploitation of prostitution and traffic in persons can constitute forms of slavery has increasingly been endorsed by the

[9] Report of the third session of the Commission on Human Rights, UN doc. E/800, 1948.
[10] Summary records of the Third Committee of the third session of the General Assembly, UN doc. A/C.3/SR.109.

international community. The Economic and Social Council (ECOSOC) has thus in relevant resolutions referred to "this form of slavery" and "the enslavement of women and children."[11]

B. The Supplementary Convention on the Abolition of Slavery, the Slave Trade, and Institutions and Practices Similar to Slavery

In 1956, a Conference of Plenipotentiaries convened by ECOSOC adopted the Supplementary Convention on the Abolition of Slavery, the Slave Trade, and Institutions and Practices Similar to Slavery. Opinions had been expressed to the effect that article 4 of the UDHR was considerably more far-reaching in its implications than the 1926 Slavery Convention, thus providing the basis for the preparation of a new instrument which would speed up the abolition of still-existing slavery and extend the scope of international concern to include other types of servitude as well as slavery.[12]

As a result of these deliberations, the 1956 Convention was so drafted as to cover in detail debt bondage, serfdom, servile forms of marriage and the exploitation of children as institutions and practices similar to slavery. The parties shall take all practicable and necessary measures for bringing about the complete abolition or abandonment of these institutions and practices "where they still exist and whether or not they are covered by the definition of slavery" as contained in the 1926 Slavery Convention. The Supplementary Convention thus leaves open another question raised during the drafting process, namely, whether or not the institutions and practices described actually fall within the scope of the definitions already contained in the 1926 Slavery Convention.

Furthermore, the Supplementary Convention provides for co-operation with and reporting between States as well as with the Secretary-General of the United Nations.

---

[11] See, for example, resolutions 1981/40 and 1983/30.

[12] Final Report of the Ad Hoc Committee on Slavery, UN doc. E/1988, para. 25.

C. The CCPR

Article 8 of the CCPR embodies the principle of freedom from slavery. To a large extent it is a repetition of the provision laid down in the UDHR. As to the distinction between 'slavery' and 'servitude' which is made in paragraphs 1 and 2 of article 8, the drafters of the CCPR pointed out that these were two different concepts and should consequently be dealt with in two separate paragraphs. Slavery was considered a relatively limited and technical notion, which implied the destruction of the juridical personality of the victim, and servitude a more general idea covering all possible forms of one person's domination of another.[13]

The only substantive difference between the CCPR and the UDHR concerns the institutions and practices of forced and compulsory labour. Paragraph 3 of article 8 in the CCPR states: "No one shall be required to perform forced or compulsory labour", albeit excluding from the rule prison work, military service or national service required of conscientious objectors, emergency or calamity work, and any work which forms part of normal civil obligations. The UDHR is silent on this point.[14]

The drafting history does not provide an explanation for the discrepancy between the two instruments when it comes to forced or compulsory labour. The main concern has most likely been one of technical nature. This has its support in the special exceptions and omissions applicable to forced or compulsory labour, but not to other forms of slavery and servitude. It is also indicated by the absence of a 'graduating' provision similar to article 5 of the 1926 Slavery Convention which requires the parties to take all necessary measures to "prevent compulsory or forced labour from developing into conditions analogous to slavery." These points, together with the lack of explicit provisions with regard to forced or compulsory

---

[13] *Annotations to the text of the draft International Covenant on Human Rights*, prepared by the Secretary-General, UN doc. A/2929, chapter VI, para. 18.

[14] None of the major UN instruments have included a definition of the term 'forced or compulsory labour', but the International Labour Organisation's Forced Labour Convention, 1930 (no. 29) defines it, in article 2(1), as "all work or service which is exacted from any person under the menace of any penalty and for which the said person has not offered himself voluntarily." This wording, however, was not considered satisfactory for inclusion in the CCPR for reasons related to the exceptions listed in para. 2 of the same article. (see also Ibid., chapter VI, para. 19.)

labour in the 1956 Supplementary Convention, support the view that, despite different terminology, it was not the intention to change or oppose in substance the understanding of the drafters of the UDHR, namely that forced or compulsory labour constitutes forms of slavery or servitude.

D. *Apartheid and Colonialism*

ECOSOC and its subordinate organs have from 1966 included apartheid and colonialism in the consideration of their agenda items relating to slavery and slavery-like practices. In 1967, ECOSOC resolution 1232 (XLII) affirmed "that the racist policies of apartheid and colonialism constitute slavery-like practices...." This is a good example of practice further expanding the anti-slavery concepts and standards.

E. *The International Labour Organisation*

Since its establishment in 1919, the International Labour Organisation has been actively involved in the abolition of slavery through the adoption of several conventions and recommendations and through its implementation machinery. Of the most relevant conventions, one can mention the Convention concerning Forced Labour, 1930 (no. 29), the Convention concerning the Abolition of Forced Labour, 1957 (no. 105), and the Indigenous and Tribal Populations Convention, 1957 (no. 107). Of particular interest with regard to the abolition of child labour is the Convention on Minimum Age for Admission to Employment, 1973 (no. 138).

IV. Implementation of Anti-Slavery Measures

By a 1953 Protocol to the 1926 Slavery Convention, it was agreed that the United Nations would take over the supervisory functions of the League of Nations.

The focal point for implementation activities in the United Nations is the Working Group on Contemporary Forms of Slavery. Appointed in 1974 by the Sub-Commission (resolution 11 (XXVII)) and authorized by the Commission and ECOSOC, the working group has the overall mandate to "review developments in the field of slavery and the slave trade in all their practices and manifestations, including the slavery-like practices of apartheid and colonialism, the traffic in persons and the exploitation of the prostitution of others" as they are defined in the 1926 Slavery Convention, the 1956 Supplementary Convention, and the 1949 Convention for the Suppression of the Traffic in Persons and of the Exploitation of the Prostitution of Others.

The working group, which is composed of five independent expert members, meets annually for five days prior to the sessions of the Sub-Commission to which it also reports.[15] Its main task in actual fact is the consideration of information submitted by non-governmental organizations concerning alleged slavery and slavery-like situations in specific countries, often resulting in recommendations to the Sub-Commission for further action. It has quite a unique potential within the United Nations and it has already become, because of its composition and specialized mandate, an excellent forum for constructive dialogue between governments and intergovernmental and non-governmental organizations. The working group has certainly raised our awareness about the many still-existing problems and practices during its 16 years of existence. Many situations which would otherwise have gone unnoticed have, because of initiatives taken by the working group, been brought to the attention of the relevant governments and international organs.

A highlight in this field of implementation efforts was the so-called Mission to Mauritania. On the invitation of the government, an expert of the Sub-Commission (Marc Bossuyt) visited the country in order to examine the prevailing situation with regard to slavery and slave trade and to study the country's needs in its struggle to end those practices. The mission and the expert's reports[16] deserve particular mentioning because they obviously

---

[15] The reports of the 15 first sessions of the Working Group are contained in UN docs. E/CN.4/Sub.2/AC.2/3, 1975; E/CN.4/Sub.2/373, 1976; E/CN.4/Sub.2/389, 1977; E/CN.4/Sub.2/410, 1978; E/CN.4/Sub.2/434, 1979; E/CN.4/Sub.2/447, 1980; E/CN.4/Sub.2/486, 1981; E/CN.4/Sub.2/1982/21 and Corr.1, 1982; E/CN.4/Sub.2/1983/27, 1983; E/CN.4/Sub.2/1984/25, 1984; E/CN.4/Sub.2/1985/25, 1985; E/CN.4/Sub.2/1987/25, 1987; E/CN.4/Sub.2/1988/32, 1988; E/CN.4/Sub.2/1989/39, 1989; and E/CN.4/Sub.2/1990/44, 1990.

[16] *Report of the Mission to Mauritania* (UN doc. E/CN.4/Sub.2/1984/23), *Interim Follow-up Report on the Mission to Mauritania* (UN doc. E/CN.4/Sub.2/1985/26), and *Final Follow-up Report on the Mission to Mauritania* (UN doc. E/CN.4/Sub.2/1987/27).

contributed to encouraging Mauritania in her efforts to abolish slavery and its consequences, and because they demonstrate one of the means for successful implementation activities.

Communications concerning individual cases of slavery can also be submitted to the Human Rights Committee, under the CCPR and its Optional Protocol. In addition, communications concerning slavery situations can be brought up in accordance with the so-called 1503 procedure established by ECOSOC resolution 1503 (XLVIII). Very few cases have been dealt with under these procedures.

V. Studies of Slavery

Several studies relating to slavery have been undertaken within the UN human rights programme. Special Rapporteurs appointed by the Sub-Commission have prepared reports on slavery (Mohammed Awad in 1966 and Benjamin Whitaker in 1982)[17] and on the exploitation of child labour (Abdelwahab Bouhdiba in 1981).[18]

In 1983, a Special Rapporteur (Jean Fernand-Laurent) appointed by the Secretary-General wrote a synthesis of the surveys and studies on the traffic in persons and the exploitation of the prostitution of others, and on this basis he submitted proposals to ECOSOC for appropriate measures to prevent and suppress those practices.[19] In 1988, a study on the legal and social problems of sexual minorities, prepared by Jean Fernand-Laurent was submitted to the Sub-Commission.[20]

In addition, the Secretary-General has prepared a few studies on specific areas within the field of slavery and slavery-like practices. As examples, one can mention reports on apartheid as a collective form of slavery (1980);[21] the sale of children (1987);[22] the legal and

---

[17] UN, *Report on Slavery*, Sales no. 67. XIV.2, and United Nations, *Slavery*, Sales no. E.84.XIV.1.

[18] UN, *The Exploitation of Child Labour*, Sales no. E.82.XIV.2.

[19] *Activities for the Advancement of Women: Equality, Development and Peace*, UN doc. E/1983/7 and Corr. 1 and 2.

[20] *The Legal and Social Problems of Sexual Minorities*, UN doc. E/CN.4/Sub.2/1988/31.

[21] *Apartheid as a Collective Form of Slavery*, UN doc. E/CN.4/Sub.2/449.

[22] *The Sale of Children*, UN doc. E/CN.4/Sub.2/1987/24.

social problems of sexual minorities (1987);[23] a survey of the recommendations made by the Working Group on Slavery and Slavery-like Practices since its inception (1988);[24] and on the adoption of children for commercial purposes and the recruitment of children into government and non-governmental armed forces (1990).[25]

VI. Other Anti-Slavery Provisions

The 1950 European Convention of Human Rights (ECHR) contains in article 4 provisions very similar to those of the CCPR although it omits prohibition of slave trade.

Article 6 of the American Convention on Human Rights (ACHR) of 1969 has provisions similar to the CCPR and, in addition, it prohibits traffic in women.

The African Charter on Human and People's Rights (African Charter) of 1981 states in article 5: "All forms of exploitation and degradation of man, particularly slavery, slave trade ... shall be prohibited", but it leaves out references to servitude and forced labour.

VII. The Nordic Situation

All the Nordic countries claim slavery, slave trade and slavery practices to be non-existent. So far, no allegations to the contrary, which have been raised at international bodies, have been determined to be well founded. In Sweden, protection against slavery, slave trade, forced labour, corporal punishment and physical integrity is guaranteed by the Constitution. Norway has similar provisions in its Penal Code, article 225. The Danish Penal Code contains safeguards against deprivation of the liberty of persons and the exploitation of the prostitution of others.

---

[23] *The Legal and Social Problems of Sexual Minorities*, UN doc. E/CN.4/Sub.2/1987/28.

[24] *Survey of Recommendations Made by the Working Group on Slavery and Slavery-like Practices since its Inception*, UN doc. E/CN.4/Sub.2/1988/29.

[25] *The Adoption of Children for Commercial Purposes and the Recruitment of Children into Government and Non-Governmental Armed Forces*, UN doc. E/CN.4/Sub.2/1990/43.

Guarantees against slavery and slavery-like practices in Finland are to be found in the Finnish Penal Code.

VIII. Conclusion

It is not difficult to conclude that international action for the abolition of slavery and the slave trade has proved successful as far as standard-setting is concerned. These provisions have acquired universal recognition. Similarly, the efforts made by the international community have led to the disappearance of slavery from national legislations throughout the world. Finally, these efforts have resulted in putting up the existing implementation machinery.

Nevertheless, all the standards and implementation efforts, notwithstanding the occasional success story, are not enough. The fact that millions of people still suffer from slavery and slavery-like practices leads inevitably to the conclusion that the implementation part has not been accomplished and that the response of the international community to these persisting problems leaves much to be desired. Even the Working Group on Contemporary Forms of Slavery, the centre of current activities, for years suffered from poor attendance and limited resources to a point where it seemed almost not worthwhile continuing. Reading its annual reports up to 1987, at least four points for relatively easy improvement came immediately to attention: consideration of too many items and too many countries at each working group session, which resulted in the working group exceeding its resources; lack of follow-up action by the working group itself; poor participation by the competent intergovernmental organizations at its sessions; and questions of coordination and co-operation between the various organs which have or should have a particular interest and influence in this field.

These shortcomings led to a growing dissatisfaction with the working group. As a result, at its 40th session, the Sub-Commission, by its resolution 1988/31, approved a programme of work of the working group for the period 1989–1991. This programme, addressing the heart of the above problems, included three main themes to be discussed in successive years: prevention of the sale of children, of prostitution of children and of the use of children in pornography (1989); eradication of the exploitation of child labour and of debt bondage (1990); and prevention of traffic in persons and of the exploitation of the prostitution of others (1991).

So far, the implementation of the above programme of work has proved successful. The number of participants of the working group has increased significantly during the last two sessions, and the efficiency of its work and quality and strength behind its recommendations to the Sub-Commission have considerably improved. Programmes of action for prevention of the sale of children, child prostitution and child pornography, and for the elimination of the exploitation of child labour have been drafted and submitted to the governments for comments. At its 46th session, the Commission, moreover, by its resolution 1990/68, on the initiative of the working group, decided to appoint a Special Rapporteur, Vitit Muntharborn (Bangkok) to consider matters relating to the sale of children, child prostitution and child pornography, including the problem of adoption of children for commercial purposes. The Special Rapporteur is expected to submit his report at the 47th session of the Commission.

With comprehensive standards in force, it is reasonable to expect that the available human and financial resources should be used for improving the efficiency of the implementation machinery. Remedying the shortcomings of the working group has already brought about a considerable improvement.

Article 5

Hans Danelius

Sweden

No one shall be subjected to torture or to cruel, inhuman or degrading treatment or punishment.

In his well-known book *Dei delitti e delle pene* ('On Crimes and Punishments'), first published in 1764, Cesare Beccaria forcefully attacked the practice of torture and pleaded for its total abolition. In his view, torture was "a secure means of acquitting strong criminals and of convicting innocent but weak persons." His pleading was well in line with the human rights ideology of the Enlightenment, and its impact was considerable.

In the course of the subsequent decades, many European countries experienced a significant development of their criminal laws away from cruel forms of punishment and towards an increased respect for individual rights. In this context, torture as a method for eliciting the truth was removed from several criminal codes. In Sweden, King Gustavus III wrote, on 27 August 1772, to the Governors of all the Swedish provinces, ordering them to destroy any torture chambers that might exist in their provinces so as to make it impossible to use them for any interrogation under torture.

The practical results of the 'human rights' movement which swept through Europe at the end of the 18th century and the beginning of the 19th century were in many respects impressive. In 1874, Victor Hugo proudly announced that "torture has ceased to exist."

Unfortunately, it appeared that these important humanitarian achievements would not be of long duration. In the wake of World War I, Europe came to know new leaders who were prepared to resort to brutal violence in order to achieve their political aims. Under the Nazi regime in Germany, torture became a means of spreading terror among the population; it was used systematically and on a large scale. The situation deteriorated even further during World War II. In concentration camps and detention centres, not only in Germany but in other countries occupied or dominated by Germany, torture became the order of the day. After the defeat of Germany, there was a widespread feeling that effective measures must be taken in international co-operation to prevent a repetition of such atrocities. It was obvious that a prohibition of torture and similar practices must be an essential element in the human rights instruments which were to be drafted.

However, the wording of such a prohibition was less obvious. It was not sufficient to merely prohibit torture; certain other cruel acts, which were difficult to define adequately, needed to be included in the prohibition. In the early discussions on this subject, terms such as 'unusual punishment or indignity' or 'cruel or inhuman punishment or indignity' were suggested, the model being to some extent the Constitution of the United States of America which prohibits "cruel and unusual punishments." It was also suggested — in the light of the experiences under the Nazi era — that there should be a specific prohibition of medical or scientific experimentation on a person against his will.

The wording which was eventually chosen for article 5 of the Universal Declaration of Human Rights (UDHR) was as follows:

> No one shall be subjected to torture or to cruel, inhuman or degrading treatment or punishment.

The same wording appears — with some variations or additions — in several subsequent instruments. Article 7 of the International Covenant on Civil and Political Rights (CCPR) reads as follows:

> No one shall be subjected to torture or to cruel, inhuman or degrading treatment or punishment. In particular, no one shall be subjected without his free consent to medical or scientific experimentation.

The importance of this provision is shown by the fact that article 7 is one of the few articles in the CCPR from which no derogation may be made, even in situations of public emergency.

Among the regional human rights conventions is the European Convention on Human Rights (ECHR) which, in article 3, provides that "No one shall be subjected to torture or to inhuman or degrading treatment or punishment." A similar provision appears in article 5, paragraph 2, of the American Convention on Human Rights (ACHR). The African Charter on Human and Peoples' Rights (African Charter), although drafted in a different manner, also prohibits in its article 5 "torture, cruel, inhuman or degrading punishment and treatment."

As in the CCPR, the prohibition of torture has been made absolute and without exception also in the ECHR and the ACHR. The fact that this prohibition has to be respected even in times of war is further emphasized by the Geneva Conventions concerning humanitarian law applicable to armed conflicts. With regard to wounded, sick or shipwrecked combatants, prisoners of war, and civilian persons in occupied territories, these Conventions make it clear that torture or inhuman treatment, including biological experiments, and the wilful infliction of great suffering or serious injury to body or health are strictly forbidden and constitute grave breaches of the Conventions which shall be punished as war crimes.

The terms 'torture', 'inhuman treatment' and 'degrading treatment' are not as such very precise, and in none of the Conventions mentioned above has an attempt been made to define them. However, in the implementation of the ECHR some precision has been given to these basic concepts. In its report on the Greek case adopted on 5 November 1969, the European Commission on Human Rights (European Commission) made a first attempt at a definition by stating as follows:

1. Article 3 of the Convention provides that: "No one shall be subjected to torture or to inhuman or degrading treatment or punishment."

2. It is plain that there may be treatment to which all these descriptions apply, for all torture must be inhuman and degrading treatment, and inhuman treatment also degrading. The notion of inhuman treatment covers at least such treatment as deliberately causes severe suffering, mental or physical, which, in the particular situation, is unjustifiable.

   The word 'torture' is often used to describe inhuman treatment, which has a purpose, such as the obtaining of information or confessions, or the infliction of punishment, and it is generally an aggravated form of inhuman treatment. Treatment or punishment of an individual may be said to be degrading if it grossly humiliates him before others or drives him to act against his will or conscience.

In the subsequent case of Ireland *v.* the United Kingdom, the European Commission found that the combined use of five interrogation techniques in Northern Ireland constituted a practice of inhuman treatment and of torture contrary to article 3 of the ECHR. The European Court of Human Rights (European Court), on the other hand, found it preferable to reserve the term 'torture' for particularly serious acts and did not consider that the use of the five interrogation techniques attained the degree of severity inherent in the term of 'torture'. It concluded:

Although the five techniques, as applied in combination, undoubtedly amounted to inhuman and degrading treatment, although their object was the extraction of confessions, the naming of others and/or information and although they were used systematically, they did not occasion suffering of the particular intensity and cruelty implied by the word torture as so understood.

While the difference between torture and inhuman treatment is essentially one of degree of severity, degrading treatment is a concept of a somewhat different character. It is the feeling of humiliation in the victim that makes the treatment degrading, but the humiliation must also attain a certain degree of severity in order to fall under the prohibition of the international instruments. The leading case brought before the European Commission and the European Court is the Tyrer case, where the issue was the infliction of corporal punishment on the Isle of Man. The European Court noted a number of elements: one human being inflicting physical violence on another human being; institutionalized violence ordered by the judicial authorities and carried out by the police authorities; an aura of official procedure attending the punishment; those inflicting it being total strangers to the offender; and delay in carrying out the punishment. All these elements taken together made the punishment degrading and in violation of article 3 of the ECHR.

Otherwise there are mainly two areas in which the European Commission has been called upon to examine whether article 3 had been violated. The first area concerns the treatment of imprisoned or detained persons. A too harsh treatment, including isolation and denial of normal prisoners' rights, could raise an issue under article 3. The second area is that of expulsion or extradition. One case belonging to the latter category — the Soering case — has also been considered by the European Court. That case concerned the intended extradition from the United Kingdom to the United States of a young man who risked being sentenced to death for murder in the latter country and being placed on 'death row' for many years, pending the outcome of various appeals and other remedies. The European Court stated that "The decision by a Contracting State to extradite a fugitive may give rise to an issue under article 3, and hence engage the responsibility of that State under the Convention, where substantial grounds have been shown for believing that the person concerned, if extradited, faces a real risk of being subjected to torture or to inhuman or degrading treatment or punishment in the requesting country." After examining a number of elements in the specific case, the European Court concluded that such a risk existed and that, therefore, the UK "decision to extradite the applicant to the United States would, if implemented, give rise to a breach of article 3."

The serious nature of torture, as well as the fact that it is so frequently practised in many different countries despite the very clear and unambiguous prohibition that is to be found in several international instruments, were reasons for some States to take further initiatives in the United Nations in order to reduce and eventually eliminate torture altogether. Although the existing international rules on this matter had not proved to be particularly effective, it was felt that their effectiveness might increase if they were supplemented by new and more extensive rules which would make the obligations incumbent on States more precise. Thus, a Declaration on the Protection of All Persons from Being Subjected to Torture and Other Cruel, Inhuman or Degrading Treatment or Punishment was adopted by the UN General Assembly in 1975. The Declaration first contains a definition of torture which, to some extent, was inspired by the general remarks on the concept of torture made by the European Commission in the Greek case. In order to prevent torture, each State should take a number of measures, including: instructing and teaching its officials; keeping interrogation methods under review; making acts of torture criminal offences; and proceeding to investigations and prosecution in appropriate cases and punishing the offenders.

The Declaration was subsequently supplemented by further instruments directed at special categories of persons: the Code of Conduct for Law Enforcement Officials, adopted by the UN General Assembly in 1979; and the Principles of Medical Ethics relevant to the Role of Health Personnel, particularly Physicians, in the Protection of Prisoners and Detainees against Torture and Other Cruel, Inhuman or Degrading Treatment or Punishment, adopted by the UN General Assembly in 1982. These instruments lay down some basic rules of behaviour for those who have particular professional responsibilities for persons deprived of their liberty and whose acts or failure to act, when torture occurs, may often be of decisive importance.

Like the UDHR, the 1975 Declaration against Torture is not a legally binding instrument. Sweden, which, together with the Netherlands, had been particularly active in bringing about the adoption of the Declaration, had always considered the Declaration as a first step on the way to a convention which could impose binding obligations on States. As early as 1977, Sweden therefore proposed that the work on such a convention should be initiated, and the UN General Assembly decided accordingly. The Commission on Human Rights (the Commission) was entrusted with the task of drawing up a draft convention against torture and other cruel, inhuman or degrading treatment or punishment "in the light of the principles embodied in the Declaration", and subsequently set up a working group to make proposals for consideration by the Commission. In the working group it was decided to work on the basis of a draft which had been presented by the Swedish delegation.

The fact that it had proved to be comparatively easy to reach an agreement on the text of the Declaration gave rise to some optimism for the further work on a convention as well. It soon became clear, however, that this would be a much more difficult operation. States were, for obvious reasons, more cautious when it came to undertaking real legal obligations and submitting to international supervision, and if the convention were to have some 'teeth', it also meant that those who feared being bitten by those 'teeth' wished to soften them as much as possible. The work on a convention, therefore, continued during several consecutive sessions of the Commission.

There were two main difficulties the work on a convention was facing. They concerned, on the one hand, the problem of the so-called universal jurisdiction and, on the other hand, the implementation machinery that was required in order to make the convention effective.

The problem of universal jurisdiction arose because Sweden had, in its draft, proposed certain provisions according to which a person suspected of torture should not be able to find a safe haven by fleeing to another country. Consequently, that country would either have to prosecute him or extradite him to a country where he would be prosecuted. This system had been inspired by similar provisions in a number of conventions dealing with different forms of terrorist crimes (for example, hijacking of aircraft, crimes against diplomats, hostage-taking). For many States applying this principle to torture created serious problems which some viewed as mainly of a legal nature while others saw political difficulties in the proposed provisions.

As regards the implementation machinery, the problems were the same as those which had also emerged in connection with many previous human rights conventions. While some States attach particular importance to effective international supervision of undertakings in this area, other States take the opposite view and consider it the exclusive task of the national authorities to guarantee the effective implementation of the international agreements and international supervision as an undesirable interference with the internal affairs of the States concerned. A compromise between these conflicting views has often been to make the complaint and investigation procedures optional in nature. In the present case, Sweden, in its draft, had wished to go one step further by permitting an international supervisory committee, on a compulsory basis, to take action whenever there was information that torture was being practised systematically in a convention State. Although limited to the very serious cases of systematic torture, this proposal created great difficulties, and it proved necessary in the end to accept making the provision optional by allowing a State which becomes a party to the convention to declare that it does not wish the procedure concerned to be applicable in relation to that State.

The Convention against Torture and Other Cruel, Inhuman or Degrading Treatment or Punishment was finally adopted by the UN General Assembly on 10 December 1984, and entered into force on 26 June 1987 after it had been ratified or acceded to by 20 States. Its introductory article contains an extensive definition of torture, based on the definition in the 1975 Declaration, but further developed and refined in some respects. The rest of the Convention is characterized by the following main elements:

1. An obligation to take effective measures against torture and to make torture a serious criminal offence punishable by appropriate penalties;
2. A prohibition against expulsion or extradition of a person to a country where he would be in danger of being tortured;
3. An obligation to apply a wide criminal jurisdiction (so-called universal jurisdiction) over the crime of torture and to prosecute or extradite a suspected torturer who is present in the territory of a Contracting State;
4. An obligation to include education and information about the prohibition against torture in the training of personnel likely to be involved in the custody, interrogation or treatment of arrested, detained or imprisoned persons;
5. An obligation to investigate all cases of suspected torture.
6. An obligation to give the victim of torture a right to fair and adequate compensation;
7. More limited obligations to prevent other acts of cruel, inhuman or degrading treatment or punishment;
8. The establishment of a Committee against Torture which shall:

a) examine reports from the Contracting States;
b) make inquiries into indications of the existence of a systematic practice of torture (unless the State concerned has declared that it does not recognize this competence of the Committee);
c) examine communications by one Contracting State against another Contracting State about violations of obligations under the Convention (provided that both Contracting States have recognized this competence of the Committee);
d) examine communications by individuals who claim to be victims of a violation by a Contracting State of the Convention (provided that the Contracting State concerned has recognized this competence of the Committee).

In the course of the work on the Convention against Torture, certain proposals were made for a more radical approach which would involve a system of international inspection through regular visits to places of detention in the Contracting States. A Swiss Committee against Torture together with the International Commission of Jurists drafted a text based on this concept which was submitted to the Commission, in the form of a draft Optional Protocol to the Convention, by Costa Rica in 1980.

In the framework of the United Nations, an international instrument based on the concept of international inspections of national prisons and other places of detention was hardly realistic. What was not possible in a worldwide forum, however, could well be achieved at the regional level. This is why efforts undertaken within the Council of Europe to draft a convention based on the same concept were more successful. The European Convention for the Prevention of Torture and Inhuman or Degrading Treatment or Punishment was signed on 26 November 1987 and entered into force on 1 February 1989. According to this Convention, a European Committee has been established with the task of examining, by means of visits, "the treatment of persons deprived of their liberty with a view to strengthening, if necessary, the protection of such persons from torture and from inhuman or degrading treatment or punishment."

The particularly abhorrent character of torture and the regrettable fact that torture is still widely practised in many countries has been a reason for the United Nations to devote special efforts to combating this evil. This has been done partly, but not exclusively, by drafting legal instruments and by adopting resolutions which condemn any use of torture. The Commission has also, since 1985, annually appointed a Special Rapporteur to examine questions relevant to torture. The Special Rapporteur has collected information about the use of torture, made occasional visits to different countries, brought cases of alleged torture to the attention of governments, and submitted annual reports on his activities to the Commission. Although the attempts to establish an office of a UN High Commissioner for Human Rights have consistently failed, it could well be said that the Special Rapporteur fulfils a similar function with regard to this one extremely important category of human rights violations.

The compassion felt for the victims of torture also prompted the UN General Assembly's decision in 1981 to establish a Voluntary Fund for Victims of Torture. The task of the Fund is to solicit voluntary contributions from governments, non-governmental organizations and individuals and to then distribute these funds as humanitarian, legal and financial aid to victims of torture and their families. Since 1983 the Fund has received substantial contributions from a large number of governments and other sources, and it, in turn, has been able to give financial support to aid programmes and projects in many different countries.

More than 40 years have elapsed since the UDHR was adopted, and we may ask ourselves what the practical effect has been, during that period, of the unequivocal prohibition of torture which was contained in article 5 of the UDHR and which has been further elaborated in a number of subsequent international instruments.

It is difficult to assess whether the use of torture has decreased during this period. The overall picture of the present situation is not particularly bright. It is a sad fact that torture is still widely used in many parts of the world. In its report 'Torture in the Eighties', Amnesty International pointed out that "While governments universally and collectively condemn torture, more than one-third of the world's governments have used or tolerated torture or ill-treatment of prisoners in the 1980s."

Nevertheless, the fact that the international community is not indifferent to the phenomenon of torture, together with the efforts that have been and are being made to eliminate torture, must in themselves be seen as positive factors whose long-term effects should not be underestimated. As the above-mentioned report from Amnesty International rightfully emphasizes:

Information leads to exposure, a key to stopping an individual's suffering and to pressing a government to abandon the practice. The increased flow of such information in the last few years indicates not only that torture remains a major international problem in the 1980s, but more positively, that those who live in fear of torture know more and more how to reach abroad quickly for help.

Article 6

Michael Bogdan

Sweden

Everyone has the right to recognition everywhere as a person before the law.

Practically identical provisions are found in, *inter alia*, the International Covenant on Civil and Political Rights (CCPR, article 16: "Everyone shall have the right to recognition everywhere as a person before the law.") and the American Convention on Human Rights (ACHR, article 3: "Every person has the right to recognition as a person before the law."). In the African Charter on Human and Peoples' Rights (African Charter), there is a partly corresponding stipulation in article 5, which gives every individual the right to the respect of the dignity inherent in a human being "and to the recognition of his legal status."

The purpose of article 6 of the Universal Declaration of Human Rights (UDHR) is to protect everyone's right to be treated as a person in the eyes of the law, i.e., to be recognized as a potential bearer of legal rights and obligations. This right to legal personality (*personnalité juridique*) includes, as a rule, the capacity to be a party to judicial proceedings (the capacity to sue and be sued). At a superficial glance, it might seem that the capacity to have obligations and be sued should not be protected as a human right since it is not an advantage from the individual's point of view, but such objection would disregard the close connection between rights and obligations. For example, the capacity to be a party to contractual relationships would obviously be purely theoretical and of little practical value if it were limited to having rights without the possibility of assuming obligations necessary for obtaining those rights.

Article 6 does not belong to those provisions of the UDHR that have attracted much attention or have been frequently invoked. Its contents are often deemed to be rather trivial and self-evident, which is the main reason why it has not been included into the European Convention on Human Rights (ECHR). Practically all States respect article 6 in their national legislation. Today there appears to be no State overtly accepting the traditional Roman law concept of slavery, degrading certain human beings to mere objects of law and denying them the status of persons before the law (in practice such treatment may occur, however, even if it violates the law of the country in question). The punishment by 'civil death', depriving to some extent the offender of his legal personality, seems not to be in use any more in any country.

The importance of article 6 lies mainly in the field of civil rights and obligations, such as contracts, property, torts, succession and family law. On the other hand, the recognition of legal personality is not a necessary prerequisite for the protection of human beings by criminal law, such as protection of human life by penalization of murder, since that law may regard the protected human beings as mere objects of protection (in the same way as animals are objects of laws forbidding cruelty to animals). Protection accorded by criminal law to property of natural persons, for example, the penalization of theft, presupposes, on the other hand, that such persons enjoy not only physical but also legal personality, since otherwise they could not have legal rights such as the right of ownership.

The recognition of legal personality must not be confused with the question of a person's capacity to handle his or her affairs. Minors or persons of unsound mind are undoubtedly entitled to have rights and obligations, for example, to own property and have debts, but their capacity to act for themselves may be limited by law, which usually provides for the appointment of someone (parent, administrator, trustee, etc.) to represent such persons. These restrictions limiting the capacity to undertake legal acts on one's own behalf are not dealt with by article 6.

Article 6 is applicable to natural persons only, i.e., not to legal entities such as corporations, companies and associations. To assert that such legal entities have the right to recognition as persons before the law would be a truism, since this right could be claimed only by legal entities which have been created as such by the law. In contrast to human beings, legal entities have no physical existence independent of legal regulation.

It can be assumed that article 6 protects every human being's right to be recognized as a person before the law during the period between his or her birth and brain death. Some legal systems do not consider a brain-dead patient to be legally dead until his heart stops beating, but this is a matter left to the discretion of domestic law. On the other hand, national legislation considering a person whose brain is still alive to be legally dead, would probably be incompatible with article 6. Similar questions arise in connection with the possibilities, varying from one legal system to another, of declaring missing or disappeared persons to be officially dead. Even this is a matter left to the discretion of domestic law, but an abuse of such declarations, for example attempts by an oppressive regime to have refugees living abroad or political opponents living in the underground declared dead, would naturally violate article 6.

Many legal systems grant certain limited legal rights to unborn children as well, for example the right to inherit. Again, this appears to be a matter not dealt with by article 6. It should be stressed that provisions of domestic criminal or administrative law protecting the life of unborn children, mainly by prohibiting or limiting abortions, do not necessarily imply a recognition of the legal personality of the human embryo, which is rather treated as an object protected by the law.

The fact that article 6 speaks of recognition 'everywhere' (*en tous lieux*) does not mean that the status with regard to legal personality of a particular person must be the same in all countries. As has been pointed out, the criteria of biological death, prerequisites of an official declaration of death, and the attitude towards the legal personality of unborn children may legitimately vary from country to country, creating the problem of 'limping personality', where the same person may in some States be considered to be alive while being deemed dead or non-existent in other countries. A further complication arising in cases having international implications is that the relevant rules on conflicts of law vary from country to country as well, some choosing the law of the person's domicile while others prefer the law of the country of citizenship or the court's own law (*lex fori*). However these problems arise in extremely rare borderline cases only.

Article 7

Jakob Th. Möller

Iceland

.

All are equal before the law and are entitled without discrimination to equal protection of the law. All are entitled to equal protection against any discrimination in violation of this Declaration and against any incitement to such discrimination.

I. The Drafting of Article 7

On its way through the drafting stages, article 7 of the Universal Declaration of Human Rights (UDHR) took many forms and was subject to many changes. There was controversy over whether it belonged in the Declaration at all, and, if so, what 'equality' actually meant, which concepts should be covered and how they should be understood. The *travaux préparatoires*, consequently, are at times rather obscure and there is still today a lively debate among scholars as to the exact meaning and scope of the principles which the article, in its final form, purports to protect, i.e., the concepts of 'equality before the law', 'equal protection of the law' and 'protection against discrimination'.[1] The present paper will endeavour to trace the article's main features from the initial stage of drafting to the final text, as adopted unanimously by the General Assembly on 10 December 1948.

---

[1] Contemporary writings focus to a large extent on the meaning and scope of the parallel article 26 of the International Covenant on Civil and Political Rights (CCPR).

A. Secretariat Draft Outline

One of the early controversies centred around the question of whether 'equality before the law' was part and parcel of, i.e., subsumed in, the general principle of non-discrimination (as finally set out in article 2, paragraph 1); whether 'equality before the law' was so closely linked to the general concept of non-discrimination that it would properly belong in the general non-discrimination clause; or whether the concept of 'equality before the law' constituted a separate principle, with a life of its own, in addition to that of non-discrimination. From the outset, it was clear, however, that the concept of non-discrimination had to be given a juridical character by affirming that equality means 'equality before the law'.[2] The initial draft outline of the International Bill of Human Rights, prepared by the Secretariat of the United Nations, proposed that "No one should suffer any discrimination whatsoever because of race, sex, language or religion or political creed. There should be full equality before the law in the enjoyment of rights enunciated in the bill of rights." At this starting point, non-discrimination and equality before the law stood together, the latter concept, it appears, giving juridical character to the first.[3]

B. Drafting Committee, First Session; Sub-Commission

The text that emerged from the first session of the Drafting Committee[4] placed the principle of 'equality before the law' in a separate article, followed by a general non-discrimination article:

Article 5:

All are equal before the law and are entitled to equal protection of the law. Public authorities and judges, as well as individuals are subject to the rule of law.

---

[2] Even before it had been decided whether the International Bill of Human Rights should comprise a declaration or a convention or both (see UN doc. E/CN.4/SR.25), the principle of equality of rights and non-discrimination had been referred to in a number of General Assembly resolutions, e.g., Res. 44(1), 56(1), 96(1) and 103(1).

[3] See UN doc. E/CN.4/AC.1/3, Annex and Add.1.

[4] UN doc. E/CN.4/21, Annex F.

Article 6:

Every one is entitled to the rights and freedoms set forth in this Declaration, without distinction as to race, sex, language, or religion.

In addition, the Drafting Committee placed expressions of the concept of equality into provisions which it numbered as article 1, on the one hand, and a suggested combination article 2, 3 and 4, on the other hand, by wording such as "all men are brothers"; "they are members of one family"; "they are free and possess equal dignity and rights" (article 1); "equal opportunity" (article 2); or, as an alternative article 2, to replace suggested articles 2, 3 and 4: "These rights are limited only by the equal rights of others." The Drafting Committee, furthermore, suggested that the general non-discrimination clause contained in its article 6 should be referred to the Sub-Commission on Prevention of Discrimination and Protection of Minorities, which, in turn, proposed the following version:[5]

Article 6:

Every one is entitled to all the rights and freedoms set forth in this Declaration, without distinction of any kind, such as race, sex, language, religion, political or other opinion, property status, or national or social origin.

C. Commission on Human Rights, Second Session

This was the state of affairs when substantive consideration of the text of the UDHR began at the second session of the Commission on Human Rights (the Commission) on 2–17 December 1947. At that time, the Commission set up three in-session working groups, to deal with the three envisaged parts of the International Bill of Human Rights, respectively, that is: a) the Declaration; b) the Convention or Conventions; and c) implementation. Upon receiving the reports of the three working groups,[6] the Commission decided

[5] UN doc. E/CN.4/52.
[6] The Working Group on the Declaration was composed of the representatives of the Byelorussian SSR, France, Panama, the Philippines, the Soviet Union and the United States. The summary records of its nine meetings are contained in UN docs. E/CN.4/AC.2/1 to 9.

to examine first the proposed articles for the Declaration, referring, however, to corresponding articles for the Convention wherever such existed. In a remarkable display of self-restraint, the Commission accepted a ruling of the Chairman that, in order to save time, only one member would be recognized to speak in favour of and only one to speak against each article or proposed amendment.

In its report to the Commission[7] the Working Group on the Declaration had proposed the following text for the general principle of non-discrimination and the more specific principle of equality before the law (at that time set out under the heading 'Articles 3 to 6'):

Articles 3 to 6:

Paragraph 1. "Every one is entitled to all the rights and freedoms set forth in this Declaration, without distinction of any kind, such as race, sex, language, religion, political or other opinion, property status, or national or social origin."

Paragraph 2. "All are equal before the law regardless of office or status and entitled to equal protection of the law against any arbitrary discrimination in violation of this Declaration."

Again, the general principle of non-discrimination and the specific principle of equality before the law had been merged to appear in the same article, albeit in separate paragraphs. The first paragraph contained, unchanged, the text proposed by the Sub-Commission to replace article 6 of the Drafting Committee's text. The second paragraph constituted a fresh attempt to express the concepts of 'equality before the law' and 'equal protection of the law', the latter concept, however, lacking considerably in clarity, i.e., 'equal protection of the law against any arbitrary discrimination'. At this point, substantive debate started in the Commission in plenary.

At the 34th and 35th plenary meetings of its second session in December 1947,[8] the Commission examined articles 3 to 6 of the draft declaration (as set out in the report of the Working Group on the Declaration, doc. E/CN.4/57), as well as the corresponding article 19 of the draft convention (as set out in the report of the Working Group on the Convention, UN doc. E/CN.4/56). A number of amendments were proposed, but only two were accepted,

---

[7] UN doc. E/CN.4/57.
[8] See UN docs. E/CN.4/SR.34 and 35.

i.e., an Indian proposal to add the words 'including colour' after the word 'race' in paragraph 1, and a Belgian proposal to add the words 'and against any incitement to such discrimination' towards the end of paragraph 2. In its edited form, the text of article 3 as adopted by the Commission's second session was set out as follows in its report to the sixth session of the Economic and Social Council (ECOSOC):[9]

Article 3:

1. Every one is entitled to all the rights and freedoms set forth in this Declaration, without distinction of any kind, such as race (which includes colour), sex, language, religion, political or other opinion, property status, or national or social origin.

2. All are equal before the law regardless of office or status and entitled to equal protection of the law against any arbitrary discrimination, or against any incitement to such discrimination, in violation of this Declaration.

No substantive consideration of the International Bill of Human Rights took place at the Council's sixth session, which confined its action to directing the Commission and the Drafting Committee to proceed with the work, as set out in Council resolution 46 (IV).[10]

---

[9] UN doc. E/600, Annex A. At this stage the text of the Draft International Declaration on Human Rights consisted of 33 articles. The representative of the United States, however, requested that the text of a shorter and less technical Declaration, which she had placed before the Commission, be included in the General Comments on the Draft Declaration, to be contained in the Commission's report. The short US version contained only ten draft articles, articles 1 and 10 of which read as follows: article 1: "Everyone is entitled to life, liberty, and equal protection under the law"; article 10: "Every one, everywhere in the world, is entitled to the human rights and fundamental freedoms set forth in this Declaration without distinction as to race, sex, language or religion. The full exercise of these rights requires recognition of the rights of others and protection by law of the freedom, general welfare and security of all." The representative of Panama, lamenting the fact that the Commission appeared to have lost track of the initial text submitted by Panama since the San Francisco Conference, *inter alia*, made the following general comment on the Draft Declaration as a whole: "2. The present draft, although it should have taken into special consideration, according to a unanimous vote by the Group that worked on the Declaration, the text submitted by the delegation of Panama since the San Francisco Conference (see document E/CN.4/53, page 3), actually has ignored the text proposed by Panama."

[10] United Nations, *UN General Assembly, Third Session, Supplement no. 3 (A/625)*, para. 128.

D. Government Comments

As had been envisaged by the fourth session of the Council, the Commission requested the Secretary-General, at its second session, to transmit the text of the Draft International Bill of Rights to governments for comments and to circulate any comments received, without delay, so that they might be taken into account by the Drafting Committee at its next session, to be convened on 3 May 1948. A compilation of the comments received was issued in UN doc. E/CN.4/85 (1 May 1948). The Netherlands made substantive comments on the text of article 3, paragraphs 1 and 2, as follows:

> The words "regardless of office or status" should be deleted. *Comment*: The use of the word "status" in paragraph 2 probably means to prohibit a distinction by race, sex, language, etc. as mentioned in paragraph 1. The word "status", however, may also be interpreted in a more restrictive sense as "civil status". Such an interpretation should be excluded, because, if accepted, discrimination on the grounds mentioned in paragraph 2, would be lawful. If the words "regardless of office or status" are deleted it is made clear that paragraph 2 has in view the prohibition of the same discrimination as paragraph 1.

An interesting comment was also made by Brazil, although in a different context. Commenting on draft article 12 (which at that time read: "Everyone has the right everywhere in the world to recognition as a person before the law and to the enjoyment of fundamental civil rights"), Brazil suggested that "Because of its broadness, the precept contained in this article should be incorporated into Article 3 of the draft, which, in accord with previous comments, would become article 1."

E. Drafting Committee, Second Session

The second session of the Drafting Committee was held from 3–21 May 1948. Owing to lack of time, it could not consider article 3. The text placed before the third session of the Commission (24 May–18 June 1948) was therefore the same as that adopted by its second session.

F. Commission on Human Rights, Third Session

The third session of the Commission was eventful. Coming back to the text of article 3, paragraphs 1 and 2, as it had left it at its second session, the Commission agreed without much difficulty on the text of paragraph 1. After accepting an amendment from the Ukrainian SSR to insert the words 'or other' between the words 'property' and 'status' (by 13 votes in favour, none against, with one abstention), the paragraph as a whole, as amended, was adopted unanimously.

Paragraph 2 gave rise to prolonged difficulties, as it transpired, again, that members did not agree on what the concepts of the paragraph were meant to protect, how they should be understood and how they differed from those in paragraph 1. The representative of Yugoslavia had observed that whereas paragraph 1 listed grounds on which there should be no discrimination, paragraph 2 was directed against unfair privileges. The debate took place mostly at the 52nd, 53rd and 54th meetings.

Some members were in favour of a more elaborate wording about equal protection against arbitrary discrimination and incitement to such discrimination (France, India, United Kingdom). The representative of the Ukrainian SSR proposed the deletion of the word 'arbitrary' before the word 'discrimination' (voted on and adopted by 9:6:1). Lebanon proposed the deletion of the words 'regardless of office or status'. The Philippines suggested the wording 'without any discrimination' instead of 'against any discrimination'. China proposed the wording 'without and against any discrimination' (adopted by 10:4:2). The United Kingdom proposed the deletion of the words 'or against any incitement to [such] discrimination' (rejected by 8:7:1). China suggested the deletion of the last paragraph '... in violation of this Declaration'. France suggested that the words 'in violation of this Declaration' should be inserted in the second line of the paragraph.

Speaking in support of or against the various proposals and suggestions made, members offered, *inter alia*, the following comments and observations in an attempt to define the meaning and scope of the paragraph. The Chairman (United States) felt that the word 'arbitrary' should be retained to give meaning to the concept of 'arbitrary discrimination', so as to explain that not all discrimination was 'invidious'. France, however, was of the opinion that 'discrimination' was equal to 'invidious distinction'. The Chairman did not share that view, explaining that in her opinion 'discrimination' had the same meaning as 'distinction' and that, therefore, 'arbitrary discrimination' meant 'invidious distinction'.

The representative of the United Kingdom felt that the word 'arbitrary' should be retained so as to preserve the notion that the provision was aimed against 'reprehensible' discrimination. As an alternative, he proposed a full stop could be put after the words '... protection of the law' (rejected by 6:8:1). Chile observed in this context that whereas paragraph 1 laid down rights and freedoms for all, paragraph 2 concerned the obligation of States to provide legal protection against discrimination. The United Kingdom then posed the question of what the meaning was of 'equal protection of the law'. Did that concept mean that laws should be applied equally?; or that all are equally entitled to whatever protection the law might provide? Addressing the question, the representative of Australia offered the following definition: "Equal protection of the law means that all are entitled to equal treatment under whatever laws that exist." The Australian member's definition of the concept of 'equality before the law' is perhaps the clearest of those that emerged during the drafting history of the provision.

At this stage, at the end of the 52nd meeting, the Chairman proposed the setting up of 'a small drafting group' consisting of China, France, and the United Kingdom, to prepare 'a final text' to be placed before the following meeting. At the beginning of the 53rd meeting, the 'small drafting group' placed the following text before the Commission:

Article 3, paragraph 2:

All are equal before the law and are entitled to equal protection of the law without any discrimination, and against any discrimination in violation of this Declaration or incitement to such discrimination.

Again, there was agreement on the text, and after Australia proposed the word 'distinction' to replace the first use of the word 'discrimination', the Chairman sent the text back to the 'small drafting group', this time to be enlarged to include the Byelorussian SSR and the Philippines.

After the enlarged small drafting group had pondered the same text (as that submitted to the 53rd meeting) it was placed before the 54th meeting, with the explanation, however, that the English and Russian versions would use the word 'discrimination', while the French version would use the word 'distinction', "since the words in question were so used in the United Nations Charter." On that understanding, the Chairman put the second part of paragraph 2 of article 3 to the vote first (i.e., from the words 'against any discrimination...'). It was adopted by 11 votes in favour, none opposed, and 5 abstentions. The representative of the United Kingdom then announced that he would be compelled to vote against paragraph 2 as a whole, because he considered that the expression 'equal protection against any discrimination' was ambiguous and the words 'without any discrimination' were unnecessary. The representative of Belgium also stated his opinion to the text which he considered "confused both verbally and in the ideas which it wished to convey." Paragraph 2 of article 3, as a whole, was then adopted by 9:6, with 1 abstention and article 3, as a whole, by 9:5, with 2 abstentions.

Although the debate on the text of article 3 was thus, in principle, over, some important tasks lay ahead, that is: the final placing of each article; and the approval of any alterations proposed by the Style Committee (an editorial body of language experts, entrusted with form and construction and the uniformity of translations).

At the 75th meeting, the representative of Ghana proposed that the two paragraphs of article 3 should become two separate articles. That proposal (together with other proposals about the placement of articles) was adopted at the 77th meeting by 9:1 with 6 abstentions. The general non-discrimination paragraph thus became article 2 of the draft declaration, while the paragraph concerning equality before the law and equal protection of the law was moved to be placed as article 6 of the draft declaration.

The Style Committee made some changes in the language of the earlier paragraph 2 of article 3. No objections were raised by the members of the Commission, and at the 78th meeting the Chairman announced that the report of the Commission to the ECOSOC "would include the Declaration in the form proposed by the Style Committee" unless there were objections to any specific changes made by the Committee.

The final text of article 6 of the draft declaration, as contained in the report of the third session of the Commission to the seventh session of the ECOSOC[11] reads as follows:

Article 6:

All are equal before the law and are entitled without any discrimination to equal protection of the law against any discrimination in violation of this Declaration and against any incitement to such discrimination.

[11] UN doc. E/800m Annex A.

G. ECOSOC, Seventh Session

In August 1948, after recalling the report of the Commission from the Social Committee because of lack of time, the Council confined its action to transmitting the text of the draft International Declaration of Human Rights, as it stood, to the General Assembly for consideration and possible adoption (Council resolution 151 [VII]).

H. General Assembly, Third Committee

The text of article 6 was examined in the Third Committee of the General Assembly at the Committee's 111th and 112th meetings. The Committee had before it various written amendments, including a proposal from the Union of South Africa[12] to delete the second part of the article ('against any discrimination in violation of this Declaration and against any incitement to such discrimination') and a proposal from Mexico[13] to include a provision concerning the individual's right to an effective remedy for violations of his fundamental rights.

The representative of the Union of South Africa, realizing that he had failed to convince the body that his proposal was motivated by a desire to strengthen the Declaration and that it was "doomed to failure" (as stated by the representative of Cuba) and seen as "defeat[ing] the purpose for which the declaration was drawn up" (as stated by the representative of India), withdrew the proposal. The Mexican proposal, on the other hand, had wide support.

Introducing his amendment, the representative of Mexico explained that it "included a statement of a fundamental right recognized by most national legislations; the right to take legal proceedings on the basis of a prompt and simple procedure which assured protection against the acts of public authorities who violated a person's fundamental rights." It was not a new idea. The constitutions of most Latin American countries included it in precise juridical terms. Further, his amendment only repeated the text of the Bogota Declaration which had been adopted unanimously by the 21 Latin American delegations. The representative, however, observing that the amendment was rather

[12] UN doc. A/C.3/226.
[13] UN doc. A/C.3/266.

in the nature of an additional article, reserved his right to submit it in the form of a separate article. Although some delegations expressed the view that the proper place for the Mexican proposal would be in the proposed Covenant and not in the Declaration (France) or that it would at least be better placed in the Covenant than in the Declaration, the thrust of this was in the end adopted as a separate article of the Declaration (article 8 of the final text).

Again, at this stage, the delegations of the Third Committee debated the meaning and scope of draft article 6, as transmitted to the General Assembly by the ECOSOC. The representative of the Philippines observed that the words 'equal protection of the law' had given rise to some confusion and that it was not clear whether they meant that there should be laws which should be applied equally or that all were equally entitled to the protection of whatever laws existed. He recalled that Woodrow Wilson had once said that 'equal protection of the law' meant that the law should be administered with an even hand. In the representative's opinion, the text of draft article 6 went further and widened the scope of the phrase. He did not elaborate, however, but the representative of Greece offered the opinion that "equality with regard to the protection of the law was not necessarily limited to the human rights defined in the declaration; it could also extend to other fields."

The representative of the United Kingdom, Mrs. Corbet, supported by Greece and Australia, suggested that the words 'without any discrimination' should be deleted from article 6. She felt that the general non-discrimination clause in article 2 applied to all succeeding articles and that the inclusion of the words in article 6 might erroneously give the impression that other articles, which did not contain these words, "tacitly permitted discrimination." In the vote on article 6 in the Third Committee, the words 'without any discrimination' were retained by 33:8, with 2 abstentions.

Referring to earlier doubts about the clarity of article 6 and the remark, in that context, of the representative of Venezuela that "some form of words should be found to make it clear that all were entitled both to equal protection of the law in general, and to equal protection against discrimination...", the representative of Australia proposed that the words 'and equal protection' should be added after the words 'protection of the law'. The Australian proposal was adopted by 34:1, with 8 abstentions.

At this stage, the Third Committee proceeded to vote on article 6, as amended. After several votes on various parts, the article, as a whole, was adopted by 45:1, with 1 abstention. The article now reads as follows:

Article 6:

All are equal before the law and are entitled without any discrimination to equal protection of the law and equal protection against any discrimination in violation of this Declaration and against any incitement to such discrimination.

Before voting, it had been agreed that consideration of the Mexican amendment, and a decision on where to place it, should be deferred. At the following meeting (113th meeting on 26 October 1948), a revised version of the Mexican amendment was adopted by 46:0, with 3 abstentions, reading as follows:

Everyone has the right to an effective remedy by the competent national tribunals for acts violating the fundamental rights granted him by the constitution or by law.

The question as to where to place the provision was still deferred, but for the time being it was included as a separate paragraph in article 6.

I. Sub-Committee 4 of the Third Committee

In this form, article 6, as all other articles and the Preamble of the Declaration, was referred to yet another drafting stage, a Sub-Committee (Sub-Committee 4) set up by the Third Committee on 30 November 1948 "to examine the totality of the Declaration of Human Rights ... solely from the standpoint of arrangement, consistency, uniformity and style and to submit proposals thereon to the Third Committee." The Sub-Committee was also asked to set up a language group of five members, one for each of the official languages, "to check and secure the exact correspondence of the text in the five official languages."

This exercise resulted in an important language polishing of article 6, which now emerged in its final form:[14]

---

[14] See Annex A to the Sub-Committee's report to the Third Committee, UN doc. A/C.3/400 and Rev.1.

Article 6:

All are equal before the law and are entitled without any discrimination to equal protection of the law. All are entitled to equal protection against any discrimination in violation of this Declaration and against any incitement to such discrimination.

There can be no doubt that the stylistic change in article 6, i.e., splitting a rather clumsy and contrived sentence into two, constituted a big improvement, and, finally, replaced confusion by clarity. It is rather astounding that nobody had had this idea before.

Further, the Mexican amendment, which the Third Committee had included as an additional paragraph in article 6, although remaining unchanged, now received a separate number as article 6 (a).

The text of the Sub-Committee was again examined in the Third Committee at its 174th–178th meetings. After 84 meetings (and 10 meetings in the Sub-Committee) the deliberations resulted in the adoption of the draft 'Universal Declaration of Human Rights'. No further changes were made in the wording of article 6, but it was renumbered as article 8, because of changes in and consequent reordering of other articles. Article 6(a), similarly, became article 9.[15]

J. General Assembly, Third Session, Plenary — Final Action

Final action on the draft UDHR was taken by the 183rd plenary meeting of the General Assembly on 10 December 1948. Articles 8 and 9 were adopted unanimously, but renumbered as articles 7 and 8, respectively (after the adoption of a UK proposal to delete draft article 3: "The rights set forth in this Declaration apply equally to all inhabitants of Trust and Non-Self-governing Territories", and to include, instead, the second paragraph of article 2).

Because of the historical drafting links between article 2, paragraph 1, article 7 and article 8, the text, as adopted, is repeated below in context:

Article 2, paragraph 1:

Everyone is entitled to all the rights and freedoms set forth in this

[15] See Report of the Third Committee, UN doc. A/777 of 7 December 1948.

Declaration, without distinction of any kind, such as race, colour, sex, language, religion, political or other opinion, national or social origin, property, birth or other status.

Article 7:

All are equal before the law and are entitled without any discrimination to equal protection of the law. All are entitled to equal protection against any discrimination in violation of this Declaration and against any incitement to such discrimination.

Article 8:

Everyone has the right to an effective remedy by the competent national tribunals for acts violating the fundamental rights granted him by the constitution or by law.

II. Article 7 of the UDHR and Article 26 of the CCPR

The concepts of article 7 of the UDHR eventually found expression in the corresponding article 26 of the CCPR, reading as follows:

Article 26:

All persons are equal before the law and are entitled without any discrimination to the equal protection of the law. In this respect, the law shall prohibit any discrimination and guarantee to all persons equal and effective protection against discrimination on any grounds such as race, colour, sex, language, religion, political or other opinion, national or social origin, property, birth or other status.

For an overview of how the concepts and principles in question have been understood, interpreted and applied, the reader may find it of interest to study the work of the Human Rights Committee, which monitors the implementation of the CCPR through the examination of State reports under the Covenant and individual complaints under the Optional Protocol. Annexed to this paper is the text of the Committee's general comments on the non-discrimination clauses of the CCPR, including article 26 (adopted at its 37th session on 9 November 1989) and a brief synopsis of the Committee's views under the Optional Protocol on a number of cases which raised issues under article 26 of the CCPR.

Annex 1

General comments of the Human Rights Committee
on the non-discrimination clauses of the
International Covenant on Civil and Political Rights
(adopted on 9 November 1989)

1. Non-discrimination, together with equality before the law and equal protection of the law without discrimination, constitutes a basic and general principle relating to the protection of human rights. Thus, article 2, paragraph 1, of the International Covenant on Civil and Political Rights obligates each State Party to respect and ensure to all persons within its territory and subject to its jurisdiction the rights recognized in the Covenant without distinction of any kind, such as race, colour, sex, language, religion, political or other opinion, national or social origin, property, birth or other status. Article 26 not only entitles all persons to equality before the law as well as equal protection of the law but also prohibits any discrimination under the law and guarantees to all persons equal and effective protection against discrimination on any ground such as race, colour, sex, language, religion, political or other opinion, national or social origin, property, birth or other status.

2. Indeed, the principle of non-discrimination is so basic that article 3 obligates each States Party to ensure the equal right of men and women to the enjoyment of the rights set forth in the Covenant. While article 4, paragraph 1, allows States Parties to take measures derogating from certain obligations under the Covenant in time of public emergency, the same article requires, *inter alia*, that those measures should not involve discrimination solely on the ground of race, colour, sex, language, religion or social origin. Furthermore, article 20, paragraph 2, obligates States Parties to prohibit, by law, any advocacy of national, racial or religious hatred which constitutes incitement to discrimination.

3. Because of their basic and general character, the principle of non-discrimination as well as that of equality before the law and equal protection of the law are sometimes expressly referred to in articles

relating to particular categories of human rights. Article 14, paragraph 1, provides that all persons shall be equal before the courts and tribunals, and paragraph 3 of the same article provides that, in the determination of any criminal charge against him, everyone shall be entitled, in full equality, to the minimum guarantees enumerated in subparagraphs (a) to (g) of paragraph 3. Similarly, article 25 provides for the equal participation in public life of all citizens, without any of the distinctions mentioned in article 2.

4. It is for the States Parties to determine appropriate measures to implement the relevant provisions. However, the Committee is to be informed about the nature of such measures and their conformity with the principles of non-discrimination and equality before the law and equal protection of the law.

5. The Committee wishes to draw the attention of States Parties to the fact that the Covenant sometimes expressly requires them to take measures to guarantee the equality of rights of the persons concerned. For example, article 23, paragraph 4, stipulates that States Parties shall take appropriate steps to ensure equality of rights as well as responsibilities of spouses as to marriage, during marriage and at its dissolution. Such steps may take the form of legislative, administrative or other measures, but it is a positive duty of States Parties to make certain that spouses have equal rights as required by the Covenant. In relation to children, article 24 provides that all children, without any discrimination as to race, colour, sex, language, religion, national or social origin, property or birth, have the right to such measures of protection as are required by their status as minors, on the part of their family, society and the State.

6. The Committee notes that the Covenant neither defines the term 'discrimination' nor indicates what constitutes discrimination. However, article 1 of the International Convention on the Elimination of All Forms of Racial Discrimination provides that the term 'racial discrimination' shall mean any distinction, exclusion, restriction or preference based on race, colour, descent, or national or ethnic origin which has the purpose or effect of nullifying or impairing the recognition, enjoyment or exercise, on an equal footing, of human rights and fundamental freedoms in the political, economic, social, cultural or any other field of public life. Similarly, article 1 of the Convention on the Elimination of All

Forms of Discrimination against Women provides that "discrimination against women" shall mean any distinction, exclusion or restriction made on the basis of sex which has the effect or purpose of impairing or nullifying the recognition, enjoyment or exercise by women, irrespective of their marital status, on a basis of equality of men and women, of human rights and fundamental freedoms in the political, economic, social, cultural, civil or any other field.

7. While these conventions deal only with cases of discrimination on specific grounds, the Committee believes that the term 'discrimination' as used in the Covenant should be understood to imply any distinction, exclusion, restriction or preference which is based on any ground such as race, colour, sex, language, religion, political or other opinion, national or social origin, property, birth or other status, and which has the purpose or effect of nullifying or impairing the recognition, enjoyment or exercise by all persons, on an equal footing, of all rights and freedoms.

8. The enjoyment of rights and freedoms on an equal footing, however, does not mean identical treatment in every instance. In this connection, the provisions of the Covenant are explicit. For example, article 6, paragraph 5, prohibits the death sentence from being imposed on persons below 18 years of age. The same paragraph prohibits that sentence from being carried out on pregnant women. Similarly, article 10, paragraph 3, requires the segregation of juvenile offenders from adults. Furthermore, article 25 guarantees certain political rights, differentiating on grounds of citizenship.

9. Reports of many States Parties contain information regarding legislative as well as administrative measures and court decisions which relate to protection against discrimination in law, but they very often lack information which would reveal discrimination in fact. When reporting on articles 2(1), 3 and 26 of the Covenant, States Parties usually cite provisions of their constitution or equal opportunity laws with respect to equality of persons. While such information is of course useful, the Committee wishes to know if there remain any problems of discrimination in fact, which may be practised either by public authorities, by the community, or by private persons or bodies. The Committee wishes to be informed about legal provisions and administrative measures directed at diminishing or eliminating such discrimination.

10. The Committee also wishes to point out that the principle of equality sometimes requires States Parties to take affirmative action in order to diminish or eliminate conditions which cause or help to perpetuate discrimination prohibited by the Covenant. For example, in a State where the general conditions of a certain part of the population prevent or impair their enjoyment of human rights, the State should take specific action to correct those conditions. Such action may involve granting for a time to the part of the population concerned certain preferential treatment in specific matters as compared with the rest of the population. However, as long as such action is needed to correct discrimination in fact, it is a case of legitimate differentiation under the Covenant.

11. Both article 2, paragraph 1, and article 26 enumerate grounds of discrimination such as race, colour, sex, language, religion, political or other opinion, national or social origin, property, birth or other status. The Committee has observed that in a number of constitutions and laws not all the grounds on which discrimination is prohibited, as cited in article 2, paragraph 1, are enumerated. The Committee would therefore like to receive information from States Parties as to the significance of such omissions.

12. While article 2 limits the scope of the rights to be protected against discrimination to those provided for in the Covenant, article 26 does not specify such limitations. That is to say, article 26 provides that all persons are equal before the law and are entitled to equal protection of the law without discrimination, and that the law shall guarantee to all persons equal and effective protection against discrimination on any of the enumerated grounds. In the view of the Committee, article 26 does not merely duplicate the guarantee already provided for in article 2 but provides in itself an autonomous right. It prohibits discrimination in law or in fact in any field regulated and protected by public authorities. Article 26 is therefore concerned with the obligations imposed on States Parties in regard to their legislation and the application thereof. Thus, when legislation is adopted by a State Party, it must comply with the requirement of article 26 that its content should not be discriminatory. In other words, the application of the principle of non-discrimination contained in article 26 is not limited to those rights which are provided for in the Covenant.

13. Finally, the Committee observes that not every differentiation of treatment will constitute discrimination, if the criteria for such

differentiation are reasonable and objective and if the aim is to achieve a purpose which is legitimate under the Covenant.

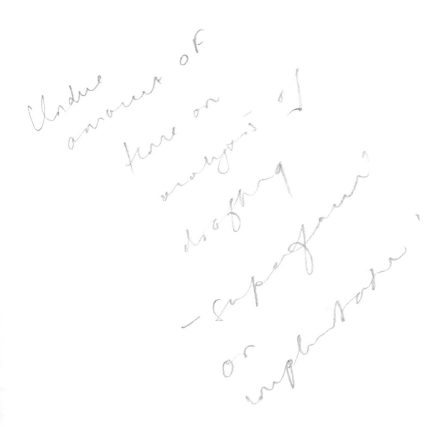

Annex 2

Case law of the Human Rights Committee on
article 26 of the International Covenant on
Civil and Political Rights

Before adopting its general comments on the non-discrimination
clauses of the Covenant, the Human Rights Committee had the
opportunity to discuss extensively the meaning and scope of article
26 in a number of cases submitted under the Optional Protocol. One
of the unresolved questions before the Committee had been whether
the principle of non-discrimination enunciated in article 26 applied
only with respect to the rights enshrined in the International
Covenant on Civil and Political Rights, or whether non-
discrimination constituted an autonomous right applicable to civil
and political rights not protected in the Covenant or even to
economic, social and cultural rights, which might be protected by
other international instruments, such as the International Covenant
on Economic, Social and Cultural Rights. While States Parties had
argued for a restrictive interpretation of article 26 on the basis that
the two Covenants established two different monitoring systems
and that a provision was made for an individual complaints
procedure only with respect to the International Covenant on Civil
and Political Rights, the Committee decided at its twenty-ninth
session with regard to communications Nos. 172/1984, 180/1984
and 182/1984 (see Annex VIII, sections B, C and D, HRC 1987
Report) that it could examine an allegation of discrimination with
regard to economic, social and cultural rights. In all three cases,
which concerned alleged discriminatory treatment in the field of
social security, the Committee observed:

> For the purposes of determining the scope of article 26, the Committee
> has taken into account the 'ordinary meaning' of each element of the
> article in its context and in the light of its object and purpose (article 31
> of the Vienna Convention on the Law of Treaties). The Committee
> begins by noting that article 26 does not merely duplicate the guarantees
> already provided for in article 2. It derives from the principle of equal
> protection of the law without discrimination, as contained in article 7 of
> the Universal Declaration of Human Rights, which prohibits
> discrimination in law or practice in any field regulated and protected by

public authorities. Article 26 is thus concerned with the obligations imposed on States in regard to their legislation and the application thereof.

Although article 26 requires that legislation should prohibit discrimination, it does not of itself contain any obligation with respect to the matters that may be provided for by legislation. Thus it does not, for example, require any State to enact legislation to provide for social security. However, when such legislation is adopted in the exercise of a State's sovereign power, then such legislation must comply with article 26 of the Covenant.

After deciding on its own competence to consider cases of alleged discrimination with regard to social security rights, the Committee examined whether certain facts constituted discrimination within the meaning of article 26 of the Covenant. In case No. 182/1984 (F.H. Zwaan-de Vries *v.* the Netherlands) the Committee found a violation of article 26:

The right to equality before the law and to equal protection of the law without any discrimination does not make all differences of treatment discriminatory. A differentiation based on reasonable and objective criteria does not amount to prohibited discrimination within the meaning of article 26.

It therefore remains for the Committee to determine whether the differentiation in Netherlands law at the time in question and as applied to Mrs. Zwaan-de Vries constituted discrimination within the meaning of article 26. The Committee notes that in Netherlands law the provisions of articles 84 and 85 of the Netherlands Civil Code imposes equal rights and obligations on both spouses with regard to their joint income. Under section 13, subsection 1(1), of the Unemployment Benefits Act (WWV) a married woman, in order to receive WWV benefits, had to prove that she was a 'breadwinner' — a condition that did not apply to married men. Thus a differentiation which appears on one level to be one of status is in fact one of sex, placing married women at a disadvantage compared with married men. Such a differentiation is not reasonable,... (see Annex VIII, section D, paragraphs 13 and 14, HRC 1987 Report).

Similarly, in case No. 172/1984 (S.W.M. Broeks *v.* the Netherlands), which involved the application of the same law in a comparable factual situation, the Committee also made a finding of a violation of article 26 (see Annex VIII, section B, HRC 1987 Report).

In case No. 180/1984 (L.G. Danning *v*. Netherlands), the Committee found that the facts did not support a finding of a violation of article 26:

> In the light of the explanations given by the State party with respect to the differences made by Netherlands legislation between married and unmarried couples ..., the Committee is persuaded that the differentiation complained of by Mr. Danning is based on objective and reasonable criteria. The Committee observes, in this connection, that the decision to enter into a legal status by marriage, which provides, in Netherlands law, both for certain benefits and for certain duties and responsibilities, lies entirely with the cohabiting persons. By choosing not to enter into marriage, Mr. Danning and his cohabitant have not, in law, assumed the full extent of the duties and responsibilities incumbent on married couples. Consequently, Mr. Danning does not receive the full benefits provided for in Netherlands law for married couples. The Committee concludes that the differentiation complained of by Mr. Danning does not constitute discrimination in the sense of article 26 of the Covenant. (See Annex VIII, section C, HRC 1987 Report.)

Following the adoption of the Committee's views in the above three cases, an increasing number of communications have been received from authors claiming violations of article 26. Most of these communications have been declared inadmissible on the ground that the authors have failed to make at least a *prima facie* case of discrimination within the meaning of article 26, or have resulted in a finding of no violation. Out of 30 final decisions adopted during this period, including the cases of Broeks, Danning and Zwaan-de Vries, 20 cases have been declared inadmissible, a finding of no violation has been made in 6 cases, while violations have been found in only 4 cases (including Broeks and Zwaan-de Vries). In the meantime (November 1989) the Committee has adopted a general comment on article 26 (CCPR/C/21/Rev.21/Add.1), which fully reflects the emerging case law. The following samples may be added, to the cases referred to above.

In case No. 212/1986 (P.P.C. *v*. the Netherlands), the author had alleged discrimination because the application of a law providing for additional assistance to persons with a minimum income was linked to the person's income in the month of September. Since the author had not been unemployed in September, the annual calculation showed a figure higher than his real income for the year in question and he did not qualify for the desired additional assistance. In declaring the communication inadmissible, the Committee stated:

The Committee has already had an opportunity to observe that the scope of article 26 can also cover cases of discrimination with regard to social security benefits (communications nos. 172/1984, 180/1984, 182/1984). It considers, however, that the scope of article 26 does not extend to differences of results in the application of common rules in the allocation of benefits. In the case at issue, the author merely states that the determination of compensation benefits on the basis of a person's income in the month of September led to an unfavourable result in his case. Such determination is, however, uniform for all persons with a minimum of income in the Netherlands. Thus, the Committee finds that the law in question is not *prima facie* discriminatory, and that the author does not, therefore, have a claim under article 2 of the Optional Protocol (see Annex VIII, section B, para. 6.2, HRC 1988 Report).

Two other cases concerned the different treatment of soldiers and civilians. In declaring communication no. 267/1987 (M.J.G. *v.* the Netherlands) inadmissible, the Committee stated:

> The Committee notes that the author claims that he is a victim of discrimination on the ground of 'other status' (Covenant, article 26, *in fine*) because, being a soldier during the period of his military service, he could not appeal against a summons like a civilian. The Committee considers, however, that the scope of application of article 26 cannot be extended to cover situations such as the one encountered by the author. The Committee observes, as it did with respect to communication no. 245/1987 (R.T.Z. *v.* the Netherlands), that the Covenant does not preclude the institution of compulsory military service by States parties, even though this means that some rights of individuals may be restricted during military service, within the exigencies of such service. The Committee notes, in this connection, that the author has not claimed that the Netherlands military penal procedures are not being applied equally to all Netherlands citizens serving in the Netherlands armed forces. It therefore concludes that the author has no claim under article 2 of the Optional Protocol (see Annex VIII, section K, para. 3.2, HRC 1988 Report).

In case no. 191/1985 (Blom *v.* Sweden), which the Committee declared admissible and examined on the merits, the main issue was whether the author of the communication was the victim of a violation of article 26 of the Covenant because of the alleged incompatibility of the Swedish regulations on education allowances with that provision. In deciding that the State Party had not violated article 26 by refusing to grant the author, as a pupil of a private school, an education allowance for the school year 1981/82, whereas pupils of public schools were entitled to education allowances for that period, the Committee stated:

> The State party's educational system provides for both private and public education. The State party cannot be deemed to act in a discriminatory fashion if it does not provide the same level of subsidy for the two types of establishments, when the private system is not subject to State supervision. As to the author's claim that the failure of the State party to grant an education allowance for the school year 1981/82 constituted discriminatory treatment, because the State party did not apply retroactively its decision of 17 June 1982 to place grades 10 and above under State supervision, the Committee notes that the granting of an allowance depended on actual exercise of State supervision; since State supervision could not be exercised prior to 1 July 1982 ..., the Committee finds that consequently it could not be expected that the State party would grant an allowance for any prior period and that the question of discrimination does not arise. On the other hand, the question does arise whether the processing of the application of the Rudolf Steiner school to be placed under State supervision was unduly prolonged and whether this violated any of the author's rights under the Covenant. In this connection, the Committee notes that the evaluation of a school's curricula necessarily entails a certain period of time, as a result of a host of factors and imponderables, including the necessity of seeking advice from various governmental agencies. In the instant case the school's application was made in October 1981 and the decision was rendered eight months later, in June 1982. This lapse of time cannot be deemed to be discriminatory, as such (see Annex VII, section E, para. 10.3, HRC 1988 Report).

In case no. 273/1988 (B.d.B *et al. v.* the Netherlands), cited above under *Right to a fair hearing* (article 14), the authors, joint owners of a physiotherapy practice in the Netherlands, also claimed to have been victims of unequal treatment under article 26, because allegedly other physiotherapy practices were not required to start paying social security contributions from the same date as they. In declaring the case inadmissible, the Committee observed:

> The authors complain about the application to them of legal rules of a compulsory nature, which for unexplained reasons were allegedly not applied uniformly to some other physiotherapy practices; regardless of whether the apparent non-application of the compulsory rules on insurance contributions in other cases may have been right or wrong, it has not been alleged that these rules were incorrectly applied to the authors following the Central Appeals Board's ruling of 19 April 1983

that part-time physiotherapists were to be deemed employees and that their employers were liable for social security contributions; furthermore, the Committee is not competent to examine errors allegedly committed in the application of laws concerning persons other than the authors of a communication (Annex XI, section F, para. 6.6, HRC 1989 Report).

In the same case, the Committee also recalled that article 26, second sentence, provides that the law of States Parties should "guarantee to all persons equal and effective protection against discrimination on any ground such as race, colour, sex, language, religion, political or other opinion, national or social origin, property, birth or other status." The Committee noted that the authors had not claimed that their different treatment was attributable to their belonging to any identifiably distinct category which could have exposed them to discrimination on account of any of the grounds enumerated or 'other status' referred to in article 26 of the Covenant. The Committee, therefore, found this aspect of the authors' communication to be inadmissible under article 3 of the Optional Protocol (Annex XI, section F, para. 6.7, HRC 1989 Report).

In case no. 218/1986 (Vos *v.* the Netherlands), the author claimed to be a victim of violation of article 26 because of the application of the General Widows and Orphans Act to her, which, as a consequence, resulted in the loss of her entitlement under the General Disablement Benefits Act. She argued that whereas a disabled man whose (former) wife dies retains the right to a disability allowance, article 32 of the General Disablement Benefits Act provides that a disabled woman whose (former) husband dies does not retain the right to a disability allowance, but qualifies instead as beneficiary under the General Widows and Orphans Act. The State Party explained that the General Widows and Orphans Act had been enacted to give widows an additional protection, which widowers do not at present enjoy. In a sense, widowers could claim unequal treatment under Dutch law, but not widows. What the author complained of was that as a result of the application of a rule of concurrence to avoid duplication of benefits she received a slightly reduced benefit. In its view, the Committee found no violation of article 26 and observed:

> In light of the explanations given by the State party with respect to the legislative history, the purpose and application of the General Disablement Benefits Act and the General Widows and Orphans Act, the Committee is of the view that the unfavourable result complained of by Mrs. Vos follows from the application of a uniform rule to avoid

overlapping in the allocation of social security benefits. This rule is based on objective and reasonable criteria, especially bearing in mind that both statutes under which Mrs. Vos qualified for benefits aim at ensuring to all persons falling thereunder subsistence level income. Thus the Committee cannot conclude that Mrs. Vos has been a victim of discrimination within the meaning of article 26 of the Covenant (Annex X, section G, para. 13, HRC 1989 Report).

A violation of article 26 was found in case no. 196/1985 (Gueye *et al. v.* France), in which the authors, retired Senegalese members of the French Army, complained that they did not receive pensions equal to those given to retired members of the French Army having French nationality:

In determining whether the treatment of the authors is based on reasonable and objective criteria, the Committee notes that it was not the question of nationality which determined the granting of pensions to the authors but the services rendered by them in the past. They had served in the French Army forces under the same conditions as French citizens; for 14 years subsequent to the independence of Senegal they were treated in the same way as their French counterparts for the purpose of pension rights, although their nationality was not French but Senegalese. A subsequent change in nationality cannot by itself be considered as a sufficient justification for different treatment, since the basis for the grant of the pension was the same service which both they and the soldiers who remained French had provided. Nor can differences in the economic, financial and social conditions as between France and Senegal be invoked as a legitimate justification. If one compared the case of retired soldiers of Senegalese nationality living in Senegal with that of retired soldiers of French nationality in Senegal, it would appear that they enjoy the same economic and social conditions. Yet, their treatment for the purpose of pension entitlements would differ. Finally, the fact that the State party claims that it can no longer carry out checks of identity and family situation, so as to prevent abuses in the administration of pension schemes cannot justify differences in treatment. In the Committee's opinion, mere administrative inconvenience or the possibility of some abuse of pension rights cannot be invoked to justify unequal treatment. The Committee concludes that the difference in treatment of the authors is not based on reasonable and objective criteria and constitutes discrimination prohibited by the Covenant (Annex X, section E, para. 9.5, HRC 1989 Report).

The Committee also found a violation of article 26 in case no. 202/1986 (Ato del Avellanal *v.* Peru), where the author had been denied the right to sue in Peruvian courts, because, according to article 168 of the Peruvian Civil Code, when a woman is married only the husband is entitled to represent matrimonial property before the courts. In its view, the Committee observed that:

> Under article 3 of the Covenant States parties undertake 'to ensure the equal right of men and women to the enjoyment of all civil and political rights set forth in the present Covenant' and that article 26 provides that all persons are equal before the law and are entitled to the equal protection of the law. The Committee finds that the facts before it reveal that the application of article 168 of the Peruvian Civil Code to the author resulted in denying her equality before the courts and constituted discrimination on the ground of sex (Annex X, section C, para. 10.2, HRC 1989 Report).

Article 8

Göran Melander

Sweden

Everyone has the right to an effective remedy by the competent national tribunals for acts violating the fundamental rights granted him by the constitution or by law.

The right to access to justice is sometimes referred to as an essential feature of any democratic society.[1] The concept of the rule of law is a general guarantee of a remedy for anyone who considers that one of his human rights has been violated. It is also generally recognized that a person who is of the opinion that he is a victim of human rights violations shall have a redress within his own State rather than resorting to international institutions. Article 8 of the Universal Declaration of Human Rights (UDHR) deals with this question in prescribing that everyone should have the right to an effective remedy by the competent national tribunals, should fundamental rights granted him have been violated.

The principle prescribed for in article 8 was inserted only at a very late stage of the drafting procedure of the UDHR. It was proposed by delegates from the Latin American countries and reflected a principle recognized by many States, in particular in Latin America.[2] An additional argument was that there was no other article in the UDHR which could be invoked by an individual against the State, if his human rights had been violated. It is obvious that the article has been strongly influenced by the principles of *amparo* and *habeas corpus*.

Provisions on domestic remedies can also be found in subsequent international instruments, although not quite identical. Article 2(3) of the International Covenant on Civil and Political Rights (CCPR)

---

[1] Council of Europe, Resolution (78)8 of the Committee of Ministers.
[2] Verdoodt 1964, p. 116.

prescribes that a State Party must ensure that a person, whose rights and freedoms as described in the Covenant are violated, shall have an effective remedy and that a person claiming such a remedy shall have his right thereto determined by "competent judicial, administrative or legislative authorities, or by any other competent authority provided for by the legal system of the State." A similar provision can be found in article 13 of the European Convention on Human Rights (ECHR) which prescribes that everyone whose rights and freedoms "as set forth in this Convention are violated shall have an effective remedy before a national authority." Provisions of domestic remedies can also be found in the American Declaration of the Rights and Duties of Man (article XVIII), in the American Convention on Human Rights (ACHR, article 25), and in the African Charter on Peoples' and Human Rights (African Charter, article 7).

The UDHR calls for remedies in the case of violations of rights and freedoms "protected by the domestic constitutions or fundamental rights granted by law." The scope of the article is, however, not described in the article. In one respect it can be said to cover a broad area of rights, in so far as reference is made to constitutions and fundamental rights granted by law. Accordingly, the article can be applied with respect to human rights not dealt with in the UDHR itself, provided such a right is protected by constitutions or by law. On the other hand, the scope of article 24 is limited in countries where human rights are not protected or insufficiently protected by the constitution (as was the case in Sweden until the adoption of the 1974 Constitution) and the domestic laws are unsatisfactory.

In contrast with article 24 of the UDHR stand the corresponding provisions of the CCPR and the ECHR. A State Party is under an obligation to guarantee effective remedies with respect to those rights prescribed for in the respective agreement. These articles can only be invoked in conjunction with another article in the treaty. In the nowadays rich jurisprudence relating to article 13 of the ECHR it has been established that the article can be invoked independently, i.e., a violation of another article in the Convention is not a prerequisite for a violation of article 13. The European Court has recently summed up the case law of the Court by stating that "where an individual has an arguable claim to be the victim of a violation of the rights set forth in the Convention, he should have a remedy before a national authority in order both to have his claim decided and, if appropriate, to obtain redress."[3]

The UDHR specifies the nature of the forum in so far as reference is made to "competent national tribunals." The expression should be compared with the broader expression used in the CCPR ("competent judicial, administrative or legislative authorities, or any other competent authority provided for by the legal system of the State") and the ECHR ("a national authority").

An ill-disposed interpretation is that access to a national tribunal must only exist when a competent court is available, and that access to a court is not needed if the domestic legal system does not offer domestic remedies.[4] Such an interpretation must be rejected, however, as it would make the article completely meaningless and be quite contrary to the intention of the authors of the article.[5]

Should article 8 be interpreted as guaranteeing a right to domestic remedies before a tribunal, it must be admitted that some countries do not live up to their international obligations. The jurisprudence under the European system, in particular cases relating to article 5 (on the right to liberty and security of persons) and article 6 (on the right to a fair and public hearing) clearly demonstrates the difficulty for States even to fulfil the obligation under the ECHR. A country like Sweden has, for example, on several occasions been found guilty of violation of article 6, as the applicant has not been granted access to a domestic tribunal.[6]

---

[3] Judgment of 25 March 1983, *Silver and others*, A.61 (1983), p. 42. See also van Dijk and van Hoof 1990, p. 522f.

[4] Robinson 1958, p. 112.

[5] Verdoodt 1964, p. 119.

[6] See, for instance, Judgment of 27 October 1987, *Pudas Case*, A.125 (1987).

References

van Dijk, Pieter, and G.J.H. van Hoof, *Theory and Practice of the European Convention on Human Rights*, 2nd ed., Deventer: Kluwer Law and Taxation Publishers, 1990.

Robinson, Nehemiah, *The Universal Declaration of Human Rights*, New York: Institute of Jewish Affairs, 1958.

Verdoodt, Albert, *Naissance et Signification de la Déclaration Universelle des Droits de l'Homme*, Société d'Etude Morales, Sociales et Juridiques, Louvain-Paris: Editions Nauwelaerts, 1964.

Article 9

Johanna Niemi-Kiesiläinen

Finland

No one shall be subjected to arbitrary arrest, detention or exile.

I. Introduction

The right to personal liberty and security, expressed in article 9 of the Universal Declaration of Human Rights (UDHR) and in all major human rights declarations beginning with the Magna Carta (1215) and the French Revolution (1789), is one of the most fundamental of human rights. Prohibition of arbitrary arrest and detention as provided for in article 9 of the UDHR shares a common history with the more broadened slogan of the right to liberty. In the words of the Magna Carta:

> No free man shall be taken or imprisoned or disseised or out lawed or exiled or in any way ruined, nor we go or send against him, except by lawful judgement of his peers or by the law of the land.

Even if the Magna Carta guaranteed rights to only a limited group of people, namely the feudal noblemen, it required that the arrest or detention be lawful and it protected a person against the excesses of his rulers.

Protection against arbitrary arrest and detention as one of the main dimensions and concretizations of the right to liberty of person was further expressed in the 17th century Bill of Rights (1688) and Habeas Corpus Acts (1640, 1679) as well as in the French Declaration of 1789 and in the constitutions of many States.[1] In the UDHR it appears in a short and programmatic version, with further elaboration left to future human rights conventions.

---

[1] For a review see UN Study, pp. 9–17.

II. *Travaux Préparatoires*

Article 9 is short and vague. It only prohibits arbitrary arrest, detention and exile without giving any guidance as to the meaning of these expressions. Several human rights conventions of more recent date have given an elaboration of this, as will be discussed later.

Early drafts of the UDHR, however, contained more precise wordings. In the first drafts before the Commission on Human Rights (the Commission) we can find the requirement of a lawful arrest; the right to an immediate judicial hearing in front of a judge; and the right to a trial within a reasonable period of time, which are all rights guaranteed by later human rights conventions.[2]

After the Commission, in its second session (2–17 December 1947), had decided that the Bill of Human Rights should include three separate instruments, (Declaration, Convention and Measures of Implementation), several proposals for inclusion of the permissible grounds for detention in the convention were presented to the drafting committee.[3] It was clear that no consensus existed on the wordings of the permissible grounds for detention.

The discussion of this article by the Third Committee of the General Assembly concerned the style of the Declaration, which "should be a brief and simple statement of general principles; precise legal provisions should rather be included in the covenant."[4] In the final vote in the Third Committee all specific limitations were defeated and thus left to the future convention.

The word 'exile' was added to the article in the Third Committee of the General Assembly after a proposal by Ecuador. Although the proposal received wide support, disagreement prevailed on whether the word 'arbitrary' should also refer to the word 'exile'. The final wording represented a compromise between a proposal 'No one may be exiled' and a proposal which would have allowed exile in accordance with the legislation.

---

[2] See, e.g., drafts before the Drafting Committee: Secretarial Draft, E/CN.4/AC.1/3 article 6, British Draft article 9–10, E/CN.4/AC.1/4, Cassin Draft article 10, E/CN.4/AC.1/W.2/Rev.1 and Commission on Human Rights at its second session article 5 Annex to E/600.

[3] List and analysis of suggested limitations to article 9 of the Covenant E/CN.4/95, pp. 20–26.

[4] Delegate of New Zealand at the Committee.

III. The Elaboration in Later Human Rights Instruments

Whereas article 9 of the UDHR is short and vague, it has been further elaborated by a number of international human rights instruments, including the International Covenant on Civil and Political Rights (CCPR) of 1966 and all major regional human rights instruments. The basic principles set out in article 9 of the UDHR are elaborated upon by several articles of the CCPR: article 9 (right to liberty and security of person); article 10 (humane treatment of those deprived of their liberty); article 11 (prohibition of imprisonment on ground of contractual obligation); and article 12(4) (prohibition of arbitrary exile).

Various human rights conventions derive from the prohibition of arbitrary arrest a number of very concrete rights. While the wordings of these instruments stress different aspects, the basic rules they set out are, in principle, the same. These rules, explained in the following sections, have been interpreted in a number of cases by the European Commission and European Court of Human Rights (European Court). The jurisprudence is not explained in detail but some general references are made.

A. Lawfulness of Detention

Article 9(1) of the CCPR provides that

> Every one has the right to liberty and security of person. No one shall be subjected to arbitrary arrest or detention. No one shall be deprived of his liberty except on such grounds and in accordance with such procedure as are established by law.

In human rights conventions the prohibition of arbitrary arrest and detention is provided in more positive terms. The requirement that the detention be lawful encompasses both the grounds for detention and the procedure to be followed: CCPR article 9(1); African Charter on Human and Peoples' Rights (African Charter) article 6; European Convention on Human Rights (ECHR) article 5(1); and American Convention on Human Rights (ACHR) article 7(2). The ACHR stresses the constitutional character of the deprivation of the physical liberty of person (article 7(2)). Article 5 of the ECHR also enumerates the permissible grounds upon which a lawful deprivation of liberty is possible.

The requirement of lawful detention does not favour any one legal tradition. Both statutory and common law systems may fulfil the requirement of the lawfulness if they satisfy the criteria of accessibility and precision set out by the European Court in the Sunday Times case (1979).

The concretization of the prohibition of arbitrary arrest and detention in the human rights instruments has meant the interpretation of the word 'arbitrary'. There remains the question, however, of whether this word has any substantive content, apart from that given it in international instruments and domestic legislation. This question was considered in the *travaux préparatoires* of the UDHR and the views were expressed that the term 'arbitrary' means the same as 'illegal' or 'unjust' or 'both illegal and unjust'.[5] In the end, none of these expressions was included in the text of the Declaration. Later, in 1965, the UN Study on this article adopted the following definition: "An arrest or detention is arbitrary if it is (a) on grounds or in accordance with procedures other than those established by law, or (b) under the provisions of a law the purpose of which is incompatible with respect for the right to liberty and security of person."[6] For international human rights to be meaningful there has to be an international minimum standard that limits the legislative power of the States.[7] Even if the content of this standard is weak, it excludes legislation which provides for a clearly arbitrary or discriminatory detention of persons.

While the human rights conventions set out a number of precise criteria for the lawfulness of the procedure to be followed, they leave — with the exception of the ECHR — the regulation of the grounds for detention to the domain of domestic legislation. An important exception, however, is the prohibition of imprisonment on the ground of inability to fulfil a contractual obligation (CCPR article 11, ACHR article 7(7) and article 1 of the Fourth Protocol to the ECHR), which is clearly prohibited.

---

[5] The Commission on Human Rights E/CN.4/SR.47, para. 43. Third Committee of the General Assembly A/4045, paras. 43–49.

[6] UN Study, p. 7.

[7] Dinstein 1981, pp. 130–131.

B. *The Right to be Informed of the Grounds for Arrest*

Anyone who is arrested shall be informed of the reasons for his or her arrest and charges against him. Although the wordings differ as to whether this must be done promptly (ECHR article 5(2), ACHR article 7(4)) or at the time of the arrest (CCPR article 9(2)), the essence is the same; the notification of the reasons for arrest must be given in connection with the actual arrest. Concerning notification of reason for arrest, there is no difference between criminal procedure and arrest on any other grounds.[8] But in criminal procedures it may take time to complete the investigation and give a detailed charge. Therefore, the detainee has a right to be informed promptly (but not at the time of arrest) of the charges he will face.[9]

C. *The Right to Judicial Control of Arrest and Detention*

This right, which is provided for in the CCPR as well as in the ECHR and the ACHR, is regulated in two separate sections of the relevant article of each instrument. The right of judicial control of arrest and detention in criminal procedures and investigations is provided for in article 9(3) of the CCPR, article 5(3) of the ECHR and article 7(5) of the ACHR. The requirement of a judicial review of deprivation of liberty provided for in article 9(4) of the CCPR, article 5(4) of the ECHR and article 7(6) of the ACHR applies to all types of deprivation of liberty.[10]

---

[8] See Human Rights Committee: General Comment 8(16) 1982 on article 9 of the CCPR para. 1.

[9] For the guidelines established in the jurisprudence of the European Commission of Human Rights see Sieghart 1983, p. 151.

[10] Human Rights Committee: General Comment 8(16) para. 2. The terminology used varies. The ACHR is most logical and uses the word 'detain' with a reference to criminal proceedings (article 7(4) and article 7(5)) and the phrase 'deprivation of liberty' in other contexts (article 7(2) and article 7(6)). The CCPR and ECHR speak of 'arrest and detention' but make a special reference to the criminal nature of it in the respective paragraphs (CCPR article 9(3) and ECHR article 5(3)). In the paragraphs with wider application "deprivation of liberty by arrest or detention" is used (CCPR article 9(4) and ECHR article 5(4)).

Logically, without this interpretation paragraphs CCPR article 9(4), ECHR article 5(4) and ACHR article 7(4) would lose most of their meaning, while the criminal arrest has to fulfil the stricter requirements in previous paragraphs. See also

The judicial control of arrest and detention in criminal procedures has two basic requirements: 1) a right to be "brought promptly before a judge or other officer authorized by law to exercise judicial power"; and 2) a right to be "entitled to a trial within a reasonable time or to release." The wording of the three instruments in this respect is identical.

The right to be brought promptly before a judge or other officer authorized by law to exercise judicial power has been interpreted in a number of decisions by the European Court and the European Commission. In the Schiesser case (1979) the Court considered what was meant by "other official authorized by law to exercise judicial power." Decisive criteria for the determination of whether an official fulfils the requirements of the ECHR is his independence from the parties, especially from the executive branch and the prosecutor.

The maximum length of detention before a judicial hearing has been discussed in the Nordic countries, notably in Sweden and Finland during the 1980s. The Human Rights Committee has in its general comment on article 9 stated that this time may not be longer than "a few days."[11] The European Court has given more exact interpretations of the word 'promptly'. No violation of the Convention was found when the time had not exceeded four days, but a longer period has been found to be unacceptable.[12]

In the cases where a claim of a breach of the requirement of a trial within a reasonable time has been made, the European Commission considers all the circumstances of the case instead of giving strict time limits. The European Court has set guidelines which should be taken into account. Detention on remand is justified in the light of the ECHR if there is a danger of absconding or repeating the offence or destroying the evidence. The length of the detention is to be considered in the light of the length and effectiveness of the investigations and the complexity of the case.[13]

Judicial review of the deprivation of liberty guaranteed in article

Pellonpää 1982. In ordinary English judicial language the word detain is by no means restricted to criminal custody. It refers to the confinement and keeping of a person in a certain place, whereas 'arrest' refers to the actual seizure of the person. See definitions adopted by the UN Study, p. 5 and, e.g., Collin 1986. See also Myntti 1988, p. 47.

[11] Human Rights Committee: General Comment 8(16) para. 2.

[12] Cases of de Jong, Baljet and van den Brink, and McGoff, all 1984, and the Case of Brogan and others, 1988.

[13] Sieghart 1983, p. 154.

9(4) of the CCPR, article 5(4) of the ECHR and article 7(6) of the ACHR is applicable to the deprivation of liberty on any grounds. In addition to the guarantees in the previous paragraphs with respect to criminal proceedings, these articles add the requirement that the authority deciding on the legality of the arrest must be a court.

The court may then without delay decide on the lawfulness of the arrest or detention and order a release if the detention is not lawful. The ACHR includes a limitation on the legislative power of the States Parties; it prohibits those States whose laws entitle anyone who believes himself to be threatened by deprivation of his liberty to recourse to a competent court, to abolish this remedy. The ACHR also allows a third person to seek these remedies.

D. Prohibition of Arbitrary Exile

'Exile' usually means expulsion of a national from his country. It is also used in a wider meaning which includes 'internal exile' or exile within the frontiers of the state. While the latter has a close connection to the right to freedom of movement, it is not discussed here.

The prohibition of exile is not listed among the rights of criminal defendants in other human rights instruments. Indeed, the word 'exile' is not even used. Instead, the provisions dealing with the right to freedom of movement guarantee everyone a right to enter his own country (CCPR article 12(4)) and also prohibit the expulsion of nationals (Fourth Protocol to the ECHR article 3, ACHR article 22(5)) which in practice make the use of exile impossible. While nationality is the essential link between the State and people under its sovereignty, it is clear that a deprivation of nationality before the expulsion cannot make exile acceptable.[14]

The absence of the term 'exile' in later human rights instruments may be explained by the prohibition of exile having become a rule of customary international law. Even if exile has not "virtually disappeared" as stated by the UN Study of the Right of Everyone to be Free from Arbitrary Arrest, Detention and Exile,[15] it is rarely used and those cases in which it has been used have been condemned by the international community.

[14] For an analysis of the relationship of exile, expulsion and nationality see Pellonpää 1984, p. 17–27.
[15] UN Study, p. 203.

IV. Special Studies

In 1956 the Commission decided to undertake studies on specific human rights or groups of rights in order to "ascertain the existing conditions, the results obtained and the difficulties encountered" in the field of human rights. The Economic and Social Council (ECOSOC) agreed to take up as a first subject of study the rights of everyone to be free from arbitrary arrest, detention and exile.

The study was carried out by a committee of four States selected from among the Member States of the Commission. The study was completed in 1965 and contains a comprehensive review of the laws on the subject in different countries.

The protection of human rights of persons suffering from mental disorders, including the procedural guarantees of article 9(4) of the CCPR and article 5(4) of the ECHR in the cases of involuntary placement in an institution, has recently been under review in both the United Nations and the Council of Europe. A special study on the subject was conducted by request of the Commission.[16] In the Council of Europe, the review has so far resulted in a recommendation by the Committee of Ministers on the legal protection of involuntary patients.[17]

V. Nordic Developments

Although it is generally believed that there are no human rights problems in the Nordic countries, the human rights protected by article 9 of the UDHR have constantly been an issue in legal policy discussions in both Finland and Sweden during the 1980s.[18]

Traditionally, in both countries the criminal police conducting investigations and, in Sweden, the prosecutor have had broad

[16] Daes 1986.
[17] R(83)2(1). Legal protection of persons suffering from mental disorder placed as involuntary patients. Of other activities in the Council of Europe see Daes 1986, p. 11.
[18] For a review of Finnish discussion see Träskman 1987, pp. 283–286. In Sweden the discussion has been more lively and only a general reference can be made here. A list of important contributions is found, e.g., in Sundberg, Jacob, p. 100–101. Since this article was written in the summer of 1988, a thorough thesis on human rights and different forms of criminal and administrative detention in Finland has been published by Myntti. This article was updated in January 1991 concerning Finnish developments after 1988.

powers to arrest and detain. The question of whether Finnish law conformed to international human rights standards was raised when Finland ratified the CCPR in 1975 and a reservation to article 9(3) was indeed made. Sweden has been a party to the ECHR since 1952, but the question of the conformity of its pre-trial detention law to the Convention did not come up until 1983 when two cases concerning Sweden were brought before the European Commission and European Court.

The European Commission reported on the Skoogström and McGoff cases against Sweden in 1983. The accused had been detained for one week in the Skoogström case and for 15 days in the McGoff case. A breach of article 5 of the ECHR was found in both cases and the cases were referred to the European Court. In the Skoogström case, the Commission also decided that the prosecutor was not an "other official authorized by law to exercise judicial power", since in the latter stage he could become a party in the trial; he did not personally hear the accused; and did not render a decision satisfying the formalities required. Thereafter a friendly settlement was reached in the Skoogström case and a judgment of the European Court was given in the McGoff case.[19]

These two cases led to a law reform in Sweden in 1987. The Code of Judicial Procedure Chapter 24 was amended to provide that the period in which the accused has to be brought before the judge may in no case exceed four days.[20]

In Finland, which has large, sparsely settled areas where transportation used to be rather slow, the court was historically not available for most parts of the year. Therefore the pre-trial detention allowed by the law was fairly long. The Finnish law on pre-trial detention of 1948[21] gave the powers of arrest and detention to the police. According to that law, an unfortunate detainee could face a fairly long pre-trial detention (even a few weeks in the countryside) before he was brought before the court. The law reforms concerning the pre-trial investigation and the coercive measures in criminal procedure which took place in the 1980s are of particular interest, while the human rights concern was decisive in the legislative

---

[19] For these two cases see Danelius 1984, p. 95 and Jacob Sundberg, pp. 66–72.

[20] Before the law was amended the courts and the prosecutors were informed of the outcome of the Skoogström and McGoff cases with a recommendation to respect them in practice. See Jacob Sundberg, pp. 69–71.

[21] Asetus rikoslain voimaanpanemisesta 20–26 § of 1889 as amended by law 515/1948.

process.

The Coercive Measures in Criminal Procedure Act (450/1987) entered into force on 1 January 1989. One of the aims of the reform was to make it possible to remove the reservation made to article 9 of the CCPR.[22] While the proposal established a basic rule that the pre-trial detention should not exceed three days, it nevertheless provided for numerous grounds on which the period could be extended. During the committee hearings in Parliament, the conformity of the proposal to the CCPR was questioned by several experts and members of Parliament,[23] which led to the modification of the proposal. As a consequence, when the Coercive Measures in Criminal Procedure Act entered into force, it still allowed numerous grounds on which the pre-trial detention time of three days could be extended, in an unfortunate case, by several days. It was generally believed that the reservation made to the CCPR could be removed.

In May 1989 Finland joined the Council of Europe and one year later became party to the ECHR.[24] A comprehensive review of Finnish legislation was made by Pellonpää in 1988 before the ratification of the ECHR, and in consequence, the ratification was accompanied by legislative amendments. In this context it is important to note that through these amendments it was assured that the legislation concerning pre-trial detention was in conformity with the Convention.[25] Also, legislation concerning judicial control of administrative detention has been under review and has led to amendments of legislation.[26]

---

[22] See Proposal of the Government HE 14/1985, p. 4.

[23] Lakivaliokunnan mietintö n:o 9 vp. 1986 hallituksen esityksen johdosta esitutkintaa ja pakkokeinoja rikosasioissa koskevaksi lainsäädännöksi s. 3–4 ja perustuslakivaliokunnan lausunto n:o 4 vp. 1986, s. 4.

[24] Law 4.5.1990/438–439, governmental proposal HE 22/1990.

[25] The Coercive Measures in Criminal Procedures Act was amended by law 30.4.1990/361 (HE 251/1989). Amendments concerning the judicial control of the loss of liberty as a criminal or disciplinary sanction were, in this context, the amendment of the Disciplinary Measures in Armed Forces Act (27.4.1990/374; HE 100/1989) and the amendment of Enforcement of Punishments Act 20.4.1990/349; HE 23/1990). See Pellonpää 1990, pp. 526–528.

[26] Amendment of the Aliens Act (4.5.1990/408; HE 29/1990) and the Mental Health Act (14.12.1990/1116; HE 201/1989).

VI. Conclusion

We have seen that the right to freedom from arbitrary arrest and detention in the Universal Declaration of Human Rights has developed into more precise international norms in international and regional human rights instruments, which in turn have had a direct impact on domestic legislation in the Nordic countries. There is no doubt that the laws and practices of these countries fulfil the requirements of the human rights conventions. Can we say that article 9 of the UDHR has fulfilled its purpose and made itself needless from the Nordic point of view? To some extent, I believe, this is the case. On the other hand, there has been a trend towards proceduralization in the regulation of detention and other forms of loss of liberty. When it comes to the material grounds for loss of liberty, we will always have to keep in mind the great ideas that lie behind the text of the Declaration.

References

Alderson, J., *Human Rights and the Police*, Strasbourg: Council of Europe Directorate of Human Rights, 1984.

Andrews, J.A. (ed.), *Human Rights in Criminal Procedure, A Comparative Study*, The Hague: Martinus Nijhoff Publishers, 1982.

Collin, P.H., *English Law Dictionary*, 1986.

Daes, Erica-Irene A, "Principles, Guidelines and Guarantees for the Protection of Persons Detained on Grounds of Mental Ill-Health or Suffering from Mental Disorder", United Nations document E/CN.4/Sub.2/1983/17/Rev.1, Sales no. E.85.XIV.9, 1986.

Danelius, Hans, Mänskliga Rättigheter, 3. upplaga Stockholm, 1984.

Dinstein, Yoram, "The Right to Life, Physical Integrity, and Liberty", in Louis Henkin (ed.), *The International Bill of Rights, The Covenant on Civil and Political Rights*, New York: Columbia University Press, 1981.

Myntti, Kristian, "Mänskliga Rättigheter och Frihetsberövande i Finland", Meddelanden från Ekonomisk-statsvetenskapliga Fakulteten vid Åbo Akademi, Institutet för mänskliga rättigheter, Ser. A:268, 1988.

Pellonpää, Matti, "Euroopan ihmisoikeussopimuksesta ja sen merkityksestä Suomelle", LM 1990.

Pellonpää, Matti, "Ihmisoikeussopimukset ja Suomi", *Perusoikeustyöryhmän muistio. Oikeusministerion lainvalmisteluosaston julkaisuja* 3, 1982.

Pellonpää, Matti, "Euroopan neuvoston ihmisorkeussopimus Suomen näkökulmasta", *Oikeusministeriän lainvalmisteluosaston julkalsu* 21, 1988.

Pellonpää, Matti, *Expulsion in International Law, a Study in International Aliens Law and Human Rights with Special Reference to Finland*, Helsinki: 1984.

Sieghart, Paul, *The International Law of Human Rights*, Oxford: Clarendon Press, 1983.

Sundberg Fredrik, "Om ingripandet mot administrativt frihetsberövande i rättighetsperspektiv", *Förvaltningsrättslig Tidskrift*, 1983.

Sundberg, Jacob W.F., *Human Rights in Sweden, The Annual Reports 1982–1984*, Institutet för offentlig och internationell rätt no. 60.

Träskman, P.O., "Brottmålsrättegången i Finland i förhållande till FN-konventionen om politiska och medborgerliga rättigheter", *Juridiska Föreningens Tidskrift*, 1987.

United Nations, "Study of the Right of Everyone to be Free from Arbitrary Arrest, Detention and Exile", Sales no. 65.XIV.2.

United Nations, "Human Rights Committee, General Comment 8(16)", 27 July 1982 on Article 9 of the CCPR.

United Nations Documents: E/CN.4/AC.1/3, E/CN.4/AC.1/4, E/CN.4/AC.1/W.2/Rev.1, E/600, E/CN.4/95, E/CN.4/SR.47, A/4045, E/CN.4/Sub. 2/1983/Rev.1.

Article 10

Lauri Lehtimaja and Matti Pellonpää

Finland

"The inn that shelters for the night is not the journey's end. The law like the traveller must be ready for tomorrow."
Benjamin Cardozo

Everyone is entitled in full equality to a fair and public hearing by an independent and impartial tribunal, in the determination of his rights and obligations and of any criminal charge against him.

I. The Emergence of Article 10 of the Universal Declaration of Human Rights

The interdependence of human rights and the rule of law is clearly recognized even in the Preamble of the Universal Declaration of Human Rights (UDHR). The right to a fair trial is an essential, if not imperative, part of any legal system purporting to be based on the rule of law, even though the precise scope of the notion 'fair trial' is fairly difficult to capture in languages other than English.

The right to a fair trial is a set of distinct, even if interrelated, rights which: "taken together, make up a single right not specifically defined."[1] This right goes under other labels, too, such as the right to a fair hearing or the right to the proper (fair) administration of justice. It is essential, however, to distinguish two aspects of it: the judicial procedure ('fair and public hearing'), on the one hand; and the organization of the judiciary ('independent and impartial tribunal'), on the other hand.

However ideally the will of the legislature may be shaped in the laws of the land, the latter may be of very limited value for the

---

[1] European Court of Human Rights, Golder judgment of 21 February 1975, Series A, no. 18, p. 13.

people whose rights depend on those laws, unless there are judges competent to interpret the laws and apply them to individual cases, and unless these judges are independent of any outside interference as well as impartial with regard to parties concerned. Similarly, justice is predicated not only on the material norms governing legal rights and obligations but also on the rules of procedure to be followed in a judicial process where those rights and obligations are determined. This is emphasized in the legal systems most directly under the influence of the Anglo-American notion of 'due process of law', but recognized by others as well. Thus, in the course of the drafting of the UDHR, there was no disagreement on the inclusion of the basic principle of fair trial by independent and impartial tribunals, both in criminal and other cases, although various views were taken as to the scope and wording of what finally became article 10.

In the first Draft Declaration, prepared by Cassin, criminal trials, on the one hand, and proceedings for the determination of one's "rights, liabilities and obligations under the law", on the other hand, were dealt with in separate articles.[2] Eventually both aspects, however, were combined into one provision. For the third session of the UN Commission on Human Rights (the Commission), it (then article 6) was submitted with the following wording:[3]

> Every one shall have access to independent and impartial tribunals in the determination of any criminal charge against him, and of his rights and obligations. He shall be entitled to a fair hearing of his case and to have the aid of a qualified representative of his own choice, and if he appears in person to have the procedure explained to him in a manner in which he can understand it and to use a language which he can speak.

In the ensuing discussion it was decided that the second sentence should be omitted, not out of disagreement as to its contents but to make the article more concise. In order to accommodate concerns raised especially by the representative of the Soviet Union, who *inter alia*, was opposed to the dropping of the reference to legal aid, a phrase emphasizing the principle of equality was added to the shortened text.[4] Another noteworthy change affected the French version of the article. In the longer version quoted above in English,

[2] UN doc. E/CN.4/21, Annex D, articles 11, 20.
[3] Report of the Commission, Economic and Social Council (ECOSOC) Official Records, third year, sixth session, E/600, Annex A.
[4] Verdoodt 1964, p. 128; UN doc. E/CN.4/SR.54, pp. 7–11.

the French text first referred to "droits et obligations *en matière civile*", but the emphasized words were finally deleted, as it was felt that they might unduly narrow the scope of the article.[5] Article 10, as finally adopted, reads as follows:

> Everyone is entitled in full equality to a fair and public hearing, by an independent and impartial tribunal, in the determination of [1] his rights and obligations and of [2] any criminal charge against him.

Thus, the right to a fair trial was expressed rather concisely in article 10. A brief provision was adopted with the understanding, recorded by the Chairman of the Commission, that more "detailed provisions belonged to the Covenant."[6] Therefore it is the International Covenant on Civil and Political Rights (CCPR) as well as the regional human rights instruments, especially the European Convention on Human Rights (ECHR), and the relevant case law that we must study in order to see how the right to a fair trial has been elaborated on the basis of the UDHR.

It should be noted that certain fundamental elements qualifying the notion of a fair trial in the UDHR have been placed outside article 10. For instance, the required 'competence' of national tribunals is mentioned in article 8. The right of the accused to be presumed innocent until proven guilty in a public trial, as well as the necessary guarantees for the defence of the accused, are mentioned in article 11(1).

II. Elaboration of the Right to a Fair Trial in Human Rights Instruments

A. Introductory Remarks

Amidst the variety of human rights, the right to a fair trial stands out as perhaps the one most inventively elaborated as well as most dynamically interpreted by the organs set up for the international protection of human rights. The right to a fair trial, as it is conceived today, is judge-made human rights law in the true sense of the word. It does not stand still but keeps developing.

As far as the various human rights instruments are concerned, there is some diversity as to the wording and systematic placement

---

[5] Verdoodt 1964, p. 129.
[6] UN doc. E/CN.4/SR.54, p. 11.

of the constituent elements of the right to a fair trial; but, on the whole, this right seems to be defined along identical lines in most instruments. It is difficult to say whether the diverse wordings reflect shifts of emphasis, or depend on regional legal traditions, drafting history or mere chance.

In the CCPR, the right to a fair trial is dealt with, among other issues, in the rather heterogeneous article 14: paragraph 1, containing the general provision; paragraph 2, the right of the accused to be presumed innocent; and paragraph 3, a list of minimum guarantees to be followed in criminal proceedings. Paragraph 5 introduces the right of a convicted person to have his conviction and sentence reviewed by a higher tribunal, while paragraph 7 concerns the prohibition of double jeopardy.

In the ECHR, the general provision for the right to a fair trial is embodied in article 6, paragraph 1, while paragraphs 2 and 3 introduce elements corresponding to the CCPR article 14, paragraphs 2 and 3. The right to have the conviction and sentence reviewed and the prohibition of double jeopardy only appear in articles 2 and 4 of Protocol no. 7 to the ECHR,[7] which entered into force on 1 November 1988.

In this commentary focusing on article 10 of the UDHR, we will only deal with the general characteristics of the notion of a fair trial as they are elaborated on, most notably in article 14(1) of the CCPR and article 6(1) of the ECHR. These provisions read as follows:

CCPR, article 14:

1. All persons shall be equal before the courts and tribunals. In the determination of any criminal charge against him, or of his rights and obligations in a suit at law, everyone shall be entitled to a fair and public hearing by a competent, independent and impartial tribunal established by law. The press and the public may be excluded from all or part of a trial for reasons of morals, public order (*ordre public*) or national security in a democratic society, or when the interest of the private lives of the parties so requires, or to the extent strictly necessary in the opinion of the court in special circumstances where publicity would prejudice the interests of justice; but any judgment rendered in a criminal case or in a suit at law shall be made public except where the interest of juvenile persons otherwise requires or the proceedings concern matrimonial disputes or the guardianship of children.

[7] European Treaty Series no. 117, 22 November 1984.

ECHR, article 6:

1. In the determination of his civil rights and obligations or of any criminal charge against him, everyone is entitled to a fair and public hearing within a reasonable time by an independent and impartial tribunal established by law. Judgment shall be pronounced publicly but the press and public may be excluded from all or part of the trial in the interests of morals, public order or national security in a democratic society, where the interests of juveniles or the protection of the private life of the parties so require, or to the extent strictly necessary in the opinion of the court in special circumstances where publicity would prejudice the interests of justice.

We must first examine the qualifications of the hearings as well as the attributes assigned to the tribunals responsible for such hearings. Then we shall discuss the different types of legal relations, bearing on rights and obligations as well as on criminal charges, that may be relevant in the protection of the basic right to a fair trial.

B. Entitlement in Full Equality to a Fair and Public Hearing by an Independent and Impartial Tribunal

The very conciseness of article 10 in the Declaration makes it necessary to assume certain implicit requirements, over and above those explicitly mentioned, in the arduous task of elaborating the constituent elements of the right to a fair trial. For instance, one must have access to a court, obviously, before the issue of a trial's fairness can be raised in the first place (for example, Golder judgment). Moreover, the mere use of the word 'tribunal' entails that certain minimum guarantees inherent in any judicial procedure must be satisfied, even if the body presented as a 'tribunal' was not named as one in the domestic legal parlance or, even by general standards, if it were no court of law in the strict and formal sense of the word.

According to the explicit wording of article 10, the tribunal must be 'independent'. This attribute has become the focus of intensive study, not only in the context of human rights case law but also in the standard-setting work of several intergovernmental as well as non-governmental organizations. At the level of the United Nations, especially the Sub-Commission on Prevention of Discrimination and Protection of Minorities, the Committee on Crime Prevention and Control, as well as the UN Congress on the Prevention of

Crime and the Treatment of Offenders, have been active in the efforts of working out standards for the independence of justice, with a view to eventually coming up with a universally acceptable declaration or convention on this topic.[8]

Given the variety of existing judicial systems, it is not easy to crystallize an exhaustive list of relevant criteria for the independence of the judiciary. Conditions of service and tenure, manner of appointment and discharge, degree of stability and non-removability of office, as well as physical, political, legal and logistical protection against outside pressures and harassment, may be named as the most crucial ones. The problems linked with the independence of judges are diverse, both in quality and quantity, in different parts of the world, ranging from salary bargaining schemes to physical disappearances.

It is interesting to note that the CCPR as well as the ECHR and the American Convention on Human Rights (ACHR) (but not the African Charter on Human and Peoples' Rights (African Charter)) expressly require that the tribunal be "established by law", i.e., the tribunal should not depend on the discretion of the executive branch but be based, as far as its organizational framework is concerned, on an enactment by the legislature. Special courts are only tolerated under exceptional circumstances.

As regards impartiality, it has been recognized that even appearances may be of great importance; a tribunal must also be *seen* to be impartial. In other words, there ought to be impartiality in the objective as well as in the subjective sense. The impartiality of the judge corresponds to the equality of the parties.

What, then, makes a hearing 'fair'? No exhaustive answer is — or will be — available. Even in criminal proceedings, the concept of 'fairness' encompasses something more than just the minimum guarantees of the defence expressly laid down in the CCPR and the ECHR. A good deal of allowance is made for the national needs and legal traditions prevailing in each country. Details and peculiarities are assessed against the overall background of each particular legal system.

Perhaps the most fundamental issue is the right to be present in person at the hearing of one's case, particularly, as it has been stressed by the Strasbourg organs, where "the personal character and manner of life of the party concerned is directly relevant to the

---

[8] Leckie 1987, p. 26.

formation of the court's opinion."[9] On the other hand, it may be debatable whether the procedure must always include an oral part, as distinct from written proceedings, which, under certain circumstances, might be argued to suffice to meet the requirement of 'fairness'. National legal traditions vary greatly on this point. In the ongoing review of the compatibility of the Finnish law with the ECHR, to which Finland has acceded, particular attention is being paid to the role of oral hearings before administrative courts as well as general courts of appeal.[10]

The fairness of the hearing may depend on a variety of issues, such as the presentation of evidence or the behaviour of the members of the court, press or the public. Even the role of lawyers is relevant, linking in many ways with that of the judges. The availability of competent legal assistance may be crucial for a successful — or even meaningful — litigation in court. The European Court of Human Rights (European Court) has held that, under certain circumstances, access to free legal aid may amount to an element of a fair trial even in civil proceedings, while it is expressly mentioned only in paragraph 3 of article 6 in the ECHR with regard to criminal proceedings.[11]

Furthermore, the hearing must be 'public'. The issue of publicity is an intricate one, in connection with legal proceedings. As the main rule, publicity is needed to protect litigants and to render the trial open to public scrutiny. Thereby, it also enhances popular confidence in the legal system as a whole. On the other hand, publicity may work in the opposite direction as well. For instance, adverse media coverage may, in some circumstances, violate the right of the accused to a presumption of his innocence and thus prejudice the fairness of the trial. It is clear that there must be room for exceptions to the requirement of publicity, such as those expressly listed in the CCPR and the ECHR. The kind and degree of publicity allowed and/or required for the purposes of the hearing and the interests of justice are eventually linked with the overall evaluation of fairness.

Unlike the CCPR, the ECHR as well as the ACHR expressly require that the hearing take place "within a reasonable time." A

---

[9] E.g., the cases cited in the *Digest of Strasbourg Case-Law relating to the European Convention on Human Rights*, vol. 2, p. 352. See also Sieghart 1983, p. 279.

[10] See Ekbatani case, *infra*.

[11] European Court of Human Rights, Airey judgment of 9 October 1979, Series A, no. 32.

delay of justice is often equal to no justice at all. It is especially
important for a person charged with a criminal offence not to
remain too long in a state of uncertainty about his fate.[12] Particular
circumstances of each case, as well as the conduct of the applicant
party himself, must be taken into account. In the Strasbourg case
law, respondent governments sometimes advance excuses such as
a stagnation of economy, adverse political climate or temporary
backlogs of business. The European Court has taken the view that,
in clear cases of delay, it is up to the government to indicate that it
has resorted to prompt remedial action to overcome all relevant and
foreseeable obstacles.

C. Determination of Rights and Obligations as well as Criminal Charges

a. General Remarks

The American Declaration on the Rights and Duties of Man (1948)
only mentions the right to a fair trial in connection with persons
accused of offences. The CCPR, and the ECHR too, are more
elaborate insofar as criminal charges are concerned. The
preoccupation of most human rights instruments with criminal
proceedings and penal issues is probably due to historical reasons.
The concern for human rights has initially been more visible in the
context of criminal law, while the emergence of the civil rights
movement represents a later stage in the legal struggle for human
rights. In a modern welfare society with a complex legal
infrastructure, the potential scope and impact of the right to a fair
trial is even broader. It is interesting to note that the ACHR (1969),
in its article 8(1), goes as far as extending the right to a fair trial not
only to the determination of rights and obligations of civil but even
"of labor, fiscal and any other" nature. On the other hand, the
African Charter (1981), in its article 7(1), only provides for
everyone the "right to have his cause heard", so as to protect his
"fundamental rights as recognized and guaranteed by conventions,
laws, regulations and customs in force." This somewhat vague
formulation may reflect the collective orientation of the last-
mentioned instrument, as also indicated in its very title.

---

[12] European Court of Human Rights, Stogmüller judgment of 10 November 1969,
Series A, no. 9.

b. Rights and Obligations

The emphasis on criminal proceedings has guided States Parties when reporting to the Human Rights Committee, the supervisory body established by the CCPR, to the extent that the Committee, in its General Comment 13(21) on article 14,[13] had to state that

> In general, the reports of States Parties fail to recognize that article 14 applies not only to proceedings for the determination of criminal charges against individuals but also to proceedings to determine their rights and obligations in a suit of law (paragraph 2).

This being the case, it cannot be said that the CCPR would have had, so far, any significant impact on the elaboration of the notion of a fair trial in proceedings other than those concerning criminal charges. Pending such elaboration by the Human Rights Committee on the basis, *inter alia*, of new reports, in which States Parties are expected to explain how they conceive of the expression "rights ... in a suit of law", the exact meaning of this phrase remains subject to debate. Although the reference to 'a suit of law' might be taken to confine the scope of the provision to private law proceedings in a strict sense, this is not the only possible interpretation. A wider notion of such a suit, indeed, seems to be inherent in a statement of the Commission. At the preparatory stage of the CCPR, the Commission emphasized the importance of article 14 on the grounds that "in the last analysis, the implementation of all the rights in the Covenant depended upon the proper administration of justice."[14]

Here we may see a clear resemblance to the views taken by the organs supervising the implementation of the ECHR. Indeed, it is in connection with this regional instrument that the right to a fair trial, especially as regards non-criminal cases, has been elaborated more than anywhere else.

Although the wording of article 6(1) of the ECHR ('civil rights ...') differs from that of article 14(1) of the CCPR ('suit of law'), no essential difference in the meaning can be inferred solely on this basis. The English wording of article 6(1) seems to have been chosen simply in order to bring the English text into harmony with the French version, which in both instruments refers to 'des

---

[13] UN doc. CCPR/C/21, Add. 3.
[14] Quoted from Fawcett 1987, p. 128.

contestations sur ses droits et obligations de caractère civil'.[15] Nor do the *travaux préparatoires* reveal any firm intention to confine the scope of the provision to private law disputes,[16] although the phrase 'civil rights', especially as compared to article 10 of the UDHR, could be taken to imply such a limitation.

Whatever the draftsmen may have had in mind, the European Court has not construed this phrase restrictively. On the contrary, in quite some similarity to the position reflected in the statement by the Commission, quoted above, the European Court has stressed that

> In a democratic society within the meaning of the Convention, the right to a fair administration of justice holds such a prominent place that a restrictive interpretation of Article 6(1) would not correspond to the aim of that provision....[17]

Proceeding from this premise, the European Court has held that 'civil rights and obligations', in the meaning of article 6(1) of the ECHR, is an 'autonomous' concept, the contents of which are not necessarily limited to what in a national legal system may be characterized as 'civil' or 'private' legal issues, as distinct from matters falling under public law. Accordingly, certain disputes ('*contestations*'), involving an individual *vis-à-vis* a public authority as parties, have been regarded as falling under 'civil rights and obligations', for the determination of which a fair trial is required. This is the case where a decision on a public law relationship, or claim, is decisive with respect to one's 'civil' rights — in a narrower sense of the term — or at least deeply affects such rights. At a relatively early stage this was found to be the case with regard to decisions whereby public officials confirm (or fail to confirm) a real estate transaction between two individuals.[18] The same has been held to be true about administrative decisions concerning expropriation proceedings, which may affect the right to enjoy private possessions.[19] By now it is also settled that, say, the revocation of a doctor's or lawyer's licence to carry on a private

---

[15] Cf. the Council of Europe Document H(70)7, p. 37.

[16] See van Dijk 1988, p. 135ff.

[17] European Court of Human Rights, Delcourt judgment of 12 January 1970, Series A, no. 11, p. 15.

[18] European Court of Human Rights, Ringeisen judgment of 22 June 1972, Series A, no. 15.

[19] See especially European Court of Human Rights, Sporrong and Lönnroth judgment of 23 September 1982, Series A, no. 52.

practice affects the person's civil rights so as to fall under article 6(1).[20]

In its evolving case law on the subject matter, the European Court has gone a step further by considering claims for social insurance benefits, at least insofar as they are to some extent based on contributions made by the insured person and thus resemble claims in connection with private insurance schemes, to fall under the notion of 'civil rights and obligations'.[21]

The Strasbourg case law on this point, while leaving many questions still open, shows the impact that binding international human rights standards may have on domestic legal systems. On the one hand, as a consequence of this judicial law-making, court control over administrative decisions has been strengthened in some countries. On the other hand, while there may be a tendency to increase the public control over affairs affecting the legal position of individuals, thus enlarging the scope of 'public law', this cannot be tolerated to happen at the expense of the individual's basic right to have his legal rights determined in a fair trial by an independent and impartial tribunal.

As far as the Nordic countries are concerned, the impact of the Strasbourg case law concerning 'civil rights and obligations' has been felt, especially in Sweden. Cases on issues such as the revocation of a traffic licence[22] and expropriation proceedings (for example, Sporrong and Lönnroth judgments), in which the remedies provided by the Swedish legal system have been mainly of an administrative nature, led to law reform work that has considerably extended the scope of judicial control over administrative decisions.[23]

The wording of article 8(1) of the ACHR quoted above is particularly interesting, because at the time of its formulation the European experience with the difficulties of giving a precise meaning to the phrase 'civil rights and obligations' was already known. The ACHR clearly reflects an intention to put it beyond doubt that (apart from criminal cases) the basic requirements of a

[20] E.g., European Court of Human Rights, König judgment of 10 March 1980, Series A, no. 36.
[21] European Court of Human Rights, Feldbrugge and Deumeland judgments of 29 May 1985, Series A, nos. 99 and 100.
[22] European Court of Human Rights, Pudas judgment of 27 October 1987, Series A, no. 125.
[23] See Danelius 1988.

fair trial should not be limited to private law disputes in a narrow sense.[24]

It may be speculated whether it is possible to envisage a future interpretation of article 6(1) of the ECHR broad enough to extend the right to a fair trial to any legal claim where an individual is contending with another individual, corporation, trade union or the government itself. This raises the question, on the one hand, to what extent the political bodies are willing to surrender decision-making power to politically independent tribunals at the national level. As far as the international protection of human rights is concerned, on the other hand, misgivings may emerge as to how profound interventions into the domestic administration will be tolerated by sovereign States in the long run. There have been voices contending that the dynamic interpretation of article 6(1) by the European Court is a 'time bomb' in this respect.

An interesting parallel can be drawn to the recent Finnish debate, where certain concerns have been expressed that the forthcoming ratification of the ECHR implies a virtual encroachment upon the powers of the Finnish Parliament, subjecting the latter to the whims of the Strasbourg judges. Whether or not these concerns are justified with respect to the right to a fair trial, the European Court may have gone further on this point than the draftsmen of the Declaration could possibly foresee in 1948. Therefore, an additional protocol to the ECHR, setting the standards of 'fairness' or 'due process' in administrative proceedings, might be welcome. It would be useful to clarify the somewhat blurred notion of 'civil rights and obligations', as opposed to issues where administrative expediency may prevail even in the absence of a fair hearing in the classic sense.

c. Criminal Charges

As far as the "determination of any criminal charge" (bien-fondé de toute accusation en matière pénale) is concerned, both the CCPR and the ECHR adhere to the original phrase coined in article 10 of the UDHR. The English term 'determination' is rather wide (see also, the somewhat narrower French expression *'bien-fondé'*), covering both questions of law and those of fact, as well as conviction and sentence, occasionally even pre-trial investigation.

---

[24] Cf. van Dijk 1988, p. 138.

The case law under article 14 of the CCPR mostly concerns defective criminal proceedings in Uruguay. The findings of the Human Rights Committee have dealt with rather 'basic' issues, involving, for example, the right to a fair and public hearing.[25]

The European Court and Commission in Strasbourg, again, have come up with more sophisticated legal distinctions, such as criminal charges *vis-à-vis* disciplinary charges, concerning, for example, offences against the internal order or proper conduct in the armed forces or other institutions. The problem has arisen whether, and to what extent, the contracting States are or should be able to circumvent the requirement of a fair trial by classifying certain proceedings of a clearly repressive nature into a 'disciplinary' category. This distinction is particularly elusive in relation to acts and omissions which may be dealt with either in a regular criminal trial or in disciplinary proceedings. According to the rulings of the Strasbourg Court, the concept of 'criminal charge' (accusation en matière pénale) is autonomous, with the effect of considering the domestic classifications only one of the relevant criteria. At the same time, due regard must be paid to the nature of the offence itself, as well as to the severity of the prescribed penalty.[26] On the other hand, no distinction in principle is drawn between proceedings of serious offences (crimes), lesser offences (*délits*) and petty offences (*contraventions*). In the Oztürk case,[27] the Strasbourg Court even extended the right to a fair trial to so-called 'regulatory offenses' (*Ordnungswidrigkeiten*). While not being opposed to the trend towards decriminalization, the Court wanted to make sure that the reclassifying of offences is not used for the purpose of excluding the operation of the fundamental procedural guarantees.

This substantive approach applies not only to charges aiming at the imposition of penalties but also to those concerning various kinds of additional restrictions of rights and freedoms, or even a crucial loss of significant privileges of a person in penal custody. The same is true about the beginning, duration and ending of criminal proceedings. A criminal charge is regarded to be there as soon as the position of the person has been substantially affected as

[25] de Zayas *et al.* 1985, p. 46.
[26] European Court of Human Rights, Case of Engel and others, judgment of 23 November 1976, Series A, no. 22.
[27] European Court of Human Rights, judgment of 21 February 1984, Series A, no. 73.

a result of the suspicion against him, no matter when the formal charge is brought.[28] The autonomy of this notion is made particularly clear in the wording of article 8(1) of the ACHR that extends the right to a fair trial to the "substantiation of any accusation of criminal nature."

With the exception of minor infractions, criminal charges must be tried 'fairly', in the sense of article 6(1) of the ECHR, all the way from the first instance to the appellate level, as long as the charge is dealt with on its merits (the Delcourt case). A recent judgment in the Ekbatani case,[29] concerning Sweden, is especially interesting from a Nordic point of view. The applicant had pleaded not guilty of the offence he was charged with in the court of first instance. Having been found guilty and convicted, he appealed to a regional court of appeal, still pleading not guilty. It was ruled that the refusal of the regional court of appeal to hold a public hearing at which the applicant would have had a right to be present and argue his case, before it confirmed his conviction, violated, in the particular circumstances of the case, the applicant's right to a fair trial. This judgment appears to have bewildered some judges especially in Finland, where courts of appeal are even less accustomed to oral hearings in public.

One of the classic notions developed in the Strasbourg case law around the concept of fair trial in criminal proceedings is known as 'equality of arms' (*égalité des armes*). It addresses the dilemma of the inherent procedural handicap facing the accused *vis-à-vis* the prosecution. The defendant must be given a full and equal opportunity to plead his case before a tribunal.[30] It is important to note that equality of arms must be pursued in the spirit of the wise slogan: justice must not only be done but it must also be seen to be done.

The right to a fair trial, as it is embodied in international human rights law, affects not only criminal charges actually made in the various criminal justice systems but also criminal justice policy-making, setting certain standards to be followed and, consequently, limiting the free margin in legislative reform. The close link between crime policy and the protection of human rights has been recognized in the inter-State co-operation at the European level in

---

[28] European Court of Human Rights, Neumeister judgment of 27 June 1968, Series A, no. 8.
[29] European Court of Human Rights, judgment of 26 May 1988, Series A no. 134.
[30] van Dijk 1983, p. 23.

particular.[31] Sometimes it is difficult to reconcile the required elements of a fair trial with the practical need to improve the efficiency of the crime control systems, such as the wish to introduce simplified or summary procedures for certain types of criminal cases, in order to speed up the proceedings or to relieve the workload of criminal courts. A special problem has emerged in connection with the movement to increase the rights of the victims of criminal offences. The strengthening of the victim's procedural position may lead, in certain cases, to a restriction of the rights of the defence, thus upsetting the delicate balance of equal protection and consequently encroaching upon the right to a fair trial.

References

Annat, Mohamed Admed Abu, "The Study of Equality in the Administration of Justice", UN doc. E/CN.4/Sub.2/296/Rev I.

Council of Europe, Document II(70)7, "Problems arising from the coexistence of United Nations Covenants on Human Rights".

Danelius, Hans, "Judicial Control of the Administration — a Swedish Proposal for Legislative Reform", in Franz Matscher and Herbert Petzold (eds.), *Protecting Human Rights: The European Dimension*, Berlin: Carl Heymanns Verlag KG, 1988.

van Dijk, Pieter, "The Interpretation of 'Civil Rights and Obligations' by the European Court of Human Rights — One More Step to Take", in Franz Matscher and Herbert Petzold (eds.), *Protecting Human Rights: The European Dimension*, Carl Heymanns Verlag KG, 1988.

van Dijk, Pieter, "The Right of the Accused to a Fair Trial under International Law", Utrecht: Netherlands Institute of Human Rights, *SIM Special* no. 1., 1983.

Dolgopol, Ustinia, "Centre for the Independence of Judges and Lawyers, its Work and its Aspirations", *CIJL Bulletin* nos. 19 & 20, 1987.

Fawcett, J.E.S., *The Application of the European Convention on Human Rights*, Oxford: Oxford University Press, 1987.

Leckie, Scott, "The United Nations and the Independence of Judges and Lawyers", Studie- en Informatiecentrum Mensenrechten, *SIM Newsletter* no. 17, 1987.

Müller-Rappard, Ekkehart, "Criminal Justice and Human Rights: the Role of the Council of Europe", *Tidskrift, utgiven av Juridiska Föreningen i Finland*, 1986.

Noor Muhammad, Haji N.A., "Due Process of Law for Persons Accused of

---

[31] Müller-Rappard 1986, p. 291ff.

Crime", in Louis Henkin (ed.), *The International Bill of Rights, The Covenant on Civil and Political Rights*, New York: Columbia University Press, 1981.

Shetreet, S. and J. Deschenes (eds.), *Judicial Independence: The Contemporary Debate*, Dordrecht: 1985.

Sieghart, Paul, *The International Law of Human Rights*, Oxford: Clarendon Press, 1983.

Singhvi, L.M., "The Administration of Justice and the Human Rights of Detainees: Study on the Independence and Impartiality of the Judiciary, Jurors and Assessors and the Independence of Lawyers", Final Report prepared by the Special Rapporteur, Draft Universal Declaration on the Independence of Justice, UN doc. E/CN.4/Sub.2/1985/Add. 5/Rev. 1 (24 August 1987).

United Nations Documents: E/CN.4/21; E/CN.4/SR.54; CCPR/C/21, Add. 3; Report of the Commission, ECOSOC Official Records, third year, sixth session, E/600, Annex A.

Verdoodt, Albert, *Naissance et Signification de la Déclaration Universelle des Droits de l'Homme*, Société d'Etude Morales, Sociales et Juridiques, Louvain, Paris: Editions Nauwelaerts, 1964.

de Zayas, Alfred, Jakob Th. Möller and Torkel Opsahl, "Application of the International Covenant on Civil and Political Rights under the Optional Protocol by the Human Rights Committee", *German Yearbook of International Law*, vol. 28, Berlin: Duncker & Humblot, 1985.

Article 11

Raimo Lahti

Finland

1. Everyone charged with a penal offence has the right to be presumed innocent until proved guilty according to law in a public trial at which he has had all the guarantees necessary for his defence.
2. No one shall be held guilty of any penal offence on account of any act or omission which did not constitute a penal offence, under national or international law, at the time when it was committed. Nor shall a heavier penalty be imposed than the one that was applicable at the time the penal offence was committed.

I. Introduction

Paragraph 1 of article 11 of the Universal Declaration of Human Rights (UDHR) concerns the basic human rights to be complied with in criminal procedures. Paragraph 2 of the same article concerns the principle of legality, which limits the application of the criminal law. In terms of the common law countries the article defines, on the one hand, procedural due process and, on the other hand, substantive due process,[1] whereas in continental legal thinking, the corresponding principles would be called those of the 'constitutionally governed State' (*Rechtsstaatlichkeit*) and 'legal security' (*Rechtssicherheit*), principles which restrain the legislative and judicial organs from misusing their repressive powers.[2]

Article 11 is not the only article in the UDHR that regulates the applicability of the principles of due process to persons accused of crimes. When the proposal for the UDHR was put before the Third Committee of the UN General Assembly, the representative for

[1] See also, e.g., Noor Muhammad 1981.
[2] See also, e.g., Jescheck 1988, pp. 21–22.

Belgium summarized the contents of this article under four basic headings: 1) the presumption of innocence until proven guilty; 2) the right to defence; 3) the right to a public hearing; and 4) the non-retroactivity of laws.[3] The reference to the right to a public hearing is problematic with respect to article 11(1) because this right is more precisely defined in article 10. It is true, however, that articles 10 and 11(1) of the Declaration are closely related.

When searching for the basis of article 11, we should begin with those documents that provided the general foundation for human rights thinking. The presumption of innocence, which is central in article 11(1), has its parallel already in 1789 in the French Declaration of the Rights of Man.[4] The prohibition of retroactivity of laws, expressed in article 11(2), was confirmed as early as 1787, in the Constitution of the United States, and even earlier in the Declarations of Human Rights passed by certain North American colonies in 1776.[5]

II. *Travaux Préparatoires*

At the first session of the UN Commission on Human Rights (the Commission), a drafting committee put forward the texts for articles 9 and 10(1), which have essentially the same contents as article 11 of the enacted UDHR. However, these draft articles also regulated principles which were later expressed in the final article 10.[6] In other words, article 9 would also have contained the requirements of an independent and impartial court, fair trial, and full hearing of the defendant. Furthermore, the prohibition of retroactivity of criminal law would have been expressed in the following article.

The above-mentioned proposal was based on a draft provided by the representative for France, Mr. Cassin.[7] According to this draft, the presumption of innocence would have been expressed at the beginning of the aforementioned articles in a separate paragraph.[8]

The second session of the Commission produced the Draft

---

[3] 3 UN General Assembly Official Records I, Third Committee, SR 115, p. 266.
[4] See also Schubarth 1978, p. 1.
[5] See Schreiber 1976, pp. 64–65.
[6] UN doc. E/CN.4/21, Annex F.
[7] Ibid., Annex D, articles 11 and 12.
[8] On the background to article 11 in general, see Verdoodt 1964, p. 131ff.

International Declaration of Human Rights of 1947, where the most important innovation with respect to the draft article in question was the following; the prohibition of retroactivity of criminal law should not "prejudice the trial and punishment of any person for the commission of any act which, at the time it was committed, was criminal according to the general principles of law recognized by civilized nations."[9]

In the third session of the Commission, this draft article was submitted in what was to be virtually its final form.[10] A member of the Commission, Cassin, summed up the issues to be considered when dealing with the article: innocence until proven guilty; public trial; guarantees of defence (the question of independent tribunals could be omitted in view of the preceding provisions); non-retroactivity of laws and punishment; and the non-applicability of those rights to war criminals.[11]

The proposal presented to the Third Committee of the UN General Assembly omitted — in connection with the prohibition of retroactivity of criminal law — the above-mentioned reference to the general principles of law recognized by civilized nations. On the other hand, the concept of offence, as used in relation to the prohibition of retroactivity, was specified in such a way that the definition of an offence could be based either on national or international law.

These changes resulted in differences of opinion at the meeting of the Third Committee of the General Assembly. The representatives for Belgium and Greece expressed their doubts as to whether the prohibition of retroactivity of laws, such as it was presented to the Committee, might be used as a basis for the argument that the trials of war criminals in general, and the trials of Nürnberg and Tokyo in particular, had been illegal.[12] Similar discussions were repeated when, in preparation of the International Covenant on Civil and Political Rights (CCPR), the necessity of the provision which later became paragraph 2 of article 15 was considered.[13]

In the course of the proceedings in the Third Committee, two

---

[9] E/600, Annex A, article 7.

[10] E/800, Annex A, article 9.

[11] E/CN.4/SR.54, p. 16.

[12] 3 UN General Assembly Official Records I, Third Committee, SR 115–116, pp. 266, 270.

[13] See Bossuyt 1987, pp. 330–333 with references, and below.

amendments were made to the prohibition of retroactivity of laws. At the instigation of the United States, the word 'penal' was inserted before the word 'offence' in order to make it clear that the paragraph related to criminal matters only. The proposal made by Panama was accepted when an additional sentence was inserted in the same paragraph, containing the principle that the penalty for any crime cannot be altered for a heavier one *ex post facto*.

III. Parallels to Article 11 of the UDHR in the CCPR, ECHR and Other Human Rights Instruments

The presumption of innocence defined in paragraph 1 of article 11 has substantively close parallels in article 14(2) of the CCPR, article 6(2) of the European Convention on Human Rights (1950, ECHR), the first sentence of article 8(2) of the American Convention of Human Rights (1969, ACHR), and article 7 (1.b) of the African Charter of Human and Peoples' Rights (1981, African Charter).

Provisions on public trial and guarantees of defence for the accused can be found in article 14 of the CCPR, especially in paragraphs 1 and 3, in article 6(1) and 3 of the ECHR, article 8 of the ACHR, and article 7(1) of the African Charter, where the basic principle is that every individual has the right to have his cause heard.

The principle of freedom from *ex post facto* laws (this term is from the ACHR), regulated in article 11(2) of the UDHR, has its equivalents in article 15 of the CCPR, article 7 of the ECHR, article 9 of the ACHR, and article 7(2) of the African Charter. The essence of the prohibition of retroactive criminal law is the same in each of these articles, but there are differences in the more precise formulation of the principle (see below).

IV. Right to a Fair Trial and Other Human Rights in the Administration of Justice

The presumption of innocence will be examined separately below. The principle of public trial and the guarantees of defence for the accused will only be briefly mentioned. This can be justified by the fact that the presumption of innocence is fundamental to the protection of human rights, as the Human Rights Committee has stated in its general comment.[14]

It must, however, be considered that all the above-mentioned principles regulating the legal status of the accused in criminal proceedings are aimed at ensuring the proper administration of justice.[15] In other words, they all concern special aspects of the general concept of fair trial in criminal cases.[16]

In the case law on article 6 of the ECHR, it has been confirmed that, although no specific right referred to in paragraphs 2 and 3 of the article has been violated, the question as to whether the trial conforms to the standard laid down by paragraph 1 must be decided on the basis of a consideration of the trial as a whole, and not on the basis of the isolated consideration of one particular aspect of the trial or one particular incident.[17]

Indeed, when discussing human rights in relation to the administration of justice, the very characteristics of fair trial and the right to judicial proceedings are those of fundamental questions. It has been justifiably maintained with respect to article 14 of the CCPR that the right to a fair hearing in court, as provided for in the article, is one of the cornerstones of the CCPR as a guarantee of the rule of law.[18] The heading of article 8 of the ACHR does explicitly express this basic principle of a 'right to a fair trial'. Consequently, article 11(1) of the UDHR must be examined in relation to article 10.[19]

Article 14(3) of the CCPR, article 6(3) of the ECHR, and article 8(2) of the ACHR all concern the minimum guarantees or minimum rights enjoyed by the accused. The lists of these rights, although the lists must not be regarded as exhaustive, are exceptionally long in comparison with the customary manner of writing down human rights. Article 14(3) of the CCPR is in some respects more explicit and thus goes further than article 6(3) of the ECHR.[20]

Such precision is understandable when we bear in mind that the application of the criminal law always has a drastic effect on the rights and liberties of the accused. The substance of article 11(1) of the UDHR has, to an unusual extent, become more concrete in the

[14] CCPR/C/21/Add.3, p. 5.
[15] CCPR/C/21/Add.3, p. 3.
[16] So, on article 6 of the ECHR, e.g., van Dijk and van Hoof 1984, pp. 262, 265.
[17] See Council of Europe, *Digest of Strasbourg Case-Law Relating to the ECHR*, vol. 2, pp. 5, 709, with references.
[18] de Zayas *et al.* 1985, pp. 44–45.
[19] See also, article 10 in this volume.
[20] Council of Europe Document H (70) 7, p. 38.

human rights conventions which have succeeded it.

On the guarantees necessary for the defence of the accused, the procedural rights known as 'equality of arms' are especially important. When this principle, which falls within the broad concept of a fair hearing, is followed, the aim is procedural equality between the accused and the public prosecutor.[21] The Human Rights Committee has stated: "[t]he accused or his lawyer must have the right to act diligently and fearlessly in pursuing all available defences and the right to challenge the case if they believe it to be unfair."[22]

When dealing with public trial, the above-mentioned articles of human rights documents contain provisions for situations where it is possible to make exceptions to this principle. Article 11(1) of the UDHR does not acknowledge such exceptions. This was criticized by the representative of the Soviet Union when the draft Declaration was discussed in the Third Committee of the UN General Assembly.[23] It must be noted, however, that there is a general limitation clause in article 29(2) of the UDHR.

With respect to exceptions to the principle of public trial, the CCPR and the ECHR do not significantly differ from each other.[24] The corresponding limitations are expressed more broadly in article 8(5) of the ACHR. Article 7(1) of the African Charter does not require a trial to be public at all; it is sufficient that a competent and impartial court or tribunal proves whether the accused is guilty or not guilty.

V. Presumption of Innocence

The presumption of innocence has been considered to be a rule of natural justice which is universally recognized.[25] For all that, its contents have been characterized as unclear until now, with the exception of the *in dubio pro reo* principle.[26]

In its general comment on article 14 of the CCPR, the Human Rights Committee has made, *inter alia*, the following statements

---

[21] See, e.g., Trechsel 1978, pp. 555–558; Opsahl 1982, p. 494.

[22] CCPR/C/21/Add.3, p. 6.

[23] 3 UN General Assembly Official Records I, Third Committee, SR 115, p. 226.

[24] Council of Europe Document H (70) 7, pp. 37–38.

[25] Trechsel 1978, p. 554.

[26] See Roxin 1987, pp. 58–59.

about the presumption of innocence: the burden of proof of the charge is on the prosecution and the accused has the benefit of doubt; no guilt can be presumed until the charge has been proved beyond a reasonable doubt; and all public authorities have a duty to refrain from prejudging the outcome of a trial.[27]

In the case law on article 6(2) of the ECHR, it has been stated that this paragraph requires that the onus to prove guilt falls upon the prosecution, and any doubt is to the benefit of the accused. Moreover, in the judgment, the accused can be found guilty only on the basis of direct or indirect evidence sufficiently strong in the eyes of the law to establish his guilt.[28]

The organs of the ECHR have taken a stand, among other things, on the admissibility of evidence of past convictions and on the imposition of costs in cases of acquittal or discontinuance of proceedings.[29] With respect to the latter issue, the interpretation of article 6(2) of the ECHR has been clarified in 1987 by the judgments of the European Court of Human Rights (European Court) in the Lutz, Englert and Nölkenbockhoff cases.[30]

In recent international practice and juridical literature, there is growing support for a broad definition of the presumption of innocence, while it is regarded as a guarantee with considerable legal consequences of varying degrees of obligation to be complied with in criminal procedure and criminal law.[31]

VI. Prohibition of Retroactive Criminal Law: *Nulla Poena Sine Lege*

In the light of its drafts, paragraph 2 of article 11 of the UDHR was created in order to signify the protection of individuals against *ex post facto* criminal laws operating to their detriment. The same is true with regard to article 15 of the CCPR.[32]

---

[27] CCPR/C/21/Add.3, p. 5; see also de Zayas *et al.* 1985, pp. 45–46.

[28] See Council of Europe, *Digest of Strasbourg Case-Law Relating to the ECHR*, vol. 2, pp. 721–722 with references.

[29] See, e.g., van Dijk and van Hoof 1984, pp. 263–264.

[30] See Westerdiek 1987. Concerning case law on article 6(2) of the ECHR in general, see especially Trechsel 1981 and Frowein 1981.

[31] See, e.g., Schubarth 1978, Trechsel 1981, Opsahl 1982, pp. 491–493, Kühl 1983, Träskman 1988.

[32] de Zayas *et al.* 1985, p. 51.

The last sentence of article 15(1) of the CCPR (as well as article 9 of the ACHR), however, prescribes the retroactive operation of a new law imposing a 'lighter penalty'. When drafting this article of the CCPR, it was regarded as a tendency in modern criminal law to allow a person to enjoy the benefit of such lighter penalties as might be imposed after the commission of the offence with which he was charged.[33]

In the case law on article 7(1) of the ECHR it has been pointed out that the paragraph does not merely prohibit — except as provided in paragraph 2 — the retroactive application of the criminal law to the detriment of the accused; it also confirms, in a more general way, the principle of the statutory nature of offences and their punishment (*nullum crimen, nulla poena sine lege*), and prohibits the extension of the application of the criminal law '*in malam partem*' by analogy. Furthermore, the paragraph includes the requirement of certainty in the criminal law; the offence shall be clearly described by law.[34]

Hence, the case law on article 7(1) of the ECHR has given an expansive interpretation to the paragraph. The prohibition of retroactive criminal law has developed into a wider concept, the 'legality principle', which is subdivided into four rules. This kind of subdivision of the legality principle is common in the judicial literature.[35]

Article 15(2) of the CCPR and article 7(2) of the ECHR include a provision which was scrutinized already in the preparation of article 11(2) of the UDHR; the prohibition of retroactive criminal law shall not prejudice the trial and punishment of any person for any act or omission which, at the time when it was committed, was criminal according to the general principles of law recognized by the community of nations (CCPR) or by civilized nations (ECHR). As discussed above, this provision was deleted from the final version of article 11(2) of the Declaration.

In the case law on article 7(2) of the ECHR it has been stated, with reference to the *travaux préparatoires* of the ECHR, that the purpose of the text is to make it clear that article 7 does not affect laws which, under the very exceptional circumstances at the end of World War II, were passed to punish war crimes, treason and

[33] See Bossuyt 1987, pp. 326–329 with references.
[34] See Council of Europe, *Digest of Strasbourg Case-Law Relating to the ECHR*, vol. 3, pp. 1–19 with references.
[35] See, e.g., Jescheck 1988, pp. 113–126, Fründe 1989.

collaboration with the enemy, and does not aim at any legal or moral condemnation of those laws.[36]

Article 15(2) of the CCPR and article 7(2) of the ECHR contain an exception to the first paragraph of the article in question. Retention of article 15(2) of the CCPR was considered to eliminate any doubts as to the legality of the judgments rendered by the Nürnberg and the Tokyo tribunals. It was also said that this paragraph of the CCPR would confirm those principles so that, if in the future crimes should be perpetrated similar to those punished at Nürnberg, they would be punished in accordance with the same principles.[37]

The expression 'according to the general principles of law recognized by civilized nations' is identical with article 38(1.c) of the Statute of the International Court of Justice. Although this requirement of the admissible legal sources would be interpreted narrowly, it is difficult to establish with any accuracy for the application of article 15(2) of the CCPR and article 7(2) of the ECHR what offences are involved.[38] Only with successful attempts to codify international crimes and to establish an international criminal tribunal can a significant improvement in this respect be achieved.[39]

VII. On Some Developments in the Implementation of Human Rights in the Administration of Justice

Norms and standards which concern human rights in the administration of justice have been the focus of continuous attention on UN activities. For example, in Resolution 41/149 of 1986 the UN General Assembly advises all bodies within its organization to keep human rights in the administration of justice under constant review and to continue to give special attention to effective ways and means of implementing existing standards and

---

[36] See Council of Europe, *Digest of Strasbourg Case-Law Relating to the ECHR*, vol. 3, pp. 34–36.

[37] See Bossuyt 1987, pp. 331–332 with references.

[38] See van Dijk and van Hoof 1984, pp. 280–281.

[39] See also, Triffterer 1966, Bassiouni 1987, United Nations, *The Work of the International Law Commission 1988*, pp. 27–30, 34–36, 121–125.

developments in this area.[40]

It may also be mentioned that the protection of human rights in criminal proceedings was one of the main topics of the XII Congress of the International Association of Penal Law in 1979. On this occasion, a resolution was adopted.[41]

The interpretation of article 6 of the ECHR has also led to very extensive practice.[42] Recently, reviews on the influence of the ECHR on the West German, UK, Italian and Swiss criminal laws and procedures have been published.[43]

Some practice also exists on article 14 of the CCPR. However, the case law under the Optional Protocol has applied the requirements of this article mainly to victims of defective criminal proceedings in Uruguay.[44] The Human Rights Committee has, moreover, issued a quite detailed general comment on the article.[45]

VIII. Nordic Events

The influence of the CCPR and the ECHR on criminal law and procedure in the Nordic countries has been discussed in the recent judicial literature.[46] In the case of Finland, only the CCPR was applicable until 1990, after which the ECHR was also ratified following Finland's membership of the Council of Europe in 1989.

The implementation of the human rights instruments in the Nordic countries has been hampered by the fact that these countries belong to the so-called dualistic system when implementing international treaties in domestic legislation. For example, the method of incorporation which is used in Finland has in practice left some discrepancies between the human rights conventions and national law. The aforementioned Scandinavian reports make it clear, however, that the positive influence of the conventions on the

---

[40] See also UN Publication ST/HR/2/Rev.2, pp. 153–156, and López-Rey 1985, pp. 59–66.
[41] See Trechsel 1978, and, on the resolution, *Revue Internationale de Droit Pénale* 1980, pp. 233–241.
[42] Council of Europe, *Digest of Strasbourg Case-Law Relating to the ECHR*, vol. 2.
[43] See the reports of Kühl *et al.*, 1988, pp. 405–732.
[44] de Zayas et al. 1985, p. 46.
[45] CCPR/C/21/Add.3.
[46] See the reports of Rehof 1987 and Nordskov Nielsen 1989 on Denmark, Träskman 1987 on Finland, Opsahl 1982 on Norway, and Danelius 1989, pp. 134–173, on Sweden.

law and practice of criminal procedure in the Nordic countries has been gaining momentum in recent years.

References

Bassiouni, M. Cherif, *A Draft International Criminal Code and Draft Statute for an International Criminal Tribunal*, Dordrecht: Martinus Nijhoff Publishers, 1987.

Bossuyt, Marc J., *Guide to the "Travaux Préparatoires" of the International Covenant on Civil and Political Rights*, Dordrecht: Martinus Nijhoff Publishers, 1987.

Council of Europe, *Digest of Strasbourg Case-Law Relating to the ECHR*, vol. 2, vol. 3; Council of Europe Document H (70)7.

Danelius, Hans, *Mänskliga rättigheter*, 4th edition, Stockholm: Norstedt Förlag, 1989.

van Dijk, Pieter and G.J.H. van Hoof, *Theory and Practice of the European Convention on Human Rights*, Deventer: Kluwer Law and Taxation Publishers, 1984.

Frowein, Jochen Abr., "Zur Bedeutung der Unschuldsvermutung in Art. 6 Abs. 2 der Europäischen Menschenrechtskonvention", in *Recht als Prozess und Gefüge, Festschrift für Hans Huber*, Bern: Verlag Stämpfli & Cie AG, 1981.

Frände, Dan, *Den straffrättsliga legalitetsprincipen*, Ekenäs, 1989.

Jescheck, Hans-Heinrich, *Lehrbuch des Strafrechts*, Allgemeiner Teil, Vierte Auflage, Berlin: Duncker & Humblot, 1988.

Kühl, Kristian, *Unschuldsvermutung, Freispruch und Einstellung*, München: Carl Heymanns Verlag, 1983.

Kühl, Kristian, Helmut Fuchs, Hans-Jürgen Schroth, Roland Riz and Stephan Trechsel, *Zeitschrift für die gesamte Strafrechtswissenschaft*, 1988.

López-Rey, Manuel, *A Guide to United Nations Criminal Policy*, Aldershot: Gower Publishing Company, 1985.

Noor Muhammad, Haji N.A., "Due Process of Law for Persons Accused of Crime", in Louis Henkin (ed.), *The International Bill of Rights, The Covenant on Civil and Political Rights*, New York: Columbia University Press, 1981.

Nordskov Nielsen, Lars, "Menneskerettighedernes Betydning for Straffeprocessen", *Nordisk Tidsskrift for Kriminalvidenskab*, 1989.

Opsahl, Torkel, "Menneskerettighetene i Straffprocessen", in *Lov og frihet; Festskrift til Johs. Andenæs*, Oslo: Universitetsforlaget, 1982.

Rehof, Lars Adam, "Straffeproces og den Europæiske Menneskerettigheds-konvention", *Nordisk Tidsskrift for Kriminalvidenskab*, 1987.

Revue Internationale de Droit Pénale, 1980.

Roxin, Claus, *Strafverfahrensrecht*, 20. Auflage, München: Verlag C.H. Beck,

1987.

Schreiber, Hans-Ludwig, *Gesetz und Richter, Zur geschichtlichen Entwicklung des Satzes nullum crimen, nulla poena sine lege*, Frankfurt am Main: Alfred Metzner Verlag GmbH, 1976.

Schubarth, Martin, *Zur Tragweite des Grundsatzes der Unschuldsvermutung*, Basler Studien zur Rechtswissenschaft, Heft 120, Basel und Stuttgart: Helbing & Lichtenhahn, 1978.

Trechsel, Stephan, "The Protection of Human Rights in Criminal Procedure, General Report", *Revue Internationale de Droit Pénal*, 1978.

Trechsel, Stephan, "Struktur und Funktion der Vermutung der Schuldlosigkeit", *Schweizerische Juristen-Zeitung*, 1981.

Triffterer, Otto, *Dogmatische Untersuchungen zur Entwicklung des Materiellen Völkerstrafrechts seit Nürnberg*, Freiburg i.Br: Eberhard Albert Verlag, 1966.

Träskman, P.O., "Brottmålsrättegången i Finland i Förhållande till FN-konventionen om Politiska och Medborgerliga Rättigheter", *Tidskrift utgiven av Juridiska föreningen i Finland*, 1987.

Träskman, P.O., "Presumtionen om den för Brott Misstänktes Oskyldighet", in *Festskrift till Lars Welamson*, Stockholm: Norstedts Förlag, 1988.

Verdoodt, Albert, *Naissance et Signification de la Déclaration Universelle des Droits de l'Homme*, Société d'Etude Morales, Sociales et Juridiques, Louvain-Paris: Editions Nauwelaerts, 1964.

Westerdiek, Claudia, "Die Strassburger Rechtsprechung zur Unschuldsvermutung bei der Einstellung von Strafverfahren", *Europäische Grundrechte — Zeitschrift*, 1987.

United Nations, *The Work of the International Law Commission*, 4th edition, New York: United Nations, 1988.

United Nations Documents: 3 UN GAOR I, Third Committee, SR 115–116; E/CN.4/21; E/600; E/800; E/CN.4/SR.54; CCPR/C/21/Add.3; UN Publication ST/HR/2/Rev.2

de Zayas, Alfred, Jakob Th. Möller and Torkel Opsahl, "Application of the International Covenant on Civil and Political Rights under the Optional Protocol by the Human Rights Committee," *German Yearbook of International Law*, vol. 28, Berlin: Duncker & Humblot, 1985.

Article 12

Lars Adam Rehof

Denmark

No one shall be subjected to arbitrary interference with his privacy, family, home or correspondence, nor to attacks upon his honour and reputation. Everyone has the right to the protection of the law against such interference or attacks.

I. Protection of Privacy

In the Universal Declaration of Human Rights (UDHR) article 12,[1] it is stated that no one should be the subject of arbitrary interference with private matters, family life, home or correspondence nor interference with honour and reputation. It is also stated that everyone has a right to be protected in law against such interference or attack. This provision covers a wide range of different interferences. The number of subtle interferences has no doubt grown considerably in the last 10 to 20 years in connection with sophisticated technological developments and thereby the increased risks of interferences such as electronic surveillance performed by either State agents or private actors. The building up of comprehensive computerized file systems and data banks is another example of modern technological developments which may entail a risk for the protection of privacy.

---

[1] Originally article 13 of the Commission on Human Rights' draft universal declaration, UN doc. A/777, and subsequently article 10 of the working document of the UN General Assembly Third Committee (as contained in UN doc. E/800). Proposed amendments to the draft by the Commission as concerns article 10 were contained in UN doc. E/800, p. 33 and UN doc. A/C.3/283/Rev.1.

A. Article 12 in the Context of the UDHR as a Whole

When discussing article 12 of the UDHR it may be fruitful to place the provision in the context of certain other clauses also found in this instrument. The right to privacy may be seen as an umbrella term for all the different rights mentioned in article 12 of the UDHR. The right to privacy is closely connected with the protection of the family, home life, place of residence, correspondence, telephone and other electronic means of communication, and physical and mental integrity. The right has to be evaluated in that context.[2]

Articles 10 and 11 of the UDHR seek to guarantee that the individual is not removed from his or her home and private sphere without certain due process requirements, including certain judicial safeguards. UDHR article 17(2) gives a certain protection against arbitrary deprivation of the actual place of habitation (house, apartment, etc., owned or otherwise disposed of by the individual).[3] Articles 18–19 of the UDHR are designed to secure the individual against interferences with the right of freedom of thought, conscience and opinion, all of which can be said to be integral and important elements of a sphere of privacy for the individual.[4]

During the debates on the draft declaration, the Cuban representative in the Third Committee of the 1948 UN General

---

[2] One may distinguish between three different spheres of privacy: (i) physical integrity; (ii) mental integrity; and (iii) a sphere of intimate relationships (from the German expression Intimssphäre). A fourth aspect could be the need for privacy protection in the workplace and other places (e.g., when sun-bathing on the beach). These three to four spheres of privacy are not necessarily located to specific places, but may 'follow' the individual.

[3] The Panamanian delegation had already at the San Francisco conference (see Documents of the UN Conference on international organization, San Francisco, 1945, vol. II, p. 266) introduced a proposal aimed at strengthening the protection of "the human person in relation to his work, his property, his actions and deeds and all his other activities" (General Assembly Official Records (hereafter Official Records), p. 276). The adopted wording of UDHR article 17 does not entail a general protection of private property. The provision only protects against arbitrary deprivation of property.

[4] Articles 18–19, of course, are specifically brought about in order to facilitate the positive aspects of individual expression, i.e., communicating with (members of) the surrounding community and the world outside. Questions of realization of the right to practice one's religion, discussions with friends, etc., can, however, be said to be closely connected to the privacy of the individual and his/her family.

Assembly, Mr. Cisneros, suggested that the provision should be divided into three separate articles. The first article should ensure "man's moral inviolability, which was based on two factors: a subjective factor, honour, and an objective factor, reputation." The second one should be concerned with inviolability of the home and the third would guarantee inviolability of correspondence and an explicit right of "free circulation of correspondence."[5]

This proposal, which was not adopted, was probably to a certain extent an expression of a Latin American preoccupation with the necessity of protecting the honour of the individual. Some delegations no doubt resisted this proposal because they feared that the consequences of a comparatively wide protection of the honour of the individual would be detrimental to the equally — or rather more — important protection of the right of free speech as touched upon below.

II. *Travaux Préparatoires*

A. Legal Safeguards — the Term 'Arbitrary' Interference

In regard to the negotiations on UDHR article 12 one of the major questions was whether the wording of the first sentence, as a restrictive qualification of the word 'interference', should include the word 'arbitrary' (french *arbitraire*) or whether it should be 'abusive' (*abusive*) or 'unreasonable' (*injustifié/injuste*).[6]

The New Zealand representative, Mrs. Newlands, said that she would prefer to replace the word 'unreasonable' with the word 'arbitrary' for two reasons.[7] First, the word 'arbitrary' should be preferred. It had already been utilized in draft articles 7 (UDHR article 9) and 13 (UDHR article 15) and: "It was extremely difficult to define the exact limits of what might be considered 'unreasonable', whereas the word 'arbitrary' signified everything

---

[5] Official Records, p. 275. A right of free circulation of correspondence can be said to be implied in the right to correspond with others.

[6] The representative from Uruguay had proposed, in UN doc. A/C.3/268, to replace the French expression '*abusive*' by the word '*injuste*' in order to reflect the concept of justice. The Saudi Arabian delegate, in drawing attention to his amendment distributed as UN doc. A/C.3/255, preferred the word 'unlawful' as it was more precise than 'unreasonable' (Official Records, p. 276). The Soviet representative found the word 'illegitimate' more suitable (Official Records, p. 306).

[7] The proposal was contained in UN doc. A/C.3/267.

that was not in accordance with well-established legal principles",[8] and, secondly, this change would mean that a higher degree of uniformity would be attained.

The British representative, Mrs. Corbet, supported the inclusion of the word 'arbitrary' which could be defined as: "Any action taken at the will and pleasure of some person who could not be called upon to show just cause for it."[9] Verdoodt concludes that the wording 'arbitrary' should be interpreted as: 'without justification in valid motives and contrary to established legal principles'.[10]

B. The Question of Legal Protection and Upholding of Freedom of Speech

In the Third Committee a lengthy argument centered around the question of whether the clause should not only contain a provision guaranteeing the individual a right of legal protection against interferences with privacy, home, correspondence, etc., but also against attacks on his/her honour and reputation.[11] This debate became confounded by the fact that the Soviet proposal, which, in the end, was accepted, turned out to have a different wording in the two — at that time — official working languages, English and French. The English version of the Soviet proposal read:

> No one shall be subjected to arbitrary interference with his privacy, family, home, correspondence, honour and reputation.[12] Everyone has

---

[8] Official Records, p. 276.

[9] Official Records, p. 306.

[10] Official Records, p. 143. See also the decision by the Human Rights Committee in case 27/1978 Pinkney *v.* Canada where a violation of CCPR article 17 was found because no statutory protection against arbitrary interferences existed.

[11] The original Soviet proposal, as contained in UN doc. E/800, p. 33, was phrased thus: "and every one is entitled to legal defence against any such interference."

[12] A conceptual issue, which has some general implications, was the question of whether the UDHR should proclaim certain positive rights or whether it should first and foremost be phrased negatively, i.e., as a guarantee against interferences. The UDHR shows examples of both wordings. UDHR articles 1–3 and 6–8 are some of several examples of the positive version, while articles 4–5, 9 and 12 are some of several illustrations of the negative version. Thus, the Chinese representative preferred the initial wording of draft article 12 to be changed to a negative formulation according to which the clause should be formulated thus: "Nul ne sera l'objet d'immixtions injustifiées dans sa vie privée, sa famille, son domicile et sa correspondance ni l'objet d'atteintes abusives à sa réputation" (UN doc. E/CN.4/SR

the right to the protection of the law against such interference.[13]

The French version, however, read:

> Nul ne sera l'objet d'immixtions arbitraires dans sa vie priveé, celle de sa famille, son domicile et sa correspondance, ni d'atteintes à son honneur et sa réputation. Toute personne a droit à la protection de la loi contre toute atteinte de ce genre.

The first sentence of this proposal was adopted by the Third Committee by a vote of 23:12, with 6 abstentions and the latter sentence by 22:12, with 11 abstentions.[14] As already touched upon, it later dawned upon the delegates that they had accepted two different versions of the same clause in as much as the English version, in the first sentence, did not contain a reference to 'attack' (*atteinte*) against honour and reputation, while the French version, in the second sentence, only spoke of protection against attacks (*atteinte*) and not against interference (*immixtion*). In the end, the French version was accepted as the 'authentic' one.

For reasons of consistency and language it was, however, pointed out that one could not, at least in the English language, 'interfere' with honour and reputation, one could, at the most, 'attack' another individual's honour and reputation. In order to correspond to the French version, the second part of the first sentence of the English version had to be altered to read: "nor to attacks upon his honour and reputation."

The final version of UDHR article 12, as we now know it, was adopted by 29:7, with 4 abstentions.[15]

55, pp. 3–5). One may, however, say that individual rights may also be derived from the negative version, even though they are only described as State obligations. In this context, the term 'rights' will also be used to cover the reflex effect of the negatively defined areas of protection.

[13] The British representative proposed the following wording (UN doc. A/C.3/319/Rev.1): "No one shall be subjected to arbitrary interference with his privacy, family, home or correspondence. Everyone has the right to the protection of the law against attacks upon his honour and reputation." This version did, as it appears, not protect honour and reputation at a par with privacy.

[14] Official Records, pp. 311–312.

[15] Official Records, p. 315.

C. The Question of the Need for Protection of Honour/Reputation

The reluctance on the part of certain delegations to include 'honour' and, to a certain extent, 'reputation' in article 12 was no doubt spurred by a premonition that these somewhat vague terms could be (ab)used as a justification for curbing free speech in some Member States, especially freedom of the press.[16] Experience, moreover, tells that polemical political debates in the media very often involve strong language bordering on questions of personal honour and reputation, but should, nevertheless, be allowed in the interests of democracy. This classical conflict between protection of free speech and protection of individuals and minorities can be found in other human rights provisions. One example could be the International Covenant on Civil and Political Rights (CCPR) article 20(2), which prohibits incitement to racial, national or religious hatred.[17] Some delegations, primarily the UK delegate, only reluctantly accepted the idea that the second sentence of the provision should contain a reference to the need for protection in domestic law.[18]

D. Permissible Limitations: the Role of UDHR Article 29

Certain delegations opposed the idea of including a qualifying adjective (for example, arbitrary, unlawful, etc.) in a description of unacceptable 'interferences'. The reason for this, advanced both by the Lebanese delegate, Mr. Azkoul, and the French delegate, Mr.

---

[16] The Cuban representative thus emphasized that "Some reputations might be justifiably attacked and it was important that the impression should not be given that the freedom of the press might be restricted" (Official Records, p. 309). The New Zealand delegate stated that she approved, in principle, of the right to protection of the law against attacks upon reputation. She was, however, doubtful whether a prohibition of attacks upon honour should be included (Official Records, p. 310).

[17] The question of the compatibility of CCPR article 20 with article 19 played a major role in the Commission; see also, Nowak 1989, p. 383. The European Convention on Human Rights (ECHR) article 10(2), also recognizes that freedom of speech may be limited in order to protect "the reputation or rights of others"; see also the similar clause in ECHR article 8(2).

[18] As mentioned, this point of view may have been motivated by the fear of possible abuse of limitations in domestic law in relation to free speech, and/or may have to be seen in the general context of a rather tense atmosphere between the Soviet and UK delegations due to the Cold War at the time.

Cassin, was that article 27 of the draft prepared by the Commission[19] had been conceived of as an exhaustive enumeration of permissible limitations. Some human rights were inalienable; others were subject to limitations.[20]

Article 8 of the UDHR seeks to ensure that the individual has access to effective means of redress for human rights violations.

III. Contemporary Legal Questions

A. *Protection of a Wider Sphere of Privacy*

According to the classical ideology of individual freedom, it is a fundamental right for the individual to have his or her private life respected: to have acceptance of a private sphere which the government or private individuals cannot touch or interfere with unless there exist well founded reasons for it, or, in some cases, consent has been given by the person affected.[21] The protection in — at least regional — international human rights law goes somewhat further by securing a right to establish and develop relationships with other people.

As mentioned below, the right to privacy is protected in legally binding instruments such as CCPR article 17, and the ECHR article 8, both of which secure respect for privacy, home and

---

[19] Article 27 of the Commission's draft Universal Declaration later became UDHR article 29, which, in para. 2, states: "In the exercise of his rights and freedoms, everyone shall be subject only to such limitations as are determined by law solely for the purpose of securing due recognition and respect for the rights and freedoms of others and of meeting the just requirements of morality, public order and the general welfare in a democratic society."

[20] Cassin was of the view that "it would be possible to delete all qualifications because they were covered by the limitations set out in article 27 — the pivotal article of the entire declaration. One reason for the confusion which existed was that the Commission of Human Rights had not yet adopted article 27 when it had voted on article 10, so that certain qualifications had been included in the latter article." (Official Records, p. 309).

[21] The question of consent to interferences with protected human rights is complicated, not only because the individual in question very often cannot be said to be in a position of free choice (free and informed consent), but first and foremost because human rights obligations are obligations on the part of the State Party. In general, the individual cannot waive the responsibility of the State by giving consent. This is particularly clear when it comes to questions of gross offences against the physical integrity of the individual, e.g., in relation to torture.

correspondence. The CCPR also protects the reputation and honour of the individual,[22] but on the other hand is restricted to interferences which are either arbitrary or illegal.

Only a few topics can be mentioned here. Such important issues as forced removal of children by Social Services officers, reunification of scattered members of refugee families, protection against expulsion of family members and other contemporary legal questions cannot, unfortunately, be dealt with in this context. Human rights obligations to respect the privacy of the individual have far-reaching application. This is clearly demonstrated by the rich case law of the Council of Europe human rights institutions. Given this background, the following can only be a subjective selection of a smaller number of current issues.

B. Positive Obligations — Protection Among Private Parties and Against State Agents

In this area one has to distinguish between two different forms of protection of privacy. One is the traditional protection of the citizens against interferences from public authorities.[23] The other is the protection against interferences perpetrated by private parties (for example, neighbours, employers, shop owners, etc.).[24] The right to privacy cannot only be seen as a right to be left in peace by others (private or public bodies), but should also be seen as an obligation on the part of the State Party — via legislation and other technicolegal means — to work for the positive protection of the privacy of the citizens.[25]

---

[22] CCPR article 17 is modelled according to the structure of UDHR article 12. ECHR article 10(2) perceives the question somewhat differently in as much as protection of reputation is seen as a possibly legitimate restriction on freedom of speech. ECHR article 8(2), does not contain a verbatim reference to the honour or reputation of others, but this may under certain circumstances be interpreted as included in the "rights and freedoms of others."

[23] Examples of this could be restrictions on the search and seizure powers of the executive (the police) and restrictions on storage of information about loaners and their reading habits in public libraries.

[24] Examples of this could be files on the use of credit card facilities and cash machines with the intention of following a certain individual's travels, pattern of consumption and other activities.

[25] This requirement is termed 'positive obligations' in the European case law, see for instance judgment no. 91 X and Y *v.* the Netherlands.

The right to privacy may not only be invoked in private relationships at home, but may also be relevant as a kind of private sphere which is inherent in the individual person when that person moves about. Looked at from that point of view, the question of privacy may also arise in the workplace, where the individual may have a legitimate claim to protection of privacy, for example, when talking on the telephone or a right not to be monitored by cameras while working. Also different modern techniques for controlling the work intensity of employees may constitute a violation of the right to privacy.[26]

C. The Right to Establish Emotional Relationships

In the regional European human rights case law it is clearly established that ECHR article 8 not only provides the individual with a right to live protected from the public in as much as that is a wish on the part of the individual, but that the provision also comprises the right to establish and develop relationships with other human beings, especially in the emotional field, for the development and fulfilment of one's own personality.[27]

Citizens have a right to live in a personal sphere, which also may include protection of the most intimate spheres, such as the sex life of the individual. In the case law, the question of the possible protection of homosexual relationships in particular has been dealt with by the European Commission and the European Court of Human Rights (European Court). This is an area where attitudes have changed in line with the generally more tolerant view on sexual minorities that can be observed in a number of Western European countries. The leading cases from the European Court of Human Rights in this respect are judgment no. 45, Dudgeon, and judgment no. 142, Norris.

In the Dudgeon case the question was whether a legal prohibition, including penal sanctions, against homosexual relationships was a violation of ECHR article 8. The European Court found that this legislation could not be seen as an expression of "a pressing social

---

[26] One may point to such examples as word processors which are able to evaluate the performance (speed, etc.) of the user, and check in/check out mechanisms using finger print identification, and DNA profiling of job applicants and employees.
[27] See Complaint no. 6862/74 X *v.* Iceland, DR 5, p. 86, and complaint no. 8257/78 X *v.* Switzerland, DR 13, p. 248.

need" and could therefore not be accepted under the ECHR. The European Court found that consenting male persons over 21 years had the right to take decisions about their own intimate lives. In the Norris case the Court found that the mere existence of penal sanctions against homosexuality — and even in the situation where these sanctions were never actually employed — could amount to a violation of article 8.[28]

The case law of the European Court as concerns the intimate sphere of privacy entails that there should be particularly serious reasons before interferences on the part of public authorities can be legitimate, and this places the burden of proof on the shoulders of the State. With regard to homosexual relationships between members of the armed forces, the European Court has earlier excepted that restrictions can be imposed on this activity.

The interception of telephone calls and the registration of other communications is undoubtedly protected by both CCPR article 17 and ECHR article 8, but interferences may often be found to be legitimate according to the criteria in article 8(2).[29]

D. Definition of 'Home' in the Sense of the ECHR

According to the case law of the European Commission, the word 'home' in ECHR article 8 comprises the residence of a person and cannot as a starting point be extended to cover, for example, a person's car. Circumstances where the complainant, because of public regulations, can no longer live in his or her prior home and where that person as a consequence thereof involuntarily has had to move to another place (for example, a tent), this place may be regarded as a home.[30] Commercial office space will not, as a starting point, be regarded as home, but especially where the offices are adjoining to the home in a strict sense (for example, the office is located in the house of the private owner) a search of the offices

---

[28] The recent judgment no. 184 in the Cossey case may, however, be seen as a step backwards in regard to equal treatment of different sexual minorities. The Court found that a transsexual male who had changed to the female sex could not demand that the birth certificate be changed in order to fulfil the legal requirements to marry a man.

[29] In the European context reference may be made to judgment no. 28, Klass; judgment no. 82, Malone; judgment no. 176–A, Kruslin; and judgment no. 176–B, Huvig.

[30] See complaint no. 7456/76 Wiggins *v.* United Kingdom DR 13, p. 40.

may amount to a violation of article 8.

Two cases concerning the circumstances on the small Channel Island Guernsey may further illustrate the concept of home. In the first case that came before the European Commission, a couple lived in a house which was owned by the husband and which was exempted from permission under the Guernsey residence regulations.[31] In 1973 the couple was separated and the woman left. The authorities then refused to uphold the permission and asked the husband to leave as well. The Commission found that this denial of permission to stay was an interference in the sense of article 8(1). The obligation to leave the island, however, was found to be justified under the terms mentioned in paragraph 2 and the case was dismissed.

In judgment no. 109, Gillow, the couple Gillow had a house built on Guernsey in 1958. They moved away in 1960 because the husband became employed in an international organization. The house was rented out and in 1979 the couple returned to their estate where they initiated negotiations with the authorities about the legality of the stay. The European Court found that the estate was the home of the Gillows notwithstanding that they had been away for almost 19 years. The European Court found that the imposition of a fine lacked the necessary proportionality and the respect of the home of the couple had been violated.

E. Definition of 'Private Life' in the Sense of the ECHR

The scope of the concept of private life and the right to a private sphere is somewhat more difficult to define in detail. Concerning searches conducted by public authorities in the house of the individual, it must be assumed that an interference with private life is present when it is stated that a person's right to respect for his home is violated. Apart from this, one may be able to envisage interferences which are not covered by the concept of home but may, because of other circumstances, amount to a violation of private life. This could, for instance, be the case when a car containing some papers of a private nature is searched by the police.

---

[31] Wiggins, case no. 7456/76, DR 13, p. 40.

F. Definition of 'Correspondence' in the Sense of the ECHR

An interference with the right of communication is not only present when letters are opened; the reading of telegrams, stopping of letters, etc., are also covered. By 'metering' is understood information concerning which telephones have been connected to which telephones. Both metering and the actual tapping of phones are covered by ECHR article 8 in accordance with judgment no. 28 in the Klass case. Also the interception of private radio communications may, in certain cases, be covered by article 8.

G. Restrictions on Prisoners and Other Inmates of Institutions

In the case law, interferences in connection with prison conditions have given rise to legal interpretations. There is no doubt that the ECHR offers a certain degree of protection to prisoners, which means that censorship and the stopping of letters from prisoners to outside persons may amount to a violation of ECHR article 8(1). This also means that each individual interference (for example, each letter opened or withheld) in order to be legitimate should fulfil the requirements in article 8(2). This is clearly stated in judgments no. 18, Golder, and no. 61, Silver.

The European Court observed in the Silver case that only those letters where threats of violence or discussions of possible crimes were mentioned could be stopped legitimately in accordance with the requirements in article 8(2). In the case of Boyle and Rice v. UK (judgment no. 131) violation of article 8 was found in as much as the prison authorities had stopped letters from a prisoner to a so-called media personality. The letters were purely personal. This was acknowledged by the authorities while at the same time regretting that a mistake had been made.

H. Body Searches and the Collection of Body Samples

Seizures of a person and closer examination of the human body (for example, involuntary examination of the colon) may also call into question ECHR articles 3 and 8. These interferences are most often employed as part of police or customs investigations. The taking of so-called body samples (for example, blood and urine tests, collection of fingernails, hair, semen) may raise questions of degrading treatment according to ECHR article 3, but especially raises questions in connection with the right to privacy of article 8.[32]

As concerns the taking of blood samples, it is settled case law that forced extraction of blood for the use of a case concerning parenthood is an interference with private life according to article 8(1), but may often be considered legitimate if the requirements in paragraph 2 are met. Also certain psychiatric investigations, for example, mental observations, may amount to a violation of article 8. The taking of fingerprints and photos are, as a starting point, also interferences covered by article 8(1).

I. Public Files and Computerized Records

With regard to the building up of public files and computerized filing systems, the different measures may also amount to an interference with ECHR article 8. In the judgment no. 116, Leander *v.* Sweden, an investigation into a secret police file concerning the applicant for a position with a naval museum was initiated. The information furnished meant that the employer terminated the employment of Mr. Leander within a short while. Mr. Leander was not given access to the contents of the files. The European Court stated that both the storage and the passing on of information about the private circumstances of the complainant amounted to an interference with his private life. However, the European Court found that the requirements in article 8(2) were fulfilled in as much as measures were necessary to preserve the security of the state.

In another judgment, no. 160, Gaskin, the complainant, asked for the files about his stay in a children's home. A majority of the individuals who had contributed to the case file and who had furnished information on Mr. Gaskin accepted that this information could be passed on to him. However, a few individuals refused to

---

[32] These procedures also often raise difficult questions of medical ethics in as much as medical personnel (doctors and nurses) are required to assist with or personally perform various examinations of suspected criminal (drug traffickers, etc.). These procedures, which cannot be described as treatment, are really police investigations performed by health professionals and may, as such, be in conflict with the ethical codes of conduct of the health profession. Also certifications stating that the individual is capable of enduring an involuntary examination may raise similar issues. This, in turn, raises the question of the need for domestic human rights protection of the health personnel, e.g., by guaranteeing a statutory right of the individual medical officer or nurse to abstain from participating.

give their consent to the passing on of information and access to the file was denied. The European Court found that this was an interference with the private life of Mr. Gaskin and the legitimacy of the interference should be found in a weighing of interests. The European Court subsequently found that the interference was not proportional in as much as it stated that "The interests of the individual seeking access to records relating to his private and family life must be secured when a contributor to the records is either not available or improperly refuses consent. Such a system is only in conformity with the principle of proportionality if it provides that an independent authority finally decides whether access has to be granted in cases where a contributor fails to answer or withholds consent."

The most important regulation concerning data security is to be found in the European Convention on the protection of individuals with regard to automatic processing of personal data (ETS 108). The Convention covers both private and public computerized and other files. In the Convention a number of requirements are established: for example, that only information which is obtained fairly and lawfully can be filed; and it is furthermore required that appropriate safeguards should be established when information about race, political affiliations, religion, health, sex life and information about previous convictions is gathered.

The Council of Europe has furthermore adopted a number of recommendations concerning data security within certain sectors, for example: Recommendation R (86) 1 concerning the protection of personal data used for social security purposes; and Recommendation R (87) 15, concerning regulation of the use of personal data in the police sector. In the Council of Europe Committee of Ministers Resolution (77) 26 concerning national identity cards, it is stated in item 14 that optically readable passports and other identity cards should not contain any information other than what is contained in the readable part.[33]

---

[33] The Commission of the European Communities recently published a draft Council directive on the protection of individuals in connection with the treatment of personalized data (EC doc. KOM[90] fin. – SYN 287, Gazette 90/C277/03 of 5 November 1990). EC regulations will undoubtedly play a bigger role in the years to come. The draft directive contains, in preambular item 7, a direct reference to ECHR article 8. In article 15 of the draft directive a number of legitimate reasons for restrictions on access to stored data are enumerated. This enumeration to a large extent is similar to the one contained in ECHR article 8(2).

IV. Concluding Remarks

The legal challenges posed by technological change and a greater degree of State involvement in the private lives of citizens necessitate a constant and dynamic development of new measures of protection within established State obligations and a wide application of the principle of privacy. This can also be observed in the development of the case law concerning the interpretation of ECHR article 8. One may, however, question whether the limits of article 8, even with a European Commission and Court willing to participate in this development, can, in the long run, satisfy the actual needs. A further elaboration of the principles enshrined in UDHR article 12 into legally binding obligations must be given high priority.

References

European Community, EC doc. KOM(90) fin. – SYN 287, Gazette 90/C277/03.

Nowak, Manfred, *UNO-Pakt über bürgerliche und politische Rechte und Fakultative-protokoll, CCPR-Kommentar*, Kehl: N.P. Engel Verlag, 1989.

Documents of the United Nations Conference on International Organization, San Francisco, 1945, vol. II.

United Nations Documents: A/777; E/800; A/C.3/283/Rev.1; A/C.3/268; A/C.3/255; A/C.3/267; E/CN.4/SR 55; A/C.3/319/Rev.1.

Article 13

Atle Grahl-Madsen

Norway

1. Everyone has the right to freedom of movement and residence within the borders of each state.
2. Everyone has the right to leave any country, including his own, and to return to his country.

I. Introduction

In two brief paragraphs, article 13 lays down no less than four distinct rights and freedoms:[1]

1) A right to freedom of movement within the borders of a particular State, which may be referred to as 'the freedom of (internal) movement';
2) A right to freedom of residence within the borders of a particular State, which we may be referred to as 'the freedom of residence';
3) A right to leave any country, including one's own, which we may refer to as 'the right to leave' or 'the right of emigration';
4) A right to return to one's country, which we may refer to as 'the right to return' or 'the right of remigration'.

The article does not mention a fifth right, namely a right to enter any country (other than 'one's own'): a right which we may label as the 'right of entry' or the 'right of immigration'.

After having examined the four rights and freedoms actually covered by article 13, we shall add some remarks about this fifth right.

The provisions of article 13 have been reiterated in Protocol no.

---

[1] See the important studies: Hannum 1987; Hofmann 1988; also Inglés, *Study of Discrimination....* (UN Sales no. 64.XIV.2 [1963]); Vasak and Liskofsky (eds.) 1972.

4 to the European Convention on Human Rights (1963, ECHR),[2] the International Covenant on Civil and Political Rights (1966, CCPR),[3] and the American Convention on Human Rights (1969, ACHR).[4]

Provisions on the freedom of movement and of residence are found in a number of conventions relating to refugees[5] and stateless persons.[6] Discrimination with respect to those freedoms is expressly prohibited by provisions in the International Convention on the Elimination of All Forms of Racial Discrimination (1965).[7]

The provisions of article 13 are related to those of article 14, dealing with the right — *vis-à-vis* one's own country — to seek and to enjoy in other countries asylum from persecution.[8]

They are also related to the provisions on family reunification contained in the Final Act of the Helsinki Conference (1975)[9] and

---

[2] Protocol no. 4 to the ECHR, securing Certain Rights and Freedoms Other Than Those Already Included in the Convention and in the First Protocol thereto (1963–09–16): Article 2 of that Protocol stipulates that everyone lawfully within the territory of a State shall, within that territory, have the right to liberty of movement and freedom to choose his residence (para. 1), and also that everyone shall be free to leave any country, including his own (para. 2). For exceptions to these rights (paras. 3 and 4), see below. Article 3 sets forth that no one shall be expelled, by means either of an individual or of a collective measure, from the territory of the State of which he is a national (para. 1). Moreover, no one shall be deprived of the right to enter the territory of the State of which he is a national (para. 2).

[3] (1966–12–16): Article 12(1) and (2) of the Covenant correspond to article 2(1) and (2) of the ECHR Protocol no. 4, while article 12(4) corresponds to article 3(1) of the said Protocol. The exceptions to paras. 1 and 2 are set forth in para. 3. There are no exceptions to para. 4.

[4] ACHR ('Pact of San José, Costa Rica') (1969–11–22): Articles 22(1) through (5) of the ACHR contain provisions corresponding to those of article 12 of the CCPR and articles 2–3 of the ECHR Protocol no. 4.

[5] Convention relating to the Status of Refugees (1951–07–28), articles 26 and 31(2); Caracas Convention on Territorial Asylum (1954–03–28), article 9; Organization of African Unity (OAU) Convention governing the Specific Aspects of Refugee Problems in Africa (1969–09–10), article II(6).

[6] Convention relating to the Status of Stateless Persons (1954–09–28): article 26; Convention on the Reduction of Statelessness (1961–08–30): articles 7–9.

[7] (1965–12–21): article 5(d).

[8] See chapter on article 14 in this publication.

[9] Helsinki Conference on Security and Co-operation in Europe: Final Act (1975–08–01) (International Legal Materials 14 (1975) 1292): (Basket One) ch. 1 (a) VII: Questions relating to Security in Europe: (Basket Four) ch. 1: Co-operation in Humanitarian and Other Fields: (a) Contacts and Regular Meetings on the Basis of

the more limited, but binding, provisions on the same topic found in the European Agreement on the Transfer of Responsibility for Refugees (1980).[10]

The right to leave a country has a counterpart in the Latin American conventions on diplomatic asylum, providing for safe conduct out of the country for persons having sought asylum at an embassy, etc.[11]

II. Freedom of Movement

The provisions of article 13 concern the basic relationship between the State and the individual. Where serfdom or bondage exists (as in Prussia and Imperial Russia into the 19th century or in Denmark in the 18th century),[12] there is no freedom of movement or of residence, not to mention any right to leave the country altogether, for those persons who are under the yoke. Dictatorships, too, tend to restrict the freedom of people to move about and to settle as they wish.

On the other hand, in a democracy the rights enumerated in article 13 are all too easily taken for granted. In a sense they are the hallmarks of a democratic society. Without the freedom to move and to take up residence without official permission, personal freedom would indeed be curtailed. There is thus a direct connection between the rights and freedoms set forth in article 13 and the reference to the necessities of a democratic society in article

Family Ties; (b) Reunification of Families; (c) Marriage between Citizens of Different States; (d) Travel for Personal or Professional Reasons; (e) Improvement of Conditions for Tourism on an Individual or Collective Basis; (f) Meeting among Young People; (Basket Four) ch. 3: Co-operation and Exchanges in the Field of Culture; (Basket Four) ch. 4: Co-operation and Exchanges in the Field of Education.

[10] European Agreement on Transfer of Responsibility for Refugees (1980–10–16), article 6: "After the date of transfer of responsibility, the second State shall, in the interest of family reunification and for humanitarian reasons, facilitate the admission to its territory of the refugee's spouse and minor or dependent children."

[11] Havana Convention on Asylum (1928–02–20), article 2(3); Caracas Convention on Diplomatic Asylum (1954–03–28), articles 11–13.

[12] Serfdom existed in Prussia until 1816, in Imperial Russia until 1861. Bondage (stavnsbånd), a legal duty to remain on the place where one was born, and to till the land, existed in Denmark between 1733–1788 for persons aged 14–36, later extended to persons 4–40 years of age. It never existed in the other Nordic countries.

29,[13] and the inclusion of article 13 in the UDHR (and of the corresponding articles in the respective human rights conventions) constitutes a tribute to democracy as the ultimate basis for government.

As a general rule, freedom of movement is simple enough. Everybody lawfully within a given territory may move about freely within that territory, without let and hindrance, and without having to ask the permission of the authorities or having to justify his/her presence in any particular place.

What constitutes the territory of a State for the purposes of article 13 and the corresponding provisions in other instruments, however, may be open to question, but this is more appropriately dealt with below in connection with freedom of residence.

A. Exceptions

While the general rule is clear, it is not, however, without exceptions. Article 13, as all the other articles of the UDHR, is subject to the provisions of articles 29 and 30.[14] Rather than trying to speculate on the effect of the exceptions set forth in these articles on freedom of movement (and the other rights and freedoms laid down in article 13), it seems more rewarding to consider the more precise exceptions spelled out in the CCPR[15] and the regional conventions[16] directly relating to these rights and freedoms.

The most elaborate enumeration of exceptions is found in Protocol no. 4 to the ECHR.[17] Article 2(3) stresses that restrictions

[13] In the ECHR Protocol no. 4 and the ACHR, the exceptions are likewise restricted to what is "necessary in a democratic society." Article 12 of the CCPR, on the other hand, does not contain this provision.

[14] See chapters on articles 29 and 30 in this publication.

[15] Article 12(3) of the CCPR.

[16] Article 2(3) and (4) of the ECHR Protocol no. 4; article 22(3) and (4) of the ACHR.

[17] Article 2(3) and (4) of the ECHR Protocol no. 4 read as follows: 3. No restrictions shall be placed on the exercise of these rights other than such as are in accordance with law and are necessary in a democratic society in the interests of national security and public safety, for the maintenance of *"ordre public"* for the prevention of crime, for the protection of health and morals, or for the protection of the rights and freedoms of others. 4. The right set forth in paragraph 1 may also be subject, in particular areas, to restrictions imposed in accordance with law and justified by the public interests in a democratic society.

ust be "in accordance with law", and that they must be necessary in a democratic society in order to safeguard certain essential interests of the State and society, to wit: national security; public safety; maintenance of *'ordre public'*; prevention of crime; protection of health and morals; or protection of the rights and freedoms of others.

Article 2(4) relaxes the requirements in particular areas by allowing restrictions that are merely 'justified' by the public interests in a democratic society. Thus, certain areas may be closed to the public, or access to them may be restricted if this is deemed to be of military importance or, for example, it is necessary to prevent the smuggling of persons or goods across national frontiers.

The State may also restrict the freedom of movement of certain individuals, for example, in order to secure their presence in criminal proceedings against them.

It is a moot point whether the freedom of movement is violated by a law closing all private land — including wilderness, forests, moors, lakes and mountains — to the public, so that people generally are confined to use only public roads, State parks, etc. Such restrictions can, however, hardly be justified as being "necessary in a democratic society", and in this modern time and age, it stands to reason that laws of trespass extending beyond the safeguarding of privacy, the needs of agriculture and other strictly legitimate needs ought to be struck down.

In the Nordic countries there is no doubt that members of the public have free access to the great outdoors — to forests, moors, islands, mountains — provided that one does not infringe upon the privacy of those who are living there.[18]

B. *Specialized Applications*

In some specialized human rights conventions, we find provisions directly bearing on the right to freedom of movement (and of residence) for the persons covered by the convention in question. Thus, article 26 of the Convention relating to the Status of Refugees (1951, Refugee Convention) makes it a duty for every Contracting State to accord to refugees lawfully in its territory the right to choose their place of residence and to move freely within its

---

[18] See also, e.g., Norwegian Act 1957-06-28, no. 16 on Outdoor Life [Lov om friluftslivet] §§ 2–4.

territory, subject (only) to any regulations generally applicable to aliens in the same circumstances.[19]

This provision was not deemed to preclude the imposition of a special restriction pertaining to refugees in article II(6) of the OAU Convention governing the Special Aspects of Refugee Problems in Africa (1969): "For reasons of security, countries of asylum shall, as far as possible, settle refugees at a reasonable distance from the frontier of their country of origin."[20]

The Convention relating to the Status of Stateless Persons (1954, Stateless Persons Convention) contains an article 26, identical to article 26 of the Refugee Convention, except that it substitutes 'stateless persons' for 'refugees'.

Articles 26 of both conventions must be read in the light of the provisions of article 31(2) of the Refugee Convention: Restrictions applied to the movements of asylum-seekers whose status has not been regularized, shall only be such as are necessary. This emphasis of necessity, as opposed to administrative convenience, etc., must clearly apply at least as much to refugees whose status has been regularized.

The International Convention on the Elimination of All Forms of Racial Discrimination (1965), obligates the States Parties to prohibit and to eliminate racial discrimination in all its forms and to guarantee the right of everyone — without distinction as to race, colour, or national or ethnic origin — to equality before the law. The first of the rights, whose enjoyment shall be particularly safeguarded, among those enumerated in article 5(d), is "the right to freedom of movement and residence within the border of the State."[21]

III. Freedom of Residence

While the right of freedom of residence is closely associated with the right to freedom of movement, the former possesses some

[19] This provision must be read in the light of article 31(2) of the same Convention, which stipulates that only restrictions which are necessary are permissible.

[20] Similar provisions are found in Latin American asylum conventions: Havana Convention, article 2(4); Caracas Convention on Territorial Asylum, article 9; and also in the OAU Convention, article II(6).

[21] This Convention merely forbids discrimination; see also Refugee Convention, article 26 and Stateless Persons Convention, article 26, mentioned above.

special aspects of its own.

The general rule is clear; any person lawfully within the territory of a given State may choose where he wants to live, whether that be in a city, a town or village, or in the countryside. He may also freely choose which city, town or village or which district he will make the centre of his life, without asking the authorities for any special permit.

As far as the metropolitan territory of the State is concerned, this right is clear. There are, of course, exceptions, similar to those applicable to the freedom of movement. One cannot demand to set up a house on other people's property, nor within a military security zone. Article 2(4) of the ECHR Protocol no. 4 (1963) may even be used to prohibit settlement in an area where this would conflict with the protection of the natural environment.

A special problem is whether the freedom of residence "within the borders of each State" extends to territories for which the State is internationally responsible, whether they are considered formally a 'part' of the State or not.

Under Danish legislation a Danish citizen is entitled to take up residence wherever he wishes within Denmark, Föroyar (the Faroe Islands) and Kalaallit Nunaat (Greenland),[22] the two latter territories being designated "self-governing communities of the Danish Realm."[23] The law recognizes the national, geographical, cultural and historical differences between the three parts of the Realm,[24] yet a Faroe Islander is legally simply a Danish citizen having his permanent residence in Föroyar,[25] and a Greenlander likewise a Danish citizen habitually residing in Kalaallit Nunaat.[26]

---

[22] There is no law restricting the freedom of movement and of residence for Danish citizens within the entire Danish Realm, consisting of three parts: Denmark proper, Föroyar and Kalaallit Nunaat; see also Danish Act 1948–03–23 no. 137 on Föroya Self-Government § 10(2); Karnovs Lovsamling (1986) 1:298.

[23] Danish Act 1948–03–23 no. 137 on Föroya Self-Government § 1 defines Föroyar as a self-governing community within the Danish Realm ("et selvstyrende folkesamfund i det danske rige"). Similarly, Danish Act 1978–11–29 no. 577 on Greenland Self-Government § 1 defines Greenland as a particular community within the Danish Realm ("et särlig folkesamfund inden for det danske rige").

[24] The preambles of Danish Acts 1948–03–23 no. 137 on Föroya Self-Government and 1978–11–29 no. 577 on Greenland Self-Government.

[25] Danish Act 1948–03–23 no. 137 on Föroya Self-Government § 10 (1)(2).

[26] Any Danish citizen having resided in Kalaallit Nunaat for six months has the right to vote in Greenland elections. Danish Act 1978-11-29 no. 577 on Greenland Self-Government § 2 (2); see also, Karnovs Lovsamling (1986) 1:300.

Under the Nordic passport and labour market agreements, citizens of the other Nordic States are also free to settle in Föroyar and Kalaallit Nunaat.[27]

This Nordic freedom to take up residence extends also to Åland, which is an autonomous community under the suzerainty of Finland. But under the Self-Government Act for Åland, there is a special 'hembygdsrätt' (the right to belong) for Ålanders, designed to preserve the Swedish character of the islands, by making it a privilege, sparingly granted, for others than those born Ålander to own real property and to vote in provincial elections.[28] It would seem that the provisions concerning the 'hembygdsrätt' do not infringe upon the right to freedom of residence as set forth in the UDHR and other relevant human rights instruments.[29] And should similar rules be adopted for Föroyar and Kalaallit Nunaat, they would undoubtedly be acceptable from a human rights point of view, particularly since they would tend to strengthen the right to self-determination of peoples, so prominently enshrined in both the CCPR and the International Covenant on Economic, Social and Cultural Rights (CESCR).[30]

IV. The Right to Leave

The right to leave any country, including one's own, is taken for granted in most countries of Western Europe and the Western hemisphere. Yet the provision was not adopted without controversy. The Berlin Wall stood as a symbol of an opposite attitude.

The right to leave is a right to depart permanently (emigration) or for a shorter or longer period, for whatever reason (with the exceptions outlined below).

It is a democratic freedom, which unlike many other human rights, is rarely mentioned in national constitutions. Statutory instruments may stipulate exceptions to the rule, but the rule itself is normally taken to be self-evident.

While Sweden is the only Nordic country having a constitutional

---

[27] See note 44 below.
[28] Finnish Act 1951–12–28 (1952:5) on Åland Self-Government §§ 3–5.
[29] The law does not restrict freedom of residence per se, but the right to own real property.
[30] Article 1 of both Covenants.

provision expressly recognizing the freedom of movement and the right to leave the country,[31] there is no doubt that this right is equally sacrosanct in the other Nordic countries.[32]

The Nordic countries filed no reservation on this point when they acceded to ECHR Protocol no. 4 or to the CCPR.

Moreover, the laws and regulations relating to passports take the right to leave (and to obtain a passport) as their point of departure. True, they authorize the denial or even the withdrawal of a passport in certain cases, but these restrictions do not go beyond the exceptions outlined above, in connection with the freedom of movement.[33]

Actually, even the denial of a passport does not necessarily prevent a person from lawfully leaving a country. In countries such as Denmark and Sweden, a person is not required to show a passport or other identity paper when departing from the country. Furthermore, citizens of the Nordic countries may cross intra-Nordic frontiers and settle in other Nordic countries without any such formality.

V. The Right to Return

In all of the Nordic countries, as in most Western countries, the right to return to one's own country is, on the whole, un-problematic.

There are, however, States that prohibit the entry of certain individuals, who formally possess the nationality (citizenship) of the State in question. This may apply to members of a dethroned royal family, former heads of State and their entourage, and other persons who are exiled or banished on political grounds. It is arguable that such special cases are covered by the exceptions in the respective human rights instruments.

A more difficult problem arises when a State refuses entry to larger groups and categories of persons possessing its nationality: for example, nationals born abroad or having lived out of the

[31] Swedish Constitution 1974 §§ 7–8. Add: Hofmann 1988, p. 223f.
[32] Hofmann 1988, pp. 189f., 214ff.
[33] Hofmann 1988, pp. 191f., 215f., 224ff.

Atle Grahl-Madsen

country for some time.[34] A national passport invalid for entry into the territory of the issuing State is surely an anomaly.[35]

There is also a problem if a State denationalizes some of its citizens — for example, on racial or political grounds — either on their leaving (voluntarily or not) their home country or while they reside abroad (for example as refugees). While a foreign State may reject such a person and demand that the country of origin take him back, this does not resolve the human rights dilemma.

The right of return does not imply that a person who has committed a crime (recognized as such in democratic societies) shall be freely entitled to return to his home country.

VI. The Right of Entry

It has been said that a right to enter a foreign country is the logical corollary of a right to leave one's own country. Yet only the latter is considered to be a human right, and perhaps rightfully so. The right to leave a territory has something to do with the person and his sense of freedom. The State does not own him. He shall not be forced to stay in a given territory against his wishes. Can he manage to find a country prepared to accept him, he ought to be free to go there. He may even wish to sail the Seven Seas, and the State should not, without valid reason, prevent him from doing so.

The question of entering a foreign country, however, relates primarily to a State's control over its territory. It is, of course, a pity for a person if he is barred from entering the country of his dreams. But this does not, after all, prevent him from going elsewhere.

Article 13 does not, as we have already observed, mention any right to enter any country other than 'one's own'. And such a right is not ordained in any other of the articles of the UDHR, nor expressly in any other international instrument, for that matter. Logic does not entitle us to infer such a right, since the right of States to control entry into their respective territories is a jealously

[34] The European Commission of Human Rights had to deal with the case of expelled Ugandan Indians with UK passports who were denied entry into the United Kingdom.
[35] This is the case with certain UK passports and certain passports issued in Taiwan; see also, the judgment of the German Federal Administrative Court in Young et al. v. Bundesrepublik Deutschland [I C 138.60] (1964-03-23), where it was held that the holder of such a passport could not be said to enjoy the full protection of the issuing government.

guarded privilege.

What comes close to a right of entry is the protection offered by the rule of 'non-refoulement', the prohibition of forcible return to a country where one would risk persecution, laid down in article 33 of the Refugee Convention.[36] But that article only applies if a person actually has set foot in the territory of a Contracting State.[37] A right of entry is implied in several provisions of the Hague Agreement relating to Refugee Seamen (1957).[38] Interesting are also the provisions of article II of the OAU Convention governing the Specific Aspects of Refugee Problems in Africa (1969).[39]

For non-refugees, a right of entry is implied in the Decision of the Council of the Organization for Economic Co-operation and Development on the Employment of Nationals of Member Countries (1953)[40] and in the European Convention on Establishment (1955).[41]

The right of entry gains another dimension by the Nordic agreements on a common travel area[42] and common labour market,[43] and by the corresponding provisions adopted within the framework of the European Communities.[44] By the provisions of those arrangements, citizens of each participating State have a right

[36] On the standing of the principle of non-refoulement outside the conventional context, see Grahl-Madsen 1985a, p. 38ff.

[37] See also, Grahl-Madsen 1972, p. 224.

[38] (1957–11–23) articles 2, 3, 6, etc. The personal scope of the Agreement was extended by Protocol to the Agreement relating to Refugee Seamen (1973–06–12).

[39] Article II(1) of the OAU Convention provides that Member States of the OAU "shall use their best endeavours consistent with their respective legislations to receive refugees...."

[40] Decision of the Council governing the Employment of Nationals of Member Countries (1953–10–30) [C(56)258], as amended, para. 1(a), provides that the authorities of any Member Country shall, as a rule, grant permits in respect of the employment in its territory, of suitable workers who are nationals of any other Member Country, as soon as it is established that suitable labour, national or foreign, forming part of its regular labour force, is not available within the country for the employment in question.

[41] (1955–12–13) articles 2 and 10; see also, Grahl-Madsen 1985b, p. 18f.

[42] Nordic Agreement on the Abolition of Passport Control at the Intra-Nordic Frontiers (1957–07–12) as amended.

[43] Nordic Agreement on a Common Labour Market (1954–05–22) as amended. See list of international instruments in Grahl-Madsen 1985b, p. 293ff.

[44] Rome Treaty on the Establishment of the European Economic Community (1957–03–25) article 48 and following ones.

to enter and settle in the territories of all participating States. In a sense, the home country has been extended. People from outside such a region, however, may well have greater difficulty in gaining access, especially for settlement.[45]

Addendum by the Editorial Committee

Since this article was written on the freedom of movement, of residence and the right to leave and return, developments have taken place in international law. Most important is that the question is presently on the agenda of the UN Sub-Commission on Prevention of Discrimination and Protection of Minorities.

A draft declaration on freedom and non-discrimination regarding the rights of everyone to leave any country, including his own, and to return to his country, has been drafted by Mr. C.L.C. Mubanga-Chipoya, Special Rapporteur to the Sub-Commission on the subject, in his Final Report to the UN Commission on Human Rights (the Commission).[46] The draft declaration has been transmitted to the UN Member States, specialized agencies and non-governmental organizations for comments. In 1989, the Sub-Commission decided to establish a sessional open-ended working group with a view to preparing a revised version of the draft declaration. The working group met for the first time in 1990 and will continue its work in 1991 with the aim, if possible, to submit a revised draft to the 1991 session of the Sub-Commission.[47]

---

[45] See also, Grahl-Madsen, 1987, p. 7ff.
[46] UN doc. E/CN.4/Sub.2/1988/35/add.1.
[47] Decision 1990/123. UN doc. E/CN.4/Sub.2/1990/59, p. 71.

References

Grahl-Madsen, Atle, *The Emergent International Law relating to Refugees: Past — Present — Future*, Bergen: University of Bergen, Institute for Public Law, 1985a.

Grahl-Madsen, Atle, *The Status of Refugees in International Law*, vol. ii, Leiden: A.W. Sijthoff, 1972.

Grahl-Madsen, Atle, *Norsk fremmedrett i Stöpeskjeen*, Bergen: Universitetsforlaget AS., 1985b.

Grahl-Madsen, Atle, *Stemming the Tide*, Bergen: 1987.

Hannum, Hurst, *The Right to Leave and Return in International Law and Practice*, Dordrecht: Martinus Nijhoff Publishers, 1987.

Hofmann, Rainer, *Die Ausreisefreiheit nach Völkerrecht und staatlichem Recht*, Berlin: 1988.

Inglés, José, *Study of Discrimination in Respect of the Right of Everyone to Leave Any Country, Including His Own, and to Return to His Country* (UN Sales no. 64.XIV.2 [1963]).

United Nations Documents: E/CN.4/Sub.2/1988/35/add.1.; E/CN.4/Sub.2/1990/59.

Vasak, Karel and Sidney Liskofsky (eds.), *The Right to Leave and to Return: Papers and Recommendations of the International Colloquium Held in Uppsala, Sweden, 19–21 June 1972*.

Article 14[*]

Morten Kjærum

Denmark

1. Everyone has the right to seek and to enjoy in other countries asylum from persecution.
2. This right may not be invoked in the case of prosecutions genuinely arising from non-political crimes or from acts contrary to the purposes and principles of the United Nations.

I. Introduction

Article 14 of the Universal Declaration of Human Rights (UDHR) marks the end of the first phase and the beginning of the second phase in the refugee policy of the 20th century.

Heinrich Böll, the German author, has declared that the 20th century will be primarily remembered as the century of the refugee: the century when refugees manifested themselves and became part of the daily consciousness of the common citizen of the world. Refugees became people for whose benefit one raised funds, people in large camps one saw on television and people who became neighbours and friends.

At the beginning of the century refugees were simply persons who, for one reason or another, had been forced to leave their country of origin and had thereby lost the protection afforded to a citizen in a specific country. It was up to them to make their way to a country which would tolerate their presence.

After a certain time, they could hope to obtain some kind of legal status in the country in question: for example, citizenship. Many of these refugee groups of the past still exist in the third and fourth generation, their legal status not yet clarified. The Kurdish refugees

---

[*] Following the limited space for this article focus has been concentrated on article 14.1.

in Lebanon can be mentioned as just one example.

In the period between the 1920s and the end of World War II, the international community dealt with the refugee situation on an ad hoc basis. In 1921, under the League of Nations, a 'High Commissioner on behalf of the League in connection with the problems of the Russian refugees in Europe' was appointed as efforts were made to give those particular refugees some legal status in the international order. The High Commissioner was Doctor Fridthjof Nansen. In 1924 the mandate of the High Commissioner was extended to Armenian refugees and in 1929 to 'other categories of refugees' including Assyrians, Assyro Chaldeans, Kurdish Syrian and Turkish refugees. In 1933 a High Commissioner was appointed to assist persons fleeing Nazi Germany. During World War II, the UN Relief and Rehabilitation Administration (UNRRA) was set up to assist and eventually repatriate those displaced during the war, and in 1946 the International Refugee Organization (IRO) was created.

In 1948, profoundly influenced by the atrocities of World War II, a number of States agreed to formulate a series of declarations on how people should behave towards each other, how power should be administered, and on what the relationship is between the values of right and wrong. These declarations were collected in the UDHR. Having chosen to condemn the exercise of certain kinds of power by formulating the UDHR, it followed logically that the international community should also request countries to afford protection to the individuals who are subject to such human rights violations. Therefore "the right to seek and enjoy asylum from persecution" became human right number 14.

The next step came in 1949 when the UN General Assembly established the office of the UN High Commissioner for Refugees (UNHCR) with the specific functions of providing international protection and of seeking permanent solutions for refugees.

The Convention relating to the Status of Refugees of 1951, (Refugee Convention) which gave substance to article 14, meant that a general refugee definition was introduced, and at the same time certain standards for the treatment of refugees by States were formulated. A refugee was defined as a person who "...owing to well-founded fear of being persecuted for reasons of race, religion, nationality, membership of a particular social group or political opinion, is outside the country of his nationality and is unable, or owing to such fear, is unwilling to avail himself of the protection of that country; or who, not having a nationality and being outside the country of his former habitual residence as a result of such events, is unable or, owing to such fear, is unwilling to return to it." In all, 104 States are now parties to one or both of these instruments.

In the postwar era the international community thus decided to define the refugee problem as a global concern, towards which the international community has a duty to find the most appropriate solution on a case by case basis without further negotiation or treaties.

International refugee work was thus finally established in the years immediately after World War II as a by-product of human rights work.

II. Legal Protection of Refugees

Refugees constitute clear evidence that human rights are not observed in all countries. Every time a person is persecuted for reasons of race, nationality, membership of a particular social group or political opinion, several civil and political rights are violated. Left-wing refugees from Chile, Christian refugees from Iran and Kurdish refugees from Iraq could be mentioned as examples; all are clearly persecuted because of attitudes, opinions or because of their nationality.

The establishment of the UNHCR meant that for the first time there was an entity to which refugees could apply concerning individual cases or general problems. But the legal status of refugees was not immediately changed through the post-war conventions or proclamations in article 14 of the UDHR.

The original draft of article 14 (originally article 12) gave refugees the right "to seek and be granted in other countries asylum from persecution." This draft thus gave the individual refugee the right to obtain asylum. The draft met with opposition and was later changed to its present wording "to seek and enjoy in other countries asylum from persecution" on the grounds that the grant of asylum is a unilateral act by the protecting State and a normal prerogative of State sovereignty.

The Refugee Convention of 1951 defines the refugee as a person unable or unwilling to return to the country of his former habitual residence owing to well-founded fear of being persecuted for reasons of race, religion, nationality, membership of a particular social group or political opinion. Thus, the Convention does not discuss the right to be granted asylum but presupposes in article 33 that individual countries will offer protection to persons who fall within the definition.

Since then, efforts have been made to give refugees a clear legal right to asylum both in the Declaration on Territorial Asylum and, for example, in the European Convention on Human Rights (ECHR). But in both cases these efforts were met with opposition and were consequently given up. The existing regulations, therefore, only give States the right to grant asylum without this being regarded as an unfriendly act towards the refugees' country of origin.[1]

Although international legislation does not recognize the individual's right to asylum, States are not free to act as they please because the principle of non-refoulement contained in article 33 of the Refugee Convention and the Declaration on Territorial Asylum limits the right to return people.

The non-refoulement article forbids a State to expel or return ('refouler') a refugee to the frontiers of territories where his or her life or freedom is threatened on account of his or her race, religion, nationality, membership of a particular social group or political opinion (Refugee Convention article 1 A) or where the refugee is not protected against return to such a country.

In effect, the principle of non-refoulement has now assumed the character of an international rule of law.[2] If States do not wish to give a refugee protection, they must send the person to another country where (s)he is not in danger of persecution on the grounds defined in the Convention, or to a country from which (s)he will not risk being sent to such a country. Although States have been unwilling to pledge themselves in international conventions to the individual's right to asylum, it is a fact that several countries in their constitutions or national legislation recognize this right.[3] Likewise, through the choice of procedures with, for instance, the opportunity to appeal to independent courts or boards of appeal, the procedure can be removed from the political process and transformed into an assessment of whether an individual fulfils the legal definition, whereby the right to asylum can truly be said to be recognized in several countries.[4]

---

[1] This is stressed in for example resolution 2312 (XXII) adopted in 1967 by the UN General Assembly — The Declaration on Territorial Asylum.

[2] Goodwin-Gill 1983, p. 97ff and 122f.

[3] Countries like The Federal Republic of Germany, Denmark and France can be mentioned.

[4] Weh 1987, p. 49.

III. Visa Restrictions and Carrier Liability[5]

Several European countries have in recent years tried to control the flow of refugees by means of a visa policy. A number of States now require that citizens from countries from which many refugees originate be in possession of a visa to enter the country of destination.

In order to make it possible for this system to function in the case of a person seeking protection in another country, six conditions must be fulfilled:[6]

1. The persecuted person must hold a valid and genuine passport or be able to obtain such from the authorities in the home country.
2. The country to which (s)he wishes to flee must have diplomatic representation in the country in question.
3. (S)he must be able to approach this representation freely and without danger.
4. (S)he must be able to wait for what could be a considerable time for the visa application to be considered in the country to which (s)he wishes to flee.
5. The authorities in the receiving country must be willing to give a visa to a person who is being persecuted in the country in question.
6. The authorities in the receiving country must be willing to accept that the applicant is not a refugee, being a resident of his home country at the moment of application, and thereby falling outside the refugee definition in the 1951 Convention.

In the majority of cases none — or only a few — of these conditions will be fulfilled. Otherwise States would have no need to impose visa restrictions.

In order to make sure that persons who are in need of protection do not try against all odds to reach some of these States by aeroplane, or other means of transportation, the carriers are threatened with fines if they carry passengers without adequate travel documents. In this way it is left to, for example, the airline companies to refuse to transport passengers who do not hold adequate travel documents and even to prevent them from boarding

---

[5] *The Role of Airline Companies in the Asylum Procedure*, The Danish Refugee Council, Copenhagen, 1988. Feller 1989. Kjærum 1990.
[6] Swart 1987, p. 95.

the plane.

Usually the refugees' only possibility will then be to try to go illegally to a neighbouring country and consider the situation from there. By far the majority of the world's refugees over the years have utilized this possibility without having been forced to do it by various restrictions. These refugees have thus found protection in the immediate vicinity of their own country, which is often the best solution — the flight should be as short as possible.

Unfortunately, however, there is a small group of refugees who for political or other reasons has no opportunity to obtain protection in a neighbouring country. This is true, for instance, for the Iranian and Iraqi refugees in the 1980s.

This comparatively small group has looked, for example, towards Western Europe for protection and they have usually found it. Visa restrictions and sanctions against airline companies are aimed at this unprotected group — other refugees rarely leave the country where they have already found protection.

In some instances neighbouring countries to 'refugee-producing' countries cannot, for political or other reasons, give protection to a number of refugees. The presence of the refugees are, though, normally accepted for transit — *en route* to a country where they can find durable protection until the situation in their home country improves.

But sanctions against carriers and visa restrictions prevent the refugees in question from moving on and the attitude in the transit countries is sure to deteriorate gradually as the number of refugees grows.

A typical precaution is to tighten up the border control so as to deny admission to persons without valid passports and often to aliens lacking adequate means. In this way persons without sufficient means are, to a large extent, prevented from leaving their home countries and reaching safety from their persecutors.

In some cases the possibilities of finding a country offering refuge determine whether persecution will merely lead to the creation of refugees or to another outcome, for example, mass murder which — put simply — can be called an extreme kind of persecution without any refugee-producing effect. The situation of European Jews in the Nazi era can be mentioned as an example of the horrors that may arise from the lack of possibilities of finding protection in another country.[7]

---

[7] Zolberg 1986, p. 154.

IV. Rejection at the Border

In spite of these barriers, a few refugees succeed in reaching countries in Europe, where they seek asylum. In order to close loopholes, Denmark became the first country in Europe to introduce the concept: return to a so-called 'safe country'.

This model of rejection is based upon the fact that a number of countries which have ratified the Convention are generally considered 'safe countries'. When an asylum seeker arrives, for example, at Kastrup airport in Copenhagen, the border authorities only look at the alien's travelling route which they compare with their list of countries which they have had 'cleared', and decide whether it is possible to return the alien. At no time do the authorities examine the alien's reasons for not seeking asylum in the country where (s)he stayed before arriving in Denmark. Nor do they examine whether the alien has close links with Denmark, for instance relatives. On the basis of this model, a 24-hour stay in a so-called 'safe country' will often be enough to make this country the country of first asylum in spite of the asylum seeker's close relationship to Denmark, for example, the presence of a sister or a brother.[8] This is called the authorization principle. One out of many examples will be mentioned:

An Iranian woman with a minor child arrived at Kastrup airport where she asked for asylum. She did not hold passport or visa. She and her husband had decided to spend the money they had got from the husband's political friends to get her and the child out of Turkey where they were by no means in safety because of their political activities in Iran. They chose Denmark because she had a brother of her own age living here.

En route from Turkey (which is not considered a safe country) she had had a transitory stay in Barcelona and the Danish authorities decided to return her to Barcelona. Before she was returned, the Spanish authorities informed the Danish authorities that they would not accept that she had closer links with Spain. She had neither relatives living there, nor did she want to stay in that country. The Danish authorities stuck to their decision.

On arriving in Spain, she was returned to Turkey. It was a well known phenomenon that Iranians who arrived at the airport at Istanbul without a passport are often sent on to Teheran. This was about to

---

[8] Castellani 1987, p. 3ff.

happen in this case, and only co-operation between UNHCR and the Danish Refugee Council prevented at the very last moment her refoulement. After some time the Spanish authorities — for humanitarian reasons — admitted the woman and the child, after they had travelled from airport to airport for 10 days. Immediately upon arrival the woman applied for asylum in Denmark via the Danish embassy in Madrid.

The authorization principle is repeated in the European Convention on Asylum — also called the Dublin Convention — which was signed by the 12 European Community countries in June 1990. The country in which the asylum seeker first arrives is to be responsible for examining the case, offering the person protection if (s)he needs it or — if not — seeing to it that the person is removed from the territory. A decision made in one of the 12 countries is binding upon the other countries.

On entering the territory, the asylum seeker knows that (s)he has but one chance and therefore (s)he will try from the very start to choose the country which is thought to be the most liberal in the eligibility procedure. Each country will therefore be encouraged to be a little more restrictive in its reception of refugees than its neighbours. This may result in a more unequal distribution than is now the case in Europe, where refugees disperse according to a series of criteria: language; relationships or other links; culture; climate; etc.

There are no doubts that some of the problems in Europe in the 1980s stemmed from the lack of clarity regarding who should be responsible for examining an asylum request. But the authorization principle may result in an increase in the downward spiral which is seen in the European refugee policy at the threshold to the 1990s.[9]

V. European Asylum Policy and Human Rights

The complicated systems mentioned above which are now being built up in various Western countries seem inconsistent in several areas with human rights and the conventions relating to them.

The right to seek asylum, established in article 14 of the UDHR, which is regarded as part of customary international law, is for some refugees suspended when they are being prevented from reaching the country where they can find durable protection. The

---

[9] Christensen and Kjærum, 1990.

right to seek asylum has, in fact, one of its bases in the 'right of emigration'.[10] In article 13(2) of the UDHR, article 12(2) of the International Covenant on Civil and Political Rights (CCPR) and Protocol no. 4 to the ECHR, the right to leave any country, including one's own, is characterized as a fundamental right, and in the last two as even having a binding nature. This right to leave one's country is a right which the countries of Western Europe have, over the years, often emphasized, especially with regard to Eastern European countries. Now the very same countries are instrumental in making it extremely difficult for persons who risk persecution to escape and find protection.

As mentioned above, no right to obtain asylum exists in international legislation, but in spite of this the right is a reality in the national legislation of several countries, or becomes a reality through the eligibility procedure offered to asylum seekers arriving in the country. These rights, contained in national legislation, are likewise suspended when the decision often takes place on the administrative level, beyond parliamentary control, by the introduction of new visa regulations. By requiring a refugee to obtain proper travel documentation before embarking on a journey to escape, governments in fact ignore the very problems which give rise to the need for refugee protection and, in effect, deny the possibility of asylum to some refugees.[11]

In a case concerning sanctions against an airline company (Lufthansa), the administrative court in Frankfurt, in a sentence from October 1987 states:

> The opinion of the respondent that the claim to asylum under art. 16 of the Constitution arises only at the moment of entering the territory of the Federal Republic of Germany, is in conformity with the jurisprudence of the Federal Administrative Court, according to which the Constitution understands as asylum the protection granted to a person who has fled persecution and reached a territory to which the pursuers have no access, and the right to asylum primarily contains a claim to protection through non-refoulement. The claim to asylum thus presupposes that protection has been sought in the country of asylum, i.e. the refugee must at least have reached its frontier. *The territorial limitation of this constitutional stipulation does not, however, permit the legislator to eliminate access to this right by administrative measures.*

[10] Grahl-Madsen 1972, p. 104ff.
[11] Feller 1988, p. 7.

In the *travaux préparatoires* to the Swedish Aliens Act of 1989, it is said that "it is difficult to establish a set of sanctions which will only curb the misusers of the right to seek asylum and not at the same time hinder people in need of protection the possibility of obtaining it" (author's translation). With this reasoning, the Swedish Government decided not to introduce sanctions on carriers.

When countries use the so-called 'safe country' or authorization principle without previous agreements with the receiving countries they run the risk that the person will be sent on to his/her country of origin without having had his/her asylum application ever tried by a competent authority. One can ask whether the first State is in conflict with the non-refoulement clause.

Pursuant to article 33, States shall not in 'any manner whatsoever' refoule a refugee. As already mentioned, the non-refoulement clause is part of customary international law. The rejection does not explicitly mean that the individual States are immediately guilty of refoulement, but instead that it may easily happen as a result of a chain of events. Each country — fully aware of the consequences of its action — may shelter behind other countries in the chain and the last country, which is typically unlikely to have a very well developed asylum procedure, will often declare that the person in question is by no means a refugee. This is how the responsibility fades away in the mist.

Pursuant to article 31 of the Vienna Convention on the Law of Treaties: "A treaty shall be interpreted in good faith in accordance with the ordinary meaning to be given to the terms of the treaty in their context and in the light of its object and purpose."

Further, article 26 states that "Every treaty in force is binding upon the Parties to it and must be performed by them in good faith."

Seen in the light of the Vienna Convention, it seems clear that countries are guilty of refoulement in cases where a refugee against his or her will is denied entry at the border, this denial of entry being repeated down through the chain causing the asylum seeker to end up in the country of origin without, at any moment, having had the opportunity of having his or her case heard by a competent authority.[12]

The country in which the alien intended to seek asylum,[13] and

---

[12] Note on International Protection, submitted by the High Commissioner, 38th session, 1987, p. 7f.

[13] UNHCR, Executive Committee 1979, no. 15 (xxx)h(iii).

which by denying entry starts the chain reaction, is ethically, morally and legally responsible for the alien in question until (s)he has obtained protection somewhere else. If the denial eventually results in the asylum seeker ending up in the home country, the country that started the chain reaction shares the responsibility together with the last country in the chain.

VI. Back to Humanitarian Principles in Asylum Law

It is difficult to understand how several European countries with a traditionally liberal attitude towards refugees can introduce the restrictive legislation described above: legislation which either leads to refugees being prevented from finding protection anywhere at all or pushes the burden onto other countries with much more limited resources with which to cope with the task. Seen against the background of the Vienna Convention, these countries must be deemed to be in conflict with both the intention and the aim of article 14 of the UDHR, article 33 of the Refugee Convention and customary international law.

At present, we are in a trough of the waves of international refugee work which began in the years after World War II. Nevertheless, seen in a wider historical perspective, the protection of refugees has gained ground during the last 40–50 years. It has gradually developed from being a purely national concern of the States bordering on refugee-producing States to something the international community has reacted to from case to case; now we have reached a general acceptance of the fact that refugees are a global responsibility, 104 States having ratified the 1951 Refugee Convention and/or the Protocol of 1967. It requires an effort, however, to get out of this trough.

Through the European Consultation on Refugees and Exiles (ECRE), non-governmental organization in Europe have proposed a comprehensive refugee policy for Europe in the document *A Refugee Policy for Europe*. In this document the elements of regional solution, resettlement in Europe, spontaneous arrivals, return to the country of first arrival, etc., are linked together in a comprehensive refugee policy where the individual elements are balanced against each other. These ideas should be developed and others should be formulated in the near future. There is not one and only one refugee policy — there are many. The common objectives, however, must be to uphold the principle of asylum and to ensure that countries fulfil their obligations in pursuance of the Refugee

Convention, the 1967 Protocol, and in accordance with other fundamental principles of international law, so that "Everyone has the right to seek and enjoy in other countries asylum from persecution."

References

Castellani, Francesco, *Expulsion of Asylum Seekers from Denmark, Current Asylum Policy and Humanitarian Principles*, Copenhagen: Danish Refugee Council, 1987.

Christensen, Arne Piel and Morten Kjærum, "Refugees and Our Role in the European House", *International Journal of Refugee Law*, vol. 2, 1990.

Danish Refugee Council, *The Role of Airline Companies in the Asylum Procedure*, Copenhagen: The Danish Refugee Council, 1988.

Feller, Erika, "Carrier Sanctions and International Law", *International Journal of Refugee Law*, vol. 1, 1989.

Feller, Erika, "Transport Carriers and Refugee Protection", in *The Role of Airline Companies in the Asylum Procedure*, Copenhagen: Danish Refugee Council, September 1988.

Goodwin-Gill, Guy, *The Refugee in International Law*, Oxford: Oxford University Press, 1983.

Grahl-Madsen, Atle, *The Status of Refugees in International Law*, Leiden: A.W. Sijthoff, 1972.

Kjærum, Morten, *Visumpolitik og luftfartsselskaber, Asyl i Norden*, Copenhagen: Danish Refugee Council, 1990.

Swart, A., *The Law of Asylum and Refugees: Present Tendencies and Future Perspectives*, Council of Europe, 1987, p. 95.

Weh, L., *The Law of Asylum and Refugees: Present Tendencies and Future Perspectives*, Council of Europe, 1987, p. 49.

Zolberg, Aristide R., "International Factors in the Formation of Refugee Movements", *International Migration Review* 20, no. 74, 1986.

Article 15

Gunnar G. Schram

Iceland

1. Everyone has the right to a nationality.
2. No one shall be arbitrarily deprived of his nationality nor denied the right to change his nationality.

I. Introduction

By the inclusion of article 15 in the Universal Declaration of Human Rights (UDHR) the framers of the Declaration emphasized the human rights aspect of nationality. Until then this concept had never received this degree of recognition. Article 15 thus constitutes a remarkable development in international human rights law, providing a foundation upon which an elaborate legal structure has since been built. The UDHR has indeed proved to be the catalyst for much of the new international law of human rights which has fundamentally changed the theory and practice of the law of nations during the last four decades.

The adoption of the UDHR was recognized as a great achievement, and from the beginning it took on a moral and political authority not possessed by any other contemporary international instrument with the exception of the UN Charter itself. It remains, as this volume bears testimony to, a living document still inspiring the efforts of the community of nations to outlaw injustice and foster the respect for fundamental rights and freedoms in a still inequitable world.

II. Constituent Elements of the Concept of Nationality

Nationality is a juridical concept possessing a dual character. It is regulated by rules of both municipal and international law as it concerns the rights and duties of both individuals and the State. The concept of nationality has been defined as the most frequent and sometimes only link between an individual and a State, ensuring that effect be given to that individual's rights and obligations under international law.[1]

In the Nottebohm case, the International Court of Justice defined nationality as follows:

> According to the practice of States, to arbitral and judicial decisions and to the opinions of writers, nationality is a legal bond having as its basis a social fact of attachment, a genuine connection of existence, interests and sentiments, together with the existence of reciprocal rights and duties.[2]

It is generally recognized that most of the rules on nationality fall within the scope of domestic jurisdiction and are therefore within the domain of municipal law. This can lead to difficulties in legal interpretation as the different rules on nationality found in the laws of various States can by no means be described as uniform. This lack of uniformity has led to problems relating, *inter alia*, to the original acquisition of nationality, multiple nationality and statelessness.

As Weis has pointed out, nationality as a term of municipal law is defined by municipal law. The meaning of the term and its content, i.e., the rights and duties which it confers, depend on the municipal law — as a rule the constitutional law — of the State concerned.[3] There is, therefore, not *one* definition of nationality as a conception of municipal law, but as many definitions as there are States, unless one wishes to choose a general definition such as "nationality denotes a specific relationship between individual and State conferring mutual rights and duties...."

While there is not *one* definition of nationality as a concept of municipal law, but as many definitions as there are States, the principle of nationality is first and foremost a matter of municipal law in each State. The concept has, nonetheless, important implications in international law. Each State, for example, is entitled to protect its subjects abroad. It is also generally accepted that the concept of nationality includes the right to settle and to reside in the State of nationality and the duty of that State to grant such rights of residence to its nationals. Finally, a State has a

[1] Starke 1977, p. 367.
[2] I.C.J. Reports 1955, p. 23.
[3] Weis 1956, p. 31.

general right to refuse to extradite its own nationals to another State requesting surrender.

III. Nationality in Municipal and International Law

When analysing the legal force and binding effect of article 15 of the UDHR in international law today, it is pertinent to ask whether States have the right to deprive their citizens of their nationality. As the regulation of nationality falls within the domestic jurisdiction of each State, it has been generally accepted that international law does not prevent States from regulating, through their own law, the acquisition or loss of nationality. However, States are not considered to have unbounded freedom in their regulation of nationality as illustrated by article 1 of the Convention on Certain Questions relating to the Conflict of Nationality Laws, signed in the Hague on 12 April 1930,[4] which provides:

> It is for each State to determine under its own laws who are its nationals. This law shall be recognised by other States in so far as it is consistent with international conventions, international custom, and the principles of law generally recognised with regard to nationality.

It can be said that this treaty provision, although only binding on parties, contains what is considered to be the current prevailing rule of customary international law. The crucial question is then whether, and to what extent, there exist such generally recognized principles of law or commonly accepted provisions of international conventions which impose limitations on the sovereign right of a State to determine the circumstances resulting in the loss of nationality.

Before World War II there were a significant number of cases where States denationalized a great number of their nationals for political reasons.[5] For example, the Soviet Union denationalized an estimated two million persons who had opposed the Bolshevik regime in 1924 and 1925 (The Union Citizenship Law of 13 November 1925, no. 581). Denationalization on racial grounds was put into effect by Germany in 1941 under the Reich Citizenship Law and by Italy in 1938 (Decree no. 1728 of 17 December).

Various endeavours were made before the war to formulate rules

---

[4] LNTS, vol. 179, p. 89.
[5] See, e.g., Hofmann 1985, pp. 128–130.

prohibiting denationalization, but these had scant results. At the International Conference for the Codification of International Law in the Hague in 1930, the parties failed to agree upon the drafting of any provisions concerning deprivation of nationality in international law that might have been included in the Convention or any of the three Protocols attached to it.[6]

At the beginning of the postwar period, States were still deemed to have the unrestricted right to deprive their nationals of their nationality without restrictions in international law. Weis, writing in 1956, gives expression to this in the following terms:[7]

> Neither the view that denationalization is inconsistent with international law because it creates statelessness nor the view that it encroaches upon the rights of the individual finds support in the rules of international law. Statelessness is not inadmissible under international law although it may be considered undesirable.

Mass denationalization of ethnic minorities took place on a very large scale immediately after the war. Acts of denationalization by Czechoslovakia affected nationals of German and Hungarian origin (Presidential Decree of 2 August 1945), while those by Poland (Law of 6 May 1945) and Yugoslavia (Law of 1 July 1948) affected nationals of German origin.

IV. Postwar Developments

Considering traditional legal theory on nationality and denationalization and the events relating to World War II, we can appreciate the great weight and impetus placed upon the creation of an entirely new framework of human rights in the world, in this instance a new approach to the question of nationality. In the light of historical developments many felt that each State should no longer be entitled to determine freely, and arbitrarily, the conditions of its nationality but that such a right should be restricted by rules of international law. Thus, individual denationalization ought only be allowed on the simultaneous acquisition of another nationality, thereby avoiding statelessness. Mass denationalization was deemed altogether contrary to the international obligations of States. In addition, States should generally avoid denationalization, which

[6] LNTS, vol. 179, p. 89.
[7] Hofmann 1985, p. 128.

constitutes an abuse of rights casting an illegal burden on the State of residence.[8]

These aims and aspirations had to be weighed against the *de lege lata* situation: that the right of a State to make rules governing the loss of its nationality was in principle not restricted by international law, unless that State had by treaty undertaken specific obligations imposing such restrictions.

The rationale behind the inclusion of article 15 in the UDHR was to effect a change in the legal parameters governing this situation. In the wording of article 15: "1. Everyone has the right to a nationality. 2. No one shall be arbitrarily deprived of his nationality nor denied the right to change his nationality."

Forty years ago, when the UN General Assembly adopted the UDHR, these provisions did not have a legally binding effect. They represented, however, the views of States as to the direction in which the new law of human rights should develop. In their own right they stood for the aims and aspirations of the international community in this important field of international law. No other document except for the Charter itself has so profoundly influenced legal relationships between nations in human rights. Since 1948, article 15 has been the basis for a number of international instruments seeking to give binding legal force to the visionary pronouncements of its basic text.

V. International Conventions Concerning Nationality

Since 1948, the United Nations has endeavoured to alleviate the plight of stateless persons. It has done this first by studying the problem and its implications, then by adopting interim measures to protect specified categories of stateless persons, and finally by taking broader action, including the promulgation of international conventions, to ensure everyone the right to a nationality.[9]

As early as 1948, by resolution 116 D (VI) the UN Economic and Social Council (ECOSOC) requested that the Secretary-General undertake two studies on the subject of statelessness. One was a study of the existing situation in regard to the protection of stateless persons; the other was a study of national legislation and international agreements and conventions relevant to statelessness.

---

[8] Hofmann 1985, pp. 129–130.
[9] UN Action in the Field of Human Rights, 1983, p. 193.

Accordingly, the Secretary-General prepared a study in two parts: improvement of the status of stateless persons; and elimination of statelessness. With a view towards eliminating the sources of statelessness, the Secretary-General suggested that two principles be universally recognized and applied; first, every child must receive a nationality at birth, and second, no person throughout his life should lose his nationality until he has acquired a new one. To reduce the number of cases of statelessness, he suggested that the governments of Member States be invited to bring their legislation into conformity with a series of principles which he presented in draft form.

A. Convention on the Reduction of Statelessness

At the request of the ECOSOC, the International Law Commission prepared in 1953 and 1954 a draft Convention on the reduction of statelessness. A UN Conference of Plenipotentiaries met to discuss the subject in 1959 and reconvened in 1961. On 30 August 1961, the Conference adopted the Convention on the Reduction of Statelessness, which entered into force on 13 December 1975.

This Convention represented a major achievement in the attempt to bring to fruition the principles of article 15 of the UDHR. It contains a number of provisions preventing statelessness resulting from loss of nationality as a consequence of any change in the personal status of a person.

Article 8 of the Convention refers to the same subject matter as paragraph 1 of article 15 of the UDHR, and in this context it is the key article of the Convention. There the following is prescribed:

A Contracting State shall not deprive a person of his nationality if such deprivation would render him stateless.

From this fundamental rule certain exceptions are recognized. A person may be deprived of his nationality if it has been obtained by misrepresentation or fraud. Furthermore, the State may retain the right to deprive a person of his nationality on the following grounds, included in its national law at that time: that, inconsistently with his duty of loyalty to the Contracting State, the person:

1.   Has, in disregard of an express prohibition by the Contracting State rendered or continued to render services to, or received or continued to receive emoluments from, another State; or

2. Has conducted himself in a manner seriously prejudicial to the vital interests of the State.

Notwithstanding these exceptions, article 8 gives effect to principles expressed in the second paragraph of article 15. Article 9 of the Convention is also of special importance here since it stipulates that a State may not deprive any person or group of persons of their nationality on racial, ethnic, religious or political grounds.

Insofar as it can be said that non-discrimination on grounds of race or religion constitutes a principle of international law, the article is in conformity with such a principle, thus making such a ban valid even upon non-contracting States and limiting the power of States to withdraw nationality. Studies of recent State practice show that while States in fact rarely resort to denationalization on racial or religious ground, denationalization for political reasons seems still to be relatively common. The legislation of the former German Democratic Republic withdrawing nationality from persons having illegally left the country is one example.[10] Other States still practise denationalization of political dissidents, for example, the Soviet Union and other East European and Latin American countries.

Apart from articles 8 and 9, the essential provisions of the Convention are as follows. A contracting State shall grant its nationality to a person born in its territory who would otherwise be stateless. It may, however, make the granting of this nationality subject to certain conditions. A child born in wedlock in the territory of a contracting State, whose mother has the nationality of that State, shall acquire at birth that nationality if it otherwise would be stateless. A foundling found in the territory of a contracting State shall, in the absence of proof to the contrary, be considered to have been born within that territory, of parents possessing the nationality of the State.

Subject to certain conditions, a contracting State shall grant its nationality to a person not born in the territory of a contracting State who would otherwise be stateless, if the nationality of one of his parents at the time of the person's birth was that of the State.

If the law of a contracting State prescribes loss of nationality as a consequence of any change in the personal status of a person such as marriage, termination of marriage, legitimization, recognition or

---

[10] Hofmann 1985, pp. 129–130.

adoption, such loss shall be conditional upon possession or acquisition of another nationality.

It is decided in article 11 of the Convention that the member States shall, after a minimum number of ratifications, establish a body to which a person claiming the benefit of the Convention may apply for the examination of his claim and for assistance in presenting it to the appropriate authority. The UN General Assembly by Resolution 3274 (XXIX) of 10 December 1974, requested the Office of the High Commissioner for Refugees to undertake this function after the convention would come into force. In a later resolution, 31/36 of 30 November 1976, the Assembly requested that the High Commissioner continue to perform these functions.

B. Convention relating to the Status of Stateless Persons

In resolution 629 (VII) of 6 November 1952, the General Assembly, expressing the desire to improve the situation of stateless persons as soon as possible, requested that ECOSOC study the text of the draft protocol prepared by ECOSOC's Ad Hoc Committee on Statelessness and Related Problems and take whatever action seemed useful, in order that a text might be prepared for signature after the Convention relating to the Status of Refugees had entered into force.

After the latter Convention entered into force on 22 April 1954, the Council in resolution 526 A(XVII) of 26 April 1954 decided that a Conference of Plenipotentiaries be convened to revise, in the light of the provisions of the Convention relating to the Status of Refugees and of the observations made by governments, the draft Protocol, and to open it for signature.

The Conference, which met at the UN Headquarters in New York 13–23 September 1954, decided to prepare a separate convention dealing with the status of stateless persons rather than a protocol to the Convention relating to the Status of Refugees. The Convention relating to the Status of Stateless Persons was adopted on 28 September 1954.[11]

The Convention relating to the Status of Stateless Persons which entered into force on 6 June 1960, applies to "a person who is not considered as a national by any State under the operation of its

[11] UNTS, vol. 360, p. 117.

law." With regard to most matters, the treatment accorded to stateless persons under the Convention is the same as that accorded to refugees under the Convention relating to the Status of Refugees.

As regards certain rights, however, the Convention relating to the Status of Stateless Persons places such persons in a position less favourable than that provided for refugees. For example, with regard to the right to wage-earning employment and the right of association, stateless persons do not enjoy most favoured nation treatment but are entitled to treatment not less favourable than that accorded to aliens.

VI. Other UN Instruments

A. Convention on the Elimination of All Forms of Discrimination against Women

The General Assembly, by resolution 3521 (XXX) of 15 December 1975, requested that the Commission on the Status of Women complete, in 1976, the elaboration of the draft Convention on the Elimination of Discrimination against Women, which had been on the Commission's agenda since 1970. The adoption of such a convention had been envisaged in the Programme for the United Nations Decade for Women prepared by the World Conference of the International Women's Year.

After receiving the draft from ECOSOC, the General Assembly, by resolution 34/180 of 18 December 1979, adopted the Convention on the Elimination of All Forms of Discrimination against Women, and expressed the hope that the Convention would be signed and ratified or acceded to without delay and would thus come into force at an early date.

Article 9 of the Convention deals with the question of nationality. The States Parties undertake to grant men and women equal rights to acquire, change or retain their nationality. They shall ensure in particular that neither marriage to an alien or change of nationality by a husband during marriage shall automatically change the nationality of a wife, render her stateless or force upon her the nationality of the husband.

B. Convention on the Nationality of Married Women

The UN Commission on the Status of Women decided as early as

1948 to study the problems arising from the nationality of married women, especially the many and varied instances of discrimination against women that resulted from conflicts in nationality laws.

At the request of ECOSOC, the Secretary-General of the United Nations prepared both a report on the legal status and treatment of women and one on the existing treaties and conventions in the field of nationality. On the basis of this documentation, the Commission on the Status of Women, at its third session in 1949, expressed the view that a convention on the nationality of married women should be prepared as promptly as possible, assuring equality with men in the exercise of this right, and especially preventing them from becoming stateless or otherwise suffering hardships arising out of conflicts in laws. This view was endorsed by the ECOSOC in resolution 242 (IX) of 1 August 1949.

In 1955 the Commission on the Status of Women completed the preparation of a draft Convention on the Nationality of Married Women and forwarded it to the Council which in turn transmitted it to the General Assembly for final approval. The Convention on the Nationality of Married Women was adopted by the General Assembly and opened for signature and ratification in resolution 1040 (XI) of 29 January 1957.

This Convention represented an important step in a development which had been foreshadowed in the Hague Convention on Certain Questions relating to the Conflict of Nationality Laws of 1930 and which tended to replace the traditional principle of the unity of the family with the principle of the independence of the nationality of the wife from that of her husband.

Article 1 of the Convention on the Nationality of Married Women:

> Each Contracting State agrees that neither the celebration nor the dissolution of a marriage between one of its nationals and an alien, nor the change of nationality by the husband during marriage, shall automatically affect the nationality of the wife.

In article 3, however, each Contracting State "agrees that the alien wife of one of its nationals may, at her request, acquire the nationality of her husband through specially privileged naturalization procedures", and that then the Convention "shall not be construed as affecting any legislation or judicial practice by which the alien wife of one of its nationals may, at her request, acquire her husband's nationality as a matter of right."

The two Covenants adopted by the UN General Assembly in 1966, the International Covenant on Civil and Political Rights

(CCPR) and the International Covenant on Economic, Social and Cultural Rights (CESCR), do not deal with the question of nationality or denationalization. It should, however, be mentioned that article 24, the first of those that deal with the rights of children, stipulates that "Every child has the right to acquire a nationality."

VII. Has the Declaration Acquired the Force of Law?

Right from its adoption, the UDHR achieved a profound moral and political authority. It became a yardstick by which the acts and conducts of governments in the field of human rights are measured, and in the 40 years that have since elapsed, it has provided standards and guidelines for States in this important field of international relations.

Not only has the UDHR served this purpose in the international community of nations, but it has also proved to be a model for a large number of treaties that have since been concluded in the field of human rights; one of the best known of these being the European Convention on Human Rights (ECHR). The two UN Covenants are other examples of such treaties with a worldwide application giving effect in detail to the provisions of the UDHR and meant to have a binding effect on the Parties. In addition, the provisions of the UDHR have been adopted in many national constitutions (for example, the Spanish Constitution of 1978) as well as in international legislation and in the decisions of both national and international courts.[12]

While all this may be self-evident on the 40th anniversary of the UDHR, there remains the crucial question: have the provisions of the UDHR themselves, such as article 15 in this instance, by now acquired the force of law as part of the customary law of nations? Initially the UDHR did not enjoy such status when it was adopted in 1948, being only a resolution of the General Assembly and thus lacking the force of law. The question is therefore whether subsequent developments have, independently of the origin of the UDHR, endowed it with the validity of a customary rule of law. Some of the arguments in favour of such an interpretation may be summarized as follows.

In a number of cases the UDHR has been considered as an authoritative interpretation of the UN Charter, which is generally

---

[12] Humphrey 1979, pp. 21–37.

accepted by States as an international treaty and therefore as having binding force. As early as 1949, the General Assembly invoked two articles (article 13 and article 16 of the UDHR), and recommended that the Soviet Union withdraw measures not in conformity with these articles. By doing so, the States voting for the resolution were using the UDHR to interpret the Charter.

The Declaration on the Granting of Independence to Colonial Countries and Peoples was adopted by the General Assembly in 1960. In its final paragraph it says that "All states shall observe faithfully and strictly the provisions of...the Declaration of Human Rights." Similar pronouncements are found in the Declaration on the Elimination of All Forms of Racial Discrimination adopted by the General Assembly on 20 November 1963, where article 11 states: "Every state shall promote respect for and observance of human rights and fundamental freedoms in accordance with the Charter of the United Nations and shall fully and faithfully observe the provisions of...the Universal Declaration of Human Rights."

On 4 December 1963 the Security Council adopted a resolution characterizing apartheid as being 'in violation' of South Africa's "obligations as a member of the United Nations and of the Provisions of the Universal Declaration of Human Rights."

Here, as in the former example, the Security Council was using the UDHR to interpret the Charter. The member States must be taken at their word. They cannot on one occasion say that the Declaration is to be fully and faithfully observed and on another that it is not binding.[13]

Further evidence of the view that by using the UDHR to interpret the Charter States recognize the binding force of its provisions, is found in the Final Act of the Helsinki Conference on Security and Co-operation in Europe of 1975. Section VII declares that "In the field of human rights and fundamental freedoms, the participating States will act in conformity with the purpose and principles of the Charter of the United Nations and with the Universal Declaration of Human Rights."

As the Charter, generally speaking, binds States to respect human rights, interpretation of the Charter by referring to the UDHR indicates that the provisions of the UDHR have achieved the status of rules of customary law. Moreover, the General Assembly Resolutions may provide the basis for common State practice which gradually transforms the substance of such resolutions into

[13] Ibid., p. 35.

customary law. Finally, it may be argued that the UDHR by now is considered as an expression of the general principles of law recognized by civilized nations in terms of article 38 of the Statute of the International Court of Justice, since certain of its fundamental rights have frequently been applied by international tribunals, for example, in cases concerning the treatment of aliens.[14]

These views carry much weight and on the basis of such arguments it may well be concluded that the provisions of article 15 have by now achieved the validity of a rule of customary law limiting the right of States to deprive their nationals of their nationality, expect in certain well defined cases as referred to in article 8 of the Convention on the Reduction of Statelessness.

References

Hofmann, Rainer, "Denationalization and Forced Exile", in *Encyclopedia of Public International Law*, 8, Amsterdam: Elsevier Science Publishers B.V., 1985.

Humphrey, John P., "The Universal Declaration of Human Rights: Its History, Impact and Juridical Character", in Bertram G. Ramcharan (ed.), *Human Rights, Thirty Years After the Universal Declaration*, The Hague: Martinus Nijhoff Publishers, 1979.

International Commission of Jurists (I.C.J.) Reports, 1955.

League of Nations Treaty Series (LNTS), Convention on Certain Questions Relating to the Conflict of Nationality, vol. 179, 89.

Salcedo, Juan Carrillo, "Human Rights, Universal Declaration, 1948", in *Encyclopedia of Public International Law*, 8, Amsterdam: Elsevier Science Publishers B.V., 1985.

Starke, J.G., *Introduction to International Law*, London: Butterworths, 1977.

United Nations, United Nations Action in the Field of Human Rights, 1983.

Weis, Paul, *Nationality and Statelessness in International Law*, Alphen aan den Rijn, The Netherlands: Sijthoff & Noordhoff International Publishers B.V., 1956.

[14] Salcedo 1985, p. 307.

Article 16

Maja Kirilova Eriksson

Sweden

1. Men and women of full age, without any limitation due to race, nationality or religion, have the right to marry and to found a family. They are entitled to equal rights as to marriage, during marriage and at its dissolution.
2. Marriage shall be entered into only with the free and full consent of the intending spouses.
3. The family is the natural and fundamental group unit of society and is entitled to protection by society and the State.

I. The Right to Marry and to Found a Family

A. *Minimum Age for Marriage*

Among the fundamental rights and freedoms included in the Universal Declaration of Human Rights (UDHR) is the right to marry and to found a family, proclaimed in article 16.

What meaning is to be given to the term 'full age'? Does the expression refer to the age of legal majority or the age of physical maturity? Countries favouring the second interpretation relate the right to contract marriage to sexual maturity or puberty, since in their opinion procreation is one of the main purposes of marriage. The term is understood as "the period of life in which the ability to procreate begins to manifest itself."[1] In Hanafi law, for example, puberty for girls and boys is presumed at the age of 15 years unless proof of earlier maturity is demonstrated, in which case the minimum ages considered acceptable are 9 and 12 years respectively.[2] The minimum age of marriage according to the

---

[1] E/CN.6/510/Add.2, p. 18.
[2] Hodkinson 1984, p. 92.

244 *Maja Kirilova Eriksson*

common law of Gambia is 12 years for women and 14 years for men.[3]

From the *travaux préparatoires*, it is apparent that this clause was designed to prevent child marriages, as further shown by the use of the phrase 'men and women.'

We may conclude that, as article 16(1) does not state what 'full age' is, the only limitation on age the UDHR seeks to impose is that of the 'physical fitness' of the prospective spouses, their capability of procreating and nothing more.[4] This is a requirement that is very easily fulfilled, and as such, it is open to criticism. Even if physical maturity is achieved, early marriages are inadvisable. The risk that lack of experience and intellectual maturity on the part of the spouses will make them incapable of meeting responsibilities associated with family life is too high. There are, thus, other more important factors to consider than mere reproductive capacity.

In a number of countries, for example in Bolivia,[5] the marriageable age is often higher for men. It is true that limitations on the grounds of sex are not explicitly forbidden in article 16(1), but the general non-discrimination article 2 in the UDHR prohibits distinctions made on that basis. In many countries, including the majority of the Nordic countries, the minimum age for marriage prescribed by national legislation is the same for both sexes.

The need for a basic requirement of minimum age for marriage found expression in the Convention on Consent to Marriage, Minimum Age for Marriage and Registration of Marriages of 7 November 1962. The convention entered into force on 4 December 1964. All the Nordic countries have ratified it. In its preamble the States are requested to take "all appropriate measures with a view to abolishing such customs, ancient laws and practices by ensuring...complete freedom in the choice of a spouse, eliminating completely child marriages and the betrothal of young girls before the age of puberty...." Article 2 of the same Convention establishes an obligation for the States Parties to take legislative action to specify a minimum age for marriage, but does not refer to a specific minimum age. According to the same article, a competent authority may grant a dispensation as to age in the interest of the intending spouses.

Principles regarding the minimum age required for marriage —

---

[3] E/CN.6/510/Add.2, Amend. 1, p. 3.
[4] Robinson 1958, p. 125.
[5] E/CN.6/510/Add.2, p. 8.

basically identical with those of the Convention mentioned above — are to be found in the Recommendation on Consent to Marriage, Minimum Age for Marriage and Registration of Marriages adopted by the UN General Assembly on 1 November 1965.[6] Principle II of the Recommendation specifically provides that the minimum age for marriage shall not be less than 15 years, except in the case where a competent authority has granted a dispensation as to age, for serious reasons, and in the interest of the intending spouses. Thus the Recommendation supplements and strengthens the Convention on Consent. The Member States of the United Nations are requested in principle III(4) to report to the Secretary General on the steps taken to give effect to the provisions of the Recommendation and on the existing rules of domestic law on the matter in the various States. In 1968, at the end of the first three-year period after the adoption of the Recommendation, only 54 out of 126 States had replied in accordance with principle III(4) regarding the national legislation and practices regulating marriage.[7] The reports showed great variations in the national legislation of the countries as to the minimum age for marriage. In eight of those States, exemptions of the recommended minimum age were obtainable in extraordinary circumstances; in five Member States these rules were applicable only to girls; and none of the States in question considered this as discriminatory against females. As regards principle III(2) and (3) of the Recommendation, 49 Member States replied on measures taken by them to bring the Recommendation before the competent authorities in their respective countries.[8]

Article 23(2), of the International Covenant on Civil and Political Rights (CCPR) is based on article 16(1) of the UDHR, and reads as follows: "The right of men and women of marriageable age to marry and to found a family shall be recognized." This provision differs in two respects from the corresponding provision in the UDHR, i.e., the use of the term 'marriageable age' instead of 'full age', and the absence of the expression "without any limitations due to race, nationality or religion." The *travaux préparatoires*[9] of the Covenant are of no help in elucidating the reason for the

---

[6] GA Resolution 2018 (XX) 1 November 1965.

[7] E/CN.6/510/Add.2.

[8] E/CN.6/510/Add.1.

[9] A comprehensive reference to all relevant documents on this question can be found in the Guide to the "Travaux Préparatoires" of the CCPR, in Bossuyt 1987, p. 454.

replacement of the term 'of full age'. The only guidance is several statements to the effect that the term 'full age' used in article 16 of the UDHR, or 'marriageable age', could refer to the age of legal majority or of physical majority.[10]

In article 16(2) of the Convention on the Elimination of All Forms of Discrimination against Women it is expressly stated that; "The betrothal and the marriage of a child shall have no legal effect." States Parties to the Convention are requested to take the necessary action to specify a minimum age for marriage.

As to the regional instruments on human rights, the right to marry exists for men and women of 'marriageable age' according to article 17(2) in the American Convention on Human Rights (ACHR) and article 12 in the European Convention on Human Rights (ECHR). The term 'marriageable age' is left to be determined by the domestic law of the States Parties, a law which can differ even within the same region. The African Charter on Human and Peoples' Rights (African Charter) does not refer to this right at all.

Moreover, we may conclude that article 16(1) of the UDHR, as other international instruments on the worldwide as well as the regional level, allows States to impose restrictions on the person's capacity to marry, if the requirement of 'full age' or 'marriageable age' is not fulfilled. The States have, however, considerable freedom in interpreting both terms. The only limitation according to the Recommendation on Consent is that the minimum age for marriage should not be lower than 15 years except when a dispensation is granted for serious reasons.

B. Consent to Marriage

Paragraph 2 of article 16 establishes the requirement that "Marriage shall be entered into only with the free and full consent of the intending spouses." The purpose of this basic principle is to ensure that marriage is entered into completely voluntarily and to prevent marriages contracted under duress or threats. The word 'free' is actually the key phrase in this paragraph, since a person can conceivably be forced to give his full consent, but not his free consent. Consequently, the use of the word 'free' is intended to eliminate "any compulsion by the parents, by the other spouse, by

[10] E/CN.4/SR.382, p. 6; E/CN.4/SR.383, p. 5.

the authorities, or anyone else."[11] Not long ago, arranged marriages were predominant in many countries and they are still practised in a number of them. An intermediary usually tries to arrange a marriage which will satisfy the two families represented, with the parents making the choice for the parties. Often economic arrangements are made. Parents, for example, usually give the daughter a dowry and the bridegroom in return makes a settlement (dower) to be used by the wife if the marriage is dissolved.

Involuntary or forced marriage has been defined as a slavery-like practice. According to article 1(c) of the Supplementary Convention on the Abolition of Slavery, the Slave Trade, and Institutions and Practices Similar to Slavery, States Parties shall take all practicable and necessary legislative and other measures to abolish or abandon institutions whereby "A woman, without the right to refuse, is promised or given in marriage on payment of a consideration in money or in kind to her parents."

The principle of freedom of choosing a prospective spouse, referred to in paragraph 2 of article 23 in the CCPR, is covered in greater detail in the Convention and Recommendation on Consent and is also stipulated in article 16(1b) of the Convention on the Elimination of All Forms of Discrimination against Women. In order to ensure the freedom of choice of the spouse, the free and full consent of both parties shall be in accordance with article I(1) of the Convention and principle I(a) of the Recommendation on Consent, expressed by both in person and in the presence of the authority competent to solemnize the marriage and in the presence of witnesses as prescribed by law.

The absolute requirement of the free and full consent of the intending spouses is also found in article 23(3) of the CCPR. Similarly, article 17(3) of the ACHR and article 10(1) of the International Covenant on Economic, Social and Cultural Rights (CESCR) — where only 'free' consent is mentioned — include this requirement, while neither the European nor the African conventions expressly mention it.

At the ninth session of the Commission on Human Rights (the Commission) it was pointed out that paragraph 2 of article 16 of the UDHR "might preclude the imposition of such requirements, as parental consent to marriage in cases where persons were under age."[12] The subsequent paragraph of the CCPR was thus amended

---

[11] Robinson 1958, p. 126.
[12] E/CN.4/SR.380, p. 13; E/CN.4/SR.384, p. 14.

to meet this objection. It is evident that consent can not be valid unless the intending spouses have reached a minimum age of maturity.

Article 16 of the UDHR does not deal with the very important question of the permissibility of marriage by proxy. Here one or both of the parties to marriage are not personally present at its celebration, "the consent of the absent party or parties being delivered by a specially authorized agent or proxy participating in the marriage ceremony on behalf of his or her principal."[13] Can the principle of free and full consent be affected by this type of marriage — *Handschuhehe* — permitted in a considerable number of countries? Since marriage is an exclusively personal transaction, it should not be possible to marry through a proxy or representative except under certain special circumstances. Marriage by proxy is further mentioned as an exception in article I(2) of the Convention on Consent and in principle I(b) in the Recommendation on the same subject. To guarantee the principle of free and full consent, the intending spouses must be present in person. By questioning the prospective spouses separately, the person who is authorized to officiate at the wedding can ascertain whether each is freely giving his or her consent. The risk of duress or even mistake is much higher when the parties are not personally present.

Article 16 of the UDHR mentions no restrictions on the right to marry and to found a family other than the requirements of full age and free and full consent. This does not mean that the right established in it is independent of national laws, and consequently, States may impose further restrictions. Thus marriage between people within certain prohibited degrees of consanguinity — or certain relationships by marriage — may be prohibited and deemed void *ab initio*.

In most countries monogamy is strictly enforced, and it is the most common form of marriage. There is a general prohibition against bigamy in the legal systems of the European countries and it is often regarded as a criminal offence, for example, in Sweden (BrB 7:1) and in Finland (SL 19:4–5).[14] The right to marry freely is restricted in a number of countries on grounds of permanent mental disorder. In Peru, for example, all marriages must be preceded by a medical examination. In Finland and Iceland impediments to marriage are mental illness, severe mental

---

[13] Pålsson 1974, p. 218.
[14] Gottberg - Talve 1986, p. 13.

deficiency and venereal illness. In El Salvador, perpetrators of, or accomplices in, the death of one of the spouses are absolutely barred from entering into matrimony.[15] The latter impediment cannot be found in the domestic legislation of the Nordic countries.

While article 16 of the UDHR does not expressly prohibit marriage by persons of the same sex, it speaks in terms of 'men' and 'women'. It is a fundamental provision in almost all States that marriage presupposes that the spouses are of different sexes.

The first paragraph of article 16 prohibits the limitation of the right to marry 'due to race, nationality or religion,' asserting that while a similar prohibition against discrimination was established in article 2 of the UDHR, article 16 would be strengthened immeasurably in the eyes of the common man, to whom the UDHR was addressed. The Pakistani delegation, in opposing the Mexican amendment, argued that "It completely disregarded the religious factor as a hindrance to marriage."[16] The representative of Egypt explained that almost all Moslem countries restrict and limit marriages of Moslem women with persons belonging to another faith. He contended that those limitations were of a religious nature, "sprung from the very spirit of the Moslem religion" and therefore could not be ignored.[17]

Article 23 of the CCPR does not contain any similar phrase. It was argued in the Commission that this type of discrimination was already covered by article 2 and that no specific provision was needed.[18] Similarly, article 12 of the ECHR also omits the provision of the prohibition of limitations of the right to marry and to found a family due to race, nationality or religion, since the draftsmen argued that article 12 is subject to the general prohibition of discrimination in article 14.

Article 12 of the ECHR is somewhat more limited in its scope

---

[15] CCPR/C/14/Add.7, p. 26.

[16] A/C.3/SR.125, p. 10; A/C.3/SR.1091, p. 152.

[17] In this connection it should be remembered that the general non-discrimination provision of article 2, includes *inter alia* the prohibition of discrimination on all religious grounds.

[18] A/2929 paras. 166–167; E/CN.4/SR.382, p. 13. That argument of course, was also raised with respect to article 16 but the outcome was different. Other delegations, e.g., the Venezuelan delegation, felt that a strongly worded paragraph condemning discrimination in marriage was important as discrimination still existed either in law or in custom. The Mixed Marriage Act prohibiting interracial marriages in South Africa was abolished as late as 1985 and practices based on racial segregation still exist in that country.

than the subsequent provisions of article 16 of the UDHR. It does not contain exhaustive enumerations of possible restrictions on the right to marry. It refers instead to the domestic law of the contracting party, leaving great freedom of choice to the States.

Article 17(2) of the ACHR stipulates that, while domestic laws may impose conditions on the right to marry, these must not be discriminatory.

The right to marry can hardly be defined as an absolute right. It is generally agreed that States may enact reasonable limitations, as long as these are legitimate and justifiable and do not make this right "illusory for large groups" of the population.[19]

In general, however, there are few remaining restrictions on the individual's freedom to marry or to choose a spouse. There has been an evolutionary development in the majority of the Nordic countries, as in most of the other European countries, of the law of marriage formation in the direction of increased freedom to marry.

II. Equal Rights to, in and after Marriage

The second sentence in article 16(1) in the UDHR provides for the principle of equal rights of the spouses relating to marriage. Women may not be put in 'a less favourable legal position' than men in contracting marriage, during marriage and at its dissolution. The principle of equality of the rights of men and women is expressly declared in the Preamble of the UN Charter, and its realization is listed as one of the main objectives of the organization. The purpose of article 16 here is to persuade States to gradually revise their legislation and practice in order to secure the legal equality of men and women as to marriage. Some delegations emphasized that the authors of the draft Declaration had for the most part only taken into consideration the standards recognized by Western civilization and had ignored more ancient civilizations, which were past the experimental stage "and the institutions of which, for example marriage, had provided their wisdom down through the centuries." The weakness of such an argument was pointed out by stressing that an international declaration should not be limited to principles that already existed in the various legal systems. Women were still frequently discriminated against in matters relating to nationality, parental control of children, the right to own property and the right

---

[19] Opsahl 1970, p. 191.

to work. An international instrument should therefore promote progress and should encourage legislators in the various countries to improve the existing laws.

Divided opinion and different attitudes emerged in the Third Committee over the inclusion in the CCPR of a provision based on article 16(1) of the UDHR concerning equal rights for men and women relating to marriage. Some delegations were for a strong, unequivocal wording of the prospective article. Others objected to the incorporation of the entire text of article 16(1) of the UDHR. The delegations of Saudi Arabia and Pakistan even expressed the view that the proclamation of equality of the rights of men and women might injure the interests of women.[20] After long discussions the difficulties were removed by a compromise, acceptable to all the delegations, which favoured a progressive application of the principle of equality. The use of the word 'steps' in paragraph 4 of article 23 of the CCPR bears witness to this idea of progressive development. The provision in question is thus meant merely as an ultimate goal rather than an immediate obligation for the States Parties to the CCPR.

The equal rights of husbands and wives upon the dissolution of a marriage are also safeguarded in the Nordic countries. Both spouses are equally entitled to bring about a divorce — in a number of countries divorce may be effected unilaterally by the husband only and not by the wife — and the father of the children does not have exclusive custody on dissolution of the marriage, as is common in a number of countries. The Swedish Marriage Code establishes that the custody of the children is the joint responsibility of the parents, even if they divorce. However, a child may live only with one of the parents.

Further development of the principle of equal rights has been achieved in the Convention on the Elimination of All Forms of Discrimination against Women. According to article 16(1e) the spouses shall have the same right to decide freely and responsibly on the number and spacing of their children.

III. The Right of the Family to Protection

Paragraph 3 of article 16 in the UDHR deals with the family as the basic unit of society. It expressly lays upon State and society the

---

[20] A/C.3/SR.1091, p. 153.

obligation to protect the family without specifying by what means that protection is to be ensured.

The family is an autonomous, separate object of protection. The object, in contrast to the others in the paragraphs of article 16, is a more collective one. The history of the drafting of this paragraph does not give any real help towards defining the scope of the provision.

The entire provision was incorporated in article 23(1) of the CCPR which was supported by the majority of the delegations. Its wording was approved without criticism, and generally seen as a preface to the rights proclaimed in the subsequent paragraphs. One proposal, implying an obligation for the States to adopt legislative measures to provide the family with special and effective protection, so as to promote its establishment and development and to ensure the fulfilment of its functions, was submitted at the ninth session of the Commission in 1953, but was rejected.[21]

In a communication submitted to the Human Rights Committee,[22] the Committee found a violation of article 23 in conjunction with articles 2(1), 3 and 26, and held that "The legal protection or measures a society or a State can afford to the family may vary from country to country and depend on different social, economic, political and cultural conditions and traditions." The Human Rights Committee, however, has not yet formulated a 'general comment' on article 23 which could provide an interpretation of the provision.

It would appear, though, that during the drafting of this provision there was a consensus on the question of safeguarding family unity as one aspect of protection.

In a section entitled 'Reunification of Families' of basket three in the Helsinki Final Act (Conference on Security and Co-operation in Europe, Final Act, Helsinki, 1975) the participating States are requested to deal "in a positive and humanitarian spirit" with applications of persons who wish to be reunited with members of their family.

While an express provision for the protection of the family is not to be found in the ECHR, the right to family life is proclaimed in article 8. There is a constantly growing body of jurisprudence on this article, in which the protection of family life is illustrated in

---

[21] E/CN.4/L. 275.
[22] No. 53/1978, Anmeemddy-Ciffrea *et. al. v.* Mauritius, HRC 1981 Report, Annex XIII, para. 9.2(b) 1–4.

many different ways.[23] The decision of the Court of Human Rights, Olsson *v.* Sweden,[24] for example, related to the taking into care of the applicants' three children and their placement in different foster homes. In the Court's opinion the splitting up of the children and their placement in different foster homes far from each other and their parents constituted a breach of article 8.

The importance of the family as an indispensable framework for the physical, emotional and social development of the individual was stressed in 1983 within the Organization of American States (OAS), when the year was proclaimed as the Inter-American Year of the Family. In the same year the Executive Committee of the Inter-American Children's Institute approved a Declaration of the rights of the family containing a number of rights of the family, such as: the right to the privacy of family life (article 3); the right to enjoy social, economic and cultural conditions that will foster their overall security and development (article 6); and the right to a decent and human abode (article 8) .

The Economic and Social Council (ECOSOC), at its 17th plenary meeting in 1987, aware of the international consensus on the importance of the role of the family, recommended to the General Assembly the adoption of a resolution[25] proposing the proclamation of an international year of the family and stressing the importance of improving the position and well-being of the family.

IV. Concluding Remarks

Article 16 of the UDHR has had a profound influence both on international and domestic law and its effect should not be underestimated. It has served as a point of departure for the drafting of international conventions, which to a great extent have further developed the principles laid down in its provisions. The process of utilizing the ideas of article 16 in creating international legal norms of both binding and non-binding nature is still continuing.

Family law is undergoing great changes in most countries of the world. Extensive reforms have been carried out and more are under consideration in the Nordic countries, where as we have seen, domestic legislation with certain minor exceptions corresponds with

---

[23] See Drzemczewski 1984. Nørgaard 1987, pp. 37–46.
[24] ECHR, Olsson Judgement of 24 March 1988, Ser. A, No. 130.
[25] E/1987/INF/5, p. 70.

the existing rules of international law. In certain areas these countries are forerunners in promoting human rights and introducing rules of law on subjects not yet covered by other countries.

References

Bossuyt, Marc J., *Guide to the "Travaux Préparatoires" of the International Covenant on Civil and Political Rights*, Dordrecht: Martinus Nijhoff Publishers, 1987.

Drzemczewski, A., *The Right to Respect for Private and Family Life, Home and Correspondence as Guaranteed by Article 8 of the European Convention on Human Rights*, 1984.

Gottberg - Talve, *Familjerättens grunder*, 1986.

Hodkinson, K., *Muslim Family Law — A Sourcebook*, 1984.

Nørgaard, G.A., "Beskyttelse af familiens rettigheder", i *Mänskliga rättigheter in Norden*, 1987.

Opsahl, Torkel, *The Convention and the Right to Respect for Family Life, particularly as regards the Unity of the Family and Protection of the Rights of Parents and Guardians in the Education of Children*, 1970.

Pålsson, L., *Marriage and Divorce in Comparative Conflict of Laws*, 1974.

Robinson, Nehemiah, *The Universal Declaration of Human Rights*, New York: Institute of Jewish Affairs, 1958.

United Nations Documents: E/CN.6/510/Add., (Amend. 1) Add. 2; GA Resolution 2018 (XX) 1 November 1965; E/CN.4/SR.380, 382, 383, 384; CCPR/C/14/Add.7; A/C.3/SR.125; A/C.3/SR.1091; A/2929; E/CN.4/L.275; E/1987/INF/5.

Article 17

Gudmundur Alfredsson[*]

Iceland

1. Everyone has the right to own property alone as well as in association with others.
2. No one shall be arbitrarily deprived of his property.

I. The Right to Property in Human Rights Instruments

The constitutions and basic laws of most if not all Western countries have long guaranteed the right to property. This right is part and parcel of their very form of government. It allows for the acquisition and ownership of private property and it protects citizens exercising this right by imposing restrictions on the State with regard to any encroachments.

Serious attempts have been made to elevate the right to property to the international level. On the success side of the story, in the United Nations system, the right to property is included in the Universal Declaration of Human Rights (UDHR); there are references in a few other instruments; and a special agency for the protection of intellectual property has been established. At the regional level, there are property rights guarantees in the Inter-American, European and African human rights instruments.

The final version of article 17 of the UDHR belies the controversy it has caused, both prior and subsequent to its adoption. Numerous proposals were made in the course of the preparatory work leading to the adoption of the article, including the complete omission of the right. The diversity of views expressed and proposals made during the legislative history, as demonstrated by the varying recommendations from the drafting bodies, tell us a lot

---

[*] The present article contains views expressed in the author's private capacity and they do not necessarily reflect those of the United Nations.

about the contents and direction of the article itself.

A drafting committee at the first session of the Commission on Human Rights (the Commission) came up with the text: "Everyone has the right to own personal property. No one shall be deprived of his property except for public welfare and with just compensation. The State may determine those things, rights and enterprises, that are susceptible of private appropriation and regulate the acquisition and use of such property."[1] At the Commission's second session, a working group suggested this wording: "Everyone has the right to own property in conformity with laws of the State in which such property is located. No one shall be arbitrarily deprived of his property."[2] This text was included in the Draft International Declaration on Human Rights, submitted by the Commission to the Economic and Social Council (ECOSOC) in 1947.[3] The working group in 1948 amended the text to read: "Everyone has the right to own such property as meets the essential needs of decent living, that helps to maintain the dignity of the individual and of the home, and shall not be arbitrarily deprived of it."[4]

At the third session of the Commission, the article had taken on its final form[5] and it passed from there to ECOSOC[6] and the General Assembly.[7] The draft still prompted extensive debates, a series of suggested amendments and votes, all the way up to and including the Third Committee of the Assembly, but the end result was article 17 as we know it: "1. Everyone has the right to own property alone as well as in association with others. 2. No one shall be arbitrarily deprived of his property."

The language of article 17 is broad and comprehensive. It applies to both individual and collective forms of property ownership. The absence of the limitations proposed in the legislative debate is noteworthy; there are no references in the article to conformity with State laws, personal property or decent living. The right is not an absolute one, however, as it is foreseen that persons can be deprived of their property under certain circumstances, but this cannot be

---

[1] E/CN.4/21, pp. 76–77.

[2] E/CN.4/57, p 10.

[3] E/600, p. 16.

[4] E/CN.4/95, p. 8.

[5] E/800, p. 10.

[6] A/625, p. 35.

[7] A/777, p. 539, and A/C.3/288/Rev.1.

done arbitrarily. The term 'arbitrarily' would seem to prohibit unreasonable interferences by States and taking of property without compensation, but a precise and agreed upon definition does not appear in the preparatory documents.

Article 17 should also be read in conjunction with other provisions of the UDHR. Articles 2 and 7, for example, provide that neither discrimination nor any distinction shall be made on the basis of property ownership or lack thereof. In his *Study of Discrimination in the Matter of Political Rights*, submitted to the Sub-Commission in 1962, Special Rapporteur Hernan Santa Cruz spoke strongly against distinctions and differentiations to the benefit of property holders.[8]

In addition to article 17, the right to property has found its way into a few other global instruments. Article 5 of the International Convention on the Elimination of All Forms of Racial Discrimination (adopted in 1965, in force since 1969) establishes the right of everyone to equality before the law without distinction as to race, colour or national or ethnic origin, including the enjoyment of "the right to own property alone as well in association with others" and "the right to inherit." Article 6 of the Declaration on the Elimination of Discrimination against Women (General Assembly resolution 2263 (XXII) of 7 November 1967) stipulates that all appropriate measures shall be taken to ensure to women equal rights in the field of civil law, such as "the right to acquire, administer, enjoy, dispose of and inherit property, including property acquired during marriage." Articles 15 and 16 of the Convention on the Elimination of all Forms of Discrimination against Women (adopted in 1979, in force in 1981) established the same rights for all women with respect to the acquisition and disposal of property. Paragraph 11 of the Declaration on the Rights of Disabled Persons (General Assembly resolution 2447(XXX) of 9 December 1975) provides for legal aid when it is indispensable for the protection of their persons and property.

A variety of standards established by the International Labour Organisation (ILO) covers property rights of trade unions and workers, of the latter with regard to home ownership and the right to own and dispose of remuneration received for their work. ILO Conventions no. 107, from 1957, and no. 169, from 1989, deal with the collective and individual rights of indigenous and tribal peoples to ownership of land and certain natural resources. The UN

---

[8] E/CN.4/Sub.2/213/Rev.1, Sales no. 63.XIV.2.

Working Group on Indigenous Populations, in its preparation of a draft universal declaration on the rights of indigenous peoples, is moving in the same direction.

In order to encourage creativity in the fields of science, technology, literature and the arts and to strengthen the contribution and participation of those involved in the economic, social, and cultural development of their countries, national laws generally accord property rights to the results of intellectual activity (industrial property, copyrights, patents, trademarks, etc.). For the international promotion and protection of these rights, there is the World Intellectual Property Organization (WIPO), a specialized agency of the United Nations, currently with about 120 Member States. A number of treaties provide substantive protection in this field, including: the Berne Convention for the Protection of Literary and Artistic Works (signed on 9 September 1886); the Paris Convention for the Protection of Industrial Property; the Rome Convention for the Protection of Performers, Producers of Phonograms and Broadcasting Organizations; the Patent Cooperation Treasury; and the Madrid Agreement Concerning the International Registration of Marks.

The International Finance Corporation (IFC), an institution affiliated with the World Bank and the International Development Association (IDA), seeks to support the economic development of States through promoting and strengthening private enterprise. It does so by providing financial and investment expertise in order to attract private investors and increase their confidence in participating developing countries. It is obviously a precondition for IFC involvement that the right to property over the means of production be recognized by the States concerned.

Regional instruments have been forthcoming on the right to property. The American Declaration on the Right and Duties of Man, which was adopted by the Ninth International Conference of American States in the spring of 1948 and thus predates the UDHR, provides in article XXIII that "Every person has a right to own such private property as meets the essential needs of decent living and helps to maintain the dignity of the individual and the home." The wording indeed resembles some of the earlier proposals for the UDHR. Article 21 of the American Convention on Human Rights (ACHR, adopted in 1969, in force since 1978) is entitled 'The Right to Property' and reads as follows:

> 1. Everyone has the right to the use and enjoyment of his property. The law may subordinate such use and enjoyment to the interest of society.

2. No one shall be deprived of his property except upon payment of just compensation, for reasons of public utility or social interest, and in the cases and according to the forms established by law. 3. Usury and any other form of exploitation of man by man shall be prohibited by law.

Article 1 of the March 1952 Protocol no. 1 to the European Convention on Human Rights (ECHR) reads: "Every natural or legal person is entitled to the peaceful enjoyment of his possessions. No one shall be deprived of his possessions except in the public interest and subject to conditions provided for by law and by general principles of international law." The article goes on to reserve to the State the right "to enforce such laws as it deems necessary to control the use of property in accordance with the general interest or to secure the payment of taxes or other contributions or penalties." A number of property rights cases have been decided by the European human rights institutions.

Article 14 of the African Charter on Human and Peoples' Rights (African Charter, adopted in 1981, in force since 1987) provides likewise: "The right to property shall be guaranteed. It may only be encroached upon in the interest of public need or in the general interest of the community and in accordance with the provisions of appropriate laws."

II. Non-inclusion of Property Rights

The listing above reflects on the instances of successful elevation of the right to property to the international level. On other occasions, similar efforts have failed and the right has come under strong criticism.

The most notable failure is the outright absence of the right in both the International Covenant on Civil and Political Rights (CCPR), and that on Economic, Social and Cultural Rights (CESCR). Notwithstanding several proposals, no such article was adopted. In lengthy debates there was disagreement on practically every aspect of the topic (E/2573, paragraphs 40–71, and Official Records of the General Assembly, Tenth Session, Annexes, agenda item 28 (part II), paragraphs 195–212), including such issues as the scope of property, conformity with State laws, expropriation and other allowable limitations, due process of law, compensation and indeed the very inclusion of the right.

As a result of this non-inclusion, the only available avenue for submitting complaints to the United Nations concerning violations of the right to property as such is the so-called 1503 procedure, established by ECOSOC resolution 1503 (XLVIII) of 27 May 1970.

An emphasis on social responsibilities and non-discrimination has brought other dimensions to the forefront of the debate. Property rights have been criticized as standing in the way of progress: from the owning of slaves to the exploitation of others through apartheid and transnational corporations. The importance of property rights is often deemed to pale against the background of other problems, such as hunger, poverty and misery. Unequal distribution of wealth tends to follow the lines of sex and race, especially affecting indigenous peoples, other groups in minority situations, rural workers and small farmers. The overall concentration of most of the world's property in the hands of a comparative few, especially in times of population growth and scarcity of resources, makes property rights seem more a part of the problem than an interest entitled to protection. For these and related reasons, international action has increasingly moved in directions not originally envisaged by the promoters of property rights in the Western sense of the concept.

Land reform, the return by museums and collectors of cultural properties, permanent sovereignty of peoples over natural resources and a new economic order are among the top items of this list of new priorities. These and similar approaches are closer to the communal and collective ownership favoured by many States in line with their traditions, customs and/or political and economic systems. One result, the cause of many disputes and the subject of much literature, has been expropriation by several governments of property owned by the few or the foreign, particularly natural subsoil or surface resources, with compensation formulas that take into account 'all pertinent circumstances'.

These approaches have found loud and clear expressions in a large number of international instruments and resolutions. These include General Assembly resolutions 1803 (XVII) of 14 December 1962 on Permanent Sovereignty over Natural Resources, 3201 (S–VI) of 1 May 1974 proclaiming the Declaration on the Establishment of a New International Economic Order, 3281 (XXIX) of 12 December 1974 containing the Charter of Economic Rights and Duties of States, and 44/18 of 6 November 1989 on the return or restitution of cultural property to the countries of origin. Similarly, article 1, paragraph 2, of the CCPR and CESCR provides that "All people may, for their own ends, freely dispose of their natural wealth and resources.... In no case may a people be deprived of its own means of subsistence." Article 25 of the CESCR and article 47 of the CCPR underscore this inherent peoples' right. Article 8 of the Universal Declaration of the Rights of Peoples, adopted by a private, albeit frequently quoted, conference in Algeria in July 1976, goes still further: "Every people has an exclusive right over its natural wealth and resources. It has the right to recover them if they have been despoiled, as well as any unjustly paid indemnities."

Article 6 of the Declaration on Social Progress and Development (General Assembly resolution 2542 (XXIV) of 11 December 1969) stipulates that "Social progress and development require...the establishment, in conformity with human rights and fundamental freedoms and with the principles of justice and the social function of property, of forms of ownership of lands and of means of production which preclude any kind of exploitation of man, ensure equal rights to property for all and create conditions leading to genuine equality among people." Article 7 goes on to say: "The rapid expansion of national income and wealth and their equitable distribution among all members of society are fundamental to all social progress...."

The activities of several UN organs and specialized agencies point in the same direction. One of the objectives of the UN Centre for Human Settlements (Habitat) is the development and use of land in a manner consistent with the interests of society as a whole, in particular for meeting the housing and land needs of the poor. In viewing the relationship between the right to land and economic and social development, as well as the role of land ownership and land tenure in ensuring the full and free participation of individuals in the economic and social systems of States, the Food and Agriculture Organization (FAO) has developed policies and engaged in activities aimed at agrarian reform and rural development. Also in this context, one should refer to UN and ILO efforts on behalf of indigenous peoples.

III. Concluding Remarks

The varying opinions on and approaches to the right to property stand as textbook examples of the different cultures and economic systems of our modern world. Rich and poor, free marketeers and socialists, all see it with their own eyes. Needless to say, the conflict remains unresolved. Recent action by the General Assembly and the Commission demonstrates the dilemma.

In resolution 41/132 of 4 December 1986, the General Assembly requested the Secretary-General to prepare a report on a) the relationship between the full enjoyment by individuals of human rights, in particular the one contained in article 17, and the economic and social development of Member States and b) the role of the right established by article 17 in ensuring the full and free participation of individuals in the economic and social systems of States. The report is available in document A/43/739. The General Assembly by resolutions 42/114 of 7 December 1987 and 43/123 of 8 December 1988 and the Commission by resolutions 1987/17 and 1988/18 have elaborated on this approach under the titles: "Respect for the right of everyone to own property alone as well in association with others and its contribution to the economic and social development of Member States." The line of reasoning emphasizes private initiative and corresponding incentives and rewards as an important contributing factor in economic and social development.

Underlining the ideological and political difficulties involved, the General Assembly in resolutions 42/115 of 7 December 1987 and 43/124 of 8 December 1988 and the Commission in resolutions 1987/18 and 1988/19 have called upon the Secretary-General to consider the impact of property on the enjoyment of human rights and on the economic and social development of States in the preparation of the aforesaid report, which should include: the New International Economic Order; the rights of peoples; the role of transnational corporations; the social functions of property; the many forms of legal property ownership (private, communal and State); and the role of the public sector. A greater emphasis was placed on article 6 of the Declaration on Social Progress and Development than on article 17 of the UDHR. The underlying tenet is the protection and promotion of the communal and collective good through guarantees of equal distribution and use.

The debate is likely to continue.

References

United Nations Documents: E/CN.4/21; E/CN.4/57; E/600; E/CN.4/95; E/800; A/625; A/777; A/C.3/288/Rev.1; E/CN.4/Sub.2/213/Rev.1, Sales no. 63.XIV.2.

Article 18

Martin Scheinin

Finland

Everyone has the right to freedom of thought, conscience and religion; this right includes freedom to change his religion or belief, and freedom, either alone or in community with others and in public or private, to manifest his religion or belief in teaching, practice, worship and observance.

I. General Observations

Freedom of thought, conscience and religion is an 'easy case' in the human rights catalogue. The right to freedom of thought, conscience and religion has long traditions both in domestic[1] and in international law.[2] There are even grounds to state that the origin of the general idea of human rights lies in the long history of protecting religious minorities.[3]

The unproblematic character of the traditional nucleus of the human right in question is apparently the reason that there has been little research regarding this right[4] and human rights complaints to supervisory international organs have relatively seldom touched on this right.[5]

States have not considered it difficult to allow their citizens the freedom to think. The difficulties start when we come to the right to *express* one's conviction, the right to *organize* as a community in order to promote a religion or belief and the right to *act* in

---

[1] See Krishnaswami 1960, pp. 4–11; and Mock 1983, pp. 120–121.

[2] See Krishnaswami 1960, pp. 11–12; Partsch 1981, p. 209; Lillich 1984, pp. 158–159; and Humphrey 1984, p. 176.

[3] See also Daes 1983, pp. 1–2.

[4] Humphrey 1984, p. 178.

[5] See de Zayas *et al.* 1985, pp. 53–54 and *Digest of Strasbourg Case-Law*, vol. 3.

accordance with one's conscience even in cases where a domestic legal system seems to require uniform behaviour irrespective of the different convictions of individuals. The real problems concerning freedom of thought, conscience and religion do not concern the nucleus of the right itself (the freedom of an inner state of mind), but issues that relate also to other human rights. In this sense freedom of conscience gives clear evidence that human rights cannot be protected as separate from each other but are realized only as a totality.

The Universal Declaration of Human Rights (UDHR) does not define the terms 'thought', 'conscience' and 'religion'. Together these terms cover "all possible attitudes of the individual toward the world, toward society, and toward that which determines his fate and the destiny of the world, be it a divinity, some superior being or just reason and rationalism, or chance", as has been stated by Karl Josef Partsch.[6] Countries differ from each other greatly on the question of relationships between the State and religious communities. Under these circumstances it is astonishing that different States have reached a common formula at all. Partsch's explanation[7] is:

> Atheists may have been satisfied to see "thought" and "conscience" precede "religion". Liberals may have been pleased to see all three freedoms on an equal level without preference to any one of them. Strongly religious people may have regarded "thought and conscience" as corresponding not only to religion generally but even to the only true religion, the one to which they adhere.

II. *Travaux Préparatoires*

Article 16 of the draft International Declaration on Human Rights, as examined by the UN Human Rights Commission (the Commission) in its second session[8] had two paragraphs which at later stages were merged into one. The draft did not include the term 'religion' at all, but on the other hand expressly emphasized the absolute and sacred character of the human right in question. The text of the article redrafted by the Drafting Committee of the

---

[6] Partsch 1981, p. 213.

[7] Ibid., p. 210.

[8] December 1947, UN doc. E/600, Annex A; for preceding stages see UN doc. E/CN.4/21.

Commission was almost identical in its wording.[9] At this stage the representative of the Soviet Union proposed an alternative text which would have clearly indicated that freedom to practise religious observances was subject to domestic law limitations.

When the Commission dealt with the draft in its third session (June 1948), the Soviet amendment was rejected by 10 votes to 5, with 1 abstention. After a lively discussion including several new proposals, a drafting sub-committee composed of the representatives of France, Lebanon, the United Kingdom and Uruguay was appointed.[10] This group unanimously recommended a one-paragraph article that was practically identical with the final wording of article 18 of the UDHR. The text was approved in the Commission by 11 votes to 0, with 4 abstentions.[11]

The Commission adopted the whole draft UDHR by 12 votes to 0, with 4 abstentions (the Soviet Union, the Byelorussian SSR, the Ukrainan SSR and Yugoslavia, which all associated with an alternative draft).[12] The Soviet representative, in the Third Committee of the General Assembly, Mr. Pavlov, explained that the Soviet Union's amendment aimed at more express guarantees for the enjoyment of freedom of thought, conscience and religion, at special emphasis on protecting scientific thinking and freethinkers, and at national legislation putting an end to religious practices dangerous for society (for example, human sacrifices).[13] Several speakers criticized the Soviet amendment as restrictive. A group of Moslem States supported a Saudi Arabian amendment deleting the words "freedom to change his religion or belief." According to Mr. Baroody of Saudi Arabia, the amendment was meant to prevent abuse of the right by missionaries who in fact were often forerunners of political intervention.[14] He did not, however, contest the individual's right to change religion.[15] Additional amendments were also proposed.

All amendments were rejected through voting in the Third Committee on 9 November 1948.[16] The article as a whole was adopted by 38 votes to 3, with three abstentions. In the final vote

---

[9] May 1948, UN doc. E/CN.4/95.

[10] UN doc. E/CN.4/SR.60.

[11] UN doc.E/CN.4/SR.62.

[12] UN doc. E/800.

[13] November 1948, General Assembly Official Records III, part I, p. 391.

[14] Ibid., p. 391.

[15] Ibid., p. 404.

[16] Ibid., pp. 405–406.

the Soviet representative voted for the article.

It is to be noted that the UDHR also contains other references to the rights mentioned in article 18. The inclusion of possible limitations of the freedoms in question in article 29, was repeatedly asserted, especially in the discussion in the Third Committee, as justification for not including special restrictions in article 18. Freedom of belief and the word 'conscience' are mentioned in the second paragraph of the Preamble, and article 1 supports the idea of the absolute character of the right in question: "All human beings... are endowed with reason and conscience...." Freedom of opinion (article 19) has a close connection with freedom of thought, and both freedom of expression (article 19) and freedom of assembly and association (article 20) strengthen the right to manifest one's religion or belief. Finally article 26, paragraph 3, proclaims that parents have a prior right to choose the kind of education their children shall receive.

The absolute character of the freedom of an inner state of mind was stressed also in the drafting of the UDHR. The decision not to include in article 18 the characterization of the right to freedom of thought, conscience and religion as 'an absolute and sacred right' shall not be read as an indication of withdrawal from this view. In particular, Mr. Cassin of France, who was a member of the sub-committee that proposed the final text, stressed the sacred and inviolable character of the right to freedom of thought, which was the basis and the origin of all other rights and had "a metaphysical significance." Mr. Malik of Lebanon (the Rapporteur) stated that the right in question was "above the law", and also Mr. Fontaina of Uruguay, a third member of the sub-committee, stressed the fundamental character of freedom of thought. Even the Soviet representative, Pavlov, supported Cassin's argument.[17]

---

[17] UN doc. E/CN.4/SR.60.

III. The Right to Freedom of Thought, Conscience and Religion in other Human Rights Instruments

A. The International Covenants of 1966

Article 18 of the International Covenant on Civil and Political Rights (CCPR) clearly follows the text of the UDHR. Paragraph 1 follows closely article 18, paragraph 3 derives from article 29 of the UDHR, and paragraph 4 concretizes article 26(3), of the Declaration. Partsch[18] stresses that understanding the CCPR requires knowledge concerning the development of the Declaration.

As in the drafting of the Declaration, the express mention of the right to change one's religion or belief also met opposition when the CCPR was drafted. The solution was to use the wording 'to have or to adopt' which was also repeated in paragraph 2 in order to give protection both *for* the individual's right to change his religion and *against* zealous proselytizers and missionaries.[19]

The prohibition of discrimination based *inter alia* on religion is stipulated in articles 2(1), 4(1) and 26 of the CCPR. Article 4(2) stresses the absolute character of the obligation of States to respect the right to freedom of thought, conscience and religion by prohibiting any derogation from this obligation during a state of emergency. Even in extreme situations only *manifestations* of religion or beliefs may be limited, and only as far as this is justified under paragraph 3 of article 18.[20] Religious minorities acquire certain special protection under article 27, which, however, is quite modest in its wording.

Article 18(4), of the CCPR is one of the links between the rights ensured in this Covenant and those covered by the International Covenant on Economic, Social and Cultural Rights (CESCR). Article 13(3), of the CESCR is for its corresponding part identical in its wording. Both provisions have their background in article 26 of the UDHR, and taken together they cover all aspects of the right of parents to ensure the religious and moral education of their children in conformity with their own convictions. Paragraph 4 was included in the CCPR at a rather late stage,[21] as the study by

---

[18] Partsch 1981, p. 210.

[19] See Bossuyt 1987, pp. 357–363; and Partsch 1981, p. 211.

[20] On the meaning of the limitation clause see, generally Kiss 1981 and Daes 1983, and specifically Partsch 1981, pp. 212–213.

[21] Bossuyt 1987, pp. 368–370.

Krishnaswami[22] had recommended this solution.

Discrimination on *inter alia* the basis of religion is also prohibited by article 2(2) of the CESCR.

B. *Some other Instruments of Universal Significance*

It is impossible to cover here all the provisions of different human rights instruments which are relevant to the protection of the right proclaimed in article 18 of the UDHR. In particular, discrimination on the basis of religion or opinion has been dealt with in several conventions, starting from article 1 of the UN Charter.

Article 5 of the International Convention on the Elimination of All Forms of Racial Discrimination (1965) includes a list of rights the enjoyment of which the States Parties undertake to guarantee without distinction as to race, colour, or national or ethnic origin. The right to freedom of thought, conscience and religion is mentioned in this list, thus allowing the international protection machinery established through the Convention to be used when this right is violated. The connection between racial discrimination and discrimination based on religion or belief is close, because ethnic or racial minorities are very often also religious minorities.

The UNESCO Convention against Discrimination in Education (1960) also prohibits discrimination on the basis of religion and political or other opinions (article 1(1)). In addition, article 5(1)(b) deals with religious or moral education and states that parents have the liberty to ensure this education in conformity with their convictions, and that no person should be compelled to receive religious instruction inconsistent with his convictions.

Religion and political opinion are mentioned also in the list of prohibited grounds for discrimination in article 1(1)(a) of the International Labour Organisation (ILO) Convention concerning Discrimination in Respect of Employment and Occupation (1958). The ILO protection machinery is available in case of violation.

A special convention on discrimination based on religion or belief has been under preparation for a long time. A detailed study in the matter including draft principles on freedom and non-discrimination in the matter of religious rights and practices was completed in 1959 by Krishnaswami. The study makes clear that the prohibition of discrimination raises special problems in the case

---

[22] Krishnaswami 1960, p. 68.

of freedom of thought, conscience and religion: "Since each religion or belief makes different demands on its followers, a mechanical application of the principle of equality which does not take into account these various demands will often lead to injustice and in some cases even to discrimination."[23] In 1981 the Declaration on the Elimination of All Forms of Religious Intolerance and of Discrimination Based on Religion or Belief (General Assembly Resolution 36/55) was proclaimed. This declaration includes also general principles relating to the right to freedom of thought, conscience and religion (article 1). The rights of children and the rights and responsibilities of parents with regard to religion or belief are developed further in article 5. The protection of different manifestations of religion or belief is dealt with in detail in article 6.

C. *Regional Instruments*

The Paris peace treaties with former allies of Nazi Germany (1947) include provisions on securing human rights, explicitly also freedom of religion, without discrimination (for example, Peace Treaty with Finland, article 6).

The European Convention on Human Rights (ECHR, 1950) contains in article 9(1) a provision almost identical with article 18 of the UDHR. A limitation clause is included as paragraph 2. In addition, article 2 of Protocol 1 to the ECHR (1952) includes the right of parents to ensure that education and teaching is in conformity with their religious and philosophical convictions. Article 14 of the ECHR forbids discrimination based on *inter alia* religion or opinion in the enjoyment of the rights set forth in the Convention. Article 9 is not mentioned in the list of non-derogable rights in article 15(2).

Article 12 of the American Convention on Human Rights (ACHR, 1969) does not mention freedom of thought, but only of conscience and religion. Restrictions of the right to maintain one's religion or belief are expressly forbidden (paragraph 2), whereas manifestations of that religion or belief are subject to limitations (paragraph 3). The issue of religious and moral education is dealt with in paragraph 4. Article 12 is mentioned in the list of rights not subject to suspension during a state of emergency (article 27).

[23] Ibid., p. 15.

The African Charter on Human Rights and Peoples' Rights (African Charter, 1981) mentions in article 8 freedom of conscience and the profession and free practice of religion, which shall both be guaranteed. A second sentence states that no one may, subject to law and order, be submitted to measures restricting the exercise of these freedoms.

Freedom of conscience, religion or belief has a special place in the Final Act of the European Conference on Security and Co-operation (1975). The Final Act's Declaration on Principles Guiding Relations between Participating States expressly mentions only this right in the heading and the first introductory paragraph of Section VII dealing with human rights and fundamental freedoms. The third paragraph deals specifically with the right to profess and practise a religion or belief, acting in accordance with the dictates of one's conscience.

IV. Possible Future Rights

A. Conscientious Objection to Military Service

The European Commission of Human Rights and, following the same line of argument, the Human Rights Committee, have interpreted freedom of conscience as not including the right to be exempted from compulsory military service.[24] The decisions have been based on the fact that both the ECHR, in article 4(3)(b), and the CCPR, in article 8(3)(c)(ii), include a special provision declaring that alternative civilian service is not to be regarded as forced or compulsory labour "in countries where conscientious objection is recognized." The latter phrase has been interpreted to indicate that States are free to decide whether they recognize conscientious objectors. This interpretation has been criticized, because the right protected and limited in these articles in question is not freedom of conscience but personal freedom,[25] and because the cited phrase itself can only be interpreted to indicate that *all* States are not under *all* circumstances obliged to recognize the right to object.[26]

---

[24] E.g., applications 2299/64, 5591/72, 7548/76, 7565/76 and 7705/76, and communication 185/1984.
[25] Eide and Mubanga-Chipoya 1985, p. 5.
[26] van Dijk and van Hoof 1984, p. 300.

It is, however, possible that the right to conscientious objection will be protected as a separate human right. The right of all persons to refuse service in military or police forces used to enforce apartheid was recognized in the UN General Assembly Resolution 33/165 (1978). The Commission has been working on the issue of conscientious objection since 1971. An important stage of this process was the study by Eide and Mubanga-Chipoya, which was completed in 1983. In March 1987 the Commission passed by 26 votes to 2, with 14 abstentions, a resolution recommending that States with a system of compulsory military service consider introducing various forms of alternative service.[27]

The right to conscientious objection has been supported by the Parliamentary Assembly of the Council of Europe in resolution 337 (1967) and recommendation 816 (1977). In April 1987 the Committee of Ministers also recommended that States recognize this right (R (87) 8).

B. The Right to Act in Accordance with One's Conscience

Freedom of conscience does not in itself include a general right of an individual to act in accordance with his conscience. The existence of a limited right in this direction is suggested by article 18, paragraphs 2, 3 and 4 of the CCPR. Paragraph 2 protects against coercion to support a religion other than one's own, for example, in the form of payment of church taxes, or (paragraph 4) obligatory religious education.[28] These provisions also assure the right to freedom *from* religion, which protects non-religious persons from obligatory religious oaths, ceremonies and other obligations.

Freedom to manifest one's religion or belief cannot be realized if there are legal obligations that prevent people from the acts that are dictated by their convictions. Paragraph 3 gives protection against these kinds of obligations to the extent they are not covered by the limitation clause in the same provision. There is some case law of the European Commission of Human Rights on the matter.[29]

A special convention against discrimination in the matter of religious rights and practices could be important for securing the right to act in accordance with one's conscience. This right cannot

---

[27] UN doc. E/CN.4/1987/L.73; E/CN.4/1989/L.11/Add.8, pp. 5–8.

[28] See Partsch 1981, pp. 211–212 and 215.

[29] See Fawcett 1987, pp. 244–250 and van Dijk and van Hoof 1984, pp. 301–304.

mean that every individual would have the complete freedom to decide the legal obligations he wishes to fulfil. There is a need for criteria that would help to determine the scope of the right. Krishnaswami's study is a valuable contribution to this goal.

V. Some Nordic Issues

In an international comparison, the Nordic countries can be regarded as secularized societies, but at the same time the connection of the State and the church is very close. This combination leads to a somewhat paradoxical conclusion: because religion is not taken very seriously, freedom of thought, conscience and religion is not protected as well as several other human rights.[30]

The case Hartikainen *v.* Finland in the Human Rights Committee (communication 40/1978) has been quite educative. At the time of the case those Finnish schoolchildren who were exempted from confessional (Lutheran) religious instruction were taught classes in 'the history of religion and ethics'. In the communication it was alleged that this alternative education was also religious in the sense of article 18(4), of the CCPR. The Human Rights Committee stated that the teaching plan appeared, "in part at least, to be religious in character", but found no violation of article 18 because the relevant provisions of Finnish legislation allowed for fulfilling the obligations set in paragraph 4, and the Committee expressed the belief that appropriate action was being taken to resolve the problem. Soon after, the problems which had originated the communication were, indeed, partly solved through administrative measures. At the same time a total revision of Finnish school legislation was under preparation, which gave an opportunity for more far-reaching reforms. Freedom from religion was realized both for schoolteachers and schoolchildren. The Parliament's Committee on Constitutional Law gave its statement on that issue as well as a bill on the educational goals of public kindergartens. In these statements (nos. 12 and 13/1982) the Committee gave a new interpretation, according to which freedom *from* religion is a constitutional right in Finland. In a decision from 1985 the Supreme Administrative Court has confirmed this interpretation.[31]

---

[30] Especially for Finland's case, see Törnudd 1986, pp. 122–129.
[31] HFD 1985, A II 54.

There is still, however, room for improvement as far as freedom of thought, conscience and religion in Finland is concerned. There are religious ceremonies in the military forces which are obligatory also for non-religious conscripts. As another example, some years ago a kindergarten teacher's assistant was given notice because she refused to participate in the preparation for religious holidays, and the Parliamentary Ombudsman saw no reason to react.[32]

VI. Conclusion

The right to freedom of thought, conscience and religion is a human right that cannot be realized separately, but only in the general context of human rights. It is also a right that crosses the traditional borderlines between different categories of human rights, because it has aspects that are highly individual ('civil' rights in this sense of the term), aspects that show that the right can be effectively realized only in an organized community with other persons possessing the same conviction (a 'political' right), and aspects that belong to the field of economic, social and cultural rights (such as matters dealing with religious or moral education).

[32] Annual Report 1984, pp. 125–131.

References

Bossuyt, Marc J., *Guide to the "Travaux Préparatoires" of the International Covenant on Civil and Political Rights*, Dordrecht: Martinus Nijhoff Publishers, 1987.

Daes, Erica-Irene A., *The Individual's Duties to the Community and the Limitations on Human Rights and Freedoms under Article 29 of the Universal Declaration of Human Rights; A Contribution to the Freedom of the Individual under Law*, UN publication E.82.XIV.1, Geneva: 1983.

Digest of Strasbourg Case-Law relating to the European Convention on Human Rights, vol. 3, München: 1984.

van Dijk, Pieter and G.J.H. van Hoof, *Theory and Practice of the European Convention on Human Rights*, Deventer: Kluwer Law and Taxation Publishers, 1984.

Eide, Asbjørn and Chama Mubanga-Chipoya, *Conscientious Objection to Military Service*, UN publication E.85.XIV.1, Geneva: 1985

Fawcett, J.E.S., *The Application of the European Convention on Human Rights*, Oxford: Oxford University Press, 1987.

Högsta förvaltningsdomstolen (HFD; Supreme Administrative Court) 1985, A II 54

Humphrey, John P., "Political and Related Rights", in Theodor Meron (ed.), *Human Rights in International Law: Legal and Policy Issues*, vol. II, Oxford: Oxford University Press, 1984.

Kiss, Alexandre Charles, "Permissible Limitations on Rights", in Louis Henkin (ed.), *The International Bill of Rights, The Covenant on Civil and Political Rights*, New York: Columbia University Press, 1981.

Krishnaswami, Arcot, *Study of Discrimination in the Matter of Religious Rights and Practices*, UN publication 60.XIV.2, New York: 1960.

Lillich, Richard B., "Civil Rights", in Theodor Meron (ed.), *Human Rights in International Law: Legal and Policy Issues*, vol. I, Oxford: Oxford University Press, 1984.

Mock, Erhard, Gewissen und Gewissensfreiheit, Zur Theorie der Normativität im demokratischen Verfassungsstaat, Berlin: Duncker & Humblot, 1983.

Partsch, Karl Josef, "Freedom of Conscience and Expression, and Political Freedoms", in Louis Henkin (ed.), *The International Bill of Rights, The Covenant on Civil and Political Rights*, New York: Columbia University Press, 1981.

Törnudd, Klaus, *Finland and the International Norms of Human Rights*, Dordrecht: Martinus Nijhoff Publishers, 1986.

United Nations Documents: E/600, Annex A; E/CN.4/21; E/CN.4/95; E/CN.4/SR.60; E/CN.4/SR.62; E/800; GAOR III; E/CN.4/1987/L.73; E/CN.4/1989/L.11/Add.8.

de Zayas, Alfred, Jakob Th. Möller and Torkel Opsahl, "Application of the International Covenant on Civil and Political Rights under the Optional Protocol by the Human Rights Committee", *German Yearbook of International Law*, vol. 28, Berlin: Duncker & Humblot, 1985.

Article 19

Lauri Hannikainen and Kristian Myntti

Finland

Everyone has the right to freedom of opinion and expression; this right includes freedom to hold opinions without interference and to seek, receive and impart information and ideas through any media and regardless of frontiers.

I. History

The roots of the right to freedom of information may be found in the struggle for the freedom of speech of legislators during the 17th century. As early as 1688, the English Bill of Rights provided "that the freedom of speech and debate or proceedings in Parliament ought not be impeached or questioned in any court or place out of Parliament." The scope of this freedom was later gradually expanded by the United States Bill of Rights added to the Constitution in 1791 and the French Declaration of the Rights of Man and The Citizen (1789). Article 11 of the French Declaration stated that "The unrestrained communication of thoughts or opinions being one of the most precious rights of man, every citizen may speak, write and publish freely, provided he be responsible for the abuse of this liberty, in case determined by law." At the end of the 19th century, the freedom of the press had been accepted in most countries. After World War II, the concept of freedom of the press, now significantly relabelled 'freedom of information' was, however, more controversial than ever.

II. *Travaux Préparatoires*

Though freedom of information and of the press are not specifically mentioned in the Charter of the United Nations, the importance of information freedoms was recognized by the United Nations from its very beginning. The discussions in San Francisco had already made it quite clear that freedom of information should be given a privileged position among fundamental human rights. In resolution 59(I), the General Assembly at its first session in 1946, proclaimed freedom of information as a fundamental human right and a touchstone of all the other freedoms to which the United Nations is consecrated. This resolution was moved on behalf of the Philippines by General Carlos Romulo, a professional newspaperman and the head of a chain of newspapers in the Philippines. Further, the General Assembly called on the Economic and Social Council (ECOSOC) to convene a conference on freedom of information.

The United Nations Conference on Freedom of Information met in Geneva from 23 March to 21 April 1948 under the chairmanship of Romulo of the Philippines. The Conference constituted a serious effort to promote peace and progress by laying down a policy for the United Nations in the field of information. The postwar climate was, however, already chilly, and the atmosphere at the Conference highly political. During the four weeks the Conference met, the positions hardened and at the end there was little room left for compromise.[1] Still, the Geneva Conference adopted and forwarded to ECOSOC three draft conventions: on the Gathering and International Transmission of News; on the Institution of an International Right of Correction; and on Freedom of Information. The draft Convention on Freedom of Information originated in a British proposal.

The Conference also adopted 43 resolutions and some draft articles for the international bill of rights concerning the freedom of information. The draft articles adopted were based on the work of the Sub-Commission on Freedom of Information and of the Press. The socialist countries, however, could approve neither the draft Convention on Freedom of Information nor the draft articles for the international bill of rights. While these drafts were based on the idea of a 'free flow' of information, according to which the right to receive and impart information is subjected to no restrictions, the socialist countries, and especially the Soviet Union, forwarded the idea of a 'balanced' flow of information or an 'exchange' of information. In the Soviet Union's alternative draft article presented at the Conference, a condemnation of warmongering was also stressed:

---

[1] Humphrey 1984, p. 53.

1. In accordance with the principles of democracy and in the interests of strengthening international collaboration and world peace, everyone must be legally guaranteed the right freely to express his opinions and, in particular, freedom of speech and the press and also freedom of artistic expression. Freedom of speech and the press shall not be used for purposes of propagating Fascism, aggression and for provoking hatred between nations.

2. For the purpose of enabling the wider masses of the people and their organizations to give free expression to their opinions the State will assist and co-operate in making available the material resources (premises, printing presses, paper, etc.) necessary for the publication of democratic organs of the press.

Four decades later, only one of the draft Conventions, the Convention on an International Right to Correction, is in force. Since the end of the Geneva Conference, the UN bodies have experienced great difficulty in clarifying and elaborating the concept of freedom of opinion and expression, its limitations and realization. The item 'Draft Convention on Freedom of Information' appeared on the agenda of the General Assembly from 1962 to 1980, but did not lead to any conclusive results. At its 29th session in 1960 ECOSOC adopted a Draft Declaration on Freedom of Information (resolution 756 (XXIX)). This item also appeared on the General Assembly's agenda from 1962 to 1980.

The text of article 19 of the Universal Declaration of Human Rights (UDHR) was, after a series of votings, adopted by the Human Rights Commission (the Commission) at its third session in 1948, according to the text submitted by the Geneva Conference, by 13 votes to 4. The proposals advanced by the Soviet delegation were all rejected by the Commission (see UN document E/800 Appendix). In the General Assembly's Third Committee, Mr. Pavlov of the Soviet Union stated that freedom of speech could not be permitted for the propagation of aggression. According to Pavlov, the United States press and their European imitators had, in disregard of General Assembly resolution 110(II), been advocating a policy of aggression, and a war psychosis had been encouraged by the reactionary press with the twofold aim of crushing the democratic forces at home and of frightening the countries with whom negotiations were being carried out. According to Mr. Aquino (the Philippines), the phrase 'regardless of frontiers' implied ideological barriers as well as physical frontiers. In Aquino's opinion, the effect of the Soviet amendment would be to create a controlled press such as existed in all 'totalitarian' countries. Finally article 17 (the future article 19) was adopted by the Third Committee by 36 votes to 6. In the General Assembly, the amendments by the Soviet delegate to article 17 (19) were on demand of Mrs. Roosevelt rejected without discussion.

Read in its ordinary meaning, article 19 of the UDHR establishes a world for the purpose of receiving and imparting information as an individual right. The aim was to promote an unobstructed flow of information in all directions and regardless of frontiers. On the other hand, even this article must be read in conjunction with other provisions of the UDHR, and especially with the conditions on duties and limitations laid down in article 29 of the Declaration.

III. Freedom of Information in Other Universal Human Rights Instruments

The right to freedom of opinion and expression as proclaimed in article 19 of the UDHR constitutes a cornerstone of democratic society. This is the reason why many human rights instruments adopted by the UN bodies since 1948 elaborate principles set out in this article.

According to paragraphs 1 and 2 of article 19 of the 1966 International Covenant on Civil and Political Rights (CCPR), everyone shall have the right to hold opinions without interference and to freedom of expression. The latter right includes freedom to seek, receive and impart information and ideas of all kinds, through any media and regardless of frontiers. Unlike article 19 of the UDHR, article 19(3) of the CCPR expressly allows for restrictions and limitations upon the freedom of expression. According to paragraph 3, the exercise of the rights provided for in paragraph 2 carries with it special duties and responsibilities and may therefore be subjected to certain restrictions. These limitations doubtlessly draw on article 29(1) of the UDHR, and they presumably include the duty to present information and news truthfully, accurately and impartially.[2] On the other hand, these limitations shall only be such as provided by law and are necessary: a) for the respect of the rights or reputations of others; b) for the protection of national security or of public order (*ordre public*); or c) for public health or morals.

---

[2] Partsch 1981, p. 219.

While article 29(3) of the UDHR contains a general provision that the rights and freedoms defined by it may in no case be exercised contrary to the purposes and principles of the United Nations, the rights laid down in article 19 of the CCPR are further restricted by article 20, according to which any propaganda for war and any advocacy of national, racial, or religious hatred that constitutes incitement to discrimination, hostility or violence shall be prohibited by law. The term 'war' in article 20 has not been defined in the CCPR, but must probably be interpreted in the sense of 'war of aggression'.[3]

During an officially proclaimed public emergency that threatens the life of the nation, article 4 of the Covenant permits the States Parties to take measures derogating from the obligations of article 19 to the extent strictly required by the exigencies of the situation, provided such measures do not involve discrimination solely on the ground of race, colour, sex, language, religion or social origin. For the uniform interpretation of limitations and derogations on the rights set forth in the CCPR, 'The Siracusa Principles' were adopted by a legal experts' meeting held in 1984. The meeting was convened by, among other organizations, the International Commission of Jurists.[4]

The question of freedom of information has formed an important part of the so-called 'Third Basket' (Co-operation in Humanitarian and Other Fields) of the Conference on Security and Co-operation in Europe (CSCE). As a result of the differences between the socialist and Western concepts regarding mass media, spread of information and the freedom to seek, receive and impart information, the East and the West forwarded diametrically opposed opinions on the improvement of exchange of information. As the Western States spoke for a free flow of information, the East European States supported a controlled and determined exchange of information. Notwithstanding these different views, the Final Act of the CSCE Helsinki Conference 1975 includes provisions on the improvement of the circulation of, access to and exchange of information, on co-operation in the field of information, as well as on the improvement of working conditions for journalists. Even though the provisions of the Helsinki Final Act were soon subjected to different interpretations in the East and the West, the concluding

---

[3] Ibid., p. 227.

[4] E/CN.4/1984/4, also published in *The Review*, International Commission of Jurists, no. 36, June 1986.

document of the Madrid CSCE follow-up meeting of 1983 also contains provisions in the field of information. The Madrid meeting was prolonged due to, among other things, different views on the issues of working conditions for journalists and deliberate interference with broadcasts, so-called jamming. Despite the Western States' strong efforts to achieve explicit provisions prohibiting jamming, such provisions were not included in the concluding document.

References to the freedom of information have also been included in several other provisions of UN instruments such as in article 9 of the 1963 Declaration on the Elimination of All Forms of Racial Discrimination and article 4 of the 1965 International Convention on the Elimination of All Forms of Racial Discrimination.

During the past few decades the question of freedom of information has been the subject of some special studies and reports within the United Nations. In 1954 Mr. Lopez, the Rapporteur of ECOSOC, presented his report entitled *Freedom of Information, 1953*[5] to the Council at its 17th session. Lopez's report dealt with contemporary problems and developments in the field of information, and contained a series of recommendations for action. A second substantive report was presented by Mr. Eek, a consultant appointed by the Secretary-General. Eek's report, entitled *Report on Developments in the Field of Freedom of Information Since 1954*,[6] dealt with matters such as facilities and obstacles for the free flow of information. From 1959 to 1965 the Secretary-General prepared and submitted to the Commission on Human Rights (the Commission) annual reports on developments affecting the freedom of information.

In the field of communication, the matter of free flow of information and space communication, UNESCO has issued a number of special studies.[7] In 1978, UNESCO adopted the "Declaration on Fundamental Principles concerning the Contribution of the Mass Media to Strengthening Peace and International Understanding, to the Promotion of Human Rights and to Countering Racialism, Apartheid and Incitement to War."

---

[5] E/2426.
[6] E/CN.4/762 and Corr.
[7] Such as *Space Communication and the Mass Media* (1964), *Communication Satellites for Education, Science and Culture* (1967), *Broadcasting from Space* (1970), *A Guide to Satellite Communication* (1972), and *Planning for Satellite Broadcasting* (1972).

IV. Regional Instruments

Not only have the principles laid down in article 19 of the UDHR of 1948 had effects on the elaboration of United Nations instruments, but the content of this article, in a somewhat modified form, appears in many regional human rights instruments as well. Provisions concerning the freedom of information are included in article 10 of the European Convention on Human Rights (1950, ECHR), article IV of the American Declaration on the Rights and Duties of Man (1948), articles 13 and 14 of the American Convention on Human Rights (ACHR, 1969, in force in 1978), and article 9 of the African Charter on Human and Peoples' Rights (African Charter, 1981, in force in 1986).

According to article 10(1) of the ECHR, everyone has the right to freedom of expression. This right shall include freedom to hold opinions and to receive and impart information and ideas without interference by public authority and regardless of frontiers. Article 10(1) does not, however, prevent States from requiring the licensing of broadcasting, television or cinema enterprises. In conformity with article 19 of the CCPR, article 10 of the ECHR also permits certain restrictions of the freedom of information. As the exercise of the freedoms set forth in article 10(1) carries with it duties and responsibilities according to article 10(2), they may be subject to such formalities, conditions, restrictions or penalties as are prescribed by law and are necessary in a democratic society, in the interests of national security, territorial integrity or public safety, for the prevention of disorder or crime, for the protection of health and morals, for the protection of the reputation or rights of others, for preventing the disclosure of information received in confidence, or for maintaining the authority and impartiality of the judiciary.

Some of the most noteworthy differences between article 10 of the ECHR and article 19 of the CCPR should here be pointed out. The right to hold opinions without interference is stated in the CCPR in a separate paragraph, paragraph 1 of article 19. It is clearly established that the restrictions of 19(3) are not applicable to this particular right. Additionally, and unlike article 10 of the ECHR, article 19 of the CCPR expressly speaks of the right to 'seek' information; on the other hand, the phrase 'without interference by public authority' included in article 10 of the ECHR is lacking in article 19. The possibility of subjecting broadcasting, television, and cinema to a licensing system is not expressly mentioned in article 19. This restriction must therefore be judged by reference to paragraph 3 of article 19. The same applies to those restrictions of article 10(2) that are not mentioned in article 19(3).[8]

V. Freedom of Information — Some Reflections

The right to freedom of opinion and expression, including the freedom of information, is an absolute prerequisite for a democratic society. Under no circumstances should a person be imprisoned for expression of his views. Unfortunately, such guarantees have not been given in all UN Member States. Through article 19 of the 1966 Covenant, the proclamations concerning the freedom of information in the UDHR have now, however, become part of a legally binding treaty for nearly 90 States. Article 19 of the CCPR maintains a clear distinction between freedom of opinion and freedom of expression. While the first right is subjected to no restrictions, the freedom of expression is subject to certain restrictions, but only in keeping with the principles of legality and necessity.[9]

The reservations to article 20(1) of the CCPR regarding war propaganda formulated by the Nordic countries and some other Western States, as article 20 was considered to endanger the freedom of speech, have sometimes, perhaps not without reason, been criticized. The legitimacy of these reservations was also questioned by the Human Rights Committee.[10] On the other hand, the term 'propaganda' for war has not been clarified in the CCPR; it is very vague and still needs refinement. The experts of the Council of Europe have expressed concern that the expression 'propaganda for war' could easily be abused; it could be invoked, for example, by a hostile critic against a scientific treatise on military matters or against a declaration on principles of national security.[11]

The explosion in communications, in particular in transnational data traffic and satellite broadcasting, has given the concept of freedom of information new dimensions. The gap between the educational and technological resources of different countries, especially between countries who control broadcast satellites and

---

[8] van Dijk and van Hoof 1984, p. 320.
[9] Partsch, 1981, pp. 221, 222.
[10] UN doc. A/34/40, para. 414.
[11] Council of Europe, Doc. CE/H (70)7, para. 180.

those who do not, underlines the problem of so-called 'cultural imperialism'. The 1966 CCPR does not include any specific reference to what has been called the 'right to communicate', but it has been suggested that this right may be seen as included in the right to freedom of information in article 19.[12] On the other hand, States are sovereign under international law. Not only are States sovereign over their territory, but they are also sovereign in the air space above their territory and their territorial waters. The principle has, however, been limited in several telecommunications conventions and radio regulations. Also the principle of freedom of outer space has its limits. The process of preparing a binding treaty on satellite broadcasting through non-binding resolutions, such as the 'Principles Governing the Use by States of Artificial Earth Satellites for International Direct Television Broadcasting' adopted by the General Assembly in 1982 in resolution 37/92, has been under way for several years. Obviously, a line has to be drawn between legitimate restrictions of the inward flow of information in the interest of protecting the cultural values of the receiving State, and straight censorship for political or ideological reasons. Historical precedents suggest that actions in order to restrict the flow of information for ideological reasons by imposing restrictions on journalists or interfering with broadcasting have been of limited value for the censor.

VI. Some Nordic Questions

In all the Nordic countries, freedom of opinion and expression is a highly respected constitutional right. Further, all the Nordic countries are legally bound by the provisions of article 19 of the 1966 CCPR. An official application for membership of the Council of Europe was made by Finland in 1988. In 1989 Finland became a member of the Council of Europe and in May 1990 Finland ratified the ECHR.

All the Nordic countries follow a dualist principle in their incorporation of treaty provisions into domestic law. However, there are certain differences between the Nordic countries as to the method of implementing treaties in domestic law. In Finland, a specific method of incorporation is followed, involving a blank legislative act — a statutory order or both law and statutory order

---

[12] Gross 1979, p. 206.

— only referring to the international treaty and incorporating the treaty. The CCPR has been incorporated through a law (no. 107/1976) and a statutory order (no. 108/1976). In the other Nordic countries neither the CCPR nor the ECHR have been incorporated, but domestic legislation has been presumed to be in harmony with these international obligations. In certain cases necessary amendments have been made to the domestic legislation. In Sweden, Denmark, Norway and Iceland the provisions of an international treaty are not, generally speaking, directly enforceable by the courts or the administrative authorities. In Finland, a more and more common opinion among the legal scholars is that individuals may invoke the 'self-executing' provisions of the third part of the CCPR before the domestic courts and administrative authorities.

Though the right to freedom of opinion and expression is considered well guaranteed by the Nordic domestic legislation, the Human Rights Committee and the European Commission have received some applications from individuals concerning alleged breaches of article 19 and 10 by certain Nordic countries.

In 1981 the Human Rights Committee gave its comments concerning a question of freedom of communication in Finland. According to the contentions of the authors of the communication (no. R.14/61), Finnish authorities, including organs of the State-controlled Finnish Broadcasting Company, had interfered with their right to freedom of expression and information, as laid down in article 19 of the CCPR, by imposing sanctions against participants in, or censuring, radio and television programmes dealing with homosexuality. The State Party rejected the allegation with reference to the restrictions included in article 19(2). The Committee found no violation of the rights of the authors. According to its view the Committee could not question the decision of the responsible organs of the Broadcasting Corporation that radio and television are not the appropriate forums to discuss issues related to homosexuality, as far as a programme could be judged as encouraging homosexual behaviour. According to article 19(3), the exercise of the rights provided for in article 19(2), carries with it special duties and responsibilities for those organs.[13]

In a case concerning access to the civil service, Leander *v.* Sweden (no. 9248/81), the applicant complained before the

---

[13] Report of the Human Rights Committee, 37th Session, Supplement no. 40 (A/37/40), Annex XIV.

European Commission that the information held on him in the secret police register had labelled him as a security risk, and that he had no remedy at his disposal which would compel the authorities to inform him of the accusations against him. The applicant alleged breaches of articles 6, 8, 10 and 13 of the ECHR. In its judgment the European Court observed that the freedom to receive information basically prohibits a government from restricting a person from receiving information that others wish or may be willing to impart to him. Article 10 does not, in the opinion of the Court, in circumstances such as those of the present case, confer on the individual such a right as access to a register containing information on his personal position, nor does it embody an obligation on the government to impart such information to the individual. According to the Court, there had been no interference with the applicant's freedom to receive information as protected by article 10.[14]

Two other Nordic applications concerning the freedom of information, the applications of Pastor X and the Church on Scientology *v.* Sweden (no. 7805/77) and X *v.* Sweden (no. 30–71/67), were declared inadmissible by the Commission, being manifestly ill-founded.[15]

The European case law relating to the right to information is extensive. In many cases the question has been the right of expression through mass media and broadcast licensing systems.

---

[14] ECHR; Leander Case 10/19–85/96/144. Judgment. Strasbourg 26 March 1987.
[15] *Yearbook of the Council of Europe*, no. 11, p. 456 and no. 22, p. 244.

References

Bloed, Ari and Pascale de Wouters d'Oplinter, "Jamming of Foreign Radio Broadcasts", in Ari Bloed and Pieter van Dijk (eds.), *Essays on Human Rights In The Helsinki Process*, Dordrecht: Martinus Nijhoff Publishers, 1985.

Council of Europe, *Yearbook of the Council of Europe*, no. 11, and no. 22. Doc. CE/H (70)7.

van Dijk, Pieter and G.J.H. van Hoof, *Theory and Practice of the European Convention on Human Rights*, Deventer: Kluwer Law and Taxation Publishers, 1984.

Eek, Hilding, *Freedom of Information as a Project of International Legislation.* Uppsala: Acta Universitatis Upsaliensis, 1953.

Gerrits, Andre and Joanka Prakken, "Madrid and the Working Conditions for Western Journalists in Eastern Europe", in Ari Bloed and Pieter van Dijk (eds.), *Essays on Human Rights in The Helsinki Process*, Dordrecht: Martinus Nijhoff Publishers, 1985.

Gross, Leo, "Some International Law Aspects of the Freedom of Information and the Right to Communicate", in Kaarle Nordenstreng and Herber I. Schiller (eds.), *National Sovereignty and International Communication. A Reader*, New Jersey: Ablex Publishing Corporation, 1979.

Humphrey, John P., *Human Rights and the United Nations: a Great Adventure*, New York: Transnational Publishers, 1984.

International Commission of Jurists, *The Review*, no. 36, June 1986.

Partsch, Karl Josef, "Freedom of Conscience and Expression, and Political Freedoms", in Louis Henkin (ed.), *The International Bill of Rights, The Covenant on Civil and Political Rights*, New York: Columbia University Press, 1981.

Rosas, Allan, *Nordic Human Rights Policies. Current Research on Peace and Violence*, 4/1986, Tampere: Tampere Peace Research Institute.

Rotfeld, Adam Daniel (ed.), *From Helsinki to Madrid. Conference on Security and Co-operation in Europe Documents 1973–1983*, Polish Institute of International Affairs Co-operative Publishers, Warsaw: 1983.

United Nations, *United Nations Action in the Field of Human Rights*, United Nations 1983, (Sales no. E/83/XIV.2).

United Nations Documents: E/CN.4/1984/4; E/2426; E/CN.4/762 and Corr.; A/34/40; Report of the Human Rights Committee, 37th Session, Supplement no. 40 (A/37/40) Annex XIV.

Verdoodt, Albert, *Naissance et Signification de la Déclaration Des Droits de l'Homme*, Société d'Etude Morales, Sociales et Juridiques, Louvain, Paris: Editions Nauwelaerts, 1964.

Article 20

Martin Scheinin

Finland

1. Everyone has the right to freedom of peaceful assembly and association.
2. No one may be compelled to belong to any association.

I. General Observations

Freedom of assembly and freedom of association, together with freedom of expression (article 19), form the core in the category of political rights. They are the legal basis for an active civil society enabling rational-collective will-formation, for the publicity of public affairs, and also for any participatory or representative democratic processes.[1]

The predominant 'political' nature of the rights proclaimed in article 20 of the Universal Declaration of Human Rights (UDHR) does not, however, justify a conclusion according to which the rights in question would have nothing to do with other categories of human rights. Freedom of association and assembly are essential for many human activities clearly relating to the private sphere. They are essential for any effective exercise of the freedom of conscience and religion (article 18) and quite important also in, for example, the field of education (article 26).

The right to form and join trade unions is included in the freedom of association, for example, in article 22(1) of the International Covenant on Civil and Political Rights (CCPR),[2] but has in human rights instruments also been dealt with as a separate issue in connection with other rights relating to work (see article 23(4) of the UDHR, and article 8 of the International Covenant on

---

[1] See, e.g., Habermas 1961 and Tuori 1990, pp. 210–211 and 269–274.
[2] See also Partsch 1981, p. 235.

Economic, Social and Cultural Rights (CESCR)). As article 23 is the subject of another study in this book, the right to form and join trade unions is not substantially dealt with here.

II. *Travaux Préparatoires*

In the early drafts for the UDHR, efforts were made to determine what kinds of assemblies would be covered by the provision on freedom of assembly. In June 1947, Mrs. Eleanor Roosevelt (USA) proposed omitting such an enumeration. In addition, there was discussion on also covering freedom of association under the same article, contrary to previous drafts treating the two freedoms in separate articles.[3]

During the second session of the Drafting Committee of the UN Commission on Human Rights (the Commission) (3–21 May 1948) a joint provision was formulated: "Every one has the right to freedom of peaceful assembly and to participate in local, national and international and trade union associations for promotion, defence and protection of purposes and interests not inconsistent with this Declaration."[4]

In June 1948, the Commission adopted, in its third session, a 'simplified' Chinese proposal on article 19, which was to become article 20, paragraph 1, of the Declaration.[5]

The word 'peaceful' in paragraph 1, as well as the second paragraph of the article were introduced as Uruguayan amendments.[6] In the Third Committee of the General Assembly the explicit provision on negative freedom of association was considered problematic by the representative of New Zealand, with explicit reference to legal provisions securing certain rights to trade union members only.

The Third Committee decided to reject the Soviet proposal on an outspoken ban on Fascist and similar organizations (by a vote of 28 to 7, with 12 abstentions). The Uruguayan proposal for a new paragraph 2 was adopted by a vote of 20 to 14, with 9 abstentions. It was criticized especially by the representatives of the United Kingdom, Australia and New Zealand. The article as a whole was

---

[3] E/CN.4/AC.1/SR.8, p. 14.
[4] E/CN.4/95, p. 9; see also E/CN.4/AC.1/SR.41, pp. 2–5.
[5] E/CN.4/SR.61, pp. 7–11 and article 18 in E/800, p. 18.
[6] A/C.3/268.

adopted by a vote of 36 to 3, with 7 abstentions.[7]

III. Freedom of Assembly and Freedom of Association in Other Human Rights Instruments

A. *International Labour Organisation (ILO) Conventions*

Freedom of association is a field where one should note that international human rights conventions already existed prior to the 1948 UDHR, even if the most important ILO conventions in the field of the right to organize were completed only after World War II.[8]

One interesting feature in the proposal of the Drafting Committee of the Commission (quoted above in section 2) was the mentioning of the freedom of international association, which did not only relate to international trade union co-operation but was general in character. In this respect, the proposal was far more modern than the final text of the UDHR, or the 1966 Covenant. As the 1990s are, at least from a European perspective, a decade for international integration, and the bells have been said to be ringing for the European Nation State,[9] the transnational or international aspect of, for example, the freedom of association becomes more and more important.

In this respect the new (1989) ILO Convention Concerning Indigenous and Tribal Peoples in Independent Countries (no. 169) has an interesting provision on the obligation of States to facilitate, 'across borders', contacts and co-operation between indigenous and tribal peoples.

B. *The International Covenants of 1966*

In the CCPR, freedom of assembly (article 21) and freedom of association (article 22) are both secured, but under separate articles. Some of the differences between the two rights are described by

---

[7] General Assembly Official Records III, part I, pp. 438–448. On the genesis of article 20 see also Verdoodt 1964, pp. 191–198.
[8] Sulkunen 1988.
[9] Rosas 1989, p. 355.

Partsch[10] as follows: "The right of association includes private informal contacts.... This may be seen as an aspect of one's privacy.... [P]ermanent associations... may present a greater danger to public safety or security and invite different regulations for public health, order, or morals than an *ad hoc* gathering for only a short time...." According to Partsch, the decision to have two separate articles in the CCPR was a political one. In reaction to a Soviet proposal aimed at enabling heavy restrictions on the rights in question, separate guarantees were designed for each of the two rights in order to reinforce them both.[11]

The decision on not to include a counterpart to article 20, paragraph 2, in the text of the CCPR cannot be read as if the right not to participate in a demonstration (negative freedom of assembly) or the right not to join an association (negative freedom of association) was not protected by the CCPR. It is true that an explicit provision was omitted because of some understanding for the closed-shop system in certain Anglo-Saxon countries, but in general the CCPR secures also the negative aspects of the rights in question.[12]

Neither article 21 nor article 22 have yet become the source for a rich jurisprudence under the Optional Protocol to the CCPR. The Human Rights Committee has not issued a general comment on either of the two provisions. One of the open questions of interpretation is what will be the actual consequences of the 'weaker degree' of protection given for freedom of assembly in article 21, compared to some other important political rights. According to the text of the CCPR, restrictions on the exercise of this right must be "imposed in conformity with the law", whereas, for example, in article 22(2) the expression "prescribed by law" was preferred.[13] Of course, the difference in wording does not necessarily imply a difference in interpretation, but the problem has not yet been answered by the Human Rights Committee.

In the field of trade union freedom, the provisions in article 22 of the CCPR cannot be read as a *lex specialis* in relation to the CESCR. On the other hand, additional rights protected by the CESCR, for instance the right to strike, cannot be subsumed under

[10] Partsch 1981, p. 231.
[11] Ibid.
[12] Ibid., p. 232, and Törnudd 1986, p. 170.
[13] See Partsch 1981, p. 233, and also Nowak 1989, pp. 400–408.

article 22 of the CCPR.[14] This line of argument has been confirmed by the Human Rights Committee which expressed, in the case J.B. *et al. v.* Canada (118/1982), the view that the right to strike is not protected by the CCPR.[15] Even the reference to ILO Convention no. 87 in article 22, paragraph 3, of the CCPR does not create any new legal obligations, since it relates to States that are also parties to the ILO Convention in question.

The CESCR has in article 8 quite detailed provisions on trade union freedoms, including the right to strike. In the context of article 20 of the UDHR it suffices to note that negative freedom of association in relation to trade union membership has a stronger foundation in article 8 of the CESCR than in article 22 of the CCPR as it secures "[t]he right of everyone to... join the trade union of his choice."[16]

C. European Regional Instruments

In the European Convention on Human Rights (ECHR) of 1950, freedom of assembly and freedom of association are treated in one and the same provision, article 11, thus following the model of the UDHR. The right to form and join trade unions is explicitly mentioned as included, but negative freedom of association is not mentioned. There is a limitation clause in paragraph 2 of the article, stating not only the 'normal' requirements for restrictions — that they must be "necessary in a democratic society", "prescribed by law" and based on certain enumerated legitimate aims — but also a second category of lesser requirements for certain groups of persons. Only 'lawfulness' is required of restrictions on the exercise of freedom of assembly and association by members of the armed forces, of the police and of the administration of the State. The two first-mentioned groups are treated in a similar way in article 22(2) (but not in article 21) of the CCPR. The ECHR appears somewhat old-fashioned also because of article 16, according to which "the political activity of aliens" may be restricted irrespective of article 11 (and articles 10 and 14).

---

[14] Partsch 1981, p. 236, who gives references to the *Travaux Préparatoires* of the CCPR.

[15] HRC Report 1986, Annex IX B; see also de Zayas *et al.* 1989, pp. 442–443, and Nowak 1989, pp. 417–419.

[16] van Dijk and van Hoof 1984, p. 325.

One future perspective for the development of the European system, and international human rights protection in general, would be the eradication of these kinds of traces of the doctrine of *'besonderes Gewaltverhältnis'*, especially now that the UN Convention on the Rights of the Child has entered into force, thus re-emphasizing the need to 'take seriously' the first sentence in article 1 of the UDHR.

Article 11 has not played a central role in the Strasbourg case law. According to van Dijk and van Hoof[17] this is at least partly due to the word 'peaceful' as a qualification for freedom of assembly in article 11(1). Because of this qualification, restrictions on freedom of assembly can often avoid scrutiny under paragraph 2.

The case Kommunistische Partei Deutschlands v. FRG (Application 250/57) concerned a decision by the German Federal Constitutional Court to declare it anti-constitutional and to dissolve and prohibit a communist party and to confiscate its property. According to the European Commission of Human Rights (European Commission) it was not necessary to decide whether the decision could be based on the limitation clause of, *inter alia*, article 11, paragraph 2, because the activities of the German Communist Party fell under article 17 of the ECHR and the application was therefore inadmissible. The Party had expressed its fidelity to the aim of establishing the dictatorship of the proletariat which, according to the European Commission, "involves the destruction of certain rights and freedoms guaranteed by the Convention."[18] Of course the decision is an anomaly in the Strasbourg case law, but perhaps the present situation in Europe is the right time to invite critical discussion on it.

The issue of negative freedom of association was raised by the case of Young, James and Webster (13.8.1981, Series A 44), which dealt with the dismissal of the applicants from British Rail on account of their refusal to join a trade union, and as a consequence of a closed-shop system. The European Court of Human Rights (European Court) did not express any opinion on whether a closed-shop system in itself is a violation of article 11. In the applicants' case, however, the provision had been violated because dismissal from work was a form of coercion that affected the essence of freedom of association. This conclusion was reached taking into

---

[17] van Dijk and van Hoof 1984, p. 321.
[18] Yearbook I of the European Convention on Human Rights, pp. 222–225, Digest of Strasbourg Case-Law, vol. 4, pp. 239–240 and 244.

account that the closed-shop agreement between the unions and British Rail had been concluded after the applicants had been employed, and that the number of unions to choose between was extremely limited.

One important feature of the European Court's judgment was that it clearly recognized the horizontal effect (*Drittwirkung*) of article 11. Even if the agreement had been made between trade unions and an enterprise, the United Kingdom was found to violate the ECHR because of its domestic law permitting such an agreement.[19]

Another important case relating to negative freedom of association is Le Compte, Van Leuven and De Meyere (23.6.1981, Series A 43), in which both the European Commission and the European Court took the position that a professional organization established by the government and governed by public law in order to promote (also) some public interests is not an association in the sense of article 11. In general, the level of protection for negative freedom of association has not been very high.[20] The Strasbourg case law on trade union freedoms in general is not dealt with in this connection.[21]

The European Court has emphasized positive State obligations when interpreting article 11. In the case of Plattform "Ärzte für das leben" (21.6.1988, Series A 139) the problem was raised whether the ECHR obliges the State to give protection for demonstrations against counter-demonstrators. The European Court gave the following answer:

> The participants (of a demonstration) must...be able to hold the demonstration without having to fear that they will be subjected to physical violence by their opponents.... Genuine, effective freedom of peaceful assembly cannot, therefore, be reduced to a mere duty on the part of the state not to interfere: a purely negative conception would not be compatible with the object and purpose of Article 11.... (§ 32)

> While it is the duty of Contracting States to take reasonable and appropriate measures to enable lawful demonstrations to proceed peacefully, they cannot guarantee this absolutely and they have a wide

---

[19] See also van Dijk and van Hoof 1984, pp. 327–328.

[20] See, e.g., the Commission report in Association *v.* Sweden, Application 6094/73, Decisions and Reports 9, p. 5, relating to compulsory membership of student unions, and van Dijk and van Hoof 1984, p. 323–324.

[21] Article 23, paragraph 4, of the UDHR, and van Dijk and van Hoof 1984, pp. 325–328.

discretion in the choice of means to be used.... In this area the obligation they enter into under Article 11 of the Convention is an obligation as to measures to be taken and not as to results to be achieved. (§ 34)

Article 5 of the European Social Charter (1961) securing "the freedom of workers and employers to form local, national or international organizations" relates more closely to article 23(4) of the UDHR than to article 20.

Article 11(2) in the Declaration of Fundamental Rights and Freedoms, adopted by the European Parliament on 12 April 1989, clearly indicates a connection between freedom of association and the right to privacy: "No one shall in their private life be required to disclose their membership of any association which is not illegal."

The Document of the Copenhagen Meeting of the Conference on the Human Dimension of the Conference on Security and Co-operation in Europe (CSCE, 1990) includes quite far-reaching commitments in the field of pluralistic and competitive democracy, including full freedom to establish political parties or other political organizations (7.6), and freedom for political campaigning (7.7).

The right of peaceful assembly and demonstration (9.2) and the right of association (9.3) are also guaranteed, the latter principle including a far-reaching qualification: "These rights will exclude any prior control." Organizations seeking the promotion and protection of human rights enjoy special protection (10.3), even for their co-operation across borders: In principle 10.4 the CSCE States express their commitment to:

> allow members of such groups and organizations to have unhindered access to and communication with similar bodies within and outside their countries and with international organizations, to engage in exchanges, contacts and co-operation with such groups and organizations and to solicit, receive and utilize for the purpose of promoting and protecting human rights and fundamental freedoms voluntary financial contributions from national and international sources as provided for by law.

This commitment is to be read in connection with principle 12 in which the CSCE States decide to accept the presence of observer representatives of non-governmental organizations at proceedings before their courts.

IV. Some Finnish Issues

A. *Experiences in Abolishing Aliens Clauses*

One peculiar feature of Finnish legislation has been that the concept of 'a Finnish citizen' has been almost systematically used as the subject of rights. This is not only the case for the present Constitution Act (1919), but also for a great part of ordinary legislation. A partial explanation can be found in Finnish history; during the time Finland was an autonomous grand duchy within the Russian empire from 1809 to 1917, the Finnish Nation State was born, and the juridical notion of Finnish citizenship was created as one of its manifestations. Especially during the russification periods in the early 20th century it was of practical significance that laws secured rights to only Finnish citizens.

Until the beginning of 1990, both the Associations Act (1919) and the Act on Public Meetings (1907), the latter act being virtually a daughter of the first russification period ending in 1905, included heavy restrictions on foreigners' rights. A foreigner could not be a member of a political party, and he could not become a board member in any association, except for special 'aliens' associations' acting under a government permit, under special supervision, and under far-reaching restrictions. The Act on Public Meetings gave only Finnish citizens the right to organize public meetings or demonstrations.

The restrictions were heavily criticized by Human Rights Committee members when dealing with Finnish reports.[22] Legal scholars[23] made efforts to show that the restrictions for foreigners had been repealed by the Peace Treaty of Paris (in 1947) and the CCPR (in 1976).

The restrictions were also challenged by test cases. In order to achieve an amendment to the Act on Public Meetings, certain individuals active in the Association for Foreigners organized a demonstration on 10 December 1988. The slogans of the demonstration were taken from the UDHR, the 40th anniversary of which was celebrated on the very same day. Quite wisely, the Helsinki police decided to tolerate the demonstration and not to enforce the law forbidding meetings organized by foreigners. The legal precedence value of this administrative decision was, of

[22] See, e.g., CCPR/C/SR.170, p. 9, and the 1986 Report of the HRC, p. 46.
[23] See, e.g., Eriksson 1983.

course, not very high.

A legal precedent in the question of whether human rights conventions incorporated by Finland had repealed the restrictions on foreigners' freedom of association was sought in a case where a student organization nominated a Turkish citizen as its Vice-President, also in 1988. The final decision was made by the Supreme Administrative Court (HFD 1990 A 125). According to the Court, the CCPR left it for the States Parties to determine the methods through which freedom of association could be implemented. Article 22, paragraphs 1 and 2, of the CCPR were expressly mentioned in the decision, but article 26, also invoked by the applicants, was not. As the Associations Act of 1919 had the system of specific 'aliens' associations', the Ministry of Justice had, according to the Court, acted properly as it had not registered a foreigner as Vice-President of an association acting without a permit from the government. In its application the association had expressly indicated that it did not intend to ask for the status of an 'aliens' association' because it had very few foreign members and such a permit would in practice lead to several restrictions on the activities of the association. The court did not treat these restrictions, and the requirement that only associations acting under a government permit may elect foreigners in their executive, as restrictions in the sense of article 22, paragraph 2, of the CCPR. This is why the court did not comment at all on the question of whether the restrictions could be "necessary in a democratic society" as required by the provision.

Before this rather disappointing court decision, the restrictions had already been repealed. Of course the criticism of Human Rights Committee members and Finnish legal scholars, as well as the test cases and their reporting in the media had created pressure, but in the last resort the necessary legal amendments were triggered off by Finland's ratification of the ECHR.[24] Part of the restrictions on foreigners' rights was abolished in the total revision of the Associations Act (503/1989), and some months later this new Act, together with the Act on Public Meetings and the Freedom of the Press Act, was amended in order to get rid of the remaining restrictions (Acts no. 1331–1333/1989).

---

[24] Pellonpää 1988, pp. 214–216, and Pellonpää 1990, pp. 57–58.

B. The Problem of Outdated Legislation

Even after the aliens clauses were abolished in the Associations Act and the Act on Public Meetings, there remained a problem relating to the latter Act. The Act on Public Meetings dates back to 1907, i.e., to a time when Finland was an autonomous grand duchy within the Russian Empire. The Act is based on a system of prior notification to police authorities of public meetings in the open air (section 3), and of public ceremonial processions and marches (section 10).

A system based on prior notification is not in itself in conflict with human rights conventions.[25] But the problem is that the outdated Act does not cope with the actual development in the public forms of citizens' activity. Thus, it has become questionable whether certain modern forms of demonstrations fall under the notification duty. And as the Act on Public Meetings criminalizes omission to notify (section 15), one can even raise the issue of analogous application of criminal law, violating the rule *nullum crimen sine lege*.

These problems became concrete in a case where a group of young people in September 1987 demonstrated against the visit of Kenyan President Daniel Arap Moi to Finland after his visits to the other Nordic countries had been cancelled because of the human rights situation in Kenya. The demonstration in question was organized in the form of distributing leaflets to the public and a single banderole with the text: "Moi, Human Rights?"

The first words in the decision by the Helsinki Court of Appeals (19.9.1989, no. 1954), in which one of the demonstrators was punished with a fine for not giving prior notification to the police, clearly illustrate the problems concerning the 1907 Act: "The Act on Public Meetings is, in the absence of other legal provisions, applicable also in the case of demonstrations...."

Efforts to modernize the Finnish legislation on public meetings and demonstrations have been made since 1973, but so far with meagre results.[26]

---

[25] See Partsch 1981, p. 234.
[26] See Hallberg 1990.

298 *Martin Scheinin*

References

van Dijk, Pieter and G.J.H. van Hoof, *Theory and Practice of the European Convention on Human Rights*, Deventer: Kluwer Law and Taxation Publishers, 1984.

Eriksson, Lars D., Ulkomaalaisten oikeuksista ja oikeusturvasta Suomessa, Lakimies 1983.

Habermas, Jürgen, Strukturwandel der Öffentlichkeit, Darmstadt: Neuwied 1981 (1961).

Hallberg, Pekka, Kokous, mielenosoitus ja ihmisoikeudet, Lakimies 1990.

Högsta förvaltningsdomstolen (HFD, Supreme Administrative Court) 1990 A 125.

Nowak, Manfred, *UNO-Pakt über bürgerliche und politische Rechte und Fakultativ-protokoll, CCPR-Kommentar*, Kehl: N.P. Engel Verlag, 1989.

Partsch, Karl Josef, "Freedom of Conscience and Expression, and Political Freedoms", in Louis Henkin (ed.), *The International Bill of Rights, The Covenant on Civil and Political Rights*, New York: Columbia University Press, 1981.

Pellonpää, Matti, *Euroopan neuvoston ihmisoikeussopimus Suomen näkökulmasta*, Publications of the Finnish Ministry of Justice, no. 21/1988.

Pellonpää, Matti, "The Implementation of the European Convention on Human Rights in Finland", in Allan Rosas (ed.), *International Human Rights Norms in Domestic Law; Finnish and Polish Perspectives*, Helsinki: Finnish Lawyer's Publishing Company, 1990.

Rosas, Allan, Stat, statsmakt, statsförvaltning — Några konstitutionella iakttagelser, in Juhlakirja, Jaakko Pajula, I, Helsinki: 1989.

Sulkunen, Olavi, Työlämän oikeudet ja Kansainvälinen työjärjestö, in Marjut Helminen and K.J. Lång, Kansainväliset ihmisoikeudet, Mänttä, 1988.

Tuori, Kaarlo, *Oikeus, valta ja demokratia*, Helsinki: 1990.

Törnudd, K., *Finland and the International Norms of Human Rights*, Dordrecht: Martinus Nijhoff Publishers, 1986.

United Nations Documents: E/CN.4/AC.1/SR.8; E/CN.4/95; E/CN.4/AC.1/SR.41; E/CN.4/61; E/800; A/C.3/268; CCPR/C/SR.170.

Verdoodt, Albert, *Naissance et Signification de la Déclaration Universelle des Droits de l'Homme*, Société d'Etude Morales, Sociales et Juridiques, Louvain, Paris: Nauwelaerts, 1964.

de Zayas, Alfred, Jakob Th. Möller and Torkel Opsahl, *Ihmisoikeuskomitea kansalais — ja poliittisia oikeuksia koskevan yleissopimuksen soveltajana sopimuksen valinnaisen pöytäkirjan nojalla*, Oikeustiede — Jurisprudentia XXII, 1989, pp. 385–454. (an updated Finnish translation of de Zayas et al., *German Yearbook of International Law*, vol. 28, Berlin: Duncker & Humblot, 1985.

Article 21

Allan Rosas

Finland

1. Everyone has the right to take part in the government of his country, directly or through freely chosen representatives.
2. Everyone has the right to equal access to public service in his country.
3. The will of the people shall be the basis of the authority of government; this will shall be expressed in periodic and genuine elections which shall be by universal and equal suffrage and shall be held by secret vote or by equivalent free voting procedures.

Article 21, so innocently appearing in the midst of a number of civil and social rights, is, in fact, a 'revolution within a revolution'. The international community has through this provision declared not only the idea of the equal and inalienable rights of the individual in relation to his or her State, but has also set minimum requirements for the structure and functioning of this State: the authority of its government must be based on 'the will of the people', and there must be a system of democratic participation with equal political rights for every citizen. Article 21 is thus primarily concerned with members of a given political community (citizens) rather than with individuals as such.

In regard to article 21, it seems especially pertinent to stress a broader framework; the modern notion of political rights is based upon the principle of equality (articles 1, 2, 4 and 7), presupposes civil rights and liberties and certain basic social rights, and is affected by the final limitation provisions (articles 29 and 30).

I. Background

It is not possible within the framework of this brief comment to analyse in depth the philosophical and political background of article 21. The idea of political democracy is ancient. Notions of popular sovereignty, coupled with the principle of equality, are particularly relevant. The American and French revolutions have offered declaratory language of interest for our theme. The idea of popular sovereignty is reflected, for example, in the Virginia Bill of Rights of 1776 and other American constitutional instruments, the French "Déclaration des Droits de l'Homme et du Citoyen" of 1789 and the abortive French Declaration of 1793.[1] There were also references especially in the French documents to the right to resist oppression, to the law being an expression of the general will; to the equal access of citizens to public service; and, of course, to the general principle of equality.

It took some time, however, before political democracy in the modern sense of the word manifested itself. The 'people' at first comprised only a small minority of the adult population, and the civil rights and liberties even of this privileged group could be fragile indeed.[2] During the 19th century the right to vote and to be elected was generally still tied to income and wealth; women were usually excluded altogether, at least from national elections. After the rise of, first, political liberalism and later, the working class movement, universal suffrage began to manifest itself. It was only after the end of the 19th century that many of the civil and social rights vital for democratic participation (freedom of speech, assembly, association, right to education, etc.) gained ground.

These gradual developments are recorded in a number of national constitutions adopted during the 19th and early 20th century.[3] At the international level, too, notions of the democratic legitimacy of governments and equal political rights of citizens began to assert themselves. There was, for instance, a tendency in the recognition policy of the Central American republics and the United States to withhold recognition of a new government deemed not to have obtained popular consent, although general international law did not come to recognize a legal duty of non-recognition.[4]

[1] Hartung 1964, pp. 36, 42, 50.
[2] See, e.g., Dahl 1971, p. 34f; Nowak 1988, p. 38f.
[3] Hartung 1964, p. 64ff.; Verdoodt 1964, pp. 199, 200.
[4] See, e.g., O'Connell 1970, p. 138f.

Democracy and the right of peoples to self-determination became key words during and after World War II. The Atlantic Charter, signed by US and British leaders in 1941, referred, *inter alia*, to the "right of all peoples to choose the form of government under which they will live."[5] The UN Charter itself does not highlight the requirement of popular sovereignty and democratic processes (for instance, article 4 on membership refers only to 'peace-loving' States), although the Charter, of course, contains some general references to human rights and fundamental freedoms and the principle of self-determination. In addition, there are some references in Chapter XI on non-self-governing territories (article 73b), and in Chapter XII on the international trusteeship system (article 76b), to the need to take into account the wishes and aspirations of the peoples concerned.

More or less in parallel with the preparation of the Universal Declaration of Human Rights (UDHR), similar preparatory work was carried out within the inter-American system. The Charter of the Organization of American States (OAS) of 1948 declares that the solidarity and the high aims it seeks "require the political organization of those States on the basis of the effective exercise of representative democracy" (article 3d).

In the American Declaration of the Rights and Duties of Man, also adopted by the Ninth International Conference of American States in 1948, there is a more elaborate provision relating to the right of all persons having legal capacity to participate in the government of their country and to take part in popular elections,[6] as well as to the political duties of citizens. This Declaration was adopted in the spring of 1948, that is, before the UDHR. There was a certain interaction in the preparation of the two instruments, as drafts and proposals concerning one instrument were available to the drafters of the other.[7]

II. *Travaux Préparatoires*

An equivalent to article 21 had already appeared in the first draft to an International Bill of Human Rights, prepared by the UN Secretariat and considered by the UN Commission on Human

[5] Osmanczyk 1985, p. 56.

[6] Article XX; *Inter-American Yearbook on Human Rights*, 1985, p. 34.

[7] See Verdoodt 1964, p. 198; Buergenthal and Norris 5, p. 15, and below.

Rights (the Commission) at its first session in June 1947.[8] There were two separate provisions, concerning respectively the right to participate in the government of the State, and the right of equal access to public functions. In addition, the outline contained an express provision on the right to resist oppression and tyranny.

This first draft underwent a number of revisions in the Commission and the Third Committee of the General Assembly.[9] In general, the original draft prepared by the Secretariat did fairly well in this flux of proposals, votes and revisions,[10] although the structure was somewhat changed and the separate draft provision on the right to resist tyranny was watered down to an indirect reference in the Preamble (see below).

There was first of all the basic choice, which came into the limelight during the third session of the Commission in June 1948, between a shorter version advanced by the United Kingdom and a more extensive version based on the original Secretariat outline and which ultimately became article 21. The shorter version did not contain any references to the will of the people as the basis of the authority of government, to elections or to equal access to public service.[11] One reason for the United Kingdom's desire for a shorter and more general text was its concern with the application of political rights in the colonies. At the insistence of France, the reference to the will of the people was kept, but the Soviet preference for keeping a reference to elections and in this context to universal and equal suffrage was not reflected in the draft adopted by the Commission.[12]

The Soviet Union again advanced this idea in the General Assembly and amendments in the same direction were also made by Cuba, France and Sweden. The final text of what became a separate paragraph 3, containing references to both the will of the people and to periodic and genuine elections, was worked out during the deliberations in the Third Committee. It was adopted by 39 votes to 3, with 3 abstentions. Guatemala, Uruguay and probably Haiti voted against, while the United States, Ecuador and probably

---

[8] UN doc. E/CN.4/21, Annex A, p. 17.
[9] For details see Verdoodt 1964, p. 198ff.
[10] Humphrey 1984, p. 192.
[11] UN doc. E/CN.4/99.
[12] E/CN.4/SR, 61–62.

the United Kingdom abstained.[13]

With respect to the reference to the 'will of the people', the US representative in an explanation of vote stated that it "proclaimed a political principle rather than a human right...." It should be noted that the new wording differed from the one proposed by the Commission, which formulated the principle as an individual right (this being in accordance with a US proposal submitted in the Commission[14]). In advocating a change to the Commission text, Professor Cassin of France claimed that for minds trained in the tradition of Roman law it was illogical to state the principle as an individual right; it was "a collective right on the part of the people as a whole."[15]

The various drafts containing express references to elections reflected a considerable variation as to what attributes these elections would possess. The requirement of 'secret ballot' first introduced in the Commission[16] raised concerns as to its applicability in the British colonies and in countries with direct forms of democracy like Switzerland, and an additional reference to 'equivalent free voting procedures' was included by the Third Committee of the General Assembly. The express requirement of 'universal and equal suffrage' was included, mainly at the insistence of the Soviet Union.

While the question of universal and equal suffrage concerns primarily what Dahl in another context has called the inclusiveness of a political regime (i.e., the extent of popular participation[17]), there were also some interesting discussions in the Commission and the Third Committee on what Dahl would term the competitive nature of a regime, that is, the actual existence of choices (public contestation).

One aspect of the question of competitiveness was the requirement in the early drafts that the elections be 'free' and 'fair', and the reference in what ultimately became paragraph 1 to 'freely chosen representatives' of the citizens. Moreover, the final text of paragraph 3 provides that elections shall be not only periodic but also 'genuine', a formulation introduced by Chile in the Third

---

[13] 3 UN General Assembly Official Records I, Third Committee, SR 132–134, pp. 448–473, explanations of vote, p. 472.

[14] E/CN.4/95, p. 9.

[15] 3 UN General Assembly Official Records I, Third Committee, SR 132, p. 450.

[16] UN doc. E/600, p. 17.

[17] See Dahl 1971, p. 7.

Committee of the General Assembly.[18]

More far-reaching suggestions did not carry the day, however. The United States at one point proposed to the Commission an express requirement of 'a government which conforms to the will of the people, with full freedom for minority opinion to persist and, if such is the people's will, to become the effective majority'.[19] The United States did not press the point but expressed its readiness to support the shorter UK proposal referred to above.[20] In the Third Committee of the General Assembly, Belgium tried to stress the aspect of public competition and pluralism by proposing an addition, according to which elections should be held 'with several lists' of candidates. This drew firm opposition from the representative of the Soviet Union, who stated that the Belgian amendment "was absolutely irreconcilable with the social structure of certain Member States." The Belgian representative immediately withdrew his amendment.[21]

Paragraph 2 of article 21, providing for the right to 'equal access to public service', caused fewer problems. The original proposal by the Secretariat contained an additional provision that 'appointments to the civil service shall be by competitive examination'.[22] France suggested an even more far-reaching text[23] but the representative of France had to admit that equality of opportunity to engage in public employment "was not, strictly speaking, a fundamental right"[24] and formulations like these were dropped from the proposal submitted by the Commission to the General Assembly.

In the Third Committee, the entire article was adopted by 39 votes to one, with one abstention (Haiti voted against[25]). In plenary, article 21 was adopted unanimously. This article thus commended broad formal support, although a number of preferences and disagreements appeared with respect to the details.

It should be recalled that the original Secretariat draft of 1947 contained a separate article on the 'right to resist oppression and tyranny'. The idea was still reflected in preliminary drafts drawn up

[18] 3 UN General Assembly Official Records I, Third Committee, SR 133, p. 463.
[19] E/CN.4/95, p. 9f.
[20] E/CN.4/SR 61, p. 13.
[21] 3 UN General Assembly Official Records I, Third Committee, SR 132, p. 453; SR 133, p. 464; SR 134, pp. 469, 471; see also Steiner 1988, p. 91.
[22] E/CN.4/21, p. 19.
[23] Ibid., p. 59f.
[24] E/CN.4/SR 61, p. 16.
[25] See 3 UN General Assembly Official Records, Third Committee, SR 134, p. 472.

within the Commission,[26] but the Commission later decided to place this right in the Preamble[27] and ultimately formulated the paragraph not as an express right but as a statement on the importance of sustaining a regime of law so as to avoid the need for rebellion against tyranny and oppression.[28] The efforts of some Latin American and Socialist States to reintroduce the idea of a separate article on the right to resist tyranny and oppression were not successful in the Third Committee of the General Assembly, and the Committee made some changes only to the text of the Preamble.[29]

III. The Universal Declaration and the Covenant

Article 21 of the UDHR has an evident counterpart in article 25 of the International Covenant on Civil and Political Rights (CCPR). It was not self-evident that the CCPR should include a separate article on political rights. The pattern of the UDHR was recommended by some European (both Eastern and Western) countries in particular, and a draft modelled along the lines of article 21 of the UDHR was ultimately presented by France and Yugoslavia.[30] In the Third Committee of the General Assembly, near unanimity was reached (by a vote of 74:0:4, in 1961). The formal consensus is underlined by the fact that only a few and marginal reservations have been made to article 25.[31] Article 25 of the CCPR reads as follows:

Every citizen shall have the right and the opportunity, without any of the distinctions mentioned in article 2 and without unreasonable restrictions:
- (a) To take part in the conduct of public affairs, directly or through freely chosen representatives;
- (b) To vote and to be elected at genuine periodic elections which shall be by universal and equal suffrage and shall be held by secret ballot, guaranteeing the free expression of the will of the electors;
- (c) To have access, on general terms of equality, to public service in

[26] E/CN.4/21, pp. 59, 79; E/CN.4/57.
[27] E/600, p. 19.
[28] E/800, p. 8.
[29] 3 UN General Assembly Official Records I, Third Committee, SR 164–165; for further details see Verdoodt 1964, p. 311ff.
[30] Partsch 1981, pp. 238, 459, note 135; Bossuyt 1987, p. 469ff.
[31] United Nations, *Human Rights-Status of International Instruments 1987*, p. 28ff.; see also Partsch 1981, p. 241.

his country.

There are a number of similarities between the two articles, but also a few interesting differences. The structure of the two articles is similar, although the order of paragraphs 2 and 3 (paragraphs (a) and (b) in the CCPR) has changed. Article 25 of the CCPR undoubtedly contains a more logical sequence.

The first paragraph of both articles speaks of the right 'to take part' in the conduct of public affairs and recognizes both direct and indirect forms of democracy, even concluding with identical language. Article 21 restricts the applicability of the right of political participation by referring to 'his' country, while article 25 of the CCPR explicitly limits this right to citizens only.

It will be noted that neither provision uses the actual concept of democracy, but instead emphasizes participation.[32] There are some references to a 'democratic society' in the two instruments (in the UDHR, article 29 only), but these appear in the context of limitation clauses. In the preparation of the UDHR, the Soviet Union called for more emphasis on the concept of democracy and, in this context, on the struggle against Fascism and Nazism[33] but these efforts were by and large unsuccessful. Undoubtedly, the choice to avoid this concept in article 21 (and article 25 of the CCPR) had to do with the divergent connotations it raised ('people's democracy', 'parliamentary democracy', etc.).

The election clauses of the two articles and their drafting history make it clear that they were intended to leave States a fair margin of choice in devising their electoral systems. Thus, a system, for example, of majority voting in one-seat constituencies, of 'indirect' elections (meaning that the voters cast their ballots for electors, not directly for the ultimate candidate), or of special ratios for minorities or other unprivileged groups, do not as such run counter to the elections clauses.[34] Of course, if such devices are applied to the extremes, so as to substitute, in fact, minority rule for majority rule, the margin of discretion may be transgressed.

A basic question concerns the degree of pluralism and public contestation (on this terminology, see above) required of a political system. The preparatory work of article 21, where the question was,

---

[32] Steiner 1988, p. 86f.

[33] See the Soviet statement made on 18 June 1948, published also as an appendix to UN doc. E/800, p. 29f.

[34] Santa Cruz 1962, p. 9ff.; see also, principle V, ibid., p. 97; see also Partsch 1981, p. 240; Törnudd 1986, p. 187ff.; Steiner 1988, p. 90; Rosas 1990, p. 40.

after all, raised, makes it clear that there was nothing near a consensus for requiring a multiparty system. During the drafting of article 25 of the CCPR, there was less open discussion on these intricate issues. In considering periodic State reports, members of the Human Rights Committee have occasionally addressed the question of competitiveness, but no definite conclusions can be drawn from these discussions.[35] The Committee has not been able to draw up so-called general comments on article 25. It has thus not been established that even an institutionalized one-party system is by definition a violation of article 25 of the CCPR. But such a system certainly raises questions as to whether the political and civil rights and freedoms available meet the requirements of the CCPR.[36]

Both article 21 of the UDHR and article 25 of the CCPR no doubt leave room for various forms of 'direct' democracy (referenda, etc.). It would seem that the term 'elections' must be construed broadly, which would imply that the election requirements apply to referenda as well.[37] On the other hand, the two articles seem to require at least some elections of decision makers, although the types of organs to be elected are not specified. At any rate, it is at the present time difficult to imagine a 'pure' system of direct democracy that could do away with elections altogether and still satisfy the requirements of these provisions.

During the drafting stages, little attention was paid to anything other than national elections, such as, for example, regional and local elections. In the preparation of the CCPR, there was a Soviet proposal concerning the right of citizens to elect and be elected "to all organs of authority." This proposal was rejected in the Commission, but this seems to have been done primarily out of concerns about extending the election requirement to the executive or the judiciary,[38] and it would seem that article 25 — and article 21 of the UDHR — have some bearing on other than national elections as well.[39] This seems more clearly enunciated in the CCPR with its reference to 'the conduct of public affairs', while the UDHR in the English version[40] speaks of 'the government of his

---

[35] Partsch 1981, p. 240ff.; Steiner 1988, p. 91f; Rosas 1990, p. 43.
[36] See also principle VIII in Santa Cruz 1962, p. 98; Partsch 1981, p. 240.
[37] Santa Cruz 1962, p. 9 and principles IV–V in ibid., p. 97.
[38] Bossuyt 1987, p. 474.
[39] Partsch 1981, p. 242f.
[40] But see also the French version and Verdoodt 1964, p. 205.

country'.

Perhaps the most striking difference between the text of the two articles is the absence in article 25 of the CCPR of the bold opening of paragraph 3 of article 21: "The will of the people shall be the basis of the authority of government." Article 25, paragraph 2, of the CCPR, on the other hand, does require that elections guarantee the free expression of "the will of the electors." As article 21 prescribes elections as the means of expressing the will of the people, and as 'the electors' mentioned in article 25 should, in view of the principles of equality and non-discrimination, comprise the entire adult population, the difference between the two articles seems more symbolic than substantial.

Moreover, the International Covenant on Economic, Social and Cultural Rights (CESCR) and the CCPR of 1966 contain an article that is not to be found in the UDHR and that might, as it were, compensate for the somewhat more bleak language of article 25. I am thinking of common article 1 on the right to self-determination. It is not possible here to go into the discussion on this rather controversial provision. Suffice it to note that I basically share the opinions of those who see also an *internal* aspect in this right, requiring some basic democratic legitimacy of a government and a political system.[41] The general comments on article 1 adopted by the Human Rights Committee in 1984 seem to presuppose internal self-determination as well.[42]

With this interpretation, there is a close link between articles 1 and 25 of the CCPR, and article 1 could be seen as an offspring of article 21, and indeed, even of the Preamble (the right of rebellion) of the UDHR. It will be recalled that the reference to the will of the people in article 21 was considered by the government representative pressing for its inclusion (Cassin of France) as a collective right. Common article 1 of the two covenants also gives expression to a collective right.

Lastly, it is to be noted that the *chapeau* of article 25 of the CCPR not only refers to the non-discrimination clause of article 2, but also recognizes the possibility of *restrictions* on the right to political participation, provided that the restrictions are not "unreasonable". In the UDHR, the possibility of restrictions is expressly recognized in the general limitation clause of article 29, paragraph 2. It is clear that both instruments leave room for certain specific restrictions, for

---

[41] See, in particular, Cassese 1979; Ramcharan 1987, pp. 12–15; Rosas 1990, p. 31.
[42] CCPR/C/21/Add. 3, p. 2.

example, on the right to vote, such as the exclusion of persons below a certain age and of special categories like the mentally ill. Sweeping exclusions, for example, of illiterates, tend to constitute violations, however.[43] The Human Rights Committee has considered several individual communications alleging unreasonable restrictions on the exercise of the political rights recognized in article 25 (especially in Uruguay) and has in most cases found a violation of this provision.[44]

IV. Other Instruments and Processes

The right of political participation has in one form or another been recognized in the regional instruments, too. I referred above to the parallel preparations of the UDHR and the American Declaration of the Rights and Duties of Man of 1948. Article XX of the latter Declaration has been followed by article 23 of the American Convention on Human Rights (ACHR) of 1969.

The similarity between this article and article 25 of the CCPR is striking, the latter undoubtedly having influenced the text of the ACHR.[45] The three paragraphs (a)–(c) of article 25 of the CCPR are repeated with some minor drafting changes only. The most apparent difference relates to the limitations clause. Paragraph 2 of article 23 of the ACHR lists as specific grounds for regulating by law the exercise of the rights recognized in paragraph 1 not only age, nationality, and civil and mental capacity but also "residence, language, education" as well as "sentencing by a competent court in criminal proceedings." This seems to be quite a far-reaching list and may allow for restrictions which would exceed the limits of the CCPR.

In the preparation of the European Convention on Human Rights (ECHR) of 1950, there was disagreement as to whether the Convention should include a provision on political participation.[46] It was not possible to agree on a provision in the ECHR itself, but

[43] Santa Cruz 1962, p. 10 and principles IV and XI, ibid., p. 97f.; Partsch 1981, p. 238.
[44] United Nations, *Human Rights Committee — Selected Decisions under the Optional Protocol 1985*, pp. 40, 57, 61, 65, 67, 76, 88, 105.
[45] On the legislative history of the provision, see Buergenthal and Norris 12, p. 124ff.; 13, p. 55f.
[46] Steiner 1988, p. 94; Nowak 1988, p. 142ff.; for details on the preparatory work see Council of Europe, *Collected Edition*.

article 3 of Protocol no. 1 to the Convention adopted in 1952 remedied this shortcoming.

This short article differs from the corresponding provisions of the UDHR, the CCPR and the ACHR above all in that it was originally devised as containing subjective rights of the individual.[47] It simply states the requirement of "free elections at reasonable intervals by secret ballot, under conditions which will ensure the free expression of the opinion of the people in the choice of the legislature". There is no general participation clause and no provision on equal access to public service, and the elections clause is limited to the choice of 'the legislature'.

Despite the fact that the election clause is formulated as an obligation of the State Party rather than as an individual right, the European Commission of Human Rights (European Commission) has through a dynamic interpretation, expressly recognized only in 1975, equated the article with the other provisions of the European system, thus granting the individual a right of complaint. There are by now a number of pronouncements by the European Commission and one decision by the European Court on the interpretation of article 3 of Protocol no. 1.[48] The Commission has interpreted the article as implying the existence of a representative legislature as well as recognition of the principle of universal suffrage and of the individual rights to vote and to stand in legislative elections. But in no case has a violation of the provision been found.

The African Charter on Human and Peoples' Rights (African Charter) of 1981 provides for a solution almost opposite to that of the ECHR. Article 13 of the African Charter contains general participation and equal access clauses but no express elections clause. As paragraph 1 of article 13 more or less repeats the wording of the UDHR and the CCPR, that citizens have the right to participate either "directly or through freely chosen repre-sentatives", the question of elections is not bypassed altogether. Paragraph 3 of article 13 contains a novelty in requiring that every individual has "the right of access to public property and services in strict equality of all persons before the law."

The right of political participation is also considered in some particular conventions, such as the International Convention on the Elimination of All Forms of Racial Discrimination of 1965 (article

[47] Nowak 1988, p. 147.
[48] Council of Europe, *Digest of Strasbourg Case-Law*, vol. 5, p. 829ff.; see also van Dijk and van Hoof 1984, p. 355ff; Nowak 1988, p. 148.

5), the Convention on the Political Rights of Women of 1952 (articles I–III), the Convention on the Elimination of All Forms of Discrimination against Women of 1979 as well as the Inter-American Convention on Granting of Political Rights to Women of 1948 (article 1).

While the general instruments considered above undoubtedly cover women and men alike, there may be some clarifications and specific additions in the gender instruments. In particular, it should be noted that article 7 of the 1979 Convention grants women the equal right to vote not only in elections but also in "public referenda", to "participate in the formulation of government policy and the implementation thereof" and to "participate in non-governmental organizations and associations concerned with the public and political life of the country", while article 8 refers to the "opportunity to represent their governments at the international level and to participate in the work of international organizations."

Finally, reference should be made to certain special studies relating to this subject which have been carried out in a UN framework. In 1961, Hernan Santa Cruz, Special Rapporteur, presented a Study of Discrimination in the Matter of Political Rights to the Sub-Commission on Prevention of Discrimination and Protection of Minorities.[49] The Sub-Commission adopted in 1962 a set of 15 General Principles on Freedom and Non-Discrimination in the Matter of Political Rights. This fairly extensive document was transmitted to the Commission, which was not able to consider it until 1973. Ultimately the study led to the adoption of the Economic and Social Council (ECOSOC) resolution 1786 (LIV), which simply draws the attention of governments and a number of other bodies to the draft general principles.[50]

A quite recent study touching upon the question of political participation is provided by a study on 'popular participation', presented in 1985 by the UN Secretary-General to the Commission.[51] This study was undertaken within the broader framework of the realization of economic, social and cultural rights and thus is not focused upon the right of political participation as such. It contains a section on the right to take part in the conduct of public affairs, however, and also alludes to the broader perspectives of political and other participation which will be touched upon

---

[49] Santa Cruz 1962.
[50] United Nations, *United Nations Action in the Field of Human Rights 1983*, p. 188f.
[51] E/CN.4/1985/10 and Add. 1 and 2.

below. Further studies containing the comments on the substantive study received from governments, organizations, etc., were submitted in 1986 and 1987[52] and the question is pending before the Commission.

V. Conclusions and Reflections

Article 21 has obviously provided a stimulus for a number of treaty-based provisions relating to political rights. But even more its text does not score at all badly in comparison with the other instruments. On the contrary, the article compares favourably with the corresponding articles of the CCPR and the ACHR, and it is certainly more comprehensive than those of Protocol no. 1 of the ECHR and the African Charter. The fact that the text of the UDHR goes further than some of the treaty provisions raises interesting questions relating to its possible status as a norm of customary international law, questions which cannot be developed in the context of this brief comment.

When adopted, article 21 (as well as article 25 of the CCPR) commanded broad formal consent from the various political groupings. The negotiating history gives ample illustration that the UDHR is not a purely 'Western' project. Article 21 came about through a kind of coalition between some Western countries, notably France, Latin American countries and socialist countries. All Western States were not that enthusiastic, as shown also by the difficulties encountered in the preparation of the political rights provision in the Western European context.

This coalition above all related to what has been referred to above as the 'inclusiveness' of a political system, for example, the question of universal and equal suffrage. With some reservations one can also detect a similar coalition behind the references in the UDHR to the basis of political authority and the ultimate right of every people to choose its own form of government ('the will of the people', the right of resistance, in the CCPR also the right of self-determination). But when it comes to the 'competitive' elements of article 21, and especially the civil liberties recognized in other articles of the UDHR, the picture is more of a Western preference and emphasis.

The real world is, as it were, conforming to this pattern, as the

---

[52] E/CN.4/1987/11; E/CN.4/1988/11.

principle of universality and equality has now gained almost universal formal acceptance, while the most notable latecomers are Western countries (Switzerland until 1974, South Africa still today). The picture is quite different, of course, when one looks at the question of public contestation and pluralism. Indicators of this type are often predominant in the numerous ratings of political systems and democracies that have been carried out especially in the West, and which usually show that only a minority, perhaps even less than one third, of the States today are really democracies.[53] At the time of writing the picture is changing, perhaps even dramatically, with important democratic processes occurring in some Eastern European and Third World countries.[54]

If one shares the present author's view that both aspects, the degree of inclusiveness as well as of pluralism, are important, it is difficult to escape the conclusion that the Nordic countries have done fairly well in a world wide survey. Universal and equal suffrage was introduced in the period 1906–1921.[55] Finland was the first country in Europe to establish full universal and equal suffrage. The Nordic democracies are also fairly comprehensive, with political participation manifesting itself not only in national elections but also at the local, and to some extent, regional level, and with opportunities for binding or consultative referenda. There is no doubt that the Nordic political systems are in an international comparison quite competitive, with free elections, a genuine multiparty system, etc.[56]

There is, of course, always room for improvements, and one way of looking at the right of political participation is to see it, partly at least, as a 'programmatic right', setting aspirations and new demands as societies change.[57] There is an ongoing debate in the West on a broader conception of political participation than mere participation in periodic elections, using concepts like 'participatory' democracy, 'strong' democracy and 'self-government'.[58] The text of the 1979 Convention on the Elimination of All Forms of Discrimination against Women and the

---

[53] See, e.g., Vanhanen 1984.
[54] Rosas and Helgesen 1990.
[55] Rokkan 1970, p. 151; Haavio-Mannila *et al.* 1985, p. 38.
[56] For a survey of Nordic democratic systems and institutions, see Friis 1981.
[57] Steiner 1988, p. 129ff.
[58] A survey, from a human rights perspective, is offered by Steiner 1988, p. 96ff.; see also, e.g., Friis 1981; Duncan 1983; Barber 1984.

ongoing UN study on popular participation to some extent seem to reflect these trends.

Thus, the concept of democracy is being related to a broader range of issues and institutions. Article 21 of the UDHR, which grants every individual the right to take part in "the government of his country", should be given a broad meaning, so as to include not only regional and local government but also various semi-public and semi-private institutions and devices[59] and, in general, all decision-making of a public interest. There should be genuine democratic participation, with open and informed discussion and interaction and effective accountability. Moreover, the population participating in decision-making should perhaps be defined more on the basis of residence than nationality and citizenship.[60]

Article 21 of the UDHR provides an inspiration and authoritative guide both in combating departures from true democracy and in setting agendas and perspectives for the future.

[59] On the semi-public and semi-private sectors see, e.g., Modeen and Rosas 1988.
[60] On the right of Nordic citizens to vote in the country of residence, see Rosas 1984; on the preparation of a Draft Convention on the Participation of Foreigners in Public Life at Local Level see Council of Europe Doc. CDLR (89)15 of 5 October 1989.

References

Allardt, Erik, Nils Andrén, Erik J. Friis, Gylfi Gíslason, Sten Sparre Nilson, Henry Valen, Frantz Wendt and Folmer Wisti (eds.), *Nordic Democracy, Ideas, Issues, and Institutions in Politics, Economy, Education, Social and Cultural Affairs of Denmark, Finland, Iceland, Norway, and Sweden*, Copenhagen: Det Danske Selskab, 1981.

Barber, Benjamin R., *Strong Democracy. Participatory Politics for a New Age*, Berkeley: University of California Press, 1984.

Bossuyt, Marc J., *Guide to the "Travaux Préparatoires" of the International Covenant on Civil and Political Rights*, Dordrecht: Martinus Nijhoff Publishers, 1987.

Buergenthal, Thomas and Robert E. Norris (eds.), *Human Rights — The Inter-American System*, Binders 1–3, Booklets 1–26, Dobbs Ferry: Oceana Publications, Inc., 1982–84.

Cassese, Antonio, "Political Self-Determination — Old Concepts and New Developments", in Antonio Cassese (ed.), *UN Law/Fundamental Rights. Two Topics in International Law*, Alphen aan den Rijn: Sijthoff & Noordhoff, 1979.

Council of Europe, *Collected Edition of the "Travaux Préparatoires" of the European Convention on Human Rights — Recueil des "Travaux Préparatoires"*, vol. I–VIII, The Hague: Martinus Nijhoff Publishers, 1975–85.

Council of Europe, *Digest of Strasbourg Case-Law Relating to the European Convention on Human Rights*, vol. 5 (articles 26–66, Protocols to the Convention), Köln: Carl Heymanns Verlag KG, 1985.

Council of Europe, Steering Committee on Local and Regional Authorities (CDLR), *Preparation of a Draft Convention on the Participation of Foreigners in Public Life at Local Level*, Secretariat Memorandum prepared by the Directorate of Environment and Local Authorities, CDLR (89)15, Strasbourg, 5 October 1989.

Dahl, Robert A., *Polyarchy. Participation and Opposition*, New Haven, London: Yale University Press, 1971.

van Dijk, Pieter and G.J.H. van Hoof, *Theory and Practice of the European Convention on Human Rights*, second edition, Deventer: Kluwer Law and Taxation Publishers, 1990.

Duncan, Graeme (ed.), *Democratic Theory and Practice*, Cambridge: Cambridge University Press, 1983.

Haavio-Mannila, Eline, *et al.* (eds.), *Unfinished Democracy, Women in Nordic Politics*, Oxford: Pergamon Press, 1985.

Hartung, Fritz, *Die Entwicklung der Menschen- und Bürgerrechte von 1776 bis zur Gegenwart*, 3, erweiterte Auflage, Göttingen: Musterschmidt Verlag, 1964.

Humphrey, John P., "Political and Related Rights", in Theodor Meron (ed.), *Human Rights in International Law: Legal and Policy Issues*, Oxford: Clarendon Press, 1984.

Inter-American Commission on Human Rights and Inter-American Court of Human Rights, *Inter-American Yearbook on Human Rights* — Anuario Interamericano de Derechos Humanos 1985, Dordrecht: Martinus Nijhoff Publishers, 1987.

Modeen, Tore and Allan Rosas, (eds., in co-operation with the International Institute of Administrative Sciences, Brussels), *Indirect Public Administration in Fourteen Countries — L'Administration Publique Indirecte dans Quatorze Pays*, Turku/Åbo: Åbo Academy Press, 1988.

Nowak, Manfred, *Politische grundrechte*, Wien: Springer Verlag, 1988.

O'Connell, D.P., *International Law*, 2nd edition, vol. I, London: Stevens & Sons, 1970.

Osmanczyk, Edmund Jan, *The Encyclopedia of the United Nations and International Agreements*, Philadelphia: Taylor and Francis, 1985.

Partsch, Karl Josef, "Freedom of Conscience and Expression, and Political Freedoms", in Louis Henkin (ed.), *The International Bill of Rights. The Covenant on Civil and Political Rights*, New York: Columbia University Press, 1981.

Ramcharan, Bertram G., "Peoples' Rights and Minorities' Rights", *Nordic Journal of International Law — Acta Scandinavia juris gentium*, vol. 56, no. 1, 1987.

Rokkan, Stein, (with Angus Campbell, Per Torsvik and Henry Valen), *Citizens, Elections, Parties. Approaches to the Comparative Study of the Process of Development*, Oslo: Universitetsforlaget, 1970.

Rosas, Allan, "Medborgarskap och rösträtt", in *Forhandlingene ved Det 30. nordiske juristmötet*, Oslo, 15–17 August 1984, Del I. Oslo, 1984: Det norske styret for De nordiske juristmoter.

Rosas, Allan, "Democracy and Human Rights", in Allan Rosas and Jan Helgesen (eds.), *Human Rights in a Changing East-West Perspective*, London: Pinter Publishers, 1990.

Rosas, Allan and Jan Helgesen, "Introduction", in Allan Rosas and Jan Helgesen (eds.), *Human Rights in a Changing East-West Perspective*, London: Pinter Publishers, 1990.

Santa Cruz, Hernan, *Study of Discrimination in the Matter of Political Rights*, (E/CN.4/Sub.2/213/Rev.1), New York: United Nations, 1962.

Steiner, Henry J., "Political Participation as a Human Right", *Harvard Human Rights Yearbook*, vol. 1, 1988.

Törnudd, Klaus, *Finland and the International Norms of Human Rights*, International Studies in Human Rights, Dordrecht: Martinus Nijhoff Publishers, 1986.

United Nations, *United Nations Action in the Field of Human Rights*, (ST/HR/2/Rev.2), New York: United Nations, 1983.

United Nations, *Human Rights-Status of International Instruments*, (ST/HR/5), Centre for Human Rights, New York: United Nations, 1987.

United Nations, *Human Rights Committee — Selected Decisions under the*

Optional Protocol, (second to sixteenth session) (CCPR/C/OP/1), New York: United Nations, 1985.

United Nations Documents: E/CN.4/21; E/CN.4/57; E/CN.4/95; E/CN.4/99; E/CN.4/SR 61–62; E/600; E/800; CCPR/C/21/Add. 3; E/CN.4/1985/10, Add. 1,2; E/CN.4/1987/11; E/CN.4/1988/11.

United Nations: 3 UN General Assembly Official Records I, Third Committee, SR 132, 133, 134, 164–165

Vanhanen, Tatu, *The Emergence of Democracy. A Comparative Study of 119 States, 1850–1979*, Commentationes Scientarium Socialium, vol. 24. Helsinki: The Finnish Society of Sciences and Letters, 1984.

Verdoodt, Albert, *Naissance et Signification de la Déclaration Universelle des Droits de l'Homme*, Société d'Etudes Morales, Sociales et Juridiques, Louvain-Paris: Editions Nauwelaerts, 1964.

Article 22

Bård-Anders Andreassen[*]

Norway

Everyone, as a member of society, has the right to social security and is entitled to realization, through national effort and international co-operation and in accordance with the organization and resources of each State, of the economic, social and cultural rights indispensable for his dignity and the free development of his personality.

I. Introduction

In the historical evolution of human rights, economic and social rights are commonly referred to as the contribution of the 20th century to the international humanitarian and human rights law.[1] During the general debate on the draft of the Universal Declaration of Human Rights (UDHR) in the UN General Assembly, stress was put on the point that one of the most important attributes by which the UDHR "represents a degree of progress over previous

---

[*] I am in dept to Professor Stein Kuhnle at the Department of Comparative Politics, University of Bergen; Director Asbjørn Eide, the Norwegian Institute of Human Rights; and to Professor Bernt Hagtvet and Researcher Hugo Stokke, and Tor Skålnes at the Chr. Michelsen Institute, Bergen, for comments on the first draft of this study. The responsibility for the end result belongs, of course, entirely to the author.

[1] It is important to recall, however, that since the adoption of the Universal Declaration of Human Rights (UDHR) in 1948 a fundamental tenet of the UN approach to human rights has been the acknowledgement of the indivisibility and interdependence of civil and political rights on the one hand and economic, social and cultural rights on the other. See "The Limburg Principle on the Implementation of the International Covenant on Economic, Social and Cultural Rights" reproduced in *Human Rights Quarterly* vol. 9, no. 2, 1987, para. 3. See Eide, *The New International Economic Order...*, E/CN.4/Sub.2/1987/23.

declarations of a similar nature" is that it includes rights to economic and social benefits.[2]

The incorporation of socio-economic rights into the International Bill of Rights was anticipated by the UN Assistant Secretary-General, Henri Laugier, in his inaugural speech at the opening meeting of the Commission on Human Rights (the Commission) on 29 April 1946, in which he addressed the Commission by saying:

> You will have to study all the declarations of rights which were born in the spirit of man and people on their march toward their liberation. You will have to show that the political rights are the first condition of liberty but that today the progress of scientific and industrial civilization has created economic organizations which are inflicting on politically free men intolerable servitude, and that therefore, in the future, the declaration of man must be extended to the economic and social field.[3]

Laugier urged the Commission to develop "a permanent guide for men of good will" by establishing a "minimum of common principles" around which the reconstruction of the world could be built. Thus, from the outset the Commission paid attention to social and economic human rights.

Since the latter part of the 19th and early 20th century, welfare rights and welfare state provisions have gradually evolved in Europe and other countries of the north-western hemisphere. Welfare state literature, however, tends to emphasize a certain ambiguity as regards the historical sources and the political justification of the modern welfare state: at an early stage welfare rights served as integrative means, and aimed at improving the political legitimacy of autocratic and authoritarian States (as in Bismarck's Germany), as well as in emerging liberal democracies. According to this view, social rights in the early phases of the modern welfare state were means to secure political stability by governments confronted with a growing and radical labour movement.

Nevertheless, the normative justification of modern social and

---

[2] Statement made by the 91st meeting of the UN General Assembly on 2 October 1948.

[3] E/HR/6, p. 2. The Commission of Human Rights, at this stage of its work was established by The Economic and Social Council (ECOSOC) as a nuclear commission in order to prepare the work of the permanent Commission which started its First Session in January 1947. See ECOSOC Official Records, first year, first edition, p. 163f.

economic human rights is different. The main justification of these rights is that they aim at securing social equality and social justice. In his inaugural lecture at the International Institute of Human Rights in July 1979, Karel Vasak argued that the economic, social and cultural rights were rights to equality, and that they constituted the "second generation" of human rights embracing "rights of credit" against the State and the organized national and international bodies as a whole.[4] In this perspective, economic and social rights represent the establishment of internationally acceptable standards for a minimum degree of social equity and solidarity in order to secure the well-being and dignity of man in societies in which traditional forms of solidarity have been substantially changed and hampered. It appears, then, that the contemporary idea of social and economic rights represents a qualitative break with the concept of social rights in the early days of the welfare state.

The formulation by the Commission of universal norms for minimum social and economic entitlements, represented an important progress in modern human rights law. Some of the members of the Commission wanted to emphasize this 'new' category of international human rights by including an introductory article to the section of the UDHR dealing with economic, social and cultural rights, and in the last phase of the Commission's work an umbrella article was formulated for this purpose. Hence, article 22 of the UDHR precedes the five subsequent articles which declare the rights to work (article 23), to rest and leisure (article 24), to an adequate standard of living (article 25), to education (article 26), and the right to participate freely in the cultural life of the community (article 27).

Although article 22 in general terms refers to the economic, social and cultural rights "indispensable for (one's) dignity and free development of (one's) personality", it also refers to "the right to social security", which entitles everyone to access to welfare state provisions. The drafting of the article, and the interpretation of it, generated a series of interventions in the Commission, expressing different political and ideological preferences. In this chapter the aim is to describe the drafting process of article 22 and to explore the intentions of the framers and their arguments and interpretations

---

[4] For a critical assessment of the terminology of 'generations of rights' and 'the status of specific emerging human rights or new formulation of existing human rights', see Alston 1982, pp. 307–322.

of the article. What were the aspirations of the members of the Commission? Who among the Commission's members took part in the drafting debates of the article, and how did the delegates argue?

During the 40 years that have passed since the adoption of the UDHR, economic and social human rights have received less legal attention than other types of rights such as civil and political rights. Therefore, in the closing section there will be a brief review of cross references to article 22 in other international human rights instruments such as the American Declaration of the Rights and Duties of Man, the European Social Charter, the International Covenant on Economic, Social, and Cultural Rights (1966, CESCR), and the International Labour Organisation (ILO) Convention no. 102 concerning minimum standards to social security, in order to elucidate the status of this category of rights within international human rights law. The section also addresses some of the main issues, and recent methodological and procedural efforts linked to the international implementation of social and economic rights internationally. In order to put this evolution of modern social and economic human rights into a Nordic context, I shall first discuss the introduction of social rights in the Nordic countries.

II. Historical Sources of Social Rights: from Territorial Citizenship to Universal Human Rights

Social and economic rights have been conceptually associated with and practically dealt with by social security policies for more than a century. The term social security, however, is recent and dates from American legislation in 1935.[5] If traced in the early social insurance legislation, it appears much older and emerged in Western European countries in the late 19th and the early 20th century as part of the extension of national citizenship by which the rights and duties of the citizen were defined.

In the tradition of the German sociologist Emile Durkheim, national citizenship is the core institution for social and political integration in modern societies. This dimension of the citizenship has also been conceived by the British social historian T.H. Marshall whose ideal–typical model of the development of the

---

[5] See the United States Social Security Act adopted on 14 August 1935.

rights of citizens in Western societies has been important for the understanding of the historical evolution of modern human rights.[6]

According to Marshall, three sets of rights have emerged in European states since the 18th century in the following order:

1. Civil rights such as "liberty of person, freedom of speech, thought and faith, the right to own property" expanded from the latter part of the 17th century and throughout the 18th century;
2. Political rights, such as the franchise and the right to access to public office developed in the 19th century;
3. Social rights ranging from "the right to a modicum of economic welfare and security to the right to share to the full in the social heritage and to live the life as a civilized being according to the standards prevailing in the society" were gradually introduced in the late 19th and early 20th century.[7]

Marshall's model, however, was developed on the basis of the British pattern of rights extension, and it does not fully reflect trends and developments in the Nordic and the European setting in general. One reason for extending social rights in late 19th century Germany was to politically neutralize a radical working class.[8] Flora and Alber conclude that the extension of social rights to the working class was a substitute for democratic reforms and the extension of political rights. It is important to observe, however, that the evolution of socio-economic rights, and the institutional breakthrough of the welfare state, varied substantially with each country in timing, and as regards their political foundation. Marshall's ideal–typical model tends to underestimate the diversity of patterns of human rights developments in Europe, although it

---

[6] Marshall 1950 and Marshall 1964.

[7] Ibid.

[8] In their analysis of the development of welfare states in Western Europe, Flora and Alber (1981) also conclude that "constitutional-dualistic monarchies tended to introduce social and insurance schemes earlier [in chronological and developmental time] than the parliamentary democracies for several reasons", primarily due to a) the greater need to solidify the loyalty of the working class, b) the higher capacity of already developed state bureaucracies, and c) because the former type of regime was dominated by landed interests that were able to shift the costs of social security schemes to the urban upper and middle classes by taxes on income and profit, as well as their ability to extract contributions both by the employers and the employees themselves. See Flora and Alber 1981, p. 70.

may be helpful in suggesting hypotheses for empirical research.[9]

III. The Nordic Pattern

When the UDHR was adopted in 1948, all Nordic countries and most countries in Europe and the Western hemisphere had introduced some form of social legislation guaranteeing social rights of the citizen. Social security programmes emerging in the Nordic countries, as elsewhere in Western Europe, addressed the major causes of social and economic insecurity; social security or insurance systems were developed in relation to industrial accidents, sickness (and invalidity), old age (including survivors), and unemployment.[10] Flora and Alber discern four phases of social security legislation in Western Europe: an introductory phase from the early German legislation during the rule of Bismarck until 1914; a phase of extension between the two World Wars extending insurance schemes to new groups and "adding the idea of a national minimum to the older concept of just wage substitution", and the outbreak of World War II all the Nordic countries had introduced compulsory accident and sickness insurance, some kind of unemployment insurance and a system providing for old age; a phase of completion, "making the catalogue of covered risks complete", immediately after World War II; and a phase of consolidation and reorganization after 1950, in which social insurance systems were made universal, in the sense of being entitlements of every citizen of the country concerned.

The legislation introduced in the first phase of welfare state

[9] The origins of public programmes of social insurance might be traced further back in European history than Marshall's theory suggests. With the support of recent re-examination of European social history, Siegel has taken issue with the influential status of Marshall's three-stage thesis: "Socio-economic rights have rather deep roots that are, in addition to being socialist, also feudal, mercantilist, Methodist, utilitarian, radical, conservative, Roman Catholic — and even liberal....The modern state's legal responsibilities to the poor are linked to obligations accepted by European feudal towns, principalities, and other local jurisdictions above and beyond those long implemented by the Church." Siegel 1985, p. 260f. See also Rimlinger 1971. Rimlinger observes two phases of 'pre history' of the modern welfare state: the 'Poor Law' period from the 16th century to the 18th and 19th centuries and the 'Liberal Break' of the 19th century. The Poor Laws, however, did not correspond to the concept of individual rights that justifies modern human rights.
[10] Flora and Alber 1981.

developments in the Nordic countries tended to converge attempts at alleviating the social costs of industrialization. The early accident insurances were limited to industrial workers in unsafe industries; later the schemes were extended to additional groups, primarily agricultural workers. In the third step the concept of industrial accidents was extended to incorporate new risks such as occupational diseases, and the last step consisted of the extension of coverage to self-employed persons. Similar step-wise extensions can be observed for the other types of insurance schemes.[11]

After having been approved at the political level, the responsibility of securing social rights in the early phase of social legislation was shared between the employer, the employee and the State. Gradually, however, the basic responsibility was one of the State, and a comprehensive public commitment to a certain minimum level of social security for every citizen was established. This extension of State (or public) obligation to safeguard socio-economic rights was inspired by the rule of uniform benefits and the idea of national solidarity as core principles of social security which were laid down in the standard-setting report 'Social Insurance and Allied Services' prepared in 1942 by Lord Beveridge, the then British Minister of Social Affairs, who assigned to the social security systems the role of guaranteeing basic egalitarian protection to the whole population.[12]

If we look at the timing of the introduction of social security legislation in the liberal democracies of the Nordic countries, we observe patterns of diffusion of policies and political learning from developments in continental Europe. Above all, the concept of State organized social insurance introduced by Bismarck in 1883, apparently exercised a catalysing effect upon the Nordic countries and inspired a number of legislative initiatives in these countries from 1884 to 1889.[13] Among the most important developments

[11] Ibid., pp. 52–54.

[12] See Perrin 1969, p. 260. For a recent study discussing the achievements of the Nordic countries in the areas of political democracy and welfare state provisions, and challenges ahead, see Grauphard 1986. An alternative (although, I think, partly complementary) perspective relates the development of economic and social rights "to the interests of the working class and other groups marginalized and exploited, hurt and hit, by the emergence of the class as a dominant class", see Galtung 1981, p. 121.

[13] Sweden, Denmark, Norway, and Finland established public commissions with the purpose of preparing State action on social insurance in the following order: Sweden in October 1884; Denmark in July 1885; Norway in August 1885; and Finland in

during the next decades, were the following:[14]

- The extent and strength of voluntary sickness funds seem to have influenced the structure of the first sickness insurance laws. In Denmark and Sweden an extensive system of voluntary sickness funds was supplemented by State funded schemes from 1892 and 1891, respectively. In Norway, on the other hand, State organized compulsory insurance was, as the main pattern, chosen from the outset in 1909;
- Laws on accident insurance had been passed in all of the Nordic countries within 20 years of the first German law. In principle, the laws introduced in Denmark and Sweden in 1916 and 1927 incorporated all employees, far ahead of corresponding laws in Norway and Finland. Old-age insurance schemes followed a similar pattern;
- Although major social security provisions were introduced on a limited scale at the turn of the century or in the first decades of our century, comprehensive reforms, including all residents of each country with an equal access to benefits, have only been operating over the last 20–35 years.

In Table 1, the introduction of insurance systems in the Nordic countries and the comparable year of introduction for Western Europe as a whole, is presented. The table also includes references to the year in which the respective laws were made universal within each country.

October 1889. See Kuhnle 1981, p. 400f.

[14] In summarizing the main trends, I primarily rely on Kuhnle 1981, p. 400f.

Year of Introduction/'Universality'[15]

	European average	Denmark	Finland	Norway	Sweden
		F/U	F/U	F/U	F/U
Accident Insurance	1914 (1898)	1898/ 1916	1895/ 1948	1894/ 1958	1901/ 1927
Sickness Insurance	1923 (1906)	1892/ 1960	1963/ 1963	1909/ 1956	1891/ 1955
Old-Age Insurance	1922 (1912)	1891/ 1964	1937/ 1957	1936/ 1957	1913/ 1946
Unemployment Insurance	1930 (1917)	1907/–[16]	1917/–[15]	1906/ 1938	1934/–[15]

Table 1: Introduction of Major Social Insurance Systems in Western Europe: year of first laws establishing compulsory systems (F=first law), and year of universal coverage (U). In the left column the year of the first law establishing a compulsory or subsidized system appears in brackets.

Social insurance legislation in Europe, in its early phase in the 1880s, was "radical as concerns the methods used, although the goals were of a conservative nature."[17] Social legislation was

---

[15] *Sources*: Flora and Heidenheimer (eds.) 1981, p. 50; Kuhnle 1983, p. 138f.; Kuhnle 1981, p. 400f.

[16] In Denmark, Finland and Sweden insurance is still in principle voluntary. Trade unions with unemployment funds, however, as a rule demand that their members take out insurance in cases of unemployment. See Kuhnle 1981, p. 406.

[17] See Kuhnle 1988, p. 187 (author's translation). Kuhnle (1983) discusses the social and political conditions for the development of the European welfare state.

conceived as important integrative measures for the support of semi- or undemocratic political regimes. In order to understand the Nordic or European experiences in extending social rights, it is, however, essential to go beyond this integrative perspective in search of additional and more comprehensive explanatory perspectives. Flora and Alber, for instance, also consider the development of modern social legislation as part of the processes of modernization and they suggest a sectoral model combining socio-economic and political developments with the evolution of social legislation and welfare state provisions. Briefly described, the model identifies three processes that are important for the development of modern welfare states: "the process of differentiation (the differentiation of individual and household income, of working and living place) creating specific labour market problems that must be solved by the state; the evolution of social rights as a consequence of (or compensation for) the institutionalization of political rights; the increasing control, substitution and supplementing of markets (and to some degree of associations) by state bureaucracies."[18] According to Flora and Alber, processes of this kind (so called 'modernization') developed social and economic problems, for example, industrial accidents, child labour and extended working hours as a consequence of free and unrestrained labour contracts, income insecurity for disabled persons, etc., and these problems created demands for social protection and reforms. The ways in which the problems were dealt with differed between countries according to the potential for social and political mobilization, main religious orientation of the society (Protestant *v.* Catholic), and notably the strength and coherence of the labour movement (the 'social question').[19]

Social security systems have been introduced or changed as a result of experiences and learning in other countries.[20] Diffusion of policies and legal reforms beyond national borders has been a recurrent phenomena, not least within the Nordic region. Within the broader international context the ILO has contributed to the development and introduction of universal and internationally integrated schemes for social legislation since the establishment of the organization in 1919. The ILO also established an effective monitoring apparatus charged with observing State compliance with

[18] Flora and Alber 1981, p. 41f.
[19] Ibid., pp. 41–43.
[20] See, for instance, Karvonen 1981; Kuhnle 1981; Perrin 1969.

its conventions.[21] The standard-setting role of the ILO in this field has been important. Equally important, the ILO has shown a great ability to extend the areas to be covered by social legislation. One of the important contributions made by the ILO is the introduction of the international doctrine drawn up by the Income Security Recommendation, 1944 (no. 67), and the Medical Care Recommendation, 1944 (no. 69) — adopted by the International Labour Conference in 1944 in Philadelphia at its 26th Session. These documents introduced a new doctrine of social protection which establishes the principle of universality. The recommendations also emphasize the unity of the role of social security in relation to the social and economic policy as a whole.[22]

In conclusion, the right to social security in the Nordic countries was introduced by step-by-step extensions of social citizenship to broader strata of the populations from the last two decades of the 19th century. A parallel development of a comprehensive system of international standards for the protection of social security through the ILO machinery occurred after 1919.

Above all, the inter-war period (1920–1940), represented a phase of rapid extension of social security legislation within the Nordic countries and Europe. At the same time, comparable developments also took place in North America, and to some degree in Latin America and a number of British Dominions.

III. The *Travaux Préparatoires* and the Components of Article 22

From the above discussion it appears that legislation to protect the individual against social hardship had emerged for decades in the Nordic countries when the drafting of a UDHR took place in 1946–1948. Equally important, the preparation of the UDHR was characterized by international aspirations of rapid and progressive

---

[21] The ILO conventions are reproduced in ILO (1982). As regards social security, see part III, pp. 515–688.

[22] This doctrine resulted from the consideration of a number of national doctrines and particularly the work of the Beveridge Commission. On the other hand, Lord Beveridge, on the behalf of the Commission, paid tribute to the assistance given by the International Labour Office in preparing the path-clearing report of the Commission (*Social insurance and allied services* (London HMSO, 1942)). See Perrin 1969, pp. 156–261.

expansion of welfare state provisions as part of the economic reconstruction after World War II. The framers of the UDHR reflected these aspirations. Throughout the drafting process, however, article 22 was rewritten and changed several times and the basic form of the article was only agreed upon by the Third Session of the Commission in June 1948. During this session it was decided to draft an introductory umbrella article which should introduce the subsequent articles 23–27. Thus, the purpose of the article was entirely changed from its first drafts.

A. The Secretariat Outline

When the Commission met for its first ordinary session (27 January to 10 February 1947) at Lake Success, New York, it confined itself to discussing the general trends and the principal foundation of a draft declaration. In order to support the Commission in its work, a Drafting Committee of three members was organized (shortly enlarged by five members). The Council also submitted a timetable for the drafting of the Declaration. The chairperson of the Commission, Mrs. Roosevelt, proposed that the UDHR was to be followed by a legally enforceable convention, in which obligations corresponding to the rights should be specified. Mrs. Roosevelt argued that the Commission should concentrate its work on formulating rights. Although this was approved by the majority of the Commission, recurrent attempts were made throughout the *travaux préparatoires*, in particular by the Soviet delegation, at defining the obligations of society and the State.

In June 1947 the Drafting Committee met to consider an Outline prepared by the Secretariat of the Human Rights Division.[23] While preparing the Outline, the Secretariat received 18 different drafts, among them a declaration presented by Panama to the General Assembly the year before, and similar proposals presented by Chile

---

[23] The Commission was set up by ECOSOC on 16 February 1946, and included from its inception 9 representatives, later extended to 18 members. In this first phase of its work the Commission appeared as a nuclear commission, with the mandate of preparing the work of the Commission. During a preparatory meeting held at Hunter College from 29 April to 20 May 1946 the final composition of the Commission was studied, and at the same time the General-Secretary (Trygve Lie) was asked to collect all possible information on the subject. This task was carried out by the newly established Secretariat of the Human Rights Division from February to June 1947. See UN 1980.

and Cuba, in addition to drafts submitted by private parties. The Secretariat also had available the texts of the national constitutions of a large number of countries.[24]

The Secretariat Outline included 48 articles of which ten dealt with the rights to social and economic benefits and security.[25] The outline did not include a prefatory article to the socio-economic rights section, but article 41 of the draft entitled everyone to the right to social security, and introduced a component which two years later was adopted as a central part of article 22. The article suggested by the Secretariat Outline declared that

> Everyone has the right to social security. The State shall maintain effective arrangements for the prevention of unemployment and for insurance against the risks of unemployment, accident, disability, sickness, old age and other involuntary or undeserved loss of livelihood.

The Secretariat, and particularly the then Director of the UN Human Rights Division, John Humphrey, played an important role at this stage of the Commission's work, a role which he himself described as being "a behind-the-scenes one."[26] We may assume,

---

[24] The following constitutions were submitted: five European States (France, Iceland, Poland, Soviet Union, Yugoslavia), 14 Latin American States (Bolivia, Brazil, Costa Rica, Cuba, Dominican Republic, Ecuador, Guatemala, Honduras, Mexico, Nicaragua, Panama, Paraguay, Peru, Uruguay), and China. The draft submitted by Chile was prepared by the Inter-American Juridical Committee, and the draft presented by Panama had been prepared by the American Law Institute.

[25] The relevant articles were the articles 35–44, see UN doc. E/CN.4/21.

[26] For an examination of the role of the various actors, see Humphrey 1984, and Philip Alston's review of the book in *Human Rights Quarterly*, pp. 224–235. In his book Humphrey, the first Director of the UN Human Rights Division, aims at revising what he consider to be the 'myth' that René Cassin (France) was 'the father' of the Declaration, and at the same time appeals for recognition of his own contribution in his capacity as the author of the first outline of the declaration (the Secretariat Outline). This outline was, undoubtedly, an important contribution and the first pillar of the UDHR, although Humphrey clearly overrates his own contribution when he writes: "It is by no means certain that economic and social rights would have been included in the final text if I not had included them in mine", Humphrey 1984, p. 32. As the subsequent pages will show, the contribution of Cassin was significant. Cassin, however, has generally been careful in acknowledging the contribution of the Secretariat (including the contribution by John Humphrey and Emile Giraud). See Alston 1984, p. 225.

As concerns the relationship between the Secretariat and the various representatives of the Commission, Humphrey puts it eloquently in the following terms: "Some [of the representatives of the Commission] were more independent [of their governments] than their colleagues and some operated without precise or any instruction from their

however, that the Secretariat was able to influence substantially the intellectual orientation and practical direction of the work at this stage. Nevertheless, when Humphrey absented himself from his office for one week in May 1947 in order to prepare the Secretariat Outline "with some help from Emil Giraud", who at the time was a member of the Human Rights Division, they frequently consulted and borrowed from national constitutions, draft declarations and private proposals referred to above.

In his memoirs Humphrey notices that the text of a draft declaration prepared by the American Law Institute (ALI) was particularly important in the preparation of the Outline, and he adds that he "borrowed freely from it."[27] In fact, article XVI of the draft of the ALI and the corresponding article of the Secretariat Outline quoted above documents considerable similarity.[28] In the field of social and economic rights, the Secretariat Outline was mainly a

governments....The Secretariat worked very closely with these delegates, who were glad to be fed ideas they could sponsor and for which they could have the credit. This was one of the ways in which we were able to make a substantial contribution." Humphrey 1984, ibid., p. 18.

[27] The text prepared by the ALI, "The Draft Declaration of the Essential Rights of Man" had been submitted by Panama to the United Nations Conference on International Organization held in San Francisco in 1945. The Conference, however, was unable to deal with the proposal because it required detailed consideration for which time was not available.

In 1946, at the first part of the first session of the General Assembly, in London, the Assembly decided not to include on the agenda a proposal by Panama to discuss a proposal on a Declaration on Fundamental Human Rights and the Rights and Duties of Nations. The Panamanian representatives then requested that the proposal should be placed on the agenda on the second part of the first session. In October 1946, the General Assembly referred the proposal to the First (Political and Security) and Third (Social, Humanitarian, Cultural) Committees, and on the basis of the joint recommendation of these committees it was decided to refer the draft Declaration to ECOSOC for reference to the Commission on Human Rights currently being set up. See UN 1980. In article 15 of the Panamanian proposal it is set out that "everyone has the right to social security." See Humphrey 1979, p. 23, footnote 7.

[28] The text of the ALI draft states that "Every person has the right to social security. The state has the duty to assist all persons to attain social security. To this end the state must promote measures of public health and safety and must establish systems of social insurance and agencies of social cooperation in accordance with which all persons may be assured an adequate standard of living and may be protected against the contingencies of unemployment, accident, disability and ill-health and the eventuality of old age. Every person has the duty to cooperate with the state according to his powers in the maintenance and administration of the measures taken to promote his own social security." E/CN.4/AC.1/3/Add.1, p. 340.

collection of core components of the ALI draft with one important exception. Differing from the ALI draft, the Secretariat Outline did not retain the obligation of the individual to co-operate with the State "according to his powers" in the promotion of his own social security. This may suggest that the Secretariat Outline was more state-centric in approaching the nature of obligations flowing from socio-economic entitlements of the individual. The ALI draft, on the other hand, strongly emphasized the obligation of the individual to take active part in promoting and fulfilling his/her own rights, and to co-operate with the State to this end.

As already observed, national legislation for social protection had become wide-spread among UN member states. More than 60 percent of the extracts of national constitutions submitted to the Secretariat referred to a minimum of four of the contingencies specified by the Secretariat draft (unemployment, accident, disability, sickness, old age).[29]

It has been argued that economic and social rights were included in the Declaration as a result of pressures and manipulations by East European Socialist countries. This theory is not verified, however, by the records of the meetings of the Commission. Right from the beginning of the Commission's work the drafts included rights to social and economic goods and benefits, and the work was inspired by a variety of sources.[30] From the outset, the right to social security was defined in terms of insurance against unemployment, accident, disability, sickness, and old age.

Nevertheless, the inclusion of social and economic rights was not uncontroversial. The UK delegate, Geoffrey Wilson, was among those who consistently called attention to the difficulties of having social and economic risks protected by human rights. Wilson suggested that the protection of the individual against such risks should be conceived as a matter of rights in the meaning of principle goals to be implemented in the long run through social and economic policies. In a rejoinder to the proposal, the US delegates, on their part, suggested considering "social rights such as the right to employment and social security and the right to enjoy minimum standards of economic, social and cultural well-being."[31]

---

[29] Ibid., pp. 341–348. See also footnote 24.
[30] See, for instance, Samnøy 1988, p. 13.
[31] E/CN.4/4, p. 2. A comparable proposal was submitted to the Commission by the representative of India. See E/CN.4/11.

In order to integrate these and other views presented in the discussion of the Secretariat's Outline, the French delegate, Cassin was asked to prepare a new draft of a Declaration on the basis of the Secretariat's draft.[32]

B. *Cassin's Review of the Secretariat Outline*

Cassin's draft emphasized that the duty to maintain effective institutions and arrangements for upholding the rights to social security is the responsibility of the State "with the participation of beneficiaries." Second, a reference was made to the need for special regard, care and resources for mothers and children.[33]

In a second (revised) draft of article 22, Cassin modified the obligation provision by adding "to the utmost of its possibilities" as regards the duty of the State.[34] This formulation introduced a limitation clause to the article, which made the State's obligation contingent upon economic and political considerations.

Cassin preferred to define obligations corresponding to the social and economic rights, although, in a previous meeting of the Drafting Committee, he had said that "the Committee would have to be prepared to make certain compromises with regard to the obligatory character of the rights" even if "the role of the Governments would be very important in this connection."[35] He explained his position by pointing to the difficulties of having different States Parties to agree on "detailed undertakings regarding

[32] In order to facilitate the work of the Drafting Committee a working group of three persons (including Cassin) was elected. The working group in turn asked Cassin to prepare a revised draft as it was felt that the work would most effectively be carried out by one person.

[33] Cassin's draft of article 22 (article 40 in Cassin's first draft) stated that "Every one has the right to social security. The state shall maintain effective arrangements for the prevention of unemployment and, with the participation of beneficiaries, shall provide for insurance against invalidity, illness, old age and all other involuntary and undeserved losses of livelihood. Mothers and children have the right to special regard, care and resources." See E/CN.4/AC.1/W.R/Rev.1, p. 7.

[34] In the revised version prepared by Cassin the draft declaration had been shortened by three articles compared with the first draft. Article 40 in the first draft appears as article 35 in the second draft. See E/CN.4/AC.1/W.2/rev.2, p. 6. The discussions in the Drafting Committee referred to the second draft, which included the limitation clause.

[35] E/CN.4/AC.1/SR.5, p. 2. Statement made in the fifth meeting of the first session of the Drafting Committee.

social security, social insurance, full employment and other undertakings."[36]

When the question of economic and social rights arose in the ninth meeting of the Drafting Committee, on 18 June 1947, the delegates of Australia and the United Kingdom reiterated their opposition against including social, economic and cultural rights. In their opinion two or three articles would be sufficient to cover "the broad principles", and these principles should be elaborated at a later stage by the United Nations and its Special Agencies. Mr. Santa Cruz, representing Chile, replied that "if the Drafting Committee did not introduce economic and social rights into the Declaration, it would not appear to the world to be acting realistically", and he urged the Commission to include rights to well-being not only in individual articles but also in the Preamble.[37] Among the Commission members, Santa Cruz was among those who most consistently supported the integration of a comprehensive list of economic and social rights. He was supported by Eleanor Roosevelt, who referred to statements made by ECOSOC stressing the importance of economic and social rights.

In the 14th meeting of the Drafting Committee, on 23 June 1947, the article was adopted with an amendment proposed by the US delegation, including the omission of the phrase "participation of beneficiaries."[38] The revised article read as follows:

---

[36] Ibid.

[37] E/CN.4/AC.1/SR.9, p. 10.

[38] The two other changes introduced were: the substitution of the phrase "the State shall maintain effective arrangements for the prevention of unemployment" by the words "the State shall undertake measures for the promotion of full employment"; and the phrase "undeserved losses of livelihood" was replaced by a reference to "all other loss of livelihood for reasons beyond his control." See E/CN.4/AC.1/SR.14, p. 9.

The US delegation also presented its own full text proposal for a draft declaration of which article 29 referred to everyone's right to "a fair and equal opportunity to advance his own physical, economic, spiritual and cultural well-being and to share in the benefits of civilization." In the following articles the rights to the highest standard of health, to education and to a decent standard of living together with the State responsibilities in these areas were spelled out. It should be recalled that the proposals presented by the US delegation were anticipated by President Roosevelt in speeches made during the war in which he explained that "true individual freedom cannot exist without economic security and independence." For instance, in a message to Congress on 11 January 1944, Roosevelt referred to a broad list of social and economic rights, and clearly presaged the later debates in the United Nations. Among the rights specifically listed we find "the right to earn enough to provide

> Everyone has the right to social security. To the utmost of its possibilities, the State shall undertake measures for the promotion of full employment and for the security of the individual against unemployment, disability, old age and all other loss of livelihood for reasons beyond his control.
>
> Mothers and children have the right to special regard, care and resources.[39]

In this text the term 'social security' referred to social situations and conditions in which the individual's livelihood may be at risk, like situations of unemployment, disability, old age, etc. This draft was submitted to the Commission for examination in its Second Session which was held at the Palais des Nations in Geneva from 2–17 December 1947. The Commission decided to set up three working groups to deal with the remaining controversies and problems of the draft declaration, the draft convention and the question of implementation respectively. The Working Group on the Declaration, composed of representatives from the Byelorussian SSR, France, Panama, the Philippines, the Soviet Union, and the United States, finished its work with the draft article 22 after a short discussion by which they decided to amend the article in accordance with a proposal made by the delegate from the Philippines which synthesized the main interventions of the debates. None of these interventions substantially changed the structure of the article.[40] The most important change compared to the draft of the Drafting Committee was the omission of the limitation clause, "to the utmost of its possibilities." Thus, the text of the article adopted by the Working Group of the Second Session of the Commission read as follows:

adequate food and clothing and recreation", "the right of every family to a decent home", "the right to adequate medical care and the opportunity to achieve and enjoy good health", "the right to adequate protection from the economic fears of old age, sickness, accident, and unemployment", and "the right to a good education." See Green 1956, p. 14f.

[39] E/CN.4/21, p. 80.

[40] All of the delegates presenting their positions, except the Soviet delegate, supported the basic text of the Drafting Committee, although they agreed to moderate the text with reference to the wording of the draft declaration presented by Panama, as synthesized by Romulo (the Philippines). See E/CN.4/AC.2/SR.8, pp. 11–13. For the full text of the respective article of the Panamanian draft, see A/148 (Statements of Essential Human Rights presented by Panama), p. 13.

Every one has the right to social security. The state has the duty to maintain or ensure the maintenance of comprehensive measures for the security of the individual against the consequence of unemployment, disability, old age and all other loss of livelihood for reasons beyond his control.[41]

The phrase "or ensure" was interpreted by the representative of Panama to provide a less state-centric structure of the obligations corresponding to the right to social security, which he deemed to be important because "in many countries social security was a matter of private initiative, and should not, in that case, be taken over by the state."[42] This approach, it appears, is particularly important in any discussion about implementation of socio-economic rights in developing countries today.[43]

In conformity with the working procedure, the draft of the working group was submitted for examination by the Second Session of the Drafting Committee which was held at Lake Success in May 1948. Due to time limits, however, the articles on social and economic rights were not examined by the Committee. In effect, the draft was submitted to the Commission for final examination by the Third Session.[44]

C. The Third Session of the Commission
— the Preparation of the Umbrella Article

In the Third Session of the Commission a request to include a prefatory, umbrella article arose and gradually gained support. A proposal to omit the term 'social security' in the redrafting of article 22 as adopted by the Second Session gave rise to strong opposition forcefully voiced by Cassin. His consistent objection to the deletion

---

[41] E/600 (Commission on Human Rights Report to the Economic and Social Council on the Second Session of the Commission), p. 18. The article appears as article 26 in the report.

[42] E/CN.4/AC.2/SR.8, p. 11.

[43] This approach has been developed in some detail by Andreassen *et al.* 1988.

[44] See E/CN.4/AC.1/SR.42, p. 2. The draft declaration as adopted by the working group of the Second Session of the Human Rights Commission was submitted to the Member States for written communications and comments. Only ten countries produced replies (Canada, the Netherlands, Australia, United States, Mexico, Brazil, United Kingdom, Union of South Africa, Egypt and Norway). See E/CN.4/85, p. 1. Only two countries (Brazil and Egypt) made remarks on the article on social security, both of a rather non-substantial nature. See E/CN.4/85, p. 42.

of the term ultimately resulted in its inclusion into the adopted prefatory article (see below).

The idea of formulating an umbrella article had been raised by the Drafting Committee in its Second Session, and it had also been referred to in the 65th meeting of the Commission, during the examination of article 23 on the right to work. Paragraph 2 of the draft article 23 referred to the obligation of State authorities to ensure the right to work: "The State has a duty to take such measures as may be within its power to ensure that all persons ordinarily resident in its territory have an opportunity for useful work."[45] Some of the delegates supported the idea of including a reference to the obligation of the State as expressed by this paragraph either into the Preamble or into article 2 of the UDHR. The representative from Egypt, Loutfi, however, proposed to prepare a separate article to be placed at the beginning of the section devoted to social and economic rights, "thus establishing a general principle" with the aim of describing the obligation of the State to take measures in order to observe and fulfil those rights.[46] Cassin, supported by Malik (Lebanon), believed that greater importance should be given to actions by individuals and groups within the society than to action by the State.[47]

In order to draft an article on the measures to be taken in order to ensure enjoyment of economic and social rights, it was decided to organize a Sub-Committee to look into the issue (composed of Mrs. Roosevelt (US), Malik (Lebanon), Wilson (UK), Fontaina (Uruguay) and Cassin (France)).[48] The Sub-Committee unanimously agreed on a text of a very general nature which was to come at the end of the UDHR expressing the right to a "good social and international order" in which all the rights enumerated by the UDHR were to be fulfilled, in order not to distinguish and give priority to any specific category of rights. This text was ultimately adopted as article 28 of the Declaration (with the word 'good' omitted!). The majority of the Sub-Committee, however, rejected

---

[45] E/CN.4/95, p. 10.
[46] For reference to the statement made by Loutfi, see E/CN.4/SR. 65, p. 4. René Cassin strongly defended the position that the individual was entitled to demand that "the State, society and international co-operation should guarantee the right in question", see E/CN.4/SR.65, p. 4. We recognize a similarity of intention and formulations used by Cassin in his proposal for a prefatory article, see E/CN.4/120. See also E/CN.4/SR. 67, p. 5, for a similar proposal.
[47] See E/CN.4/SR.65, p. 5.
[48] Ibid., p. 11.

a proposal by Cassin for a separate article intended to precede the articles on social and economic rights. As a result, the French delegation submitted Cassin's text for examination by the Commission. The text formulated by René Cassin stated that

> Everyone as a member of society has the economic, social and cultural rights as enumerated below, whose fulfillment should be made possible in every State or by international collaboration.[49]

Several delegates supported the proposal warmly (Jockel (Australia), Sender (American Federation of Labour) and Steyaert (Belgium)) and argued that it was "very complete" and "much more important and of greater scope than the one agreed upon by the Sub-Committee."[50] Representing the opinion of the majority of the Sub-Committee, Malik of Lebanon, argued that Cassin's proposal was redundant because it was already covered by the text proposed by the majority, and he feared that a special umbrella article to the social, economic and cultural rights would favour these rights in comparison with other rights.[51]

In the 70th and 71st meetings of the Commission, a proposal to amalgamate the draft articles 25 and 26 (on the right of everyone "to the preservation of his health", and "the right to social security...", respectively), was presented.[52] The essential part of the proposal stated that "Every one has the right to social security. This includes the right to a standard of living and social services adequate for the health and well-being for himself and his family and security in the event of unemployment, sickness, disability, old age." The proposal generated a long debate about the interpretation of the term social security.[53] In previous drafts the term had a narrow and technical meaning. In the present draft of the Sub-Committee, however, the interpretation of the term was substantially changed. Metall, the representative of the ILO, proposed to delete the reference to 'social security' because "the

---

[49] See E/CN.4/120.

[50] E/CN.4/SR.65, p. 5.

[51] The report of the Sub-Committee unfortunately does not exist, so we can not detail the discussion of the Committee. This is even more regrettable in so far as we cannot trace the origin of what seems to be an 'inconsistency' in the position taken by Malik. The various positions presented are taken from the plenary debate of the Commission in its 67th, 70th, 71st, and 72nd meetings. See also Verdoodt 1964, p. 213.

[52] See E/CN.4/127 and E/CN.4/SR.70, p. 7.

[53] See E/CN.4/127.

Commission was placing a new definition on the words 'social security' and was giving it the same meaning as the right to a standard of living and adequate social services."[54] Therefore he suggested that the first sentence of the revised and amalgamated article 25/26 should read: "Everyone has the right to a standard of living...." Metall was able to achieve wide support from, among others, Mrs. Roosevelt, who argued "that it would be unwise for the Commission to use the term social security in a different sense from that in which it was used by the ILO."[55] Wilson (UK) concluded from a debate that may be seen as confusing, that the discussion had convinced him that it was undesirable to include the concept of social security in the UDHR "in view of the difficulties of interpretation to which they were bound to give rise."[56]

When a vote was taken, the draft article 23 was amended as proposed by the ILO by 8 votes to none, with 6 abstentions. Cassin abstained from voting because the article did not contain any reference to social security, and he added that "the world public opinion would fail to understand why such an omission had been allowed to occur, and reserved the right to raise the whole question again when the umbrella clause came under discussion."[57]

He returned to the question in the subsequent meeting of the Commission during his presentation of the draft umbrella article, and argued that it would be "a grave error to omit from the Declaration the modern and widely accepted concept of social security."[58] Malik, on the other hand, said that he had failed to find any parallel article on the general nature of obligations as regards civil and political rights. Therefore, he was worried that "the adoption of the French proposal would mean that economic and social rights, the importance of which none could deny, would be given preferential treatment over other rights of equal importance."[59] It is interesting to observe that the delegate of the Soviet Union, Pavlov, and the liberal Malik, agreed that "it would be incorrect to have a covering article stressing the realization of economic and social rights unless the other rights mentioned in the Declaration were mentioned as well. When he had voted in favour

[54] See E/CN.4/SR.70, p. 9.
[55] Ibid.
[56] E/CN.4/SR.71, p. 11.
[57] E/CN.4/SR.71, p. 15.
[58] E/CN.4/SR.72, p. 4.
[59] Ibid.

of a covering article, he thought that it would apply to all rights, though particular emphasis would be placed on the realization of economic, social and cultural rights, which, historically speaking, had been more recently recognized."[60]

Cassin, on the other hand, wanted to refer to social security in the umbrella article "because the welfare of workers had since long ceased to be a purely national concern; the mass unemployment of 1932 showed that action was needed on an international level."[61] Cassin argued that the clause referring to "international co-operation" in his proposal would meet that request. Hence, the omission of the term resulting from the amalgamation of articles 25/26 gave Cassin the opportunity to establish a broader international framework for considering the right to social security, and economic and social rights in general.

In a previous meeting, Loutfi (Egypt) had proposed to amend the umbrella article with a sentence referring to the economic and social resources of each State, and responding to the various positions, Eleanor Roosevelt suggested that the article should start with "every person has the right to social security" and that the proposal by Loutfi should be kept. When a vote was taken this proposal was approved, and an umbrella article was adopted by 12 votes with 5 abstentions. The text of article 22 as adopted by the Commission was the following:

> Everyone as a member of society has the right to social security and is entitled to the realization, through national effort and international co-operation, and in accordance with the organization and resources of each State, of the economic, social and cultural rights enumerated below.[62]

The inclusion of the term 'social security' was the result of the initiative of Cassin. No attempt was made at defining the term, however, and it is quite clear that the reason for including the term into the 'umbrella article' was the omission of it from article 26. Ambiguity as to the interpretation of the term gave rise to a debate on the principal foundation of the article during the examination of the Draft Declaration in the Third Committee of the General Assembly in December 1948. Different interpretations of the term in various national legislations added to this ambiguity.

---

[60] Statement by Pavlov, see ibid., p. 8.
[61] Ibid., p. 9.
[62] Ibid., p. 10. See also E/CN.4/148/Add. 1, in which the full text of the Draft Declaration as adopted by the Third Committee is displayed.

D. The Final Debate: 'Social Security' or 'Social Justice'?

The draft text of article 22 examined by the Third Committee under the General Assembly, and finally approved by the General Assembly, included three main components:[63]

- "the right to social security" and "the economic, social and cultural rights enumerated below";
- a modest formulation, although a formulation of potentially great importance, referring to the scope of the provision stating that every one "is entitled to the realization through national effort [in accordance with the organization of each State] and international co-operation";
- a limitation clause making the realization of the rights enumerated conditional on the "resources of each State".

Most of the contributions and statements made during the debate of the Third Committee addressed the first part of the first component. On the other hand, little attention was paid to the request for international co-operation in fulfilling economic and social rights. A major controversy revolved around operationalization and identification of obligations and duty-holding parties corresponding to the respective rights. According to Eleanor Roosevelt, the Commission "had [...] effected a compromise between the view of 'certain' Governments, which were anxious that the State should give special recognition to the economic, social and cultural rights of the individual and the views of Governments, such as the Government of the United States, which considered that the obligation of the State should not be specified."[64] The governments that she referred to were apparently the Governments of the Soviet Union and Eastern Europe whose representatives throughout the *travaux préparatoires* had consistently insisted that the obligations of the State should be precisely defined in the text of the UDHR, as well as in the draft convention under preparation. The final text of the umbrella article certainly reflected a compromise between different ideological and political positions: "One, the tenuous majority position that there should be no reference to the obligations of States in the Declaration, and the

---

[63] Article 22 of the UDHR appears as article 20 of the draft declaration adopted by the Third Session of the Commission and discussed by the Third Committee of the General Assembly.
[64] E/800, p. 501.

other that obligations should be spelled out in detail."[65]

Nevertheless, it was the term social security that generated the most profound debate within the Third Committee. As we have seen, in previous drafts of article 22, social security referred to the protection of the individual from want in the narrow technical sense, described as protection of the individual against the consequences of unemployment, sickness, invalidity, old age, etc. In the umbrella article, however, social security appears to mean social justice in a "broad and humanitarian sense." The French representative, Grumbach, explained what seems to be an inconsistency in the interpretation of the article: "The discussion on the term 'social security' had shown that the members of the Committee were in complete agreement on the substance of the question, but differed in the way in which they wished to express that idea. The French delegation was ready to accept the term social security [although] it would [...] prefer the word 'social justice'. That term was included in the Constitution of the International Labour Office and it was the most general term."[66] Statements by other representatives lend support to the same conclusion. The Belgian delegate, de Wiart, argued that 'social security' should be retained. At the same time he suggested interpreting the term more inclusively by adding the words 'social justice'.[67] The article proposed by the Commission was finally adopted with an amendment proposed by the delegate of Cuba which substituted the words "set out below" with "indispensable for his dignity and the free development of his personality."

The main purpose of inserting an umbrella article in the UDHR was a desire by the majority of the Commission "to work out a special article concerning the measures to be taken in order to ensure economic and social rights",[68] and to emphasize that "it was not enough to enumerate economic and social rights, but [it was also important to make clear] that society itself should be of such a nature as to ensure the observance of those rights."[69] It can be concluded, however, that this task was hardly fulfilled by the

---

[65] Eide 1987, p. 21, see footnote 2.

[66] E/800, p. 509. The term as included in the ILO Constitution (in the first sentence of the Preamble) is not defined, however, in any specified way. See ILO 1952, p. 3.

[67] Ibid., p. 512. A similar proposal to substitute the term 'social security' with 'social justice' by the Syrian delegate was rejected by 26:8 with 8 abstentions.

[68] This wording was used when the Sub-Committee for drafting a separate article was appointed, see E/CN.4/SR.65, p. 11.

[69] Statement by Malik (Lebanon), see E/CN.4/SR.65, p. 3. Parenthesis added.

Commission. A definition of the obligatory nature of socio-
economic rights remained extremely vague in the adopted text of
the umbrella article, and the problem of agreeing upon such
definitions was rooted in ideological disagreement on the role and
nature of the State in economic and social life. It is also
questionable whether the use of the words 'social security' was
consistent with the intention of expressing in general terms the
societal conditions for implementing the economic, social and
cultural rights of the UDHR. In most countries these terms have an
entirely technical and narrow meaning, and the correct term would
apparently have been 'social justice'.[70] The purpose of keeping the
former term, however, was the omission of it from article 26, where
it actually belonged, and the consistent pressure exercised by
Cassin to have the term included 'somewhere else' in the
Declaration. One may say, perhaps, that the outcome reflects how
the human rights norms are created through negotiation and
diplomacy, for better and for worse; realistic achievement is the
reaching of compromises, often at the expense of clarity and
consistency. This conclusion probably reflects the difficulty of
framing human rights instruments and the stubborn problem of
having States Parties agree upon such unique things as human
rights norms.

The only reference that was made to the important second
component of the article was a statement at one point by Mrs.
Roosevelt noting that the essential elements of the article were "the
two phrases 'through national effort and international co-operation'
and 'in accordance with the organization and resources of each

[70] On the term 'social justice', see Rawls 1971, ch. 1. In modern political thought
social justice refers to the virtue and functioning of social institutions and the rules
and laws directing their work. John Rawls, for instance, concludes that principles of
social justice "provide a way of assigning rights and duties in the basic institutions
of society and they define the appropriate distribution of the benefits and burdens of
social cooperation", see Rawls 1971, p. 4. Social justice, then, is a set of principles
guiding the discussion about and agreements obtained as to the proper distribution
of goods and benefits in the society. Economic and social rights as laid down in the
International Bill of Rights aim at securing for the individual a minimum share of
certain crucial good and benefits which are appropriate for the dignity and well-being
of the individual in his or her social setting. Within this perspective 'social justice',
as distinguished from the more narrow and technical term 'social security', provides
a reference to some basic principles for the societal structure, notably the distributive
dimension, in which socio-economic rights, as well as political freedom and rule of
law, are to be implemented and secured.

State'."[71] According to Mrs. Roosevelt, these phrases had intended to make the article an introduction to the subsequent articles, but no effort was made by the Commission to explicate any interpretation of the term "international co-operation" and corresponding international obligations to socio-economic rights fulfilment. In the 40 years that have passed since the adoption of the UDHR, the importance of international co-operation in addressing serious socio-economic rights problems in all parts of the world, for example, the poverty problem of the South, environmental issues, natural (and man-made) disasters, etc., has been recognized. On the other hand, the human rights foundation of obligations to assist people beyond national borders has so far not been either developed theoretically or in practical terms, although one of the most important attributes of article 22 was to emphasize the need for linking national and international efforts in securing and fulfilling economic and social rights.[72]

IV. Cross References to Article 22, Monitoring Procedures and Main Challenges

Although a series of international conventions and recommendations has been formulated in the field of economic, social and cultural rights since the adoption of the UDHR more than 40 years ago, not least by the ILO, many of the main controversies within the Commission remain significant analytical and practical challenges. Among the most important ones is the operationalization of the obligations of States Parties (and other duty-holding parties) to the various human rights norms.

The article of the UDHR relating most explicitly to article 22 is article 25(1), in which large components of early drafts of article 22 are included. Article 25 entitles everyone to "the right to a standard

---

[71] E/800, p. 501.

[72] The same concern is formulated in article 28 of the UDHR stating that "Everyone is entitled to a social and international order in which the rights and freedoms set forth in this Declaration can be fully realized." Similar concern is also expressed in article 2 and article 11(1) of the CESCR, and in article 4 of the Declaration on the Right to Development. For a thorough analysis of the various dimensions of international obligations, e.g., the obligation to respect the self-determination of other peoples over natural resources, the obligation to co-operate in the protection against exploitative patterns, and the duty to assist by developing aid and other means, see Eide 1987, E/CN.4/Sub.2/1987/23, ch. V. See also Mower 1985.

of living adequate for the health and well-being of himself and of his family, including food, clothing, housing and medical care and necessary social services, and the right to security in the event of unemployment, sickness, disability, widowhood, old age or other lack of livelihood in circumstances beyond his control." Other articles of the UDHR with an explicit link to article 22 are: article 23 (the right to work and rights corresponding to that right); article 24 (the right to rest and leisure); article 26 (the right to education); article 27 (the right to participate freely in the cultural life of the community); and article 28 entitling everyone "to a social and international order" for the realization of the rights set forth in the UDHR. A cross reference may also be made to the general limitation provision set forth in article 29 ("everyone has duties to the community in which alone the free and full development of his personality is possible"), and the non-discrimination clause of article 2.

Cross references should also be made to the CESCR, in particular article 9 and article 2(1). Article 9 says that "States Parties to the present Covenant recognize the right of everyone to social security, including social insurance." Article 2(1) refers to the international obligations of States Parties and requires that steps be taken "individually and through international assistance and co-operation, especially economic and technical" with a view to achieving progressively the full realization of the rights recognized in the CESCR. Other articles corresponding to article 9 are articles 6–11 (the right to work, the right to the enjoyment of just and favourable conditions of work, the right to health, the right to housing, and the right to food, respectively).

The short form of article 9 of the CESCR is worthy of a brief remark. When the Commission resumed its standard-setting work shortly after the adoption of the UDHR in 1948, and began drafting a human rights convention, the delegates from the United States and the United Kingdom were strongly against the incorporation of social and economic rights. Their main argument was that these socio-economic rights are not enforceable, and that some of the rights were more far-reaching than most existing national constitutions.[73] This position, however, was not approved by the majority, and it was decided to deal with socio-economic rights in a separate covenant. Surprisingly, the US and the UK delegates

[73] See Alston 1979, p. 5. See also A/C.3/L.111 (17 November 1950) for details of the debates in the Third Committee.

achieved support for their position from the ILO observer, whose position reflected a controversy between two schools of thought about how articles on substantive rights of international human rights instruments ought to be drafted: "One school held that each article should be a brief clause of a general character — another school was of the opinion that each right, its scope and substance, its limitations as well as the obligations of the State in respect thereof, should be drafted with the greatest possible precision."[74] The Governing Body of the ILO was of the opinion that "economic and social rights should be excluded on the basis that responsibility for their implementation rested primarily with the [specialized] agencies",[75] but during the drafting process the ILO changed its position and favoured the former of these schools, i.e., each right should be stated as "brief clauses of a general nature." It appears that the ILO wanted as much power as possible to design "precise and detailed provisions necessary for effective implementation."[76] Thus, the degree to which the specialized agencies succeeded in maintaining influences and powers in the drafting process was reflected in the formulation of the articles of the CESCR. The lobbying of the ILO was successful, a fact which explains why article 9, a key right within the working area of the ILO, is the briefest article in the entire CESCR.

On the other hand, since the ILO was established in 1919, the organization has performed extensive activity in the field of social security policies, reflected in 24 Conventions and 11 Recommendations referring especially to social security policies.[77]

---

[74] A/2929 1955, pp. 24–25. See also Alston 1979, p. 7, note 17.

[75] Alston 1979, p. 5.

[76] A/2929 (1955), pp. 24–25.

[77] The following instruments refer to social security provisions within the ILO machinery (C - refers to Convention; R - refers to Recommendation and figures refer to the respective number of the instrument concerned): On social policy, see C:117: Social Policy (Basic Aims and Standards), 1962; R:127: Co-operatives (Developing Countries), 1966. On comprehensive standards, see R:67: Income Security, 1944; C:102: Social Security (Minimal Standards), 1952; C:118: Equality of Treatment (Social Security), 1962. On protection in the various Social Security Branches, see the respective instruments under the following subheadings: 1. Medical care and sickness benefit: C:24: Sickness Insurance (Industry), 1927; C:25: Sickness Insurance (Agriculture), 1927; R:69: Medical Care, 1944; C:130: Medical Care and Sickness Benefits, 1969; R:134: Medical Care and Sickness Benefits, 1969; 2. On old age, invalidity and survivors' benefit: C:35: Old-Age Insurance (Industry, etc.), 1933; C:36: Old-Age Insurance (Agriculture), 1933; C:37: Invalidity Insurance (Industry, etc.), 1933; C:38: Invalidity Insurance (Agriculture), 1933; C:39: Survivors'

These Conventions and Recommendations are subject to procedures of annual reporting and to supervision of the implementation carried out by the independent Committee of Experts on the Application of Conventions and Recommendations which formulates questions and comments, and which may submit requests to the governments for additional information.[78]

In addition to the International Bill of Rights and the ILO system, three regional instruments deal explicitly with the right to social security, i.e., the American Declaration on the Rights and Duties of Man (articles XVI, XXXV, and XXXVI), the European Social Charter (article I (12–15), and the African Charter on Human and Peoples' Rights (African Charter, articles 13(1), 18(4), and 29(6)). The most comprehensive of these is the European Social Charter (entered into force in 1965), which requires the Contracting Parties to undertake "to maintain the social security system at a satisfactory level at least equal to that required for ratification of International Labour Convention (no. 102) concerning Minimum Standards of Social Security, and to endeavour to raise progressively the system of social security to a higher level" (article II, 12 (2–3)).

Until recently, the reporting procedure of the CESCR has been substantially different from the ILO approach. Throughout the drafting of the CESCR it was stressed that the reporting procedure was "intended to represent a system of mutual aid and progressive promotion of human rights, rather than a machinery of enforcement."[79] Therefore, the CESCR only requires the States

---

Insurance (Industry, etc.), 1933; C:40: Survivors' Insurance (Agriculture), 1933; C:48: Maintenance of Migrants' Pensions Rights, 1935; C:128: Invalidity, Old-Age and Survivors' Benefits, 1967; R:131: Invalidity, Old-Age and Survivors' Benefit, 1967; 3. On employment insurance benefits: C:12: Workmen's Compensation (Agriculture), 1921; C:17: Workmen's Compensation (Accidents), 1925; R:23: Workmen's Compensation (Jurisdiction), 1925; C:18: Workmen's Compensation (Occupational Diseases), 1925; C:19: Equality of Treatment (Accident Compensation), 1925; C:42: Workmen's Compensation (Occupational Diseases) (Revised), 1934; C:121: Employment Injury Benefits, 1964; 4. Unemployment benefit: C:44: Unemployment Provision, 1934; R:44: Unemployment Provision, 1934; 5. Maternity benefit: C:3/103 (revised): Maternity Protection, 1919/1952; R:95: Maternity Protection, 1952. See ILO 1982.

[78] See the Report of the Committee of Experts on the Application of Conventions and Recommendations (Geneva: International Labour Office), annual issues. Ratification of an ILO Convention involves an immediate obligation to ensure compliance with its provisions. For a study on the experiences of the ILO in the supervision of international labour standards, see for instance ILO 1977, and Haas 1970.

[79] A/2929 (1955), p. 341.

Parties "to take steps, individually and through international assistance and co-operation ... to the maximum of its available resources, with a view to achieving progressively the full realization of the rights recognized...."[80] The CESCR itself makes no provision for establishing a supervisory body. In May 1985, however, the ECOSOC of the United Nations organized a new expert Committee on Economic, Social and Cultural Rights, with the aim of monitoring States Parties' compliance with their obligations under the Covenant.[81] From 1979 to 1986 a sessional working group assisted the ECOSOC in the consideration of reports due under the CESCR, but criticism of the working group led to the upgrading of it into a Committee.[82] Philip Alston, the Rapporteur of the new Committee, has summarized the principle challenges confronting the Committee as follows:

1. Clarification of the normative content of each of the relevant rights;
2. Encouragement of more meaningful reporting by states parties;
3. Improved co-operation with relevant UN bodies, including the specialized agencies;
4. Facilitation of greater input from non-governmental organizations;
5. More streamlined working methods; and
6. More effective follow-up to the examination of State reports.[83]

Today, a critical conceptual challenge confronting the UN bodies as well as the human rights research community is to identify obligations inherent in the CESCR's respective articles, and to specify minimum requirements with which every State Party is bound to comply. In recent years these problems have achieved

---

[80] Article 2(1) of the CESCR. The implementation provisions of the CESCR is covered by the articles 16–22 in Part IV.

[81] E.S.C. Res. 1985/17. Earlier proposals for an expert committee date back to 1951, moved by the Lebanese representative in the Commission (see UN doc. E/CN.4/570 (1951)), in 1954 by the French representative (see UN doc. E/CN.4/L388 (1945)), and two final attempts in 1966, one by the Italian representative, and the other by the United States (see UN doc. A/C.3/L.1358 (1966) and UN doc. A/C.3/L.1360 (1966), respectively).

[82] The main shortcomings of the now defunct working group have been summarized in Eide, E/CN.4/Sub.2/1987/23, p. 53f. A critical appraisal of the work of the working group in its first three sessions, identifying a number of substantive shortcomings, was made by the International Commission of Jurists (ICJ), see ICJ 1981, p. 26. On the establishment and mandate of the new Committee, see OBJECTIVE: JUSTICE, October, 1986, p. 25ff.

[83] Alston 1987a, p. 351 and pp. 351–379.

more attention. Models have been developed for examination of different levels of positive State action required by the CESCR. One approach distinguishes three levels of obligation. At a minimalist level the State is required to respect the right of the individual, i.e., to avoid doing anything that violates the integrity of the individual; at an intermediary level there exists an obligation of the State to protect the individual from deprivation of his rights and freedoms, by means of appropriate measures; and at a maximalist level of State duties the obligation to ensure and fulfil requires the State to take the appropriate steps in order to secure the satisfaction of all basic needs of each person within its jurisdiction, either partly or completely by its own help, or by positive State action.[84] These distinctions do not apply unconditionally to all economic and social rights. Whereas the rights to social security, health care and compulsory primary education are good examples of obligations to fulfil, more complex rights such as the rights to work, to an adequate standard of living and to freedom from hunger require combinations of the different levels of obligation. Perhaps the most important attribute of typologies of this kind is their function of serving as important methodological tools for the purpose of monitoring and analysing economic and social rights in different political, economic and social contexts.

Yet another basic problem in assessing social and economic rights concerns the definition of levels of achievement by the CESCR. There is still little consensus as to which goods and benefits one is entitled to (and how much). Nevertheless, within the area of labour legislation and social security policies, the ILO Recommendations and Conventions and the European Social Charter have defined a series of minimum international standards of achievement.

It is important to observe, however, that according to article 2(1) of the CESCR, States Parties are obliged to take steps immediately, although the full realization is admitted to come about gradually. The ambiguous character of this provision is seen in the context of poor countries in which the mobilization, distribution and organization of the material resources are inadequate for meeting the requirements of the CESCR.

In 1986 a group of experts on international law formulated a set

---

[84] For a comprehensive presentation of this typology of obligations, see Eide E/CN.4/Sub.2/1987/23, pp. 10–16. For a typology of basically the same kind, see Shue 1980, ch. 2. See also Alston 1987b, pp. 183–186. On the juridical status of the UDHR and other human rights instruments, see Sieghart 1983, para. 6.2, p. 53ff.

of principles (the Limburg Principles) with the aim of defining the scope and nature of obligations of States Parties to the CESCR.[85] Discussing what amounts to a failure to comply with an obligation contained in the CESCR, the principles conclude that "It must be born in mind that the Covenant affords to a State Party a margin of discretion in selecting the means for carrying out its objects, and that factors beyond its reasonable control may adversely affect its capacity to implement particular rights" (paragraph 71); but that a State Party will be in violation of the Covenant, *inter alia*, if "it fails to take steps which it is required to take by the Covenant; it fails to remove promptly obstacles which it is under a duty to remove to permit the immediate fulfilment of a right; it fails to implement without delay a right which it is required by the Covenant to provide immediately; it wilfully fails to meet a generally accepted international minimum standard of achievement, which is within its power to meet; it applies a limitation to a right recognized in the Covenant other than in accordance with the Covenant; it deliberately retards or halts the progressive realization of a right, unless it is acting within a limitation permitted by the Covenant or it does so due to a lack of available resources or *force majeure*; [or] it fails to submit reports as required under the Covenant" (paragraph 72).

As part of generating methodological and conceptual tools for determining violations of economic and social rights, a major conceptual challenge in this field relates to the importance of developing analytical frameworks for non-discriminatory distributions of rights-related goods and benefits in the economic and social realm in order to protect the individual from 'intolerable servitude' and want.[86]

V. Concluding Remarks

Robinson has summarized the intention of inserting an umbrella article covering the socio-economic rights sector and the status of the article in the UDHR: "In general the article was drafted more in the manner of a preamble than a legal provision. It carries general implications for the scope of the individual's economic, social and

---

[85] See *Human Rights Quarterly*, 1987, pp. 121–135.
[86] A theoretical approach for analysing economic and social rights in poor countries is proposed in Andreassen *et al.* 1988.

cultural rights 'indispensable for his dignity and the free development of his personality'. However, these rights are not defined in any precise way because such a specification is impossible, since the expressions 'dignity' and 'free development of the personality' of the individual are extra-legal concepts."[87]

Robinson fails to observe, however, that the article in addition to introducing economic, social and cultural rights in general terms, also includes a reference to the right to social security, which is, perhaps, one of the main standards of the ILO machinery of conventions and recommendations.

The incorporation of the article, as an umbrella article was controversial and implied conceptual problems about the scope and nature of corresponding obligations, both nationally and internationally. The quest for an international distributive justice to establish a fair division of income and wealth among the citizens of different societies, did not motivate any debate at all. Since the late 1960s, however, this dimension has become one of the important issues of the human rights community and international relationships, and highlights core problems of North–South relations, transfers of development aid, unjust international trade systems, etc.

This review of the origin of article 22 (and the corresponding development of social security systems in the Nordic countries) has also shown that the framers of the article deliberately avoided defining a minimum core of the social and economic rights indispensable for the dignity and personal development of any individual. Thus, the definition of minimum entitlements to social and economic goods and services, and the corresponding obligations of the State and society to provide and secure these minima, remain as major challenges to the human rights research and action-taking community.

---

[87] Robinson 1958, p. 133.

References

Alston, Philip, "Making and Breaking Human Rights. The UN's Specialised Agencies and Implementation of the International Covenant on Economic, Social and Cultural Rights", *Working Papers* no. 1., London: Anti-Slavery Society, 1979.

Alston, Philip, "A Third Generation of Solidarity Rights: Progressive Development or Obfuscation of International Human Rights Law?", *Netherlands International Law Review*, vol. XXIX, issue 3, 1982.

Alston, Philip, Book Review of: "Human Rights and the United Nations: A Great Adventure", *Human Rights Quarterly*, vol. 6, no. 2, 1984.

Alston, Philip, "Out of the Abyss: The Challenges Confronting the New UN Committee on Economic, Social and Cultural Rights", *Human Rights Quarterly*, vol. 9, no. 3, 1987a.

Alston, Philip, "The Nature and Scope of State Parties' Obligations under the International Covenant of Economic, Social and Cultural Rights", *Human Rights Quarterly*, vol. 9, no. 2, 1987b.

Andreassen, Bård-Anders; Tor Skålnes; Alan G. Smith and Hugo Stokke, "Assessing Human Rights Performance in Developing Countries: The Case for a Minimal Threshold Approach to the Economic and Social Rights", in Bård-Anders Andreassen and Asbjørn Eide (eds.), *Human Rights in Developing Countries 1987/88*, Copenhagen, Akademisk Forlag, 1988.

Eide, Asbjørn, *The New International Economic Order and the Promotion of Human Rights, Report on the Right to Adequate Food as a Human Right*, E/CN.4/Sub.2/1987/23.

Flora, Peter and Jens Alber, "Modernization, Democratization, and the Development of Welfare States in Western Europe", in Peter Flora and Arnold J. Heidenheimer (eds.), *The Development of Welfare States in Europe and America*, New Brunswick: Transaction Books, 1981.

Galtung, Johan, "What Kind of Development and What Kind of Law", in ICJ *Development, Human Rights and the Rule of Law*, Oxford: Pergamon Press, 1981.

Grauphard, Stephen R., (ed.), *Norden — The Passion for Equality*, Norwegian University Press: Oslo, 1986.

Green, James Frederick, *The United Nations and Human Rights*, Washington: The Brookings Institution, 1956.

Haas, E.B., *Human Rights and International Action: the Case of Freedom of Action*, Stanford: Stanford University Press, 1970.

Human Rights Quarterly, vol. 9, no. 2, May 1987.

Humphrey, John, "The Universal Declaration of Human Rights: Its History, Impact and Juridical Character", in Bertrand G. Ramcharan (ed.), *Human Rights Thirty Years after the Universal Declaration*, The Hague: Martin Nijhoff Publishers, 1979.

354   *Bård-Anders Andreassen*

Humphrey, John, *Human Rights and The United Nations: A Great Adventure*, Dobbs Ferry: Transnational Publisher, 1984.

ICJ, "Implementation of the International Covenant on Economic, Social and Cultural Right: ECOSOC Working Group", *ICJ Review*, no. 27, 1981.

ILO, *The Constitution of the International Labour Organisation*, Geneva: International Labour Office, 1952.

ILO, *The Impact of International Labour Conventions and Recommendations*, Geneva: International Labour Office, 1977.

ILO, *International Labour Conventions and Recommendations 1919–1981*, Geneva: International Labour Office, 1982.

Karvonen, Lauro, *Med vårt västra grannland som förebild. En undersökning av policy diffusion från Sverige til Finland*, Åbo/Turku: Åbo Akademi, 1981.

Kuhnle, Stein, "Grenser for velferdsrettighetene? Sosiale og økonomiske rettigheter i et utviklingsperspektiv", in Bernt Hagtvet (ed.), *Menneskerettighetene som forskningstema og politisk utfording*, Internasjonal perspektiver, Oslo: Ad Notam, 1988.

Kuhnle, Stein, *Velferdsstatens utvikling. Norge i komparativt perspektiv*, Oslo: Universitetsforlaget, 1983.

Kuhnle, Stein, "Welfare and the Quality of Life", *Nordic Democracy*, Copenhagen: Det Danske Selskap, 1981.

Marshall, T.H., *Citizenship and Social Class and Other Essays*, Cambridge: The University Press, 1950.

Marshall, T.H., *Class, Citizenship and Social Development*, Garden City, N.Y.: Anchor Books, 1964.

Mower, Glenn A., *International Cooperation for Social Justice. Global and Regional Protection of Economic/Social Rights*, London: Greenwood Press, 1985.

OBJECTIVE: JUSTICE, October, 1986.

Perrin, Guy, "Reflections on Fifty Years of Social Security", *International Labour Review*, vol. 99, no. 3 (March) 1969.

Rawls, John, *A Theory of Justice*, Cambridge, Mass.: Harvard University Press, 1971.

Rimlinger, Gaston V., *Welfare Policy and Industrialization in Europe, America, and Russia*, New York: John Wiley & Sons, 1971.

Robinson, Nehemiah, *The Universal Declaration of Human Rights*, New York: Institute of Jewish Affairs, 1958.

Samnøy, Åshild, "Historisk Prolog: Då Menneskerettsærklæringa vart til, 1945–48", in Bernt Hagtvet (ed.), *Menneskerettighetene som forskningstema og politisk utfordring. Internasjonale perspektiver*, Oslo: Ad Notam, 1988.

Shue, Henry, *Basic Rights. Subsistence, Affluence, and U.S. Foreign Policy*, Princeton: Princeton University Press, 1980.

Siegel, Richard L., "Socioeconomic Human Rights: Past and Future", *Human Rights Quarterly*, vol. 7, no. 3, 1985.

Sieghart, Paul, *The International Law of Human Rights*, Oxford: Claredon Press, 1983.

United Nations, *United Nations Action in the Field of Human Rights*, New York: United Nations, 1980.

United Nations Documents: E/CN.4/AC.1/3/Add.1; E/CN.4/4, E/CN.4/11; E/CN.4/AC.1/W.R/Rev.1; E/CN.4/AC.1/W.2/rev.2; E/CN.4/AC.1/SR.5; E/CN.4/AC.1/SR.9; E/CN.4/AC.1/SR.14; E/CN.4/21, E/CN.4/AC.2/SR.8; A/148; E/600; E/CN.4/AC.1/SR.42; E/CN.4/85; E/CN.4/95, E/CN.4/SR.65, E/CN.4/120. E/CN.4/SR.67; E/CN.4/127; E/CN.4/SR.70, E/CN.4/SR.71; E/CN.4/SR.72; E/CN.4/148/Add. 1; E/800; E/CN.4/570 (1951); E/CN.4/L388 (1945); A/C.3/L.1358 (1966); A/C.3/L.1360 (1966); A/2929 (1955); A/C.3/L.111 (17 November 1950); E/HR/6.

Verdoodt, Albert, *Naissance et Signification de la Déclaration Universelle des Droits de l'Homme*, Société d'Etudes Morales, Sociales et Juridiques, Louvain-Paris, Editions Nauwelaerts, 1964.

Article 23

Kent Källström

Sweden

1. Everyone has the right to work, to free choice of employment, to just and favourable conditions of work and to protection against unemployment.
2. Everyone, without any discrimination, has the right to equal pay for equal work.
3. Everyone who works has the right to just and favourable remuneration ensuring for himself and his family an existence worthy of human dignity, and supplemented, if necessary, by other means of social protection.
4. Everyone has the right to form and join trade unions for the protection of his interests.

I. Introduction

Article 23 establishes four principles:

a) the right to work principle;
b) equal pay principle;
c) just remuneration principle;
d) freedom of association principle.

The right to work principle includes several elements. The article establishes the right of every resident — not only citizens — to get access to the labour market. This goal can be reached by vocational training, labour agencies and sometimes economic support in order to assist an individual to enter the labour market. The right to work means that the individual should be able to choose employment without interference from the authorities. Forced work, in all its forms, is rejected. However, access to the labour market is worthless if the working conditions are not acceptable. Wages and the working environment must rise to a certain level before the right to work has any real meaning. The same can be said about the free choice of employment in relation to protection against unemployment. Free choice cannot exist if the unemployed are left unprotected. The right to work can be regarded as a prerequisite for the protection against discrimination, the freedom of association and other economic and social rights of the employees.

Since the four principles enumerated above are quite disparate, and have at least partly different backgrounds, they will be dealt with separately as to their historical background, their implementation and their impact on national law.

II. The Historical and Ideological Background of the Article

A. The Right to Work Principle

The characterization of the right to work as a social right of an individual is closely linked to modern industrialized society. Historically, it is only during this century that this concept has become important in society and in politics. In the Western industrialized countries, salaried work has become the most important way to distribute the national income among the members of society, and the right to work has therefore grown more and more politically significant.

The right to work principle is closely related to salaried work in a modern sense. In a non-industrialized society this kind of work is less important. During the Roman Empire work was primarily performed by slaves. The obligation to work was also a way of imposing taxes on groups in a society without a common currency.[1] This kind of taxation survived the Empire and was in practice for centuries. Considering this background, it is no mere coincidence that the Latin word 'labor' has two meanings: work and sufferance.

In medieval thought, man had his fixed position in a system decreed by the Lord. Religious dogma held that man was condemned to work because of his sins, and it was during this period that compulsory work for free men was introduced in the Nordic countries, as in the rest of Europe. Following the Renaissance, with the loss of political power by the Church, compulsory work became more and more a part of the social order,

---

[1] Nilsson 1921, p. 168ff.

and a cornerstone of society according to mercantilism. The mercantilists even argued that the more skilled the workers were, the more important it was to keep them in hard work.[2]

Compulsory work for members of society was the prevailing principle in the Nordic countries until the breakthrough of industrialism and liberalism during the 19th century. During this entire epoch, only privileged individuals were exempted from a regime that imposed a general obligation to be employed by someone the law recognized as an employer. A person without such an employer and not belonging to a group exempted from compulsory work was regarded as a vagabond who could be condemned to military service (in Sweden this matter was regulated in 1846; and compulsory work statutes were not abolished until 1885).

Even though the declaration of rights in the French Constitution (article 21 in the Declaration of Rights of 1793) and the Constitution of the Second Republic of 1848 included provisions pertaining to the right to work, article 23 of the Universal Declaration of Human Rights (UDHR) owes its origins more to the experience of the economic crises during the interwar period. Unemployment during this period is regarded as an important cause of the popular support of the Nazis in Germany. Politicians can choose mobilization and war as a way to deal with unemployment, and are tempted to solve internal economic problems by expanding the war industry. After World War II, unemployment has apparently been viewed not only as a threat against the existence of the individual, but also against democracy itself.

B. Freedom of Associations Principle

The right to equal pay for equal work and the right to form and join labour unions ('freedom of association') are to an even greater extent than the right to work principle products of modern thoughts. The right to form unions without interference from the State is a basic principle of the constitution of the International Labour Organisation (ILO), which was formed in 1919. This principle is contradictory to the basic principles of the liberal society of the 18th and 19th centuries. The Combination Acts of England and Loi Chapelier of France (1799 and 1792, respectively) made all

---

[2] Adlercreutz 1954, p. 99ff.

agreements between employees for advancing their wages or improving their working condition illegal. The constitution of the ILO is the international breakthrough for the recognition of labour unions.[3] At that time unions were accepted in a majority of the Western countries but the real expansion of unionism came during the 1930s. The revival of the ILO after World War II and the new interest in freedom for the organizations on the labour market, expressed in the Declaration of Philadelphia of 1944, were also related to the experiences of European labour unions during the interwar period. The unions could be a safeguard against dictatorship, but could also be an instrument of oppression in the hands of anti-democratic powers, and thus a threat to democracy.

C. The Just Remuneration Principle

According to mercantilism, it was important to keep the cost of production low and in order to achieve this goal, wages were regulated by the authorities. Even if the wage level was probably fixed at the lowest possible level, one could assume that some idea of a decent wage level existed. The idea of a decent wage level is probably very old. During the liberal period, this public wage regulation was replaced by a 'free' market pricing. The consequences in terms of poverty, child labour, etc., of this free employment contract and the omissions of the State to regulate wages and working conditions is well known. It became the main objective of the labour movement to establish a minimum wage by collective agreements and in this way restore the public regulation of wages.

The just remuneration principle became one of the cornerstones in the Constitution of the ILO (such as freedom of association and equal pay). It was obvious that a minimum standard of life is a precondition for all other worker's rights. During the interwar period a convention and a recommendation were signed in order to promote minimum wage legislation (convention no. 26 of 1928 (Minimum Wage-Fixing Machinery Convention) and recommendation 1928 no. 30). This kind of legislation was introduced in several European countries (France, Luxembourg, the Netherlands, Portugal and Spain) after World War II.

---

[3] See Valticos 1983, p. 70ff.

D. *The Equal Pay Principle*

This principle, which is now enshrined in numerous international documents, has its origin in the ILO Constitution of 1919. The doctrine, embodied in Part XIII of the Treaty of Versailles, that "men and woman should receive equal remuneration or work of equal value", was acknowledged as a basic principle in regulating labour conditions in all industrial communities. During the interwar period little happened with respect to the programme due at least partly to the severe international depression during the 1930s which made it difficult, especially for women, to compete on the labour market. People in most countries felt that women should care for the home and children and not compete with men for work outside the home.[4] This illustrates well that the right to work is fundamental for other workers rights.

III. *Travaux Préparatoires*

A. *Right to Work*

The drafting of the UDHR has been thoroughly described by Cassin, Robinson and Verdoodt.[5] As Cassin, who was a member of the Drafting Committee, has pointed out, the provisions of article 23 represented economic, social and cultural rights, then entirely new in international documents.[6] The UDHR regards human rights as divided into two groups: civil and political rights on the one hand and economic, social and cultural rights on the other hand. These two groups differ as to the obligations they impose on the Contracting States. Civil and political rights basically create an obligation for the State to refrain from certain activities, while economic, social and cultural rights often impose an economic burden on the Contracting States. Articles 22–27 of the UDHR are of the latter group. Among these articles, the right to work provision in article 23 was the one which was subject to the most intensive debate and the most changes before it reached its final wording.

The first question at issue in this context was whether the right to

---

[4] Schmidt (ed.) 1978, pp. 137ff.
[5] Cassin, p. 241ff.; Robinson 1958; and Verdoodt 1964.
[6] Cassin, p. 278.

work should be combined with an obligation for the individual to perform work which is useful for society.[7] The combination of the right to work with an obligation to perform useful work is known from the constitution of the Weimar Republic of 1919 (article 163), and it is apparent that this duty to work harks back to the ideas of earlier centuries, mentioned above. In the final version, article 23 of the UDHR confined itself to the right to work in an economic sense, and should be construed not as a right of the individual but rather as the responsibility of the State to give individuals free access to the labour market. Thus the right to work is an economic right and not a civil right, though it does not directly impose an economic burden on the State. The authorities must refrain from disturbing the market and the distribution of work in society as a whole should be governed by the free choice of the individuals and not by the government. The 'free choice of employment principle' should also be construed in this context. Accordingly, it is not a 'right' for the individual to choose but it represents a prohibition against compulsory work or assignments of work by the authorities.[8]

It is not surprising that the former socialist States were opposed to this kind of provision. The Soviet delegate argued that the right to work should be regulated in a way that emphasized the obligation of the State to use all its power to create work for all its citizens. This proposal was repudiated on merely formal grounds.[9] The majority of the Drafting Committee argued that article 23 would be confined to protection against unemployment for working people, while article 25 would deal with the social benefits in the event of unemployment.

B. *The Equal Pay and the Just Renumeration Principles*

The equal pay principle raises several questions. The *travaux préparatoires* deal with the problem of what circumstances shall be allowed as grounds for differentiation in pay. Robinson emphasizes that the principle of equal pay in article 23(2) should not be construed so rigidly as to prohibit reasonable disparity such as higher pay to workers with more seniority or those working in areas

---

[7] Verdoodt 1964, pp. 217 and 226.
[8] Robinson 1958, p. 134.
[9] A/C3/SR 140, p. 11.

with a higher cost of living.[10] By equal pay, the UDHR means that the pay should be commensurate with the work done and should not depend on the specific characteristics of the worker. As already pointed out, article 23(3) goes further as it seeks not only to ensure for the worker equal pay but also adequate salaries. According to the UDHR, an employer should consider the family obligations of the worker. Thus, it is not considered discriminatory to pay higher wages to a man with a family than to a woman who, for example, has a wage-earning husband. Here the UDHR is probably not in accordance with the view prevailing on the labour market of the Nordic countries. At least in Sweden the equal pay principle has been a part of the wage policy (often called solidarity wage policy) and in this context the principle is construed more rigidly than in the UDHR. The unions in Sweden have opposed different wage scales regardless of purpose. Otherwise, the unions have argued, it would be more favourable to hire workers belonging to certain groups.

IV. Global Documents Concerning Article 23

The provisions of article 23 of the UDHR are partly included in the International Covenant on Economic, Social and Cultural Rights of 1966 (CESCR) and in the International Covenant on Civil and Political Rights (CCPR) of the same year. In the CESCR, the right to work is provided for in article 6, the right to adequate salaries and other working conditions, as well as the equal pay principle, in article 7, and finally the right to organize, in article 8.

There are some differences between the UDHR and the CESCR. Firstly, the right to work is more precise in the Covenant. While the right to work as expressed by the UDHR only implies free entry to the labour market for the individual, the Covenant adds provisions aimed at creating a well functioning and balanced market, and these include vocational guidance, employment services and guidelines to promote full employment. While the principle of full employment is established as a basic principle, this principle may not come into conflict with the fundamental political and economic freedoms of the individual (article 6(2)). In other words, the price of full employment can not be allowed to rise to a level where the burdens upon the individual jeopardize free enterprises and free

---

[10] Robinson 1958, p. 135.

markets.

The equal pay principle has also undergone a significant change in the CESCR. The principle established in the UDHR was "equal pay for equal work." In the CESCR, the wording has been changed to "equal remuneration for work of equal value", reflecting the principle of "equal remuneration for men and women workers for work of equal value" of the Equal Remuneration Convention from 1951 (ILO Convention no. 100).

"Equal pay for equal work" is far narrower than "equal pay for work of equal value" (also known as 'comparable work'). The first principle is designed mainly to combat dual pay scales for men and women. As mentioned earlier, collective agreements from the beginning of the century often comprised different wage scales, one for men and one for women, as well as one scale for married and one for unmarried workers. The husband was regarded as the principal breadwinner for the family and this method of setting wages reflected the 'payment in accordance with need' principle. Clauses of this type in collective agreements are thus violations of ILO Convention no. 100 but not necessarily a violation of the UDHR. The principle of equal pay for work of equal value goes further and aims to avoid even indirect violations of the equal pay principle. It is, for example, a well known fact that women are often concentrated in certain occupations, such as teaching, nursing and secretarial work. Although these types of work require a high level of skill, they often pay relatively low wages. ILO Convention no. 100 seeks to establish equal pay for comparable, albeit not exactly similar, work, in order to create equal conditions for men and women. The Convention advocates a system of objective appraisal of the requirements of various types of work without taking the sex of the workers into consideration when determining the pay scales.

Like several other ILO Conventions, Convention no. 100 can be brought into operation by means of either national laws or regulations or by collective agreements, and the undertakings contained in the Convention are fulfilled if most of the labour market is covered by collective agreements which do not take gender into account when determining pay scales. It is up to the parties on the labour market to decide the methods used in the appraisal of jobs, and if this appraisal is based on objective grounds, differences in wages between workers cannot be considered as being contrary to the principles of Convention no. 100 (article 3(3)).

Other forms of discrimination of workers are covered by the ILO Discrimination (Employment and Occupation) Convention (no.

111) and Recommendation (no. 112) of 1958. This Convention is designed to create equality of opportunity and promote equal treatment in employment, and aims to combat all kinds of exclusions and preferences made on the basis of race, colour, sex, religion, political opinion, national origin or social class (article 1(1a)). The ILO conventions are designed to implement rights in the field of working conditions and other matters concerning the labour market. The implementation of human rights has become especially efficient in this field because of the scrutiny to which national legislation is subjected within the procedures of the different bodies of the ILO.

The most important ILO conventions for the protection of workers' rights are the Freedom of Association and Protection of the Right to Organise Convention of 1948 (no. 87) and the Right to Organise and Collective Bargaining Convention of 1949 (no. 98). These conventions were formulated prior to the UN covenants but have their origin in the same period as the UDHR. These conventions are of great significance since the obligations in them are more specific than those in the UDHR or the UN covenants, and the ratification of ILO conventions creates an obligation to follow a procedure for regular international supervision and control.

The main differences between Convention no. 87 and the UDHR and the 1966 covenants relate to the nature of the freedom of the worker and employer to exercise their rights to organize freely in the place of work. The right to organize in the UDHR and the covenants is primarily an obligation upon the State to refrain from any interference with labour organizations and their activities. This obligation is expressed more precisely in Convention No. 87, which makes it a violation, for example, to make the legal organization of trade unions dependent on the approval of public authorities (article 7). However, the ILO Convention no. 87 goes even further. It not only imposes obligations on public authorities, but also specifies that workers' and employers' organizations shall enjoy adequate protection against any act of interference by each other or each others' agents or members. This means that the Convention is intended to affect the civil law in countries that have ratified it.

The ILO conventions on the right to organize freely are effective not only because their provisions are more precise than those of, for example, the UN covenants but also because of the special machinery set up within the ILO to deal with matters concerning freedom of association. Two bodies, the Fact-Finding and Conciliation Commission, and the Freedom of Association Committee of the Governing Body, perform this task. The

Commission is composed of independent experts assigned to carry out an impartial examination of complaints concerning alleged infringements of trade unions' rights.

The Committee was established by the Governing Body of the ILO to carry out preliminary examinations of complaints on behalf of the Governing Body, and by 1985 had made 1300 decisions.[11] Many of these decisions contain important principles, not only on trade union rights but also on the international protection of human rights in general.

V. Regional Documents Concerning Article 23

The Council of Europe has implemented the UDHR with two separate documents: the European Convention on Human Rights (ECHR) and the European Social Charter. The ECHR signed in 1950, shortly after the UDHR, proved easier to formulate than the European Social Charter, which was not signed until 1961, following several years of intensive preparatory work.

As mentioned, human rights can be divided into two categories, on the one hand civil and political rights, and on the other hand economic, social and cultural rights. The Council of Europe has pursued the same plan as the United Nations in this respect. Thus the CCPR has its counterpart in the ECHR, while the CESCR has its counterpart in the European Social Charter. Experience of international law shows that achievements relating to economic, social and cultural matters are generally more difficult than those relating to political rights and consequently, it is not surprising that the European Social Charter took longer to formulate than the ECHR. The cautiousness of the governments of the Council of Europe is demonstrated by the fact that the Charter was drafted so that its objectives are to be attained by persuasion, with no State subjected to binding decisions.[12]

[11] ILO 1985, p. 2.
[12] Parliamentary Assembly, Document 5374, 1985, p. 5.

A. The Freedom of Association Principle

The freedom of association is a civil and political right as well as a social and cultural right, and is thus included in the ECHR as well as in the European Social Charter (article 11 of the ECHR and article 5 of the Charter). Article 11 of the ECHR is organized in the same way as article 22 of the CCPR. The interpretation of this type of international convention, however, is not strictly dependent on the preparatory work, and the ECHR has at least partly been construed differently from the CCPR. As mentioned, the UN documents in question only protect against State interference with union activity. The ECHR, however, is broader, allowing complaints to be brought against States whose courts accept, for example, employer interference in union matters.

This broader scope becomes even more apparent when considering the right of workers to remain outside the union. The regulation of freedom of association in the UDHR and in the CCPR of 1966 has deliberately left this question unresolved. The provision in article 20(2) of the UDHR against compulsory membership in organizations is not applicable to unions or other organizations which are formed in the interest of the worker.[13] In the British Rail case, the European Court of Human Rights (European Court) held that the workers' right to remain outside the union, at least to a certain extent, is protected even if it cannot be based on the wording of article 11 of the ECHR. According to the European Court, an employee cannot be dismissed for his refusal to join a certain union. The freedom of association is thus wider than the wording of the article suggests.[14]

Although freedom of association is regulated by both the ECHR and the European Social Charter (article 11 and article 5), for the individual the provision in the ECHR is the more important one. According to this convention, an individual who claims that a public authority or an employer has interfered in his right to organize freely can bring his case to the European Commission of Human Rights (the European Commission). The European Commission may decide to refer the case to the European Court. As the European Commission functions basically as a court, there is a system of two fora within the organization of the Council of Europe.

---

[13] Robinson 1958, p. 131.

[14] Evju 1982, p. 37ff., with a comment on the British Rail Case.

The provisions of the European Social Charter are more elastic than those of the ECHR. The Committee of Ministers, which has the power to issue recommendations (article 29), has so far not taken any action against any of the contracting nations. The most important source of the interpretation of the Social Charter is the Conclusions of the Committee of Independent Experts. The governments of the Contracting States are obliged to submit a report to the Council of Europe every other year, covering the measures taken in order to reach the goals set forth in the Social Charter. These reports are scrutinized by the Committee of Independent Experts, and the Conclusions of the experts often contain precise interpretations of the articles of the Social Charter. While it is true that the statements of the Governmental Committee, which at least formally is superior to the Committee of Independent Experts, are 'softer' than the statements of the experts, the great authority of the Committee of Independent Experts is demonstrated by the many instances in which the Contracting States have changed their legislation after the Committee of Independent Experts has pointed out imperfections. This is at least the Swedish experience.[15]

B. *The Right to Work Principle*

The goals of the European Social Charter look more ambitious than those set forth in the UDHR and the International Covenants of 1966. The right to work principle of the Social Charter goes further than that of the CESCR since it characterizes full employment as the leading principle of economic policy. The reservation that the right to work is not allowed to infringe on fundamental political and economic freedoms for the individual in article 6(2) of the CESCR is not repeated in the Social Charter. The regulation of the right to work is a good example of the functioning of the Social Charter. The Social Charter establishes the goals but not the means to attain them. It is up to the governments subject to the Social Charter to decide on the means and to report to the Council of Europe the steps taken. The weakness of these provisions is obvious, since the whole system relies on the willingness of the politicians to pursue the principles of the Social Charter.

---

[15] The implementation of the European Social Charter has been studied in Jaspers and Betten 1988.

C. *The Equal Pay Principle*

The principle of equal pay has been thoroughly discussed by the Committee of Independent Experts and of the Parliamentary Assembly of the Council of Europe. The Committee concluded that the Social Charter goes further than the Equal Remuneration Convention (ILO Convention no. 100). As mentioned, this ILO Convention relies on collective bargaining to create equality between the sexes in this respect. The Committee has stated:

> Dans un Etat, qui a accepté cet engagement, il n'est pas possible d'assurer le plein exercice du droit à l'egalité de rénumeration à tous les travailleurs par le seul jeu des conventions collectives, cet Etat est tenu d'intervenir, soit au moyen des méthodes légales de fixation de salaires, soit de tout autre manière appropriée.[16]

This interpretation of the Social Charter, however, has been contested by the Governmental Committee which expressed the opinion that the Social Charter does not go further than the Equal Remuneration Convention (First Report of the Governmental Committee § 13). It is typical of the Social Charter that provisions can be construed differently and that there is no organ that has the power to make a final determination. The issues are left for continued discussions.

The administration of the Social Charter is also important since statements are made which can illuminate the provisions of other conventions. Debates in the Parliamentary Assembly, for example, have included interpretation of the concept of 'work of equal value', also used in ILO Convention no. 100 as well as in the Social Charter. The Parliamentary Assembly has stated that the application of ILO Convention no. 100 implies inclusion of "work of equal value" in the term "the same work".[17] This means that in practice when the "objective appraisal" provided in article 3(3) of ILO Convention no. 100 has not been carried out, the ILO Convention and the Social Charter have the same effect as the UDHR, i.e., only to combat different pay scales for men and women.[18]

---

[16] Conclusions of the Committee of Independent Experts II, pp. 18–19.

[17] Parliamentary Assembly Report Doc. 5374, p. 8.

[18] The ILO Conventions has been discussed, *supra* note 4.

D. The Freedom of Association Principle

Freedom of association is regulated in the Social Charter along the same lines as in article 11 of the ECHR. The difference between them concerns primarily procedures and the nature of supervision. The ECHR procedure is triggered by a complaint by a subject of a Contracting State normally submitted to the European Commission, which in principle functions as a court. The Social Charter functions differently. The Council of Europe has no effective legal sanction at its disposal and the only obligation for the Contracting States is to explain the legal or social situation to the organ of the Council of Europe. This lack of legal sanctions, however, is compensated for by the public nature of the proceedings before the Committee of Independent Experts, which exposes the legal and social situation in a country to the international community. This publicity can be as effective as legal sanctions in forcing a country to change its policy.

VI. The Treaty of Rome

Labour law has not been high on the agenda of the European Community. But there are indications that this situation could change. The most important provision in the Treaty of Rome concerning labour is article 119 which establishes the principle of equal pay for equal work. This article is a result of a goal of the Treaty of Rome to avoid situations in which a country suffers a competitive disadvantage because another country allows the employment of women at lower wages than men. Primarily, this is not a question of human rights but rather a way of dealing with imperfections in the functioning of the market. In the Treaty of Rome, a well functioning market is regarded as a condition for social progress and improvement of living conditions.

Article 119 goes further than other conventions on equal pay, by imposing a duty on the national courts to ensure the protection of individuals against direct discrimination, whether it originates in legislative provisions or in collective labour agreements.[19] However, this is not only a question of individual rights but also an undertaking to create equality between the sexes in the economic

---

[19] See the Defrenne case, the Courts of Justice of the European Communities 8 April 1976; Schmidt (ed.), p. 140ff.; and Nielsen 1989, p. 137ff.

system as a whole.

As mentioned, the European Community regulations have the objective of creating a common market for labour and a prerequisite for this is a certain equality in the social structure. Equal conditions for men and women is, for instance, important as it disturbs competition if one country allows the employer to pay women less than men. In the same way a market cannot work if the standard of living goes below a certain level — free movement of labour demands employment agencies and that the unemployed person can afford to move. Aware of this, the Commission of the European Communities has drafted a Charter of fundamental social rights. The Community Charter is, to a large extent, based on the Social Charter of the Council of Europe and on the conventions of the ILO. In the Preamble to the Community Charter it is emphasized that the European Economic Community Treaty has the objective "to promote improved living and working conditions" and that "the internal market is the most effective means of creating employment and ensuring maximum well-being in the Community."

The substantive rules of the Community Charter are not in any sense more far reaching than the European Social Charter and the ILO Convention mentioned above. The impact of the Community Charter depends highly on its implementation. The Charter has not been accepted as a binding document by the members of the Community. The Commission of the European Communities has produced an action programme relating to the implementation of the Charter (Com (89) 568 final 29 November 1989). As to the right to work principle it is important that the Charter creates an obligation to give first priority to development and creation of employment. However, this is the very meaning of the right to work principle in the European Social Charter and all other conventions dealing with the right to work. As to the fair remuneration principle, the Community Charter does not add anything except a statement that workers subject to other terms of employment than an open-ended full-time contract shall benefit from an equitable reference wage (article 5(ii)). The provisions in the Community Charter concerning equal treatment for men and women are the most elaborated ones. The implementation of article 119 in the Treaty of Rome should be intensified, not only as to equal remuneration but also as to access to employment, social protection, education, vocational training and career development. It is also provided that measures should be developed enabling men and women to reconcile their occupation and family obligations (article 16).

372 *Kent Källström*

Among the Nordic countries, the Treaty of Rome concerns only Denmark.[20]

VII. Nordic Compliance with Article 23

A. The Right to Work Principle

The principle of the right to work is included in the Constitutions of Denmark, Finland, Norway and Sweden (§ 75 Grundloven, 6 § Regeringsformen, § 110 Grunnloven, 1:2 Regeringsformen, respectively). In all cases it is not merely a moral duty for the public authorities to do their best to help individuals enter the labour market, but it is also a question of political responsibility. The Constitution of Finland differs from the Scandinavian countries in the scope of its application. The Finnish Constitution only protects citizens, and this is a difference compared with the right to work provision in the UDHR which covers all residents. In the Danish Constitution the expression 'borger' is used concerning the right to work, probably the same as legal residents.[21]

It is obvious that the discussions within the United Nations concerning the right to work have had an influence on the Constitutions of the Scandinavian countries. The discussions concerning § 110 in the Norwegian Constitution went along the same lines as those in the preparatory work of the UDHR. Some politicians argued that the Constitution should guarantee the right of the individual to work. This suggestion was repudiated by the majority, which argued that inclusions of such a right could imply an obligation for the individual to work, which was not regarded as fitting in a democratic society.[22]

The fact that the right to work has been inserted in the Constitutions of the Nordic countries is not only political rhetoric but also a commitment to make it possible to give everyone access to the labour market. The labour market policy in these countries is based on the knowledge that the efficacy of union rights depends on how well the labour market works. If large crowds of workers are

[20] Autumn 1991 the EFTA-states are negotiating with the European Community in order to reach an agreement about an European Economic Space (EES). Such an agreement may affect all parts of the legal system of Finland, Norway and Sweden.
[21] Zahle 1989, s. 227.
[22] *Mennesker og Rettigheter*, 1982, p. 46.

out of work the bargaining system and the union rights are always at stake.

The right to work principle is construed in the Nordic countries not only as a matter of giving workers access to the labour market on the same conditions. The goal is to assist every person to get a job on the regular market. This implies not only vocational training but also different kinds of support to partially disabled persons. This question has been discussed in the preparatory works of the Norwegian Constitution. According to § 110 Grunnloven every human being ('arbeidsdyktig Menneske') has the right to work to the extent that he is able to perform work.[23] The goal is to make it possible for everyone who can work to enter the labour market and to take part in the social life at regular places of work and in unions.

The governments in the Nordic countries have chosen different ways to implement the right to work. The labour market legislation in Sweden is very ambitious but the effectiveness of the legislation can be, at least partly, questioned. In Norway and Sweden the employment agencies have an important position. Employers who want to hire must notify the public employment agency.[24] In Sweden the legislation also makes it possible for the authorities to impose an obligation on an employer who discriminates against old or partially disabled persons, to hire workers through the public employment agencies.[25] The right to work legislation also comprises different kinds of support to individuals belonging to groups generally known to have a high risk of unemployment (young or elderly persons and partially disabled). Special employment for young persons (under the age of 20) has been introduced in the public sector.[26] Employers who hire partially disabled persons can receive financial support from the labour market authorities.[27] It should be mentioned that the group of partially disabled person is wide according to the right to work legislation. This group comprises persons with both physical and social defects.[28]

The fact that there is a consensus among the political parties to give priority to the right to work and full employment does not

---

[23] Andenæs and Willberg 1983, s. 151.
[24] SFS 1976:157, and Sysselsättningsloven of 1947.
[25] § 12 SFS 1974:13.
[26] SFS 1989:425.
[27] SFS 1984:519.
[28] 3 § SFS 1984:519.

mean that this policy has been successful. From time to time the number of persons out of work has increased. From a Nordic perspective, these figures have been especially high in Denmark. The Committee of Independent Experts of the Council of Europe has noticed the high unemployment rate in Denmark and has requested information on the position of the Danish Government with respect to 'work sharing' and the reduction of working hours.[29] These measures have not come into practice in the Nordic countries as the unions have so far opposed them. Work sharing perhaps does not seem adequate in societies like the Nordic ones where such a high percentage of the population perform salaried work.

B. The Equal Pay Principle

The principle "equal pay for work of equal value" is inserted in the legislation of the Nordic countries.[30]

As mentioned above, the change from 'equal work' to 'work of equal value' has its background in the fact that the labour market is at least partly segregated and that women are still concentrated in certain sectors (health care, secretarial work, etc.) and that work performed by women is generally lower paid than work performed by men. A change from 'equal work' to 'work of equal value' makes it possible to compare work which is not identical. The Danish legislation, earlier based on "equal pay for equal work" was changed after remarks from the Court of Justice of the European Community.[31]

It has already been pointed out that the ILO Convention recommends that equal conditions for men and women should be promoted by an objective appraisal as a part of the collective bargaining procedure. The wage systems in the Nordic countries are built on industry-wide collective agreements which are not based on any kind of objective appraisal. Wages are determined by union

---

[29] Conclusions of the Committee of Independent Experts IX, p. 118.
[30] 1 § lov nr 244/1989 om ligebehandling af mæend og kvinder med hensyn til beskæftigelse og barselorlov mv, Denmark, 8 § 1986 års lag om jämställdhet mellan kvinnor och män, Finland, lag nr 65/1985 om kvinnors och mäns lika ställning och lika rätt, Iceland, Lov 1978 om likestilling mellom kjønnene, Norway, and lag 1979 om jämställdhet mellan kvinnor och män i arbetslivet, Sweden.
[31] Andersen and Nielsen 1986, p. 151.

power, employer's interest and market influences. In the preparatory work of the Swedish Act (lag 1979 om jämställdhet mellan kvinnor och män i arbetslivet) it is stated that the pricing of a job, made by the collective parties, cannot be regarded as discriminatory by the courts. It was assumed that the unions refuse to assist in a discriminating wage system. Some might say that this assumption is false and that it opens the field for traditional discriminating evaluations of work within the unions. The sovereignty of the collective parties in these matters is not as clearcut as in the other Nordic countries, though the practice in the labour market is much the same. The experiences of these countries are that it is difficult to shape a legal system which at the same time allows the unions to act freely without possibilities for the courts to control the operations and guarantees of the individuals right. The difficulties are particularly large in cases where wage discrimination is claimed to be based on sex. These cases often concern individual rights and group interests as well. It is easy to claim that the wage has been determined by other factors than gender. This conclusion is confirmed when looking at the decisions of the Swedish Labour Court (for example, AD 1984, no. 140). In 1991 the Swedish Parliament passed an Act on Equal Opportunities for Women and Men. The article about wage discrimination in the act of 1979 has been reshaped in order to, at least to some extent, remove the sovereignty of the collective parties and thus bring the regulation in accordance with the Danish Act on Equal Treatment of Women and Men (244/1989), the Finnish Act on Equal opportunities for Women and Men of 1986 and the Norwegian Act on Equal Opportunities for both Sexes of 1978. It seems that the legislations of all the Nordic countries should be construed in the same way as article 119 in the Treaty of Rome and directive (75/117/EC) on equal pay.

The legislation in Finland differs somewhat from the other countries as to the legal control of the unions and the employers. Unions in Finland are subject to a certain control by the courts according to an Act of 1989 (previous — lag 1919 om föreningar). Finland is also the only country with statutory protection against all kinds of discrimination of the employees (17 § arbetsavtalslagen).

The strategy of the legislators of the Nordic countries is to achieve equality in wages between the sexes by attacking the segregation of the labour market. In order to avoid segregation of the labour market, the legislations of the Nordic countries impose an obligation on employers to take active measures to help to increase in number the minorities (men or women) in a place of work and to attain better conditions. This active work for equality between the sexes is to a large extent performed independently from the unions and supervised by public authorities.

C. The Just Remuneration Principle

International undertakings concerning adequate remuneration imply certain problems for the Nordic countries. In the collective bargaining system of these countries, working conditions are regulated in collective agreements, and Sweden, especially, has a tradition of non-interference by the State in wage determination.[32] Consequently, the government is not responsible for the outcome of the negotiations on the labour market. This has caused Denmark and Sweden to reject some provisions in the European Social Charter which concern matters that are subject to collective bargaining in these countries (for example, article 4(2), 4(4) and 4(5)). The position of the Swedish Government has been that while Sweden complies with these articles, Swedish public authorities should not be burdened with an obligation of supervising the bargaining system.[33]

D. Freedom of Association

The principle of freedom of association is protected in the legislation of Finland and Sweden (paragraph 17 arbetsavtalslagen, paragraphs 7–9 medbestämmelseslagen). The principle has been accepted in collective agreements in all the Nordic countries since the beginning of the century. Nevertheless, there have been discussions about the absence of statutory protection of this freedom in Denmark and Norway. As only the European documents protect freedom of association as a civil law right (i.e., protect it against infringements from other than public authorities) the ECHR and the Social Charter are the most interesting in this respect. The Committee of Independent Experts of the Council of Europe has questioned whether this lack of statutory protection is contrary to article 5 of the Social Charter. The Governments of Denmark and

---

[32] The Swedish pattern of collective bargaining is thoroughly described by Elvander 1988.
[33] Government Bill 1962:175 p. 7ff.

Norway have explained that collective agreements cover most of the labour market and that in practice most of the workers are protected under these agreements. This argument has also been accepted by the Council of Europe.

In Sweden, two complaints concerning the freedom of association have gone to the European Commission and to the European Court. In neither of these cases did the European Court hold that there had been a breach of article 11 of the ECHR, (decisions of the European Court, 19 January and 6 February 1976). The decisions of the European Court have been criticized by Schmidt as being at least partly based on a mis-characterization of the function of Sweden's labour market.[34]

References

Adlercreutz, *Kollektivavtalet*, 1954.

Andenæs and Willberg, *Grunnloven*, 1983.

Andersen and Nielsen, *Ligestillingsloven*, 1986.

Bergqvist, Olof, *Sverige inför den europeiska domstolen i Strasbourg*, SvJT, 1976.

Cassin, *La Déclaration Universelle et la Mise en Oevre des Droits de l'Homme*, Recueil de Cours 1951-II Academie de Droit International de la Haye.

Elvander, Nils, *Den svenska modellen*, 1988.

Evju, *Organisasjonsfrihet, tariffavtaler og streik*, Oslo: 1982.

ILO, *Freedom of Associations, Digest of decisions and principles of the Freedom of Associations*, Digest of decisions and principles of the Freedom of Association Committee of the Governing Body of the ILO, 3rd. ed., 1985.

Jaspers and Betten, *25 Years European Social Charter*, Deventer: Kluwer Law and Taxation Publishers, 1988.

Mennesker og Rettigheter, 1982.

Nielsen, *EF-arbejdsret*, Gylling: 1989

Nilsson, Martin P., *Den romerska kejsartiden*, II, Lund: 1921.

Robinson, Nehemiah, *The Universal Declaration of Human Rights*, New York: Institute of Jewish Affairs, 1958

Schmidt (ed.), *Discrimination in Employment*, Stockholm 1978.

Schmidt, *Law and Industrial Relations in Sweden*, Stockholm 1977. (Schmidt II).

United Nations Document: A/C3/SR 140.

Valticos, Nicolas, *Droit International du Travail*, Paris: 1983.

Verdoodt, Albert, *Naissance et Signification de la Déclaration Universelle des*

[34] Schmidt II 1977, p. 103ff. See also Bergqvist 1976, p. 399.

Droits de l'Homme, Société d'Etudes Morales, Sociales et Juridiques, Louvain-Paris: Editions Nauwelaerts, 1964.

Zahle, *Menneskerettigheder*, Copenhagen: 1989.

Article 24

Göran Melander

Sweden

Everyone has the right to rest and leisure, including reasonable limitation of working hours and periodic holidays with pay.

Article 24 of the Universal Declaration of Human Rights (UDHR) is concerned with the more general problem often referred to as just conditions of work. The provision should be read in conjunction with article 22, prescribing for a State's general obligation to guarantee social security and, in accordance with the resources of each State, economic, social and cultural rights.

The rights mentioned in article 24 are among the original concerns of the labour movement and among the early standards established by international labour law.[1] In some countries the right prescribed for in the article is considered to be a fundamental right and may be embodied in constitutions.

The principle embodied in article 24 has been expressed in universal and regional human rights treaties. According to the International Covenant on Economic, Social and Cultural Rights (CESCR) the States Parties recognize the right to rest, leisure and reasonable limitation of working hours and periodic holidays with pay, as well as remuneration for public holidays (article 7, paragraph d). The situation prescribed for in article 24 of the UDHR is also referred to in the 1989 Convention on the Rights of the Child: "States Parties recognize the right of the child to rest and leisure, to engage in play and recreational activities appropriate to the age of the child" (article 31). The following article on child labour gives provisions on the State's obligation to protect children from engaging in work that constitutes a threat to their health, education or development, to set minimum ages for employment,

---

[1] See, Harris 1984, p. 37.

and to regulate conditions of employment. It may be seen as a peculiarity that there is no direct provision on just conditions of work in the UN Convention on the Elimination of All Forms of Discrimination against Women. The provision closest to the right concerning just conditions of work is the general provision on equality with men in the political, social, economic and cultural fields (article 3).

It is, however, first and foremost within the International Labour Organisation (ILO) that various aspects of just conditions of work have been of interest. In the Preamble of the Constitution of the ILO it is prescribed: "And whereas conditions of labour exist involving such injustice, hardship and privation to large numbers of peoples to produce unrest so great that the peace and harmony of the world are imperilled; and an improvement of those conditions is urgently required; as, for example, by the regulation of the hours of work, including the establishment of a maximum working day and week,...." Just conditions of work are certainly referred to in the 1944 Declaration concerning the aims and purposes of the ILO (article III) and several of the ILO Conventions and Recommendations refer explicitly or implicitly to the problem.

On the regional level, parties to the European Social Charter undertake obligations similar to the CESCR (article 2 paragraph 5). There is, however, no corresponding provision in the Organization of American States (OAS) human rights convention, nor in the African Charter on Human and Peoples' Rights (African Charter).[2]

The drafting history of article 24 clearly explains the difference between 'rest' and 'leisure'. The word 'rest' is close to the limitation of working hours and is intended to guarantee a real cessation of activities, giving the individual a possibility to regain his strength. 'Leisure' on the other hand should make it possible for the individual to cultivate his mind and interests. From the *travaux préparatoires* it is also clear that the explicit mentioning of limitation of working hours that is implied in the right to rest, was added in order to limit to persons having paid work the right to periodic holidays with pay.[3]

---

[2] Article 15 of the African Charter prescribes that every individual shall have the right to work under equitable and satisfactory conditions.

[3] Verdoodt 1964, p. 231f. The proposal to add periodic holidays with pay in the article prescribing for rest and leisure was met with the objection that such a provision could be invoked by housewives which raised the question of responsibility for paying.

Accordingly, from the *travaux préparatoires* it follows that there are three problems prescribed for in UDHR article 24: weekly rest, limitation of working hours and holidays with pay.

The right to weekly rest is probably one of the less controversial human rights provisions. It is a generally accepted principle in almost all countries and in all cultures. It is also significant that the ILO Conventions relating to the question of weekly rest have been ratified by a considerable number of States. In many instances the right to weekly rest goes back to religious conceptions. As such there are certain connections with the right to freedom of religion.

On the national level the vast majority of States have introduced legislation to give effect to the principle of weekly rest. In other countries it is governed by decrees or ordinances. A third alternative is that the principle of weekly rest is applied by means of collective agreements or arbitration awards.[4]

According to the European Social Charter, the Contracting Parties undertake "to ensure a weekly rest period which shall, as far as possible, coincide with the day recognized by tradition or custom in the country or region concerned as a day of rest." In practice this may place immigrants or minority group workers at a disadvantage if it is assumed that a part of the purpose of the day is to allow a worker to practise his religion.[5]

If there is a basic unanimity with respect to the principle of weekly rest, the same does not apply concerning limitation of working hours. The subject of working time is of course a continuous task of the ILO and many instruments adopted within the organization deal either directly with working hours or contain provisions relating to working hours. Only few of the ILO conventions limiting working hours have, however, entered into force, and if so the number of ratifying States is limited. For example, the Forty-Hour Week Convention (No. 47) 1935 has only been ratified by eight states and the Hours of Work and Rest Periods (Road Transport) Convention (No. 153) 1979 by five states. Accordingly, the most important instrument in this respect is the Reduction of Hours of Work Recommendation, 1962 (No. 116).[6]

The question of working time must be considered in relation to a

---

[4] International Labour Conference 1984, p. 65f.

[5] Harris, *supra* note 1, p. 43.

[6] For instance, The Hours of Work and Rest Periods (Road Transport) Convention (No. 153) and Recommendation (No. 161), 1979. The Special Youth Schemes Recommendation, 1970 (No. 136) advocates the limitation of daily and weekly work.

number of factors, such as the effect of new technology and national employment policy objectives. It is against this background that the wording of the European Social Charter should be seen, in which it is prescribed that the working week should be reduced "to the extent that the increase of productivity and other relevant factors permit." In a general survey by the ILO Committee of Experts on the application of ILO Recommendation 116 some of these factors have been stressed, for example "the country's capacity, given its level of development, to bring about a reduction of hours of work without adversely affecting productivity, industrial development and competitiveness in international trade and without creating inflationary pressures which would ultimately reduce the workers' real income."[7] Other factors mentioned have been new technology and management techniques, the need for improving standards of living in developing countries, and the preferences of employers' and workers' organizations.

The same survey demonstrates that the level of normal hours of work is variable in most countries according to industry or activity. In some countries it varies according to time of year. Special protection is often provided for young persons by laying down reduced normal working hours to apply to them. Similarly special protective measures in favour of women, in particular for pregnant and nursing mothers, are prescribed for. Where activity involves strain or health risks for the workers in general there is often a reduction in normal working hours. Night work is often distinguished from daytime work as regards hours worked. White-collar workers often have shorter basic hours than blue-collar workers. Generally speaking the countries that appear to have relatively long working hours are the developing ones.

The ILO survey concludes that the trend leads towards lower levels of actual hours of work which reflects new methods of arranging working time and new thinking on the conditions and quality of life.[8]

The third principle prescribed for in UDHR article 24 relates to holidays with pay. Once again the subject has been of great interest to the ILO and it has frequently been discussed by the International Labour Conference. The most important instruments are the Holidays with Pay Convention (No. 52) and the Holidays with Pay (revised) Convention (No. 132).

---

[7] International Labour Conference, *supra* note 4, p. 21.
[8] Ibid., p. 54.

The question of holidays with pay seems to be a field in which there has been considerable development during the past few decades. As has been reported by the ILO, there were in 1934 only 12 countries with holiday legislation applying to wage and salary earners in general. At the present time such legislation exists in the vast majority of States.

Also the duration of holidays with pay has been prolonged. While in 1934 the duration was between four days and three weeks, the present duration is mostly between two weeks and four weeks, in some countries even longer.[9] It can be noted that according to the ILO Convention 132 the minimum length of basic holiday is three working weeks for one year of service. The general trend towards the prolongation applies to both industrialized and developing countries, although it is more marked among the former countries.

References

Harris, David, *The European Social Charter*, Charlottesville: University Press of Virginia, 1984.

International Labour Conference, 70th Session, *Working Time*, 1984.

Verdoodt, Albert, *Naissance et Signification de la Déclaration Universelle des Droits de l'Homme*, Société d'Etudes Morales, Sociales et Juridiques, Louvain-Paris: Editions Nauwelaerts, 1964.

[9] Ibid., p. 90.

Article 25

Asbjørn Eide

Norway

1. Everyone has the right to a standard of living adequate for the health and well-being of himself and his family, including food, clothing, housing and medical care and necessary social services, and the right to security in the event of unemployment, sickness, disability, widowhood, old age or other lack of livelihood in circumstances beyond his control.
2. Motherhood and childhood are entitled to special care and assistance. All children, whether born in or out of wedlock, shall enjoy the same social protection.

I. Significance and Sources

Article 25 is one of the key components of economic and social rights. Contrary to what is often thought, there was no significant controversy surrounding the adoption of article 25 or the other economic and social rights. As will be pointed out below, the initial drafts emerged from circles within the United States, and in the negotiations leading up to the Universal Declaration of Human Rights (UDHR), the US delegation was consistently in favour of article 25 and the other economic and social rights.

Controversies concerning this matter arose later, and have focused in particular on the question of State obligations in regard to economic and social rights. To this we will return below, under section III.

Among the four freedoms enunciated by Franklin D. Roosevelt in 1941, 'freedom from want' stood out as the most innovative in the new international humanitarian order envisaged by him to be established when World War II was over. Traditional thinking on 'natural rights' (18th century) or 'civil rights' (19th century) had not incorporated concern with the satisfaction of basic needs. It was therefore an innovation, but this innovation was not, as is often claimed, brought into the international arena by socialist States.

Doubts have been raised whether article 25 and similar provisions relating to social and economic rights are human rights properly speaking. To address this issue, some comments are appropriate at this stage.

Human rights do not necessarily constitute rights as understood in positive law. We do not assume that all human rights are presently enforceable. In their positivistic sense, rights are often understood as enforceable claims on the delivery of goods, services, or protection by specific others. Rights, in this understanding, exist when one party can effectively insist that another deliver goods, services, or protections, and third parties will act to reinforce (or at least not hinder) their delivery.

Human rights start out as moral rights and over time become to some extent enforceable rights in the positive law of different societies. Two questions arise. How do they become enforceable? What content has to be given to enforceable law in order to have it correspond to a full implementation of the human right?

The process of enforceability has proceeded both at the national and the international level, through idealization, positivization and realization.

At the present time the idealization and the process towards enforceability are to a large extent promoted by the international community. Some rights were made enforceable in some States prior to the efforts at the international level, but no State had made all modern human rights enforceable inside their society prior to the adoption of the UDHR.

The process of absorbing human rights into national law is still occurring. It meets more or less acceptance or resistance, depending on both the cultural traditions and the predominant political ideology. Social and economic rights meet resistance in the legal system of the United States, but are acceptable in others, including the welfare states of Western Europe; equality of rights between men and women meets resistance in Muslim States but is generally acceptable both in the Western and the socialist countries of Europe; freedom of expression and opinion are strongly endorsed in the United States, generally acceptable in most West European countries and have met, in the past, strong resistance in the so-called socialist States of Central and Eastern Europe; and minority rights have generally been endorsed in Central and Eastern Europe but have met resistance in some Western States deeply wedded either to the ideology of the unitary nation-state or to the notion of the 'melting pot'.

A. The Nature of Obligations for Economic and Social Rights

Traditional wisdom will have it that economic and social rights have to be provided by the State, over its budget, and for this reason they are costly and lead to an overgrown State apparatus. This view results from a very narrow understanding of the nature of these rights and of the corresponding State obligations.

Fundamental to a realistic understanding of State obligations is that the individual is the subject of all economic and social development. This is stated in the following terms in the Declaration on the Right to Development, article 2.[1]

> 1. The human being is the central subject of development and should be the active participant and beneficiary of the right to development.
> 2. All human beings have a responsibility for development, individually and collectively, taking into account the need for full respect of their human rights and fundamental freedoms as well as their duties to the community, which alone can ensure the free and complete fulfillment of the human being....

The individual is expected, whenever possible through his or her own efforts and by the use of his or her own resources, to find ways to ensure the satisfaction of his or her own needs, individually or in association with others. Use of the own resources, however, requires that the person has resources that can be used — typically land or other capital, or labour. It could include the shared right to use communal land, and the land rights held by indigenous peoples. Furthermore, the realization of economic, social and cultural rights of an individual will usually take place within the context of a household as the smallest economic unit, although aspects of female and male division of labour and control over the produce, as well as various forms of wider kinship arrangements may present alternative alliances.

State obligations must be seen in the light of the above. States must, at the primary level, *respect* the freedom of the individuals to take the necessary actions and use the necessary resources — alone or in association with others. It is in regard to the latter that *collective* or group rights become important: the resources belonging to a collective of persons, such as indigenous populations, must be respected for them to be able to satisfy their needs by those resources. Similarly, the rights of peoples to

---

[1] Adopted by the General Assembly on 4 December 1986, res. 41/128.

exercise permanent sovereignty over their natural resources may be essential for them to be able, through their own collective efforts, to satisfy the needs of the members of that collective.

State obligations consist, at a secondary level, of the protection of the freedom of action and the use of resources against other, more assertive or aggressive subjects (more powerful economic interests, protection against fraud, against unethical behaviour in trade and contractual relations, against the marketing and dumping of hazardous or dangerous products — to mention some examples from different fields).

Probably this is the most important aspect of the right to food and other survival rights: not the State as provider, but as protector. This is a function similar to the role of the State as protector in regard to civil and political rights: protecting the right to life, to freedom from slavery and servitude, from violence and maltreatment by third parties.

Significant components of the obligation to *protect* are spelled out in existing law. Much more could be elaborated on the significant components, however. When further developed, such legislation becomes manageable for judicial review, and therefore belies the argument that economic and social rights are inherently non-justiciable. Legislation of this kind must, of course, be contextual, i.e., it must be based on the specific situational requirements in the country concerned. To take one example: legislation requiring that land can be owned only by the tiller of the land is essential where agriculture is the major basis of income, but may be much less relevant in highly industrialized technological societies where only a small percentage lives off the land. For groups of people whose culture requires a close link to the use of land, protection of that land is even more important as an obligation to realize the right to food — again, the indigenous peoples serve as the clearest example.

At the tertiary level, the State has — as a last resource — the obligation to *fulfil* the expectations of all for the enjoyment of the right to satisfaction of basic needs (in the following called livelihood rights), to be the provider. This may take two forms:

1. assistance in order to provide *opportunities* for those who have not;
2. direct *provisions* of food or resources which can be used for the satisfaction of basic needs (direct aid, or social security) when no other possibility exists, for example: 1) when unemployment sets in (such as under recession); 2) for the

disadvantaged, and the elderly; 3) during sudden situations of crisis or disaster (see further below); and 4) for those who are marginalized (for example, due to structural transformations in the economy and production).

It may now have become clearer why the allegation that economic and social rights differ from the civil and political in that the former require the use of resources by the State, while the obligation for States to ensure the enjoyment of civil and political rights do not require resources, is such a gross oversimplification. The argument is tenable only in situations where the focus for economic and social rights is on the tertiary level (the obligation to fulfil), while civil and political rights are observed on the primary level (the obligations to respect). This scenario is, however, arbitrary. Some civil rights require State obligations at all levels — also the obligation to provide direct assistance, when there is a need for it.[2] Economic and social rights, on the other hand, can in many cases best be safeguarded through non-interference by the State with the freedom and use of resources possessed by the individuals.

B. On the Contents of Article 25

The four elements contained in article 25 are:

1. Paragraph 1 provides for a standard of living "adequate for the health and well-being" of every individual. This includes, but is not limited to, food, clothing, housing, medical care and necessary social services. This right can be enjoyed when the person concerned has resources by which to be self-employed (land for cultivation, access to fishing and hunting grounds, the use of property as a source of income, fair wages in the sense used by the UDHR article 23, or through social security);

---

[2] The General Comment of the Human Rights Committee in regard to the right to life, article 6 of the International Covenant on Civil and Political Rights (General Assembly Official Records, Supplement No. 40, A/37/40, 1982, p. 93) refers, *inter alia*, to widespread and serious malnutrition leading to extensive child mortality, as a non-fulfilment of the right to life. Remedies to counteract child malnutrition often require government organized provisions. In a field more wellknown to lawyers, equal access to justice (which is essential for the protection of civil and political rights) requires legal aid to those in the lowest income brackets, another illustration that the State may have to be a provider in order to complete its range of obligations also in regard to civil and political rights.

2.   The second element in paragraph 1 deals with this second aspect — the right to security in the event of unemployment, sickness, disability, widowhood, old age and other lacks of livelihood — and is therefore closely related to article 22, which deals generally with the right to social security;
3.   The first element of paragraph 2 of article 25 contains the entitlement of special care and assistance for motherhood and childhood;
4.   The second element provides for equal enjoyment by children, whether born inside or outside wedlock, of social protection.

II. Drafting

In 1942, soon after the 'Four Freedoms Address' by Franklin D. Roosevelt, the American Law Institute convened a committee of experts, intended to cover the main cultures of the world, to draft a proposal for an international Bill of Human Rights. The majority of the members were experts from the United States.

In 1944, the draft was finished. In line with predominant thinking at the time, both in the United States and elsewhere, the draft contained a number of economic and social rights: right to work, right to food and housing, and right to social security.

It was not formally adopted by the American Law Institute, but was subsequently distributed by an organization called 'Americans United for World Organization', New York.[3] It was to have considerable impact on the subsequent drafting of the UDHR, though not in the way intended.

On the right to food and housing, the American Law Institute draft had the following text:

Article 14
Everyone has the right to adequate food and housing. The State has a duty to take such measures as may be necessary to insure that all its residents have an opportunity to obtain these essentials.

Social security was dealt with in the next article:

Article 15

---

[3] The document was later presented to the General Assembly of the United Nations and was given the symbol A/148, under which it can be retrieved.

Everyone has the right to social security. The State has a duty to maintain or ensure that there are maintained comprehensive arrangements for the promotion of health, for the prevention of sickness and accident, and for the provision of medical care and of compensation for loss of livelihood.

In the commentary to the text, it was stated that the duties imposed on the state by article 15 were to see that the resources of society are organized:

1. To raise standards of health;
2. To prevent sickness and accident;
3. To provide medical care wherever needed, including maternity cases;
4. To provide for the financial support of persons deprived of earnings, who lack means of livelihood, including the involuntarily unemployed and their dependents, the aged, widows and orphans.

The commentary also added the following:

The wording of the article leaves full scope to private initiative, in countries where this is considered desirable, to accept as much of the responsibility as it can and will....

Panama presented the draft at the founding conference of the United Nations in San Francisco in 1945, seeking to include it as a bill of rights in the Charter of the Organization. This was not accepted, but it was agreed that a Commission on Human Rights (the Commission) should be established with the task of drafting an international bill of rights. Panama then took the matter to the General Assembly in 1946, seeking to have the Assembly adopt it there and then as its Bill of Rights. The General Assembly declined to do so, in the light of the fact that the Commission had been provided for in the Charter, but transferred the draft to the Commission. Within the Secretariat of the new organization, the Division of Human Rights under its Director, the Canadian Professor John Humphrey, prepared the first draft for the Commission. In regard to the sources used by the Secretariat, Humphrey has subsequently made the following observation: "The best of the texts from which I worked was the one prepared by the American Law Institute, and I borrowed freely from it. This was the text that had been unsuccessfully sponsored by Panama at the San Francisco conference and later in the General Assembly. It had been drafted in the United States during the war by a distinguished group representing many cultures, one of whom was Alfredo

Alfaro, the Panamanian Foreign Minister."[4]

The draft prepared by the Secretariat (the Division of Human Rights) had several articles related to what subsequently became UDHR article 25. Among the Secretariat provisions of relevance here are articles 35 ("Everyone has the right to medical care. The State shall promote public health and safety."); article 39 ("Everyone has the right to such equitable share of the national income as the need for his work and the increment it makes to the common welfare may justify"); article 40 ("Everyone has the right to such help as may be necessary to make it possible for him to support his family"); article 41 ("Everyone has the right to social security. The State shall maintain effective arrangements for the prevention of unemployment and for insurance against the risks of unemployment, accident, disability, sickness, old age, and other involuntary or undeserved loss of livelihood"); and article 42 ("Everyone has the right to good food and housing and to live in surroundings that are pleasant and healthy").

In the Commission, several elements of the Secretariat draft were brought together into what became UDHR article 25. One initial focus was on the right to health, which was understood not only to require access to medical care, but also adequate food and nutrition, clothing and housing. During the negotiations, the UK representative underlined that these requirements could be met only to the extent that the level of available resources in the country concerned made it possible.[5]

At the third session of the Commission, in May–June 1948, a new approach was chosen, moving beyond the question of an adequate standard of living for the maintenance of health and well-being. It was decided to combine elements of the then draft article 22 with article 25. This is why, in paragraph 1, the final part "and the right to security in the event of unemployment..." was added. In one sense, this elaborates on the provision of article 22. It emphasizes the conditions under which security shall be provided. On the other hand, article 25 abstains from using the word *social* security.

The Indian representative, Mrs. Mehta, during the first session of the Commission proposed the addition of the words "motherhood and childhood are entitled to special care and assistance." This addition met with no opposition, and was included in the draft.

The final addition to article 25(2) "All children, whether born in

---

[4] Humphrey 1984, p. 32.
[5] E/CN.4/SR 40, pp. 16/17.

or out of wedlock, shall enjoy the same social protection," did not emerge during the drafting in the Commission, but instead in the Third Committee of the General Assembly during the final drafting of the Declaration in the autumn of 1948. The initiative was taken by the Yugoslav representative, whose proposals were modified by the Norwegian representative, Lunde. Two elements were involved in their proposal: that children born out of wedlock should have the same rights as those born in wedlock, and that they should enjoy the same social protection. The first part of the proposal met with some resistance. Some States were not prepared to give juridical equality to children outside or inside marriage. The first part of the proposal was therefore rejected by a very narrow vote in the Third Committee (18:18, with 9 abstentions). A large majority, however, accepted the principle of equality in regard to social protection.

III. The Covenant on Economic, Social and Cultural Rights (CESCR) and other International Instruments

The initial debate in the working group on economic, social and cultural rights set up by the Commission in 1951 (E/CN.4/AC/14) was faced with a set of proposals made between 1949 and 1951 by the United States, the Soviet Union, Yugoslavia, Denmark, Egypt, Australia and in some cases by specialized agencies. The drafts did not refer to specific basic needs, but only to an 'adequate standard of living'. The one exception was the Soviet draft which included the right to decent housing. While the other drafts sought to base the right around the obligation of States to promote social and economic conditions to advance the standard of living, the Soviet draft was somewhat more direct; the obligation of the State should be to ensure to everyone the right to work and to choice of profession "with the object of creating conditions which will remove the threat of death by hunger or by inanition."

The draft by the Soviet Union on housing had the following language: "The State shall take all the necessary steps, especially legislative measures, to ensure to everyone living accommodation worthy of man." Because of the reference to the responsibility of the State, this was rejected. The United States introduced a draft with the following language: "The States Parties to the Covenant recognize the right of everyone to adequate housing." An amendment presented by Egypt, to change 'adequate housing' into 'living accommodation worthy of man' (thus introducing part of the

Soviet proposal into the text) was also rejected, and the proposal by the United States was then adopted by a large majority.

Simultaneously, the Commission discussed another provision dealing with an adequate standard of living. An Australian text formed the basis of the discussion: "The States Parties to the Covenant recognize the right of everyone to an adequate standard of living." Yugoslavia presented a proposal to add "and the continuous improvement of living conditions." This was adopted, and the Australian draft with the Yugoslavian addition was adopted by a large majority. This became draft article 24, presented by the Commission in 1951.

In 1952 the Commission was faced with a new situation. The General Assembly had finally agreed that there should be two Covenants, and therefore a separate Covenant on economic, social and cultural rights had to be drafted. The UK proposed to delete the article on adequate housing, article 23, as it had been adopted in the 1951 draft. The argument was that adequate housing was included in the concept of adequate standard of living, which was to be covered by the subsequent article and therefore would be redundant and beyond the scope of the article on adequate standard of living. Others differed, claiming that there was a need to express the right to certain basic needs, and some of them even wanted to add other things to 'adequate housing'. China presented a draft proposing to add "food, clothing and..." before housing. A large majority accepted this proposition.

As a consequence of the division into two Covenants, article 23 of the 1951 draft became article 11. It required the States Parties to recognize the right to adequate food, clothing and housing. In this formulation, there is a general recognition of the right to basic needs.

Separate from article 11, there was a discussion of article 24 of the 1951 draft, on an adequate standard of living, which was unanimously adopted with the same text as in 1951, now having the number article 12 of the new Covenant.

While some found the expression "adequate standard of living" very vague, the majority argued that any definition would be restrictive and should be avoided.

The additional concern with "continuous improvement in the standard of living", which had been proposed by Yugoslavia and adopted, was somewhat more controversial.

Articles 11 and 12, as adopted in 1952, formed the draft presented by the Commission to the General Assembly. They were discussed by the Third Committee in 1957. At that time, there was general agreement that the two articles should be combined, since they were closely interrelated. Adequate food, clothing and housing were seen to be elements in an adequate standard of living. However, a Philippine amendment proposed to replace the word 'adequate' with the word 'decent'. Supporters of that amendment argued that 'decent' indicated a higher standard than merely 'adequate'. The latter, it was argued, might be interpreted to cover only basic needs, and the word 'decent' had also been used in article 7, where 'decent living' was the expression. There were others, however, who argued that 'decent' had additional connotations, not all of them relevant in the present context. They argued that 'adequate' had a clear and well understood meaning, and it was therefore adopted.

In 1963, the Director-General of the Food and Agriculture Organization (FAO) was invited to address the Third Committee, and made an impassioned plea for "a vast collective movement of aid and solidarity, to help the millions unable to attain the degree of development that the progress of science ought to enable them to achieve. But that aid must be given with full respect for the liberty of the developing peoples. They must feel themselves principally responsible for their economic and social progress." (Third Committee, 1232nd meeting, paragraph 7).

In March of that year, a manifesto had been issued by world-renowned statesmen who had met in the Special Assembly on Man's Right to Freedom from Hunger at the FAO headquarters. A declaration had also been issued by the World Food Congress in June of the same year. That declaration had stated that the persistence of hunger and malnutrition was unacceptable morally and socially, and was incompatible with the dignity of human beings; the elimination of hunger was the primary task of all men and women.

He proposed a new draft article to be included in the Covenant, whereby the States Parties to the Covenant would recognize the right of everyone to be free from hunger, and to undertake development programmes aimed at achieving freedom from hunger within the shortest possible time.

The intervention was followed up by a number of draft proposals (Saudi Arabia, Chile, Colombia, Ecuador and Uganda, and eventually a joint proposal by Afghanistan, Chile, Colombia, Ecuador, Guatemala, Nigeria, the Philippines, Saudi Arabia, Sudan, Syria, Uganda, and the United Arab Republic). This resulted in the addition now found in paragraph 2 of article 11 of the CESCR.

The addition was adopted without any votes against and only one (Pakistan) abstention. In spite of this, however, there were some reservations concerning the usefulness of adding the article, a point which has more to do with the question of State responsibility than with the appropriateness of recognizing the right to be free from hunger.

Two very different approaches confronted each other. The initial proposal by the Soviet Union concerning the right to 'living accommodation worthy of man' started with the formulation "the State shall take all the necessary steps, especially legislative measures, to ensure to everyone...." This formulation of State responsibility caused the draft to be rejected, and the US draft which contained no reference to State responsibilities to be adopted.

The approach by the United States was to avoid any formulation of State responsibility in connection with the separate articles, but to adopt a general umbrella article, which was to precede all the individual articles and to contain whatever reference to State responsibility there was in the Covenant. The initial US proposal for such an umbrella clause was rather perfunctory: "Each State Party to this Covenant undertakes, with due regard to its organization and resources, to promote conditions of economic, social and cultural progress for securing" ... and then the different "rights".

In the Commission, all efforts to include responsibilities in the individual articles were rejected. However, in the Third Committee, discussing article 11, there was a Polish amendment to add the phrase "and will take appropriate steps to secure conditions for the fulfilment of this right." Chile and Japan added another suggestion, which was to recognize the particular importance of international co-operation in ensuring the exercise of this right.

Western countries argued that it was unfortunate to include these elements in the draft, arguing that one should not specify obligations of States since these were dealt with in article 2, the general umbrella clause applying to all articles. They also argued that in article 2, States had only the obligation to 'achieve progressively' the realization of the rights, whereas the new draft proposed concerning article 11 did not refer to 'progressively'. That might be interpreted, it was said, as binding on States to ensure an adequate standard of living for everyone immediately.

Those supporting the article with the addition argued that the right was so fundamental that there could be no valid objection to the inclusion of an implementation clause in this article. It was also argued that the inclusion of a reference to international co-operation in this article which dealt with the question of the standard of living was particularly essential since some countries, especially those that were underdeveloped, would not be able to provide their people with adequate food, clothing and shelter without international assistance. Finally, the text of the article as a whole was adopted by 48 votes to none, with 16 abstentions. This text is identical to article 11(1) of the text contained in the CESCR.

When, in 1963, the Third Committee adopted a second paragraph to article 11, dealing with the freedom from hunger (see above), a number of measures to be undertaken by States were included in the article. This not only included improvement in the methods of production, conservation and distribution of food, but also developing or reforming agrarian systems. Also included were programmes to ensure an equitable distribution of world food supplies in relation to need.

These proposals were met with some resistance. Pakistan proposed the enumeration of measures, apparently concerned primarily with the undesirability of including the question of land reform. (Third Committee, 1264th meeting, paragraph 4.) This seems to have been the reason why Pakistan, as the only country, abstained in the voting.

Others intervening in the debate addressed the importance of land reform. This included in particular Chile (1266th meeting, paragraph 55) who quoted the former Chairman of the Council of FAO, Josue D. Castro, who had said that hunger could not be combated effectively by paternalistic measures designed solely to mitigate the gravity of the problem and to avert the revolt of the starving. "For an effective remedy to that evil it was essential to accelerate economic development in general and agricultural production in particular. *It was therefore essential to carry out effective agrarian reform*, to apply modern techniques to the extraction of natural wealth, to train technical and administrative personnel in sufficient quantities and, in addition, to inculcate sound nutritional principles in the people."

Some Western countries, including the Netherlands (1266th meeting, paragraph 57) expressed misgivings. "There should be a clear distinction between the enunciation of a right and a summing-up of the various means of realizing it, and he doubted whether the latter should be included in the draft Covenant" (paragraph 59). The UK, on the other hand, commented favourably on the measure to reform agrarian systems (1267th meeting, paragraph 5).

These quotes have been given since they indicate the diversity of opinion on the inclusion of responsibilities in connection with the different articles. It clearly emerges that there are strong disagreements on the inclusion of responsibilities, even when there is general acceptance of the inclusion of the right as such.

The concerns reflected in UDHR article 25(2) (special protection of motherhood and childhood; equality of children born in or out of wedlock) were given a separate article in the CESCR (article 10) which deals with the protection and assistance to the family.

IV. Follow-up in Other Instruments

Were we to explore all the instruments which directly or indirectly recognize the freedom from want, the list would become very long, far beyond the scope of the present study. Some illustrations can be given of the ways in which these concerns have found recognition in international law. This does not imply that all elements referred to below contain legally binding obligations of States; some of them are recommendations only, contributing to the recognition of the right but leaving the obligations still in abeyance. Most of the recommendations and conventions seek in one way or another to secure the conditions under which livelihood can be ensured. The full implications of these provisions are too extensive to be examined in this brief study.

Apart from the basic provisions in the UDHR, article 25, and in the CESCR article 11, the concern with food, freedom from hunger, and other basic needs required for an adequate standard of living has been reviewed by Tomasevski (1987) and appears at least in the following contexts: freedom from hunger;[6] safeguarding of the right to food in armed conflict;[7] providing food for refugees;[8]

[6] Universal Declaration on the Eradication of Hunger and Malnutrition, adopted by the World Food Conference in 1974 and endorsed by the General Assembly in resolution 3348 (XXIX) of 17 December 1974.
[7] The Geneva Convention of 1949 Relative to the Treatment of Prisoners of War, articles 26 and 51, the Geneva Convention Relative to the Protection of Civilian Persons in Time of War, articles 23 and 55, Protocol Additional to the Geneva Conventions, and Relating to Victims of International Armed Conflict, articles 54, 69 and 70, Protocol Additional to the Geneva Conventions, and Relating to the Protection of Victims of Non-International Armed Conflicts, articles 14 and 15, Declaration on the Protection of Women and Children in Emergency and Armed Conflict, p. 6.
[8] Statute of the Office of the United Nations High Commissioner for Refugees, Convention Relating to the Status of Refugees, chapter IV.

disaster relief;[9] providing food for prisoners;[10] international crimes involving deprivation of food;[11] access to food and adequate nutrition;[12] minimum wages;[13] social security and social assistance;[14] adequate nutrition for infants;[15] consumer protection;[16] food strategy;[17] population policy;[18] natural resources;[19] fisheries;[20] prohibition of slavery and forced

[9] There is no explicit recognition of the obligations to give, or to receive, in times of disaster. But steps in this direction have been taken by the decision to establish the office of a United Nations Disaster Relief Coordinator, and subsequent resolutions by the General Assembly in this area. See General Assembly resolution 2816 (XXVI), 1971, establishing UNDRO, and resolutions 36/225, 1981 and others strengthening the United Nations system to respond to natural disasters and other disaster situations.

[10] United Nations Standard Minimum Rules for the Treatment of Prisoners, European Standard Minimum Rules for the Treatment of Prisoners.

[11] Convention on the Prevention and Punishment of the Crime of Genocide article II (c), International Convention on the Suppression and Punishment of the Crime of Apartheid, article II (a) (iii).

[12] World Food Conference 1974 resolution V: Policies and Programs to Improve Nutrition; Mexico Declaration of the World Food Council.

[13] ILO Convention No. 131, 1970: Minimum Wage-Fixing Machinery (Agriculture) Convention; ILO Recommendation No. 135: Minimum Wage-Fixing Machinery (Agriculture) Recommendation.

[14] ILO Social Security (Minimum Standards) Convention; ILO Social Policy (Basic Aims and Standards) Convention; World Employment Conference: Basic Needs Strategy; Inter-American Charter of Social Guarantees; OAS Charter: Right to Nutrition and Well-Being; European Social Charter; European Convention on Social and Medical Assistance.

[15] Declaration of the Rights of the Child, Principle 4; International Code of Marketing of Breast-milk Substitutes, adopted in May 1981 as a Recommendation under article 23 of its constitution by the WHO conference.

[16] Code of Ethics for International Trade in Food, adopted by the Codex Alimentarius Commission of the FAO; Legal Protection of Collective Interests of Consumers by Consumer Agencies — Recommendation R (81)2 by the Council of Europe, Committee of Ministers.

[17] World Conference on Agrarian Reform and Rural Development, convened by FAO in Rome, 12–20 July 1979; Food Strategy Guidelines, contained in Program of Action, paras. 51–65.

[18] World Food Conference 1974 resolution VIII: Achievement of desirable balance between population and food supply; International Conference on Human Rights, Teheran 1968: Human Rights Aspects of Family Planning; World Population Conference, Bucharest 1974: World Population Plan of Action Section C.

[19] General Assembly resolution 1803 (XVII): Permanent Sovereignty over Natural Resources; General Assembly resolution 3281 (XXIX): Charter of Economic Rights and Duties of States; General Assembly resolution 37/7, 1982 (Annex): World

labour;[21] special categories of agricultural workers;[22] education
and vocational training in agriculture;[23] rural organizations and
associations;[24] elimination of discrimination against women;[25]
elimination of racial and ethnic discrimination;[26] and rights of the
child.[27]

The relevance of the Convention on Elimination of
Discrimination against Women (CEDAW) is the aim to avoid
motherhood contributing to discrimination of women. Two
provisions can be mentioned here: CEDAW article 5(b) requires
States to take all appropriate measures to ensure that family
education includes a proper understanding of maternity as a social
function and the recognition of the common responsibility of men
and women in the upbringing and development of their children.
CEDAW article 11, dealing with prevention of discrimination in
employment, provides in its paragraph 2 for a number of measures
to be taken by States in order to prevent discrimination against
women on the grounds of pregnancy or of maternity leave. This
includes the prohibition of dismissal on the grounds of pregnancy
or maternity leave; prohibition of discrimination on the basis of

Charter for Nature; Declaration of the United Nations Conference on Desertification:
Plan of Action to Combat Desertification; General Assembly resolution 39/208:
Countries Stricken by Desertification and Drought.

[20] United Nations Convention on the Law of the Sea, 1982: Fishing Rights, articles
62 and 63.

[21] Slavery Convention, 1926; Supplementary Convention on the Abolition of Slavery,
the Slave Trade, and Institutions and Practices Similar to Slavery, 1956; ILO Forced
Labour Convention (Convention No. 29), 1930; ILO Abolition of Forced Labour
Convention (No. 105), 1959.

[22] Plantations Convention and Recommendation; Protocol to the Plantations
Convention; see also, Tomasevski 1987.

[23] Human Resources Development Convention and Recommendation; Special Youth
Schemes Recommendation; Vocational Training (Agriculture) Recommendation.

[24] Co-operatives (Developing Countries) Recommendation; Rural Workers'
Organisations Convention.

[25] International Convention on the Elimination of All Forms of Discrimination
Against Women (1979), articles 11 *et seq.*, in particular article 14; World Food
Conference 1974: Resolution on Women and Food; General Assembly resolution
37/59, 1982: Improvement of the Situation of Women in Rural Areas; World
Conference on the United Nations Decade for Women, Copenhagen 1980: Women
and Nutritional Self-sufficiency; World Conference of the United Nations Decade for
Women, Copenhagen 1980: Women in Agriculture and Rural Areas.

[26] International Convention on the Elimination of All Forms of Racial Discrimination,
1965, particularly article 5.

[27] Convention on the Rights of the Child, adopted by the General Assembly on 20
November 1989.

marital status; introduction of maternity leave with pay; and encouragement of necessary supporting services such as child-care facilities.

The Convention on the Rights of the Child, adopted by the General Assembly in 1989, is a wide-ranging elaboration of the protection of the child, but more importantly, it emphasizes the child as a separate and independent holder of those rights, not simply as an appendix to the family. It would go beyond the scope of the present study to go into the details of that significant new convention, however.

V. Nordic Policies in Regard to Article 25

Nordic implementation of the rights contained in article 25 has been carried out through a wide range of laws and administrative arrangements. The rights contained in this article were already by 1948 central elements in the established legal systems of the Nordic countries, and have since been further developed.

The right to an adequate standard of living is at the heart of the Nordic welfare society which has been developed over a century, and the structure of the social legislation is quite similar in the five different Nordic countries. It is composed of several elements:

- social welfare law;
- health law;
- social security law;
- workers' protection.

The overall development has been described in the previous articles and will not be reviewed here.

Of special relevance for article 25 are the laws on social welfare and social security. Some illustrations can be given, however, by the case of Norway.

Social welfare law includes the Act on Social Welfare of 5 June 1964, no. 2 and the Act on Child Welfare of 17 July 1953, no. 14. These laws are administered by elected local authorities — the social welfare boards and the child welfare boards. Social security law comprises the national insurance system, personal injury insurance, and public service pension schemes.

Central to the system is the National Insurance Act of 17 June 1966, no. 12. The entire Norwegian population is covered under this law.

Protection of maternity and childhood, and more generally the

Asbjørn Eide

protection of the family as provided for in article 25 paragraph 2 and in CESCR article 10 is based on a very extensive legislation in all the Nordic countries.

During the last century, however, substantial changes have taken place in attitudes towards the family. It has proceeded from paternalism, through equal partnership in parental authority, to an increasing recognition of the rights of the child, even when the child is in conflict with the parents. The culmination of this process might well be illustrated by the establishment in Norway, in 1981, of a special Ombudsman for children. The task given to the Ombudsman is to ensure that the needs, rights and interests of children are given the necessary consideration in all areas of society. The Ombudsman does not have the authority to decide or set aside decisions made in the administration, but he does have the authority to lobby for the interests of the children and to receive communications directly from them.

The Ombudsman's competence does not include the handling of specific conflicts between a child and its parents or other guardians, regarding parental responsibility and similar matters. Nevertheless, in practice, this issue could not be avoided.

The social context of families, and therefore also of maternity and childhood, has undergone considerable changes since the adoption in 1948 of the UDHR. Four major elements in these changes can be mentioned: the declining size of families, many of which are now single-parent; the increasing number of families consisting of unmarried, co-habitating couples; the steep increase in the number of working mothers, with a corresponding increase in the establishment and use of day-care centres, and the substantial benefits of a financial nature to families with children; and the decreasing time spent by parents with their children due to the conditions of work.

The implementation of the provisions in article 25(2) have mainly taken four directions. First, there is a very extensive network of health care for children and mothers, in all the Nordic countries, largely available free of charge. Secondly, there are provisions for financial security for the families with children, including child allowances, special allowances for the single mother, and allowances for widows and young children.

A third direction is the promotion of equality between men and women, which also requires special protection against discrimination of pregnant women and mothers of young children.

Finally, the fourth direction is an increasing protection of the rights of the child, as a separate subject from that of the family, which corresponds to the direction taken by the new UN Convention on the Rights of the Child.

The success in regard to child protection through health care and social security can be demonstrated by the exceptionally low infant mortality rate. This is achieved, *inter alia*, by prenatal and postnatal protection and assistance, including extensive medical and health care and maternity and other benefits, which are given irrespective of marital status.

The maternity and child health-centre activities throughout the Nordic countries are key elements in this protection.

Maternity, paternity and parental allowances are provided for in the sickness insurance acts and similar legislation in the respective countries. Social assistance is provided to secure the necessary maintenance and care of an individual or a family, whenever that person is not able to secure it through work, through private means, or in other ways. Social assistance services aim at maintaining or reviving a person's own initiative when (s)he is temporarily unable to secure the necessary maintenance. The purpose is also to keep the family intact in these situations. Maintenance aims at providing conditions for adequate nourishment, clothing, hygienically satisfactory living conditions, necessary sanitation, and special care necessitated by illness or disability.

Equality in the protection of children, whether born in or out of wedlock, has been a feature of Nordic legislation for nearly a century. The right of a child born out of wedlock to inherit from her or his father is the same as that of a child born in wedlock.

References

Humphrey, John, P., *Human Rights and the United Nations: a Great Adventure*, Dobbs Ferry: Transnational Publishers, Inc., 1984.

Tomasevski, Katarina (ed.), *The Right to Food: Guide through Applicable International Law*, Dordrecht: Martinus Nijhoff Publishers, 1987.

United Nations Documents: E/CN.4/SR.40; A/148; General Assembly resolution 41/128; General Assembly resolution 3348 (XXIX); General Assembly Official Records, Supplement No. 40, A/37/40, 1982;

Verdoodt, Albert, *Naissance et Signification de la Déclaration Universelle des Droits de l'Homme*, Société d'Etudes Morales, Sociales et Juridiques, Louvain-Paris: Editions Nauwelaerts, 1964.

Article 26

Pentti Arajärvi

Finland

1. Everyone has the right to education. Education shall be free, at least in the elementary and fundamental stages. Elementary education shall be compulsory. Technical and professional education shall be made generally available and higher education shall be equally accessible to all on the basis of merit.
2. Education shall be directed to the full development of the human personality and to the strengthening of respect for human rights and fundamental freedoms. It shall promote understanding, tolerance and friendship among all nations, racial or religious groups, and shall further the activities of the United Nations for the maintenance of peace.
3. Parents have a prior right to choose the kind of education that shall be given to their children.

I. Article 26 of the Universal Declaration of Human Rights

A. The travaux préparatoires

In the report of the Drafting Committee on an International Bill of Human Rights, in Annex A,[1] which was prepared by the Secretariat, education is mentioned in article 21. According to this article: "Everyone has the right to establish educational institutions in conformity with conditions laid down by the law." Furthermore, according to article 36(1) in the same document: "Everyone has the right to education", and (2): "Each State has the duty to require that every child within its territory receive a primary education. The State shall maintain adequate and free facilities for such education.

---

[1] UN doc. E/CN.4/21, p. 8.

It shall also promote facilities for higher education without distinction as to race, sex, language, religion, class, or wealth of the person entitled to benefit therefrom." Article 46 of the draft declaration mentions some educational rights for minorities.

"All persons have an interest in learning and a right to education. Primary education is obligatory for children and the community shall provide appropriate and free facilities for such education," according to article 41 in Annex D (p. 48) of the same document, drafted by Professor Cassin on the basis of discussions. An enactment for access to higher education without discrimination as well as access to general vocational and technical training was suggested in the same article. Article 44 granted rights for ethnic, linguistic and religious minorities to establish and maintain schools.

Annex F of the same document (p. 73) contains the suggestion of the Drafting Committee for an International Declaration on Human Rights to be adopted by the Commission on Human Rights (the Commission). At this stage the enactments on the right to education have been formulated in article 31, according to which: "Everyone has the right to education. Primary education shall be free and compulsory. There shall be equal access for all to such facilities for technical, cultural and higher education as can be provided by the State or community on the basis of merit and without distinction as to race, sex, language, religion, social standing, political affiliation or financial means." Article 36 includes a provision on the right of ethnic, linguistic or religious minorities to establish and maintain schools and other institutions of their own. The Drafting Committee, though, suggested that taking into consideration the importance of this article, further preparations should be made by the Commission and suggested that it might, if necessary, be referred to the Sub-Commission on Prevention of Discrimination and Protection of Minorities for examination of the minority aspects.

Already at this stage consideration had also been given to almost all aspects of the right to education as mentioned in the Universal Declaration of Human Rights (UDHR) as well as in other declarations and conventions. Since then, basic enactments on the content of education have been developed most.

The Commission decided during its second session to use the above mentioned Annex F as drafted by the Drafting Committee as the basis of their further work on the UDHR. A special working group was assigned to this task. The right to education was included in articles 27 and 28 of the work of the Commission.[2] Article 27 almost exactly corresponds to that of the Drafting Committee.

Article 28 prescribes the content of education. According to the above article, "education will be directed to the full physical, intellectual, moral and spiritual development of the human personality, to the strengthening of respect for human rights and fundamental freedoms and to the combating of the spirit of intolerance and hatred against other nations or racial or religious groups everywhere."

Article 31 contains enactments regarding the rights of minorities. The Commission did not deal with them, but left them for later preparations. One of the texts was based on that of the Drafting Committee and the other one on the text prepared by the Sub-Commission for Prevention of Discrimination and Protection of Minorities. Neither of these texts are included in the UDHR.

In meetings 67–69 of the third session of the Commission, the Commission discussed the right to education and how to take into consideration the ethical principles of the content of education based on the experiences of World War II and especially the education of the Nazis. The wordings of the articles were agreed upon article by article.

The Commission decided not to include in the article a prohibition of discrimination, as there already was a general clause forbidding the same. Nor was the right of parents to choose the quality of the education nor the school for their children approved. The articles 27 and 28 were combined, and the paragraph concerning the content of the education was notably improved.[3]

The proposal of the Commission to the Economic and Social Council (ECOSOC) for article 23 reads:

1. Everyone has the right to education. Elementary and fundamental education shall be free and compulsory and there shall be equal access on the basis of merit to higher education.
2. Education shall be directed to the full development of the human personality, to strengthening respect for human rights and fundamental freedoms and to combating the spirit of intolerance and hatred against other nations and against racial and religious groups everywhere.[4]

---

[2] UN doc. E/600, p. 18.
[3] UN doc. E/CN.4/SR 67 to 69.
[4] UN doc. E/800

During the third session of the UN General Assembly the Third Committee discussed the UDHR based on the proposal by the ECOSOC.[5]

The discussion dealt basically with the right of parents to choose the education of their children, prohibition of discrimination and the content of education. While discussing the content of education the question of the aims and principles of the United Nations also arose. The meeting thus wanted to extend the concept of promoting peace as the basis of all the activities of the United Nations.

The 148th meeting of the Third Committee voted on the content of article 23. The proposal made by the Soviet Union stressing the prohibition of discrimination was rejected. The expression of article 23(2) that "Education shall be directed to combating the spirit of intolerance and hatred against other nations and against racial and religious groups everywhere," was changed to the positive expression: "It [education] shall promote understanding, tolerance and friendship among all nations, racial or religious groups...." Furthermore the criteria for the content of education was agreed upon as: "[It] shall further the activities of the United Nations for the maintenance of peace." Also a third paragraph concerning the right of parents to choose the education of their children was approved. The UDHR was thus finalized.

B. The Right to Education

According to the first sentence of the article, "Everyone has the right to education." This right refers both to adults and to children and the word education is to be understood in a broad sense. It should not be limited to only general education.

"Education shall be free, at least in the elementary and fundamental stages." Most probably 'free' is to be understood as the education being free of charge, but to be able to participate in the education the pupil might have to cover his or her own expenses, such as transportation to the school. The fundamental stage of education is most probably to be defined by the States themselves, but it should contain basic knowledge and skills essential for functioning in society, which differ in various societies. Elementary education is part of the fundamental education.

As "elementary education shall be compulsory," also adults who

---

[5] UN doc, Third Committee, pp. 579–607.

have not received elementary education must be educated. There is no fixed border between elementary and fundamental education. Elementary education includes fundamental education such as literacy, arithmetic and basic orientation into society. The compulsion obliges society to attend to the existence of access to schools and to see to it that either through the education offered by the society or otherwise the knowledge and the skills provided by the elementary education are received.

"Technical and professional education shall be made generally available and higher education shall be equally accessible to all on the basis of merit." This enactment prohibits unjustified requirements for access to this education. The requirements could, though, be based on the educational system, for example, in order to receive a basic education. The only criteria for selecting students for higher education mentioned is merit, which should be understood as the ability to absorb the education.

C. The Content of Education

The notion "education shall be directed to the full development of the human personality" indicates the general ethical aim of education which would influence the individual. The development of the entire personality includes all the dimensions of the human being: physical, intellectual, psychological and social. The aim is that each individual could develop himself or herself according to his or her abilities and talents, to a harmonious person.

"Strengthening of respect for human rights and fundamental freedoms" requires at least an education that is not in contradiction with the UDHR or any other human rights or fundamental freedoms included in other international conventions or declarations.

The notion "education shall promote understanding, tolerance and friendship among all nations, racial or religious groups and shall further the activities of the United Nations for the maintenance of peace," also includes an indirect prohibition of discrimination. The provision calls for the existence of different views, coexisting side by side as well as within each other. The content of education should also take into consideration the principles of the UN Charter and the functions of the special agencies of the United Nations.

D. The Choice of Education

The notion of "a prior right of parents to choose the kind of education that shall be given to their children" does not give parents the right to choose not to give their children any education at all. This is very clear regarding elementary education. On the other hand, the right of parents to choose the quality of education includes among other things the choice of philosophical, ethical or religious principles or educational methods. The enactment does not require society to provide the education desired by parents nor to finance it. That kind of obligation is found nowhere in any of the declarations or conventions between States. The States should, though, allow such education.

II. Global Declarations and Conventions

A. The Declaration of Geneva

The Declaration of Geneva regarding the status of the child adopted by the League of Nations in 1924 provided the background for the drafting of the Declaration of the Rights of the Child. The Declaration of Geneva does not specifically mention education, but among other things the first part notes that "The child must be given the means requisite for its normal development, both materially and spiritually." Part V among other things notes, concerning the content of education, that "The child must be brought up in the consciousness that its talents must be devoted to the service of its fellow men."[6]

B. The Declaration of the Rights of the Child

A first draft of the Declaration of the Rights of the Child (1959) was prepared in 1950 by the ECOSOC's Social Commission. ECOSOC forwarded the draft to the Commission for comment in view of its close relationship with the UDHR.[7]

---

[6] *Official Journal*, p. 43.
[7] UN 1959, pp. 192 and 193.

a. The Right to Education

According to principle 7 of the Declaration of the Rights of the Child: "The child is entitled to receive education." The Declaration of the Rights of the Child is more restrictive than the UDHR as the former requires that the education shall be free at least in the elementary stages. There is, however, no difference regarding the compulsory education, both the UDHR and the Declaration of the Rights of the Child require that, at least at the elementary stages. The Declaration on the Rights of the Child does not include any provisions on the quality of the education nor on providing education according to merit.

b. The Content of Education

The Declaration on the Rights of the Child requires that "He shall be given an education which will promote his general culture, and enable him, on a basis of equal opportunity, to develop his abilities, his individual judgement, and his sense of moral and social responsibility, and to become a useful member of society." The background for this expression lies in article 29(1) of the UDHR, the ideas of which should also be part of the contents of education. The aims at an individual level will correspond to those of the full development of the human personality as noted in the UDHR. The sense of morality and social responsibility as well as being a useful member of society correspond to the requirements of strengthening the respect for human rights and fundamental freedoms. These aims furthermore promote understanding, tolerance and friendship as mentioned in the UDHR.

c. The Choice of Education

The principle of the right of parents to choose the quality of education of their children as noted in article 26(3) of the UDHR has also found its way into principle 7(2) of the Declaration on the Rights of the Child. As a matter of fact, the expressions are the same. There is, though, one difference, as the Declaration on the Rights of the Child states that "The best interest of the child shall be the guiding principle of those responsible." As and when parents interpret what is in the best interest of the child, there will in fact be no difference. A new view on education is submitted by the Declaration on the Rights of the Child, that of play and recreation.

C. The UNESCO Convention against Discrimination in Education

a. The Right to Education

The UNESCO Convention against Discrimination in Education (1960) stresses that the UDHR asserts the principle of non-discrimination and proclaims that every person has the right to education. This Convention puts into effect the aim of a specific prohibition of discrimination in education expressed by some States while drafting the UDHR.

Article 1 of the Convention gives a very broad definition of discrimination both regarding its grounds, expressions and implications. The purpose of the Convention is not, however, to create a uniform educational system based on article 2. Establishing and maintaining different educational systems or institutions is not considered as discrimination, "if the education provided conforms with such standards as may be laid down or approved by the competent authorities in particular for education of the same level." The establishment or maintenance of separate educational systems for pupils of the two sexes are required to "offer equivalent access to education, provide a teaching staff with qualifications of the same standard as well as school premises and equipment of the same quality, and afford the opportunity to take the same or equivalent courses of study." Also establishing or maintaining separate educational systems for religious or linguistic reasons are similarly approved, "if participation in such systems or attendance at such institutions is optional and if the education provided conforms to such standards as may be laid down or approved by the competent authorities, in particular for education of the same level."

Article 3 of the Convention provides for actions in order to eliminate discrimination. A provision implying free and compulsory primary education is included in article 4 of the Convention. Secondary education has to be generally available and accessible to everyone and higher education equally accessible to everyone on the basis of individual capacity. The States Parties are also bound to assure compliance by all with the obligation to attend school as prescribed by law. The obligation to attend school is also fulfilled by compulsory education. The State should further "ensure that the standards of education are equivalent in all public education institutions of the same level and that the conditions relating to the quality of the education provided are also equivalent."

b. The Content of Education

Article 5 of the Convention includes regulations regarding the content of education. The first paragraph (a) is identical to that of article 26(2) of the UDHR. The principles of the UDHR have thus been included in the Convention.

Also article 6 refers to the content of the education, as "in the application of this Convention, the States Parties to it undertake to pay the greatest attention to any recommendations hereafter adopted by the General Conference of UNESCO defining the measures to be taken against the different forms of discrimination in education and for the purpose of ensuring equality of opportunity and treatment in education." The various instruments adopted by UNESCO are mentioned by Törnudd.[8]

c. The Choice of Education

The chapter regarding the right to education also refers to the possibility of the State to maintain separate educational systems based on language or religion. These do not depend on the minority status of the groups in question. For example, Belgium and Switzerland have declared that they have no national minorities. This understanding has also been expressed regarding the Swedish speaking Finns but not regarding the Samis.[9]

In Finland, both a Finnish language and a Swedish language educational system are maintained in bilingual and some other minicipalities, and the pupil can enter either of these two systems depending on his/her better language ability. Only when the child has an equal ability to study in either language is the guardian allowed to choose the language of instruction. The Convention is not clear about the implementation of the optionality relating to language. Does only the minority in a specific area have the right to participate in the education with the optional language of instruction or does this right exist within at least all the parts of the State where schools with both languages of instruction are maintained? This question is relevant in Finland, where in some parts of the country the Finnish speaking population is in the minority, although the Swedish speaking population is in the

[8] Törnudd 1986, p. 195.
[9] Törnudd 1986, p. 263 and Modeen 1976, p. 163.

minority in the country as a whole.

The above mentioned provision of the Convention is not to be understood as minority protection, as it only indicates that the procedure is not to be considered as discrimination and thus should be generally implied. The provision may only refer to an education according to the wishes of parents, but not to a system based on the Finnish legislation (which even so implements the wishes of parents). There are usually no problems in choosing the language of instruction. Modeen, among others, finds it clear that the children will attend school according to their own language, so there would have been no need for Finland to ratify the Convention.[10] The background for the denial of the right to choose in Finland is the aim of safeguarding that the child receives education in a language he or she understands.[11] The Finnish solution is contrary to a broad interpretation of the Convention.

In the home district of the Samis in Finland, education is given in the Sami language. Sami as a language of instruction is not compulsory, and it can be applied only to students with a sufficient ability to understand the Sami language. If parents so wish, the State has to provide for such instruction. The reason is similarly to be able to guarantee that the child is able to understand the instruction. These proceedings are acceptable as regards article 2 of the Convention.

Establishing and maintaining private educational institutions is not considered as discrimination under article 2(c), provided that "The object of the institutions is not to secure the exclusion of any group but to provide educational facilities in addition to those provided by public authorities." Furthermore, education has to conform to such standards as may be laid down or approved by the competent authorities.

Article 5(1)(b) calls for the State to respect the liberty of parents and guardians to firstly choose for their children institutions other than those maintained by the public authorities but conforming to such minimum educational standards as may be laid down or approved by the competent authorities and secondly to ensure, in a manner consistent with the procedures followed in the State for the application of its legislation, the religious and moral education of the children in conformity with their own convictions. The latter provision enforces in a Convention the provision in article 26(3) of

---

[10] Modeen 1976, p. 160.
[11] Arajärvi 1985, pp. 52, 60, 61.

the UDHR regarding education in accordance with one's convictions. Article 18 of the UDHR includes a latter part, according to which no person or group of persons should be compelled to receive religious instruction inconsistent with his or their convictions.

Modeen stresses that the notion in article 5(1)(b): "States agree that it is essential to respect the liberty of parents or guardians firstly to ensure the religious and moral education of the children in conformity with their own convictions," does not include a declared right to take care of their own educational activities. Their right is a negative one, as they cannot be forced into a certain religious or moral education.[12] Indirectly an opportunity for such an educational activity may arise, as they have the freedom of choosing from schools other than those provided for by the public authorities. The national minorities have the right to maintain schools of their own. Nor is the establishing or maintaining of separate educational systems, among others for religious reasons, to be considered as discrimination according to article 2.

According to article 5(1)(c) of the Convention, it is essential to recognize the rights of members of national minorities to carry on their own educational activities, including the maintaining of schools and the use or teaching of their own language, provided, however, that this right is not exercised in a manner which prevents the members of these minorities from understanding the culture and language of the community as a whole and from participating in its activities, or which prejudices national sovereignty. The standard of education shall not be lower than the general standard and the attendance at such schools shall be optional.

Article 5(1)(c) mentions the term 'national' minority instead of that of 'ethnic' or 'linguistic' minority, as the Contracting Parties did not want to extend the right to establish schools of their own to immigrants.[13] The importance of this provision is weakened by the fact that the Convention also gives an opportunity for only the teaching of the language of a national minority.

The first of the restrictions regarding educational activities of the national minorities and the use of their own language as the language of instruction or the teaching of their language is the fact that this right should not be used to prevent understanding of the culture of the society as a whole, or its language, as well as the

---

[12] Modeen 1976, p. 144.
[13] Ibid., p. 145.

participation in its activities, or harm the national sovereignty. According to Modeen, this restriction gives the provision a tone of hatred against minorities. He thus suggests that the provision should have been drafted in a positive way: the minority schools are not permitted to hinder the understanding of the whole of the culture of society.[14]

Modeen's remark is appropriate regarding relatively equal groups or in the case where the minority is also a minority in terms of power. But in those cases where the national minority is suppressing the majority, the implication of the provision is different, as it does not approve of the isolation of the minority.

Article 5(1)(c)(iii) requires that attendance at minority schools is optional. According to Modeen the majority schools should function in the same districts as the minority schools. This principle, according to Modeen, weakens the main provision in (c), as there is no provision in the Convention providing for a right for the minorities to maintain educational activities of their own, excluding the majority schools in their area, so that the status of the language of the minority would be strengthened. The provision also bars assimilation into the minority and further might lead to the minority sending their children for opportunistic reasons to majority schools.[15] The denial of majority schools might lead to unreasonableness and maybe even to violations of human rights relating to religion. Furthermore it might result in denial of minority schools in the area of the majority.

Modeen also refers to the requirement of free elementary education and that the national minority is forced to finance themselves their own schools, which might result in the favouring of the majority and violate the requirement of equality as prescribed in the Convention as well as violate article 3 of the Convention, which forbids the authorities to create funding systems which would result in discrimination or dividing the students solely on the grounds of belonging to a certain group. Modeen does not interpret article 5(1)(c) as requiring the State to provide for minority schools, as the provision only includes private schools.[16] Modeen seems also to indicate another interpretation regarding the financing of private education.[17]

---

[14] Ibid., pp. 145 and 146.
[15] Ibid., pp. 146 and 147.
[16] Ibid., pp. 147–149.
[17] Modeen 1987, pp. 85.

D. The International Covenants of 1966

The International Covenant on Economic, Social and Cultural Rights (CESCR) and the International Covenant on Civil and Political Rights (CCPR) are ratified by all Nordic countries.

a. The Right to Education

In the CESCR, article 13 recognizes the right of every one to education. This expression corresponds to that of the first sentence of article 26(1) of the UDHR, although literally they are not exactly the same. Article 13(2) of the Covenant corresponds to the latter part of article 26(1) of the UDHR: "Primary education shall be compulsory and available free to all."

The CESCR article 13(2)(d) emphasizes everyone's right to education, stating that fundamental education shall be encouraged or intensified as far as possible for those persons who have not received or completed the whole period of their primary education.

The Covenant also relates to the requirement of organizing education in such a way that the development of the educational system at all levels will be pursued, as well as improving the fellowship programmes for the students and the material conditions of the teaching staff.

The UDHR states that technical and professional education shall be made generally available, while the CESCR emphasizes that secondary education in its different forms shall be made generally available and accessible to all by every appropriate means, and in particular by the progressive introduction of free education. Thus, the aim of a free education goes beyond that of the UDHR.

Higher education is presumed to be equally accessible by everyone on the basis of capacity. In this respect also the approval of the *numerus clausus* system has been questioned.[18] In addition, higher education should gradually become free of charge.

b. The Content of Education

The latter part of article 13(1) regarding the content of education emphasizes as a convention rather literally the content of article 26(2) of the UDHR. The differences are the following: education

[18] Guradze 1971, p. 253.

shall be directed, not only to the full development of the human personality, but also to the sense of its dignity. To broaden the statement would indicate a new dimension of the human value. Education shall enable all persons to participate effectively in a free society, too. This binds the objective of education and at the same time limits the recipient of education. Ethnic minorities are added to the groups among whom understanding, tolerance and friendship are to be promoted.

c. The Choice of Education

According to article 13(3), parents and, when applicable, legal guardians, have the liberty to choose for their children schools other than those established by the public authorities, which conform to minimum educational standards. The difference between the CESCR and article 26(3) of the UDHR is that the CESCR grants the right to choose the school, while the UDHR grants the right to choose the kind of education. In practice there is not necessarily a great difference, though as a principle the difference is considerable. The limitation of the freedom of choosing the school is the necessity of the curriculum of the schools to conform to minimum educational standards laid down or approved by public authorities. The requirement is thus close to, in Nordic countries generally, an approved understanding of the necessity of completing the compulsory education either within the school system or through private teaching.

In the same paragraph 3 the States Parties undertake to have respect for the liberty of parents to ensure the religious and moral education of their children in conformity with their own convictions. This provision is close to article 26(3) of the UDHR as, in practice, the most important right for parents to choose education would be regarding religion and morals.

Article 18 of the CCPR has connections with education, though its main connection is with article 18 of the UDHR. The actual content of article 18(4) is very close to article 13(3) of the CESCR.

A new aspect of education laid down in a convention is found in article 13(4) of the CESCR, guaranteeing the liberty of individuals and bodies to establish and direct educational institutions. The UNESCO Convention also guarantees the right to choose institutions other than those provided for by the public authorities and a right of the national minorities not only to choose their own educational system but also to maintain their own schools. The

CESCR mentions two limitations. First, the education must observe the principles set forth in article 13(1). Secondly, the education given in such institutions shall conform to such minimum standards as may be laid down by the State. In this regard article 13(4) as mentioned above corresponds to the UNESCO Convention and is closely linked to the freedom to choose the school.

Article 14 of the CESCR refers basically to developing countries, as the States Parties undertake, at the time of becoming a Party to the CESCR, to work out a plan to gradually, within a reasonable period of time, organize compulsory and free primary education.

E. The Convention on the Rights of the Child

The latest of the international conventions relating to education is the Convention on the Rights of the Child of 20 November 1989. The Preamble of the above mentioned Convention refers to the UDHR and the two International Covenants on Human Rights. The Convention on the Rights of the Child is also a successor to the Declaration on the Rights of the Child and the Declaration of Geneva. An indication of development can be found in the fact that the Declaration of Geneva understood the child as an object as indicated in the expression 'it', while the Declaration on the Rights of the Child understand the child as a subject and as a male person 'he'. The Convention on the other hand already gives the child a sex, 'he or she'.

According to article 4, the States Parties shall among other things undertake all appropriate legislative, administrative and other measures for the implementation of the CESCR rights to the maximum extent of their available resources and, where needed, within the framework of international co-operation. Article 14 of the Convention on the Rights of the Child corresponds with article 18 of the CCPR regarding freedom of thought, conscience and religion. Closer links with principles of education are found in article 18 of the Convention of the Rights of the Child, according to which "parents and, as the case may be, legal guardians have the primary responsibility for the upbringing and development of their child."

a. The Right to Education

In article 28(1) States Parties recognize the rights of the child to an education. The Convention is another example of how the principles of the UDHR have been transferred into binding Conventions. The importance of attending school is stressed in article 32, according to which the child has the right to be protected from performing any work that is likely to be hazardous or to interfere with the child's education.

Article 28(1)(a) of the Convention on the Rights of the Child confirms again the principles of a compulsory and free primary education. States Parties shall, in particular, encourage the development of different forms of secondary education, make them available and accessible to every child, and take appropriate measures such as introducing free education and offering financial assistance in case of need.

New elements to organize education are dissemination of guidance and knowledge as well as promotion of the regularity of school attendance and reduction of the disruptions of school attendance. This is an indication of the concern the States Parties have for the children that have been deprived of their education.

In article 28(2) we find a new element, the requirement of guaranteeing that the human dignity of the child is respected in maintenance of discipline. Although indications of the same principle are found in the CCPR and the UDHR, the direct mentioning of this fact promotes human rights and abolishes punishments relating to shame.

b. The Content of Education

Provisions relating to the content of education are found in article 29. As stated in earlier declarations and conventions, education shall be directed towards the development of the child's personality, talent and mental and physical abilities to their fullest potential. In line with the UDHR is the notion of directing education to a respect for human rights and fundamental freedoms, and for the principles enshrined in the UN Charter.

The provision of directing education to the development of respect for the child's parents, his or her own cultural identity, language and values, for the national values (both of the country in which the child is living and as the case may be, the country from which the child may originate) and for other civilizations is a new aspect of the aims of education. This will also develop a sense of opposing discrimination. "The preparation of the child for responsible life in a free society" is better than the expression used in the CESCR, that of enabling "all persons to participate effectively in a free society." Equality between the sexes and respect for the natural environment are new values to be included in the contents of education.

c. The Choice of Education

Article 29(2) is equal to the CESCR in questions of liberty of individuals and bodies to establish and direct educational institutions.

F. Some Other International Conventions

The United Nations and its specialized agencies have adopted numerous conventions, which partly refer to the right to education. Provisions relating to education in the International Labour Organisation (ILO) Convention (no. 117) concerning Basic Aims and Standards of Social Policy, the International Convention on the Elimination of All Forms of Racial Discrimination, Convention on the Elimination of All Forms of Discrimination against Women, Convention relating to the Status of Refugees and the Convention relating to the Status of Stateless Persons will be dealt with hereafter.

The ILO Convention prescribes in articles 15 and 16 education and training. Adequate provisions shall be made for the progressive development of a broad system of education, vocational training and apprenticeship, with a view to the effective preparation of children and young persons of both sexes for a useful occupation. National laws and regulations shall prescribe the school leaving age and the minimum age for, and conditions of, employment. Keeping children of compulsory school age at work during school hours shall be prohibited, so that the children are able to utilize the offered education. Training in new techniques of production shall be provided in order to secure high productivity through the development of skilled labour.

The Convention on the Elimination of Discrimination against Women explicitly obliges the States Parties to ensure for women equal rights with men in the field of education, such as the same conditions for access to studies and for the achievement of diplomas in educational establishments of all categories. Education shall be on a basis of equality of women and men also in questions of standards and quality. The aim is also the elimination of any stereotyped concept of the roles of men and women.

Under the International Convention on the Elimination of All Forms of Racial Discrimination, States Parties undertake to prohibit discrimination in all its forms and to guarantee the right of everyone in the enjoyment of, among other things, the right to education and training.

Stateless persons and refugees shall enjoy the same treatment as that accorded to nationals with respect to elementary education and, in any event, not less favourable than that accorded to aliens generally in the same circumstances, with respect to other education.

III. Regional Conventions

A. Conventions of the Council of Europe

The Statute of the Council of Europe (1949) includes no references to economic, social and cultural rights. Nor does the European Convention on Human Rights (ECHR) of the Council of Europe (1950) include any provisions relating to the right to education. But the First Protocol to the ECHR (1952) is in fact the first internationally binding document after the UDHR to include education.

At the time of the adoption of the First Protocol to the ECHR, the development of the right to education after the UDHR had only reached a negative definition, as "no person shall be denied the right to education." This was the first time a convention provided that "In the exercise of any functions which it assumes in relation to education and teaching, the State shall respect the right of parents to ensure such education and teaching in conformity with their own religious and philosophical convictions."

The European Social Charter (1961) includes provisions relating to education. Article 7 treats the right of children and young persons to protection. In this respect the article also includes provisions regarding the working conditions of young people as well as emphasizing that persons who are still subject to compulsory education shall not be employed in such work as would deprive them of the full benefit of their education. The working hours of persons under 16 years of age shall be limited in accordance with the needs of their development, and particularly with their need for vocational training.

Article 10 treats the right to vocational training, and the States Parties undertake to provide or promote, as necessary, the technical and vocational training of all persons and to grant facilities for access to higher technical and university education, based solely on individual aptitude. The Convention also includes elements of the right to education, financial support for education and education being free of charge. Article 15 aims at granting physically or mentally handicapped persons, among other things, the right to vocational training, if necessary through special institutions.

B. The American Convention on Human Rights

The States Parties to the American Convention on Human Rights (ACHR, 1969) undertake in article 26 to adopt full realization of the rights implicit in the economic, social, educational, scientific, and cultural standards set forth in the Charter of the Organization of American States (OAS). In practice these are closely linked to the CESCR.[19]

C. The African Charter on Human and Peoples' Rights

Article 17(1) of the African Charter on Human and Peoples' Rights (African Charter, 1981) reads as follows: "Every individual shall have the right to education." The African Charter does not include any other articles about education, but in the African Charter there are many rules about the duty of the States Parties to assist values of community, and to ensure the elimination of discrimination, equality of people and equal rights, etc. Those rules can be viewed as a matter of the content of education.

[19] Kutzner 1971, p. 285.

IV. The Nordic Constitutions

A. The Provisions in the Constitutions

Provisions relating to education are found in the Nordic countries in the Constitutions of Denmark, Finland, Sweden and Iceland. The educational systems are, regardless of the provisions in the respective constitution, very similar.[20]

According to article 76 of the Constitution of Denmark, all children of compulsory school age have the right to free education in primary school. Parents or guardians who themselves take care of the education of their child conforming to the general aims of the primary school, are not obliged to send their children to primary school.

Education is mentioned in the Finnish Constitution Act Part VIII articles 77–82. Two of the articles define the right of citizens to education, one the sovereignty of the University of Helsinki and the others the obligation of the State or municipalities to organize education. These last ones indirectly grant citizens a right to education.

Directly relating to the rights of the citizen is article 80(2) of the Constitution Act, according to which education in primary schools shall be free for all, as well as article 82, according to which provisions shall be made by law regarding the right to establish private schools and other private educational institutions and to organize education within them. The same article also states that instruction at home shall not be subject to the supervision of the public authorities. Article 80(1) of the Constitution Act states the obligations of the citizen, according to which general compulsory attendance at school is prescribed by law.

The same provision included in the Finnish Constitution Act is in the Danish Constitution mentioned *expressis verbis*; there is general compulsory school attendance. Education is free according to both Constitutions. Furthermore, the Danish Constitution explicitly states that parents are not obliged to send their children to school if the children are otherwise receiving an education according to aims corresponding to the requirements of primary school. Similar provisions are not included in the Finnish Constitution. The situation is, though, factually the same in Finland, where the legislator is

[20] Faerkel 1975, p. 244; Helgesen 1975, p. 262; Hiden 1975, p. 280; Petren 1975, p. 270; Törnudd 1986, pp. 197–199; Vilhjalmsson 1975, p. 231.

obliged to enact regarding the right to establish private schools and other educational institutions. Instruction at home is not supervised by the public authorities, but the outcome of education, i.e., realization of compulsory education, is controlled.

Exceptional among the Nordic Countries are the provisions in the Finnish Constitution regarding the obligation of the State and the municipalities to organize education. Under article 78 of the Finnish Constitution Act, the State shall provide for research and higher education in technical, agricultural, and commercial sciences and in other applied sciences as well as the training and teaching of fine arts. The State should, for the above mentioned sciences, establish special colleges or financially assist private institutions for the above mentioned purpose, in such case as there are not yet any such colleges or institutions at the university level. All higher educational institutions for science and arts are nowadays State institutions.

The State should maintain or financially assist, if necessary, general higher education and popular higher education under article 79 of the Finnish Constitution Act. Similarly, the same applies to the institutions for technical occupations, agriculture and its secondary occupations, trade and shipping, as well as fine arts, according to article 81 of the Constitution Act. In accordance with these provisions, general education after primary education has been worked out so as to be provided for by the municipalities. Vocational training in Finland is maintained by private institutions, municipalities and the State. The State pays for more than half of all the costs of these institutions.

Furthermore, article 80 of the Finnish Constitution Act states that the basis for the organization of primary education as well as the obligation of the State and the municipalities is prescribed by law. The basis of this organization includes the functions, structures of the educational institution, the subjects and the central administrative bodies. The municipalities maintain the primary schools. The State, though, pays for more than half of their expenses.

Due to historical reasons, the Constitution Act includes a special provision, article 77, granting Helsinki University certain privileges. The University of Helsinki is granted self-government, the mode of organization of the University is prescribed by law and the Consistory of the University shall have given its statement regarding all legislation relating to the University. The self-government includes a right to decide their own affairs, administer their property, to sue and to stand trial, freedom of teaching and exemption from taxation and some other duties. The basis of the organization of the university includes the central bodies of the administration. None of the other 16 universities and colleges have similar constitutional privileges.

According to article 2 of Part 1 of the Swedish Constitution, the basic aim of public activities should be among other things the cultural well-being of the individual. In particular the public authorities have to grant the right (...) to education (...). The enactment provides for an obligation of the State, especially as it is included in the first part, the title of which is the Basis of the Form of Government, instead of in the second Part, the title of which is Fundamental Freedoms and Rights.

The Constitution of Iceland includes the following provision in article 71: "If parents cannot afford to educate their children, or if the children are orphaned or destitute, their education and maintenance must be defrayed from public funds." The wording of this article goes far back in history.

B. *The Freedoms and Obligations of the Individual Regarding Education*

Often the provisions in the constitutions regarding education, and generally economic, social and cultural rights as well as the right to education as per provisions in conventions, are considered to be norms of obligations only for the legislator, although the specialization is often many-sided.[21] On the other hand, similar provisions to those in Finland, according to which the State has an obligation to assist financially both the student and the educational institution, will finally also lead to the full realization of the content of the right.

The upbringing of the child and his or her education brings the problems of individual freedoms and State requirements. Parents have a general responsibility for the upbringing of the child, as the State is interested in guaranteeing the necessary upbringing and education from the point of view of society. Also the possible need of protecting a person under age from his or her own parents should be noted. The sensitive issue of possible state propaganda is closely linked to this question, which in a democratic society is contrary to the freedom of the parents or the child to decide about the life of the child. Thus it is important to notice the freedom to provide

---

[21] Guradze 1971, pp. 250 and 251; Törnudd 1986, pp. 8–13; Vierdag 1978, p. 103.

elementary education through private tuition or in private institutions at the same time as it is important to fulfil the general standards of society.[22]

Ross also describes the obligation of parents to teach. In his opinion, parents or guardians are obliged to ensure that the child receives a regular and full education during a certain period of life. This obligation does not imply compulsory school systems, but the provisions in the Danish Constitution lead to the fact that most children do complete primary school.[23] The situation is the same in Finland, where education is compulsory, and its implementation is controlled. The necessary knowledge and skills can be acquired in schools provided by society, in private schools or through instruction at home.

The obligation of the authorities to provide education implies the obligation of public organizations to provide to all school-age children an open opportunity to free education. Thus parents have an opportunity to fulfil their educational obligation by sending their children to a school maintained by the public authorities.[24] The Finnish system differs as there are no provisions at the constitutional level regarding an educational obligation for the parents, only an obligation of education for the children. The final result is, however, the same.

The freedom to choose the school or education or not to choose a school at all gives parents a right to fulfil their educational obligation through instruction at home or to educate their children in private schools. The principle of freedom of education also gives parents an opportunity to choose an educational institution following a certain philosophy of life. The student could also be only partly exempted from regular schooling. A typical example of such a possibility would be exemption from ideological education such as religion.[25] The arrangements in the Nordic countries are corresponding in this regard also.

---

[22] Ross 1980, pp. 786 and 787.
[23] Ibid., pp. 787 and 788.
[24] Ibid., p. 788.
[25] Ibid., pp. 789–794.

428   *Pentti Arajärvi*

References

de Revue des Droits de l'Homme, VIII–1, 1975.

Guradze, Heinz, "Die Menschenrechtskonventionen der Vereinten Nationen vom 16 Dezember 1966", in *Jahrbuch für internationales Recht*, 15. Band. Göttingen: Vandenhoeck & Ruprecht, 1971.

Helgesen, Jan Erik, "The Protection of Economic, Social and Cultural Rights in Norway", in *The Protection of Human Rights in the Nordic Countries, Extrait de Revue des Droits de l'Homme*, VIII–1, 1975.

Hidén, Mikael, "The Protection of Economic, Social and Cultural Rights in Finland", in *The Protection of Human Rights in the Nordic Countries, Extrait de Revue des Droits de l'Homme*, VIII–1, 1975.

Kutzner, Gerhard, "Die Amerikanische Menschenrechtskonvention", in *Jahrbuch für internationales Recht*, 15. Band. Göttingen: Vandenhoeck & Ruprecht, 1971.

Modeen, Tore, "Unesco-konventionen mot diskriminering inom undervisningen och Ålandsöarna", *Tidskrift, utgiven af Juridiska föreningen i Finland* 3, 1976.

Modeen, Tore, "Rätten till privat skolundervisning. Bidrag till tolkningen av RF 82 och 79", in Kristian Myntti (red.), *Finländska mänskorättsperspektiv, Meddelanden från ekonomisk-statsvetenskapliga fakulteten vid Åbo Akademi, Ser. A:242*, publikation nr. 5, Åbo: Institutet för mänskliga rättigheter, 1987.

Official Journal, Special Supplement no. 21, October, 1924.

Petren, Gustaf, "The Protection of Economic, Social and Cultural Rights in Sweden", in *The Protection of Human Rights in the Nordic Countries, Extrait de Revue des Droits de l'Homme*, VIII–1, 1975.

Ross, Alf and Ole Espersen, *Dansk statsforfatningsret* II, København: Nyt Nordisk Forlag – Arnold Busck, 1980.

Törnudd, Klaus, *Finland and the International Norms of Human Rights*, Dordrecht: Martinus Nijhoff Publishers, 1986.

United Nations Documents: E/CN.4/SR.67; E/800; E/CN.4/21; E/600; Official Records of the third session, Social, Humanitarian and Cultural Questions, Third Committee, September – December 1948.

United Nations, *Yearbook of the United Nations*, 1959.

Vierdag, E.W, "The Legal Nature of the Rights Granted by the International Covenant on Economic, Social and Cultural Rights", in *Netherlands Yearbook of International Law*, volume IX, The Hague: T.M.C. Asser Institute, 1978.

Vilhjalmsson, Thor, "The Protection of Human Rights in Iceland", in *The Protection of Human Rights in the Nordic Countries, Extrait de Revue des Droits de l'Homme*, VIII–1, 1975.

Article 27

Göran Melander

Sweden

1. Everyone has the right freely to participate in the cultural life of the community, to enjoy the arts and to share in scientific advancement and its benefits.
2. Everyone has the right to the protection of the moral and material interests resulting from any scientific, literary or artistic production of which he is the author.

Article 27 of the Universal Declaration of Human Rights (UDHR) prescribes for the enjoyment of cultural rights, i.e., that everyone has the right to participate in all forms of cultural life. As such the article reflects one of the most important purposes and principles of the United Nations as described in the UN Charter article 1(3). The General Assembly should promote initiatives in the cultural field (article 13(1b)). The United Nations should promote international cultural co-operation (article 55(b)). A specialized agency, *inter alia* responsible for cultural questions, was foreseen and in 1946 UNESCO was already established. Particular competence has been given to the Economic and Social Council (ECOSOC) with respect to cultural activities (article 62(1)).

In spite of the impression given by reading the UN Charter, stressing cultural rights as an essential part of UN activities, it must be admitted that little attention has been paid to cultural rights, at least in comparison with other human rights. As will be mentioned later, there are numerous international instruments mentioning cultural rights and even describing them. Still the range of cultural rights can by no means be considered as definitely settled.

A variety of explanations can be found for the luke-warm interest in cultural rights within the United Nations. It is certainly a right closely linked with the protection of minorities, an old human rights problem which is still unsolved. To describe in legal terms the concept of the term 'culture' is in itself an almost impossible task.

Generally speaking, cultural rights refer to a variety of aspects, including the right to education. In interpreting article 27 of the UDHR, at least one delimitation is possible. In view of article 26 of the UDHR which explicitly deals with the right to education, it must be concluded that this aspect is not covered by the present article. Accordingly, article 27 deals with cultural rights with the exception of the right to education.

The two paragraphs of article 27 concern separate aspects of cultural rights. Paragraph 1 deals with the enjoyment of rights and as such it can be interpreted as prescribing for both group rights and individual rights. Paragraph 2, on the other hand, clearly prescribes for individual rights.

The enjoyment of cultural rights has, after the adoption of the UDHR, been expressed in numerous human rights agreements, both on the universal and on the regional level. Article 15 of the International Covenant on Economic, Social and Cultural Rights (CESCR) prescribes that everyone is entitled to take part in cultural life and to enjoy the benefits of scientific progress and its application. Article 5 of the UN Convention on the Elimination of All Forms of Racial Discrimination prescribes that everyone without any distinction as to race, etc., is entitled to equal participation in cultural activities. Of the regional agreements, it is primarily the African Charter on Peoples' and Human Rights (African Charter) which explicitly makes reference to the enjoyment of cultural rights (article 27(2)).

Respect for the right for culture is certainly a primary task of UNESCO, whose Constitution states that the wide diffusion of culture and the education of humanity for justice and liberty and peace are indispensable to the dignity of man and constitute a sacred duty which all the nations must fulfil in a spirit of mutual assistance and concern. At the 20th anniversary of the foundation of UNESCO in 1966, the General Conference of UNESCO adopted the Declaration of Principles of International Co-operation which proclaims in article 1:

1. Each culture has a dignity and value which must be respected and preserved;
2. Every people has the right and the duty to develop its culture;
3. In their rich variety and diversity, and in the reciprocal influence they exert on one another, all cultures form part of the common heritage belonging to all mankind.

As distinguished from most of the other articles of the UDHR the following agreements do not shed light on the interpretation of

UDHR article 27. In this respect it should be noted that the draft Declaration was so worded that everyone had the right to participate freely in the cultural life of 'society'. At a later stage the word 'society' was replaced by the word 'community', although there is no clear explanation for the amendment. As has been pointed out, this substitution may be connected with the discussion on including minority rights in the UDHR. It may be that reference to the 'culture of the community' serves to replace the inclusion of 'national culture'.[1] Should minority rights be included in UDHR article 27, the provision is of extra-ordinary wide application.

Article 27, paragraph 2, is less complicated. Everyone has a right to the protection of moral and material interests resulting from scientific, literary and artistic production of which he is the author. The paragraph is in fact a declaration of copyright which has been given the rank of a human right.[2]

The sub-paragraph is unique also in the respect that copyright existed not only on the national level but also on the international level long before the adoption of other international human rights instruments. Various copyright conventions had already been adopted during the 19th century and have been revised and complemented during the 20th century. It is, however, interesting to note the wording of copyright interests in various human rights instruments. According to the CESCR, article 15(1c) everyone is entitled to benefit from the protection of the moral and material interests resulting from any scientific, literary or artistic production of which he is the author.

As has been stressed this sub-paragraph prescribes for a clear individual right, and as such the paragraph is more similar to a civil and political right. This right is clearly possible to implement and it has certain similarities with property rights. It is also symptomatic that provisions prescribing for copyright can be found in Bills of Rights in constitutional law. For instance, the Swedish Constitution of 1974 prescribes that authors, artists and photographers have a right to their production in accordance with provisions laid down by law.

It may be surprising to find an article on copyright in the UDHR. It would perhaps have been more logical to find a provision on the right to creative activities, as it can be argued that such a right is closely related with cultural rights. On the other hand, such a right

---

[1] Szabó 1974, p. 45.

[2] Ibid., p. 46.

is equally an individual right, imposing certain restrictions on a government not to create obstacles for an individual. As such it bears certain similarities with the right to freedom of expression and the right to freedom of thought, conscience and religion, i.e., rights that are mostly considered as civil and political rights.

There may be several explanations for the inclusion of copyright as a human right in the UDHR. It has been suggested that the early international interaction has been of significance. Presumably the struggle launched as early as just after World War I for the international enactment and safeguarding of the 'droits intellectuels' had a part to play in so laying down the right to active culture; the Institut International de Coopération Intellectuelle, a French-inspired organization, had become active at an early period and, reappearing again after World War II, energetically acted in the interest of securing copyright within the scope of intellectual rights.[3]

Reference

Szabó, Imre, *Cultural Rights*, Leiden: 1974.

---

[3] Ibid., p. 46.

Article 28

Asbjørn Eide

Norway

Everyone is entitled to a social and international order in which the rights and freedoms set forth in this Declaration can be fully realized.

I. Introduction

Article 28 cannot, even by the most imaginative judge, be handled as a justiciable and enforceable subjective right for individuals, and yet it has had a follow-up of considerable significance.

Reflection on article 28 may also help remind us of one important point. As brought forth in the introductory section under the discussion of article 25, the notion of human rights does not necessarily correspond to the notion of rights as understood in positive law. We do not assume that all human rights are presently enforceable, nor that they can ever become enforceable in all their aspects.

Article 1 of the Universal Declaration of Human Rights (UDHR) presents the basis of contemporary human rights — that all persons are born free and equal in dignity and rights and that they should act towards one another in a spirit of brotherhood. We know that human beings very often do not act in that way. Conflicts are widespread and often cruel. The conditions under which human beings live, and the ideologies or idiosyncracies that guide their behaviour, make article 1 little more than a pious wish. Article 28 presents us with the opposite requirement, which is that conditions both inside the national society and in the world at large should be shaped and transformed in such a way that the rights can be enjoyed in fact.

II. Drafting

The proposal to include the provision now found in article 28 emerged within the Drafting Group of the UN Commission on Human Rights (the Commission) in May 1948, a late stage in the Commission's drafting of the UDHR. Neither of the drafts which had existed before the Commission started its work, nor the draft presented by the Secretariat, nor any other major drafts had contained anything pointing in the direction of what later became article 28.

The proposal for a text which was to become article 28 emerged as a consequence of a substantial change of approach which took place in the drafting of the UDHR at the third session of the Commission, in May 1948. During the previous sessions of the Commission, held in 1947, it had been assumed that the UDHR would include not only the individual rights but also the corresponding obligations of States. While this would not require detailed elaboration in regard to most of the civil rights, the obligations required in order to give content to economic, social and cultural rights might have to be spelled out in some detail. The draft of the UDHR adopted in its first reading by the Commission in December 1947 therefore included obligations in several of the articles containing rights.

In May 1948 the approach was reversed. There was an increasing resistance by some Western members, particularly the United States, to include formulations of State obligations in the UDHR. The issue became significant during the discussion on what became article 23, the right to work. The formulation of that right became controversial primarily because it brought to the fore different conceptions of the role of the State in regard to the individual. The solution to the controversy was in effect postponed by an agreement not to include any obligations of States in the UDHR. The majority accepted that the UDHR should contain only general principles, providing abstract formulations only of the rights to be included, without formulating the corresponding obligations. This was done on the assumption that the UDHR would soon be followed by one or more conventions which would spell out the obligations in detail.[1]

---

[1] There was a growing reluctance by the United States, however. A few years later it announced its intention not to ratify any human rights conventions. There was at least a double reason for this: first, a reluctance to submit to international monitoring

Members of the Commission were painfully aware that the economic and social rights included in the UDHR would appear rather abstract. As a result, a working group was established to explore ways in which a formulation could be found whereby these rights could be given reality.

Two proposals emerged in the working group, one by Cassin[2] and another by Malik of Lebanon.

Cassin was concerned with the need to reflect in some form the obligations of States to ensure the enjoyment of economic and social rights. His draft was finally worked out as a *chapeau*, or general clause, which was inserted at the beginning of the section of the UDHR dealing with economic and social rights.[3] Malik had a broader perspective. His view was that the enjoyment of human rights depended on the quality of social and international relations. His draft read:

> Everyone is entitled to a good social and international order in which the rights and freedom set forth in this Declaration can be fully realized.

His draft was accepted by the working group and the Commission and was presented, as article 26, to the General Assembly in 1948. In the Third Committee opinions on it were divided.[4]

Some argued that it was redundant. Egypt[5] had proposed the deletion of the article, which was supported by Ecuador. The representatives of several other States (Norway, Australia, Saudi Arabia) were also of the opinion that it could be deleted, but without holding strong opinions either way. New Zealand (Ms. Newlands) understood the article as an 'umbrella' provision and as a compromise measure to avoid any specific reference to the duties of the State.[6] She therefore would not raise any objections to the article.

The Lebanese representative (Azkoul, not Malik) stated in support of the draft that while the preceding articles dealt with individual rights, article 26 was concerned with general principles.

and supervision of implementation, and secondly, an unwillingness to accept specific obligations on how to fulfill the various rights.

[2] UN doc. E/CN.4/SR.67.

[3] Cassin's proposal corresponds in essence to what became article 22.

[4] The discussions took place in the Third Committee at its 152nd meeting (General Assembly Official Records, Third Committee, SR 152).

[5] UN doc. A/C.3/264.

[6] General Assembly Official Records, Third Committee, p. 641.

It set forth the ultimate conditions necessary for the realization of those rights.

He made a somewhat surprising additional statement. Certain rights, he said, had to be curtailed, during wartime, for reasons of national security. "It was necessary, however, to ensure that the basic rights laid down in the Declaration would be guaranteed in any circumstances. That was the purpose of article 26." On the face of it, he appeared to be concerned with the issue of non-derogable or absolute rights. But this is not the concern of article 28, and none of the other speakers took up the issue.

Cassin supported the article and opposed its deletion, though he was not happy with its form. He underlined that it was a general principle rather than an individual right.

Then Pavlov (Soviet Union) sparked off an interesting discussion by proposing the elimination of the word 'good' as a qualification of 'social and international order'. His proposal was accepted, but for conflicting reasons. In introducing his amendment, Pavlov thought the word 'good' should be deleted:

> Because, even should all the rights and freedoms set out in the declaration be fully realized, there was still no ground to conclude that the resulting social and international order would necessarily be good.

He argued that the formal proclamation and even the formal realization of a right did not necessarily mean much in practice. The principle of equality had once been of the greatest importance; it had led to the abolition of serfdom and slavery. There existed at present a formalized concept of equality which was generally accepted. It was a far cry, however, from that equality — the equality of the rich and the poor, of capital and labour — to real social justice and a really good social order. The same might be said of a number of other rights contained in the UDHR such as the right to freedom of association; it, too, would be devoid of meaning unless proper facilities were available for its realization.

In the view of the Soviet delegation, as long as society was divided into exploiters and the exploited, as long as there was private ownership of the means of production, the social order could not possibly be a good one.

The Soviet Union was not asking the Committee, he said, to approve its social order. What it did ask was that, since two conflicting views were involved, there should be no moral evaluation in the declaration of either order and that the final verdict should be left to history. It would be preferable to avoid an ideological discussion and to delete the word 'good', because it represented an evaluation which the new democracies, in the name of millions of workers and indigenous inhabitants of colonies, in the name of posterity itself, felt bound to reject.

Maybank (Canada) disagreed with the reasons given. Should the rights set forth in the UDHR be achieved, the social and international order would be good, whether it came within the framework of capitalism, Communism, feudalism or any other system. On that understanding, he would vote for the Soviet amendment.

Mrs. Roosevelt (USA) considered that a good social and international order was necessary for the achievement of the rights set forth in the UDHR. She had no objections to the Soviet amendment, although she considered it unnecessary. Any order which permitted individuals to achieve the rights and freedoms set out in the UDHR would obviously be a good one and the adoption of the Soviet amendment would not mean the endorsement of any particular political or social system. If the wording of the article would thereby be improved, she was prepared to accept the Soviet amendment.

Azkoul (Lebanon) understood the expression 'good social and international order' not to apply to any particular system, whether capitalist or socialist. It was possible that no good order had as yet been found, but it was appropriate to state that human beings had faith and hope in the possibility of such an order being established.

Few representatives appear to have felt strongly about the retention or deletion of the article. For those who were sceptical, it was probably seen as rather harmless; for those who favoured it, they do not appear to believe that it would lead to substantial action. The divisions did not follow ideological or regional lines. The draft which became article 28 found support as well as opposition within the same regions. The strongest support as well as the strongest opposition came from the Arab countries; article 28 was proposed by the Lebanese delegation and was supported by Syria; the proposal for deletion came from Egypt, supported by Saudi Arabia. Also in Latin America there were voices in favour (Uruguay, Peru) and against (Ecuador). The socialist countries were reluctant, and Western countries were split; the French (Cassin), the United Kingdom, and the United States were in favour whereas Norway and Australia were sceptical.

It may be quite significant that it emerged from one of the few participants from the non-Western world. It foreshadowed concerns from the Third World which have since become much more prominent, but it also reflected a concern with domestic social

438   *Asbjørn Eide*

conditions which did have support in some of the Western
countries.

III. Background and Follow-up

A. *'The Four Freedoms' and the Purpose of the United Nations*

Article 28 calls for reform at the national and international level. In
so doing it corresponds to the visions underlying the formation of
the United Nations, first presented by the then President of the
United States, Franklin D. Roosevelt in his 'Four Freedoms'
address in 1941:

> In the future days, which we seek to make secure, we look forward to
> a world founded upon four essential human freedoms[7] ... That is no
> vision of a distant millennium. It is a definite basis for a world
> attainable in our own time and generation.

Freedom from want, he said, would mean:

> Economic understandings which will secure to every nation a healthy
> peace-time life for its inhabitants — everywhere in the world.

Freedom from fear would mean:

> A world-wide reduction of armaments to such a point and in such a
> thorough fashion that no nation would be able to commit an act of
> physical aggression against any neighbor — anywhere in the world.

Around the conceptions in the Four Freedoms address, preparations
for the postwar institutional structures and legal order were
started.[8] The United Nations was established in order to provide
the institutional framework for the creation of an international order
in which these freedoms could be achieved. Thus, from the very
inception of the idea of the United Nations, there was a concern
with the need for a fundamental restructuring of national and
international relations, in the economic as well as the political
fields. In many ways, the Roosevelt conception of the United
Nations can be seen as a projection to the international level of the
concerns underlying his national New Deal policy. While there is

---

[7] The four freedoms were freedom of speech and belief, and freedom from fear and
from want.
[8] The history of these preparations has been described in great detail by Russell 1958.

not any direct link between the vision presented by Roosevelt in 1941 and the proposal by Malik in 1948 for what became article 28, both reflect a general concern: the need actively to restructure society, at the national and international levels, in such a way that the equality and dignity of the human being can be transformed from rhetoric to reality.

The same concern can be found in the Declaration of Philadelphia, adopted by the General Conference of the International Labour Organisation (ILO) in 1944, which subsequently found its way into the constitution of the ILO in 1946. The declaration recognized that the individual had the right not only to material but also to the non-material aspects of development, and that development of the individual must take place within the broader framework of development which alone can provide the individual with economic security. Such development will require the application of the principles of social justice and equity. Development and respect for human rights are interdependent. Freedom and dignity should be the condition, and the end, of development. All national and international policies, in particular those of an economic and social character, should be judged in this light and accepted only in so far as they may be held to promote and not hinder the achievement of this objective.

Important also is the Charter of the United Nations. In the statement of its purposes, article 1(3) refers to "the achievement of international co-operation in solving international problems of an economic, social, cultural or humanitarian character, and in promoting and encouraging respect for human rights and fundamental freedoms for all." Article 55 spells out what is also the main thrust of the UDHR article 28, that the United Nations, in order to create conditions of stability and well-being which are necessary for peaceful and friendly relations, shall promote: a) a higher standard of living, full employment, and conditions of economic and social progress; b) solutions of international economic, social, health, and related problems, and international cultural and educational co-operation; and c) universal respect for human rights without discrimination.

Dilemmas had to be faced in this effort. What should be the role of the State in regard to the domestic social order? Market-oriented liberal thinking clashed with policies more or less oriented towards planned or directed social and economic development. The yet uncharted task of international planning was looming on the horizon; human rights activities would by necessity be influenced by them. Unfortunately, for many decades the United Nations was to create artificial institutional divisions between agencies dealing with development and with human rights; the same division has emerged in national governmental institutions and in the world of non-governmental organizations. For the realization of article 28 there is a strong need for the close collaboration between those concerned with human rights and those whose focus is on development.

B. *Follow-up in the Covenants*

The Preamble of the International Covenant on Economic, Social and Cultural Rights (CESCR) rephrases article 28 in its third paragraph:

> Recognizing that, in accordance with the Universal Declaration of Human Rights, the ideal of the free human beings enjoying freedom from fear and want can only be achieved if conditions are created whereby everyone may enjoy his economic, social and cultural rights as well as his civil and political rights,...

Under article 2 of the same Covenant, the States Parties promise to take steps to achieve progressively the full realization of the rights contained in the CESCR. This is to be done separately and through international assistance and co-operation, to the maximum of the available resources.

One step further is taken in article 11 of the CESCR, where the States Parties to the CESCR oblige themselves to:

> Take appropriate steps to ensure the realization of this right (to an adequate standard of living), recognizing to this effect the essential importance of international co-operation based on free consent.

Article 11(2), dealing with freedom from hunger, establishes requirements, *inter alia*, of land reform (restructuring of the national social order) and the ensuring of an equitable distribution of world food supplies in relation to need (international order). Both requirements are hedged around with modifications which empty the obligations of most of their substance, however.

C. *Exploring the Obstacles and their Remedies*

The International Conference on Human Rights, celebrating the 20th anniversary of the UDHR, was held in Teheran in 1968, at a time when the composition of the United Nations had changed so that African and Asian members constituted more than one-half of the membership.[9]

In the Proclamation of Teheran[10], adopted on 13 May by the Conference, the major obstacles to the realization of human rights were underlined. Among those listed are apartheid (paragraph 7), other forms of racial discrimination (paragraphs 8 and 11), the remaining pockets of colonialism (paragraph 9), the massive effects of aggression and armed conflicts, and occupation (paragraph 10).

In paragraph 11, the Conference points to the increasing gaps between the rich and the poor countries as a major obstacle to the realization of human rights. The focus of structural injustice at the global level was coming to the forefront of the attention of the United Nations.

The widening gap between the rich and the poor countries of the world became a dominant preoccupation of the majority in the subsequent years. While the Proclamation of Teheran underlined the indivisibility of human rights, which has also been regularly expressed in General Assembly resolutions since 1952, a new twist was given to it in paragraph 12:

> Since human rights and fundamental freedoms are indivisible, the full realization of civil and political rights without the enjoyment of economic and social rights is impossible.

This formulation, which is filled with ambiguity, was to become a major source of controversy within the human rights bodies of the United Nations in the subsequent years.

The ambiguities include the following:

a) What would be required in order to ensure the enjoyment of economic and social rights? Were those States who apparently proclaimed the need to give substance to economic and social rights, prepared to do so themselves? Were they prepared to

---

[9] Whereas, in 1948, African and Asian States together formed only 29 percent of the UN membership, in 1968 they formed 54 percent.

[10] The text is found in the publication by the UN Centre of Human Rights 1988, p. 43ff. in the English edition.

ensure the necessary combination of measures required, such as respecting and protecting the freedom of the individual to engage in economic activity and to unfold her or his creativity in this regard, together with the adoption of the necessary measures for social justice, such as land reform?

b)   While the full enjoyment of civil and political rights might not be possible without some basic enjoyment of economic and social rights, did this give any justification for the government to adopt measures violating the civil and political rights? If so, exactly which rights should be limited and how would that contribute to the realization of economic and social rights?

Unfortunately, the debate within the United Nations was for nearly two decades polarized on this matter, and pursued at a level of generalization which made it near impossible to discuss the real issues. A cleavage emerged in the Commission between two basically different approaches to the further realization of human rights.

The predominantly Western approach was to concentrate on civil and political rights, and to search for the establishment of machineries which could serve either as a recourse procedure or as a control mechanism. The relationship between these two sets of machineries remained vague, due to different priorities, but one proposal dominated the thinking in the Western group for some time: the possible establishment of a High Commissioner for Human Rights.

The other approach took its inspiration from the Proclamation of Teheran, focusing on measures to transform social and international conditions in order to make the enjoyment of human rights for all a possibility.

From 1973, these two approaches were merged into one agenda item called 'Alternative ways and means ... for the promotion of human rights by the United Nations'. Under this heading, widely differing conceptions such as the Human Rights Commissioner and the pursuit of structural transformation were debated. By 1976, the dominant trend was to insist on structural changes as the major road in the implementation of human rights. The 'right to development', to which we return below, was first expressed in a resolution by the Commission in 1977.

D. *Declaration on Social Progress and Development*

The Declaration on Social Progress and Development, adopted by the General Assembly in 1969, can be seen as a significant step in the follow-up of the UDHR. This Declaration did not emerge from the Commission on Human Rights, but from the Commission on Human Development. It gives broad attention to human rights, and is one of the few early UN instrument to bring together human rights and development.

In the Preamble of the Declaration on Social Progress and Development, the General Assembly declares itself convinced that "man can achieve complete fulfilment of his aspirations only within a just social order...."

> It is consequently of cardinal importance to accelerate social and economic progress everywhere, thus contributing to international peace and solidarity.

The Assembly recognized that the primary responsibility for the development of the developing countries rests on those countries themselves, but pointed to the pressing need to narrow and eventually close the gap in the standards of living between the economically more advanced countries and the developing countries

To that end, Member States shall, according to the Preamble of the UDHR, have the responsibility to pursue internal and external policies designed to promote social development throughout the world, and in particular to assist developing countries to accelerate their economic growth.

The Declaration on Social Progress and Development underlines the need to transfer resources from armament and conflict to peaceful activities and social progress. It also states that the primary task of all States and international organizations is to eliminate from the life of society all evils and obstacles to social progress, particularly such evils as inequality, exploitation, war, colonialism and racism.

In the operative part, a conception of development is presented and the consequences drawn are as follows:

> Social progress shall be founded on respect for the dignity and value of the human person and shall ensure the promotion of human rights and social justice, which requires...the final elimination of all forms of inequality, exploitation of peoples and individuals,...and the recognition and effective implementation of civil and political rights as well as

economic, social and cultural rights.

E. The Right to Development

On 4 December 1986, the General Assembly in resolution 41/128 adopted the Declaration on the Right to Development. It was the result of many years of negotiations, sometimes very conflicting. In its Preamble, it refers implicitly to UDHR article 28 by:

Considering that under the provisions of the Universal Declaration of Human Rights everyone is entitled to a social and international order in which the rights and freedoms set forth in that Declaration can be fully realized.

The General Assembly goes on to state, in the Preamble, that it is:

Concerned at the existence of serious obstacles to development, as well as to the complete fulfillment of human beings and of peoples, constituted, *inter alia*, by the denial of civil, political, economic, social and cultural rights, and considering that all human rights and fundamental freedoms are indivisible and interdependent and that, in order to promote development, equal attention and urgent consideration should be given to the implementation, promotion and protection of civil, political, economic, social and cultural rights and that, accordingly, the promotion of, respect for and enjoyment of certain human rights and fundamental freedoms cannot justify the denial of other human rights and fundamental freedoms.

In operative article 3, the Declaration on the Right to Development asserts that States have the primary responsibility for the creation of national and international conditions favourable to the realization of the right to development, but that States have the duty to co-operate with each other in ensuring development and eliminating obstacles to development. States should realize their rights and fulfil their duties in such a manner as to promote a new international economic order based on sovereign equality, interdependence, mutual interest and co-operation among all States.

F. The General Norms and the Supporting Instruments

Taken together, the Declaration on Social Progress and Development and the Declaration on the Right to Development can be held to constitute the normative framework for the transformation of the 'right' contained in article 28 of the UDHR to social reality.

They are both formulated on a general level, but numerous building blocks have been established which can serve as pillars for their realization.

In a paper[11] prepared for a global consultation on the right to development, held by the UN Centre for Human Rights in Geneva on 8–12 January 1990, Kunanayakam has provided an overview of these instruments. They include, in addition to what has already been mentioned above (the UN Charter, the ILO Constitution, the two Covenants on Human Rights, the Declaration on Social Progress and Development, and the Declaration on the Right to Development) at least the following: ILO Convention no. 87 on the Freedom of Association and the Right to Organise (1948); the Declaration on the Granting of Independence to Colonial Countries and Peoples (General Assembly resolution 1514 (XV), 1960); the Declaration in Permanent Sovereignty over Natural Resources (General Assembly resolution 1803 (XVII), 1962); Final Act of the First United Nations Conference on Trade and Development (E/Conf.46/141, 1964); the International Covenant on the Elimination of All Forms of Racial Discrimination (1965); Declaration on Principles of International Law concerning Friendly Relations and Cooperation among States in accordance with the Charter (General Assembly resolution 2625 (XXV), 1970); the Universal Declaration on the Eradication of Hunger and Malnutrition (adopted by the World Food Conference 1974, endorsed by General Assembly resolution 3348 (XXIX), 1974); Charter of Economic Rights and Duties of States (General Assembly resolution 3281 (XXIX), 1974); ILO Convention no. 141 on Rural Workers (1975); Declaration of Principles and Programme of Action of the World Employment Conference (E/5857, 1976); Report of the World Conference on Agrarian Reform and Rural Development (A/54/485, 1979); Convention on the Elimination of All Forms of Discrimination against Women (1979); ILO convention no. 169 on the Rights of Indigenous and Tribal Peoples in Independent Countries (1989); and the Convention on the Rights of the Child (1989). Many more could be added. Space does not allow a survey here on the commitments expressed in these documents towards the building of a social and international order in which all human rights can be fully enjoyed. The problem at this

---

[11] Kunanayakam, UN doc. HR/RD/1990/Conf.1.

stage, however, is not the lack of texts but of their effective implementation.

IV. Future Implementation

While article 28 is phrased in general and vague terms, the subsequent normative elaboration referred to above provides a composite and detailed framework for its operationalization.

Implementation of the obligations and commitments contained in the many instruments reviewed (many of them containing only moral and political, not strictly legal obligations) have to be taken more seriously than they have been so far, and to be carried out both at the national and the international level.

It should not be overlooked, however, that major achievements have already been made since the adoption of article 28. The international order has been substantially changed by the successful process of decolonization; most cases of gross racial discrimination have been brought to an end. Namibia has become a fully independent State; South Africa is in a process of transformation; all the major elements of apartheid legislation have been eliminated except that universal franchise has not yet been adopted; the process of social and political transformation of South Africa is now beginning. With regard to the relationship between the rich and poor countries, changes have occurred but they are going in different directions. Some newly industrialized States have appeared and are doing relatively well; in most Third World States, however, poverty is still very serious and in some places worsening, affected by both the debt crisis and by devastating internal conflicts.

It would be recommendable, first, that all States at the national level seek to implement the Declaration of 1969 on Social Progress and Development. In so doing, they should recognize that democracy both at the national and local levels are essential to development, and that structural inequalities have to be removed through the operation of open and pluralistic democratic processes. A fair distribution of economic and political power among the different sections of society is both an aim of, and a conducive factor to, a healthy democratic development. The recognition that the individual, each and every human being, is the subject of development and not a mere object, is a prerequisite for moving towards the goal outlined in article 28.

At the international level there is an urgent need to relate development activities with the promotion and protection of human rights. This is still in its infancy stage, but the trend is going in the right direction. Both the World Bank and the UN Development Programme have, in the past few years, given indications of interest in the human rights aspects of their work. Human rights bodies, in turn, should take more interest in how development processes in different parts of the world affect the human rights situation.

Obligations of international co-operation by States for the dual task of promotion of human rights and of development, referred to in the UN Charter article 55, need to be given concrete and at least potentially acceptable content and made subject to control mechanisms. This will be the major challenge of the next few years to come, but the instruments already adopted provide a wide set of building blocks which can be joined together for that purpose.

References

Kunanayakam, Tamara, "Annotations to the Declaration of the Right to Development and Related United Nations System Instruments, Resolutions and Reports", HR/RD/1990/Conf.1.

Russell, Ruth, *A History of the United Nations Charter. The Role of the United States 1940–1945*, Washington: The Brookings Institution, 1958.

United Nations Centre of Human Rights, *Human Rights: A Compilation of International Instruments*, Geneva: United Nations, 1988.

United Nations Documents: E/CN.4/SR.67; A/C.3//264; General Assembly Official Records, Third Committee, SR.152.

Articles 29 and 30

The Other Side of the Coin

Torkel Opsahl

Norway

What the Universal Declaration of Human Rights (UDHR) has told us so far is, in a sense, too good to be true. No State would have approved the 28 previous articles without reservation, not even as only 'a common standard of achievement'. The two final articles serve the purpose of meeting needs felt by States, not by undoing everything, but in going some way to redress the balance. In the UDHR itself they occupy a modest position, rather like an afterthought. Their importance has shown itself later, in the context of obligations and their implementation. Here the claim to 'universality' is put to its most critical test.

Article 29: Duties and Limitations

1. Everyone has duties to the community in which alone the free and full development of his personality is possible.
2. In the exercise of his rights and freedoms, everyone shall be subject only to such limitations as are determined by law solely for the purpose of securing due recognition and respect for the rights and freedoms of others and of meeting the just requirements of morality, public order and the general welfare in a democratic society.
3. These rights and freedoms may in no case be exercised contrary to the purposes and principles of the United Nations.

I. General

Article 29 somehow represents the other side of the coin. It reminds us that the individual has not only rights, but also duties (paragraph 1), and that limitations on rights not only may (paragraph 2) but also must (paragraph 3) be drawn. None of these matters, however, are spelt out in any detail. The proclamation of rights in previous articles of the UDHR is thus accompanied by three caveats, brief, but meaningful and very important.

Two of these ideas seem to be obvious and necessary: that the corollary of rights is duties, and that rights are not unlimited. Otherwise, no social balance and harmony would be possible.

However, since the UDHR does not list the duties of the individual, there is no such thing as fundamental or 'human' duties in the same meaning as there are rights. Any catalogue of duties to the community — as one finds in some constitutions — would therefore be to some extent arbitrary, or rather, a matter for domestic law and politics.

Next, it is worth noting that experience has shown the crucial importance of the so-called limitations, sometimes described as restrictions, or even forthright exceptions from rights. Although the terminology differs, the issue of permissible limitations sometimes overshadows the basic principle that a right is supposed to exist, both on the 'domestic' or 'national', and on the international level.

The third element is less obvious. In fact, in the last paragraph it could seem that the parent organization somewhat self-righteously takes the opportunity to claim priority for its own purposes and principles. That the exercise of rights should yield to such considerations might appear doubtful if one thinks of similar statements in a national declaration in favour of the purposes and principles of the nation or its constitution. But it is obviously necessary to balance the exercise of rights with the interests of the world community which the United Nations claims to represent. Maybe the UDHR on this point says either too much or very little.

The three subjects are sufficiently different to be discussed separately (sections II–IV), and another, less visible, ought to be added (section V). But first let us have a look at the background, in particular the *travaux préparatoires*.

Based on statements at the first session of the Commission on Human Rights (the Commission), as well as various constitutions before it, the original Secretariat draft proposed two terse articles on the substance which became article 29, one on the duty of loyalty towards the State and the United Nations, and one on limitations on rights by those of others and the just requirements of the State and the United Nations.[1] Cassin, charged by the Drafting Committee with preparing a draft, then produced three articles, somewhat more flowery, on the task of society being to permit all to develop their personality, without one being sacrificed for others, on man's dependence on society and thus duties toward it, and on limitations of everyone's rights by those of others.[2] A working group of that Committee omitted the 'sacrifice' clause as redundant, and another member (Harry, Australia) proposed a shorter formula expressing the two ideas of duties and limitations. Both versions came before the Commission at its second session, and in its working group Romulo (Philippines) and Amado (Panama), preferring the latter, proposed further drafting amendments which were adopted by the group and the plenary Commission, resulting in a text which became draft article 2 of the UDHR.[3]

The Commission at its third session decided at the request of Chang (China) to move it from the second article to the next to last one, because it was not logical to foresee limitations before mentioning the rights. Also the order of the sentences (later paragraphs) on limitations and duties was reversed on the suggestion of Cassin, and there was a debate on whether to prefer the term 'general welfare' as the basis of restrictions, rather than 'democratic State' which had no commonly accepted definition (Chile, United Kingdom, India), but Eastern European members (Byelorussia, Yugoslavia) recalling threats to democracy said that the term should be preserved; 'democratic society' was then suggested instead of 'democratic State' by Hood (Australia), but Pavlov (Soviet Union) wanted both of these terms included. Cassin assured him that respect for the law was included in general welfare; later, however, the words 'morality' and 'public order' were nevertheless added to the limitation clause, as well as the mention of 'in a democratic society' at the end.[4] Without explanation, duties to the 'community' came instead of 'society' in the first paragraph.

Coming before the General Assembly the draft thus adopted by the Commission went through further significant changes. After a debate about the situation of Robinson Crusoe between the Belgian

---

[1] Verdoodt 1964, pp. 262–264, with quotations.
[2] Quoted by Verdoodt 1964, p. 264.
[3] Quoted by Verdoodt 1964, p. 266.
[4] For details see Verdoodt 1964, p. 267.

and Soviet members, the Third Committee, by a vote of 23:5:14, adopted the latter's proposal (first made by Watt, Australia, but withdrawn when opposed) to insert after 'community' the words 'in which alone' full personal development 'is possible'. Conflicting statements were made about the interpretation of this clause.[5] And the limitation clause was supplemented, as argued by Jimenez de Arechaga (Uruguay), by the words 'established by law...(etc.)' and only for the said purposes. Beaufort (the Netherlands) supported this on the condition that the law could include also regional or local measures but above all that it referred to a democratic country, not a dictatorship where public opinion did not influence the law. The addition was adopted by a vote of 21:15:7. Proposals to include references to more purposes of limitation, such as national sovereignty, solidarity or security, or loyalty and good faith, were not insisted upon because others felt they were already covered by 'general welfare', or 'morality'. The latter term in return was feared by some but they were silenced by the observation that 'welfare' was too materialist to stand alone.[6] Suggestions and comments were also made about the term 'democratic society' as covering both community, State and international order.

Finally, the third paragraph proposed by Cassin and Hamdi (Egypt), referring to the purposes and principles of the United Nations was added after a vote of 34:2:6.

Thus the article, as quoted above, was adopted by the Third Committee (41:0:1) and the Assembly (unanimously).

Although the UDHR is not as such a legally binding instrument, it is possible and perhaps useful and necessary to interpret it, as any other recommendation, for various purposes: to give it the weight it (still) deserves as a recommendation; to measure the achievement of it everywhere as 'a common standard'; or to preserve it as an ideal, perhaps unattainable, which should nevertheless not be diluted. For purposes of the law it serves also as a background and historical source to binding provisions in regional, global and functional instruments to which some references will be made below, as throughout this book. Otherwise its recommendations today are primarily relevant in areas or countries not yet covered by such instruments, or for new issues where its spirit may offer guidance.

---

[5] Verdoodt 1964, p. 268.
[6] Verdoodt 1964, p. 296.

The UDHR is still fundamental because of its prestige, and because what it says to a large extent is still evident in the prevailing opinion. But this position of the document and its message is only preserved on a general level. The issues have changed. And the authority of the message could be challenged on various grounds.

Basically the UDHR is a recommendation by a General Assembly 40 years ago, composed of the relatively few (56) governments then voting in the World Organization. Many of them were governed by regimes whose legislation and recommendations have since long lost their persuasive force. The style of international and national discourse has developed and many more actors now have a say. The world's women were poorly represented, and very many of the world's nations and peoples were subject to foreign domination. The matters dealt with in the earlier articles are easier to specify, illustrate and visualize than the very abstract notions of article 29. One must wonder what kind of universality can be achieved through interpretation in this respect. Maybe it should be admitted that universality did not pre-exist, and cannot be imposed, but must be created, in this regard.

Verdoodt,[7] basing himself on the *travaux préparatoires*, has offered an interpretation reflecting the developments and elements summarized above. But the UDHR has to be regarded as a living instrument, to be understood and applied today in the light of later practice and experience as well.[8]

II. Duties

The "duties to the community" referred to in article 29(1) of the UDHR are not listed as are the rights. Thus we do not find there any international basis for singling out 'fundamental' or 'human' duties in the same meaning as there are rights. However, the African Charter on Human and Peoples' Rights (African Charter), for instance, has codified such duties. Some national constitutions have them, too. Domestic law and politics are very often concerned with individual duties, towards others as well as towards the public, on loyalty, military and other service, or taxes. Generally, the

---

[7] Verdoodt 1964, pp. 270–271.
[8] On the dynamic interpretation of the Declaration, see for instance Alston 1983, p. 60ff.

situations within the nations differ. The Nordic States have made extensive use of the legislative power in this respect.

In fact, it may be argued that although a balance is required between rights and duties, it is no task for international instruments to deal with them in equal depth. In almost any society the balance of power is overwhelmingly in favour of the State. That is why the individual needs international protection for his fundamental rights and freedoms. Usually there is no corresponding need for an international protection of a State's claims against individuals.

As no authorized international catalogue of the individual's duties to his community exists, any analysis, listing or classification should serve some purpose. The following observations concern first the meaning of article 29(1), and next how the same idea is reflected elsewhere, especially in related instruments.

According to Wieruszewski[9] there was agreement that there should be some provision on the duties of man, but the controversy was who should be the counterpart: society or community — meaning the non-organized collective. The second point of view prevailed. Another point of controversy was whether the duties should be formulated in detail. One of the viewpoints expressed was that it should be mentioned precisely what duties were meant. It was also said that rights and duties should be expressed more clearly. The final result was a compromise. The doctrine claims that article 29 should be interpreted in accordance with article 30, i.e., not to limit the human rights of the individual. And as remarked by Verdoodt[10], the *travaux préparatoires* suggest an interpretation based on the terms in paragraph 1 about personal development, to the effect of recognizing otherwise an implicit right to revolt, of which the Preamble speaks openly.[11]

A. Follow-up to the Duties Approach

The Preambles to both International Covenants of 1966 refer to the individual's "duties to other individuals and to the community to which he belongs" (fifth preambular paragraph in both Preambles). Wieruszewski sees this as evidence that the authors of the

[9] Wieruszewski 1984, p. 48.
[10] Verdoodt 1964, p. 270.
[11] On the drafting history of the proposed right to resistance against tyranny, see Rosas, chapter on Article 21.

Covenants supported the idea expressed in article 29. This is not surprising. But they have not made the idea much more specific, nor have they (unlike the idea of limitations, below, section III) included it among the binding provisions. The latter course would be difficult; a listing of duties would arguably have to be seen as exhaustive and thus limit the national lawmaker more than States would be likely to accept.

A survey from 1976 of national responses — comments by governments to a questionnaire — although incomplete, reveals interesting features.[12] They range from such observations as that the "Constitution does not set fundamental rights against 'basic duties', but this does not mean that...legislation does not impose duties on citizens (for example, compulsory military service)" (Austria); "The duties of the individual to the community are not codified as such" (Barbados); and even that "the law...does not impose on the individual any specific duties towards the community" (Mauritius); to detailed lists of solemnly worded provisions ('honour and sacred duty' to work, do military service, etc.). Supplementing these responses, a review of other countries' constitutions and legal systems gave further material,[13] some with a rather harsh flavour, such as: "Those who lay hands on social property are enemies of the people," and: "Betrayal of the people is the greatest felony" (Albania, Constitution articles 35 and 36, on the duties to safeguard social property and do military service). The link between rights and duties is sometimes stated directly: "Citizen's exercise of their rights and freedoms is inseparable from the performance of their duties and obligations" (Soviet Constitution of 1977, article 59).

Daes states a number of obligations which in her thinking somehow seem to be implicit in article 29. However, the precise status of her catalogue is unclear, perhaps deliberately.[14] The list begins with a detailed statement of the duty to respect peace and

---

[12] Daes 1983, pp. 21–31.

[13] Daes 1983, pp. 32–38.

[14] The catalogue summarized here is preceded by the following comments: "227. The basic difference between law and morality is that morality is conceived as a system composed of duties. 228. Law is the synthesis of factors including morality. The Special Rapporteur does not believe that an antithesis between law and morality exists. 229. With these principles, preconditions and considerations in mind, as well as those mentioned earlier (reference), the duties and responsibilities discussed in section G below should, in conclusion, be considered as the individual's basic duties to the community." Daes 1983, p. 53.

security, the question of a duty to refrain from any propaganda for war, and advocacy of national, racial or religious hatred, duties to humanity, observance of international law, respect for general welfare, to review and resist, etc., including obedience to the law — with reservations. She also distinguishes categories in her list. Duties to the community and to other individuals are set out separately. Some are linked to rights, for example, to work and to education, some to special instruments, in particular the list of duties set out in the American Declaration of the Rights and Duties of Man. Duties of aliens, refugees and stateless persons are also mentioned, as well as miscellaneous duties provided for by national legislation. The down-to-earth nature of the latter list (including 'pay taxes') in comparison to some other items, is striking, and it ends with other 'law-made' duties without specification. Many of the statements by Daes seem open to further debate. The merit of her survey lies in its variety which provides food for thought. Daes applies a very broad concept of obligation. Wieruszewski finds her distinction between obligations toward individuals and towards society imprecise.

The attempt demonstrates disparity rather than universality in the area of duties to the community.[15]

Other relevant instruments are, as already suggested, more specific. Besides the list of duties in the American Declaration,[16] the African Charter deserves particular attention. In its Chapter II — Duties, article 27(1) states that every individual "shall have duties towards his family and society, the State and other legally recognized communities and the international community", a principle which obviously cannot be regarded as self-executing; article 28 states a duty to "respect and consider his fellow beings without discrimination" and to "maintain relations aimed at...mutual respect and tolerance", which is also not very precise; while article 29 of the Charter lists these duties:

[15] Daes recommended preparation of a draft declaration on the principles governing the responsibilities of the individual. This was authorized by the Sub-Commission in its resolution 1982/24 and the Commission by decision 1984/52 established a Working Group which as of 1988 had not completed the draft, see United Nations 1988, pp. 51–52.
[16] On the other hand the American Convention on Human Rights (ACHR) of 1969 only contains a short article 32 on duties and limitations generally, in substance if not in terms quite close to article 29(1) and (2) of the UDHR.

1.   To preserve the harmonious development of the family and to work for the cohesion and respect of the family; to respect his parents at all times, to maintain them in case of need;
2.   To serve his national community by placing his physical and intellectual abilities at its service;
3.   Not to compromise the security of the State whose national or resident he is;
4.   To preserve and strengthen social and national solidarity, particularly when the latter is threatened;
5.   To preserve and strengthen the national independence and the territorial integrity of his country and to contribute to its defence in accordance with the law;
6.   To work to the best of his abilities and competence, and to pay taxes imposed by law in the interest of the society;
7.   To preserve and strengthen positive African cultural values in his relations with other members of the society, in the spirit of tolerance, dialogue and consultation and, in general, to contribute to the promotion of the moral well-being of society;
8.   To contribute to the best of his abilities, at all times and at all levels, to the promotion and achievement of African unity.

Much could be said about this list and its possible use, or even abuse, by States and governments. Here it must suffice to note that it would not look good to enforce it or any part of it directly as the sole basis, for example, for trial and punishment. The condition 'imposed by law' linked to taxes in paragraph 6 (above) ought to apply more generally to the whole list of duties.

A non-governmental initiative to draft a universal declaration on the duties of man was launched by the Armand Hammer Foundation in 1981. Authors tried to work out a catalogue drawn from different constitutions. A draft was circulated for comments in 1982. Its whereabouts and later fate are unknown to the present author.[17]

However, the moral and political appeal of the idea of basic duties should not be ignored. As an illustration one might recall Mahatma Gandhi's response to UNESCO's inquiry in 1947 when he and other moral and cultural leaders were asked to comment on the project of a UDHR. Declining to give a substantial answer he observed briefly that "All rights to be deserved and preserved came

[17] The information is based on a correspondence from the said Foundation, later discontinued.

from duty well done. Thus the very right to live accrues to us only when we do the duty of citizenship of the world. From this one fundamental statement, perhaps it is easy enough to define the duties of Man and Woman and correlate every right to some corresponding duty to be first performed. Every other right can be shown to be a usurpation hardly worth fighting for."[18]

This brings up the legislative needs of mankind today. They are often said to concern values that have been expressed in human rights terminology, sometimes called a 'third generation' or 'dimension' of human rights, respectively 'collective' or 'solidarity' rights. Behind this terminology are serious concerns such as development, security, peace, and environment. But the legislative needs cannot simply be met by recognizing new individual rights; rather there is a need for more international law, setting out more duties and responsibilities of individuals, as well as for groups and States.

B. *The Nordic Countries*

Despite differences in the constitutional history of the Nordic countries there is broad parallelism between them as regards duties of individuals; the constitutions do not refer to many of them. More generally, they must either follow from the law or be freely undertaken, as contractual obligations. The law can only impose duties in the ways and by the authorities provided for by a constitution based on democratic principles. Usually they are derived from legislative acts of parliament, even though other constitutional procedures also exist.[19] The prevailing attitudes in such matters as criminal, fiscal and administrative policies are largely similar in the Nordic countries. Therefore the person facing sanctions for an offence, the taxpayer, or the enterprise or person subject to administrative requirements, can expect comparable outcomes although procedural arrangements may differ. There are safeguards and remedies against any arbitrary or unreasonable imposition of duties.

[18] UNESCO 1949, p. 18.
[19] The Norwegian Constitution, for instance, recognizes special procedures different from ordinary legislation, for imposing taxes and provisional ordinances, and accepts considerable delegation of legislative functions from the legislature to the executive.

All of this can be assumed to be in the spirit of the UDHR when article 29(1) is read in its context, although it does not say anything about it.

III. Limitations of Rights

The UDHR sometimes, even today, is presented and relied on as if its rights were absolute and did not allow for any limitations.[20] This, of course, was never true. With hindsight anyone must see how crucial the limitation issues are. While the UDHR saves them to the end, and almost hides them in article 29(2), they turn up in the front line in all the conventions and in the practice of their implementation. What is true is that they often present difficulty, on many levels, not only in law, but also from the moral point of view. The balance between the individual and society can be struck in many ways, and universal agreement is as difficult to achieve or create here as concerning duties to the community.

Obviously, each system implementing the programme of the UDHR more or less defines the rights it protects. To define a right is in fact at the same time to limit it: it excludes what it does not cover. What is positively described as its content indicates its limits.

However, limitations are expressed in other ways as well, familiar to anyone with some experience of legal texts. Many alternatives exist, explicitly described as limitations, restrictions, exceptions or in terms such as "shall, however, not include." The logic is often the same, whatever drafting is adopted.

In making human rights binding, nationally and internationally, lawmakers have resorted to many such techniques of limitation. At first sight they may appear deceptive, like the small print on the back of the standard contract formula. Some are politically controversial, or perhaps overcautious. But only the most naïve

---

[20] The author has experienced this with some spokesmen of non-governmental organizations, e.g., as regards freedom of expression (article 19), and even government representatives, such as the chief US delegate to the Conference on Security and Co-operation in Europe (CSCE) Vienna meeting, as regards freedom of belief (article 18), according to press reports in the *International Herald Tribune*; on the latter point a compromise statement in the Concluding Document of January 15, 1989, Principles, no. 17 seems to contain a "contradiction of sorts" apparently reflecting that position, see Tretter 1989, p. 264.

could say that all such techniques should be avoided.

The technique adopted in the UDHR, instead of raising the limitation issue at every point, is first to refer only to rights in 28 articles altogether, and then to add, once and for all, article 29 as set out above.

As for limitations it refers, more precisely, only to the exercise of rights, thus implying, perhaps, for instance that the rights themselves cannot be limited in substance. But it is submitted that there is no real difference between the substance and the exercise of a right. Similarly, although article 29, which we must remember is primarily a recommendation, only speaks about 'limitations', it also must apply equally to 'restrictions', 'exceptions', or the like.

It is important to note the difference between limitations that an international text itself makes, and limitations that text allows States to make for purposes of their own domestic law. Article 29(2) refers to the latter category.

The reasons which may justify such domestic limitations are basic values 'in a democratic society'. This clause apparently intends to bar rulers without a genuine mandate from the people from invoking morality, public order and the general welfare. The limitations must also be based on law in the wide sense discussed in the General Assembly (above under section II). But when these conditions are met, the universality of human rights yields to national standards.

On the national level the constitution may recognize human rights, generally or in specific terms, and at the same time permit restrictions or limitations. Very often these are not determined by the constitution itself, but laid down in ordinary legislation or perhaps even in other ways.

Previous chapters in this book have considered a number of norms of international human rights law where this point is further illustrated. Following the pattern laid out in article 29(2), a common feature of such norms is their reference to national law which may lay down limitations in further detail. Central among the binding international instruments are the two 1966 International Covenants, together with the regional and specialized conventions. But their drafters have had to be more specific. Unlike the UDHR, most other instruments of human rights deal with the issue of limitations in the context of each right, thus bringing it to attention more directly.[21]

---

[21] Sieghart 1983, pp. 89–90, has tried to group and table these clauses in the main instruments.

Some examples are the articles on freedom of movement in the International Covenant on Civil and Political Rights (CCPR), article 12(3); European Convention on Human Rights (ECHR), Fourth Protocol, article 2; European Social Charter articles 18 and 19; ACHR article 22(3) and (4); and the African Charter article 12(2); or on conscience and religion, the CCPR article 18(3); ECHR article 9(2); ACHR article 12(3);and African Charter article 8. Similarly for the articles, for example, on privacy, opinion and expression, assembly and association, property and fair trial. The terms used in these limitation clauses vary in significant details, but follow the pattern of the UDHR article 29(2) as regards the general conditions (law, necessity, democratic society) and specific justifications (national security, public safety or order, health, morals, rights and freedoms of others, etc.).

On the other hand, some convention rights are drafted in more absolute terms, such as the prohibition against torture and related treatment (CCPR article 7, ECHR article 3). The nature of the UDHR did not make it necessary to distinguish systematically between rights which can be limited ('by law', etc.) as article 29 says, and rights which in this sense are more absolute; nor does the UDHR classify rights as 'derogable' and 'non-derogable' ones. While limitations are permissible in normal conditions, the latter distinction refers to departures from the normal protection in times of emergency (below under section V).

The convention provisions recognizing national limitations are often interpreted and applied by competent international organs acting under the conventions (below). Moreover, experts have sought to 'codify' unofficial guidelines in this area.[22] Such attempts are clearly more inclined to favour the individual than one can expect the competent international bodies to be. This can probably be demonstrated in a study of the cases decided by them. There are, however, a considerable number of cases where the restriction relied on by a State was found by the European Commission and Court of Human Rights or the Human Rights Committee under the CCPR to go beyond what the relevant provision allows, correctly applied.

The international review of the application of national limitation clauses, in practice, typically takes place, for instance, as follows. A complaint against Sweden of an interference in family life by the

---

[22] See, in particular "The Siracusa Principles", *Human Rights Quarterly*, 1985, and *The ICJ Review*, no. 36, June 1986.

authorities depriving a parent of custody, was met with the argument that the measure was lawful and necessary in the interest of the children because of insufficient parental care. The European Court of Human Rights (European Court) accepted the need for placing the children in foster homes. However, the way the measure was carried out went too far; the children were separated far from each other and the parent, in breach of ECHR article 8 and its right to respect for family life by making family visits and possible reunification more difficult than necessary.[23] The seizure of a paper in the United Kingdom and prohibition of its publication of certain articles about pending proceedings before national courts, was in the government's view justified as being in accordance with the law on 'contempt of court'. The European Court, however, found this to be a breach of the right to freedom of expression and information under ECHR article 10 because in all the circumstances the measures were not necessary in a democratic society.[24]

Through these and many other cases certain maxims have been laid down by the independent international organs. The law on which an interference is based, must be accessible and foreseeable. The enumeration in the conventions of recognized purposes is exhaustive. Other purposes, such as the wish to save money and achieve administrative efficiency, cannot be pursued. And the necessity of applying a limitation depends on whether there is a reasonable proportion between the purpose to be achieved and the measures adopted.[25] Non-discrimination is an additional condition for accepting limitations otherwise allowed. Doctrines originally suggesting 'inherent limitations', or 'inherent features of deprivation of liberty' as a sufficient basis for restrictions not covered by the express clauses, have been discarded in subsequent practice. On the other hand, the internationally competent organs accept that States have a 'national margin of appreciation' in these matters.

---

[23] The Olsson Case, European Court of Human Rights, Series A No. 130 (1988).

[24] Many arguments had to be examined and the European Court was divided (11 against 9 judges), The Sunday Times Case, European Court of Human Rights, Series A No. 30 (1979).

[25] While prosecution for blasphemy may be justifiable under ECHR articles 9 and 10 and CCPR articles 18 and 19, capital punishment would in most countries today seem to be out of proportion to this kind of offence; but the Salman Rushdie affair has shown that Islamic law as understood in Iran requires such penalty for this offence.

In the Nordic countries the individual does not have to accept interferences with his rights and freedoms without a basis in the domestic law, any more than he has to accept duties arbitrarily imposed on him. But legislation balancing the rights and freedoms of the individual against social concerns of the kinds accepted in article 29(2) and the conventions based on its precepts, is complex and contains many limitations requiring difficult assessments. For two reasons there is always the possibility that an international review may find against even a correct national application of such legislation, as in one of the examples mentioned above. In the first place, the international human rights law to this day has not been clearly considered to be directly applicable in four of the Nordic countries (all except Finland). Secondly, when the requirement 'necessary in a democratic society' is reviewed internationally, it may in some cases lead to an adverse finding although the national law as such conforms to the international norms allowing for limitations of rights.

IV. Priority for United Nations Purposes and Principles

In the drafting history the proposed concept of 'duties to the State and the United Nations' appeared at one stage. Only a 'world law' or 'world federal government' could have implemented such a concept. Instead, it was reduced to duties to the community (paragraph 1), as well as the third paragraph of article 29. In the present stage of international law and organization this is the logical outcome. But it raises certain problems of interpretation.

It is not evident when or how the exercise of human rights could possibly be contrary to the purposes and principles of the United Nations. Such a prohibition could not, even if appearing in a binding instrument, be regarded as self-executing.

Jimenez de Arechaga (Uruguay) voting against this clause, envisaged an example. He explained his fear that the provision would make it possible to prohibit criticism of the United Nations, which should be freely discussed in view of the freedom of speech.[26] However, in the light of article 30 (below) the prohibition against exercising rights contrary to the purposes and principles of the United Nations cannot mean that there should be

---

[26] Verdoodt 1964, p. 269.

no freedom of expression on this point, for instance as regards criticism and reform of the United Nations.[27]

'Purposes and principles' seem not to be limited to those laid down as such in the Charter of the United Nations, or later amendments. Any codifications or general practices in other forms which define or redefine fundamental policies of the United Nations ought to be treated likewise—in areas such as say, racial integration, protection of minorities, disarmament, development or environment — as being 'purposes and principles' of the organization. Admittedly, this might seem to go too far, and trying to answer these questions is of limited interest. Like the rest of the UDHR they do not concern applicable law, but rather metalegal issues. And the principle would need to be made more specific before it could become operational, in matters such as crimes against peace, war crimes, terrorism, dictatorship, apartheid, denial of political rights, or abuse of rights (which rather should be considered under article 30, below).

V. Derogation?

An extreme sort of limitation not discussed above is the emergency derogation of human rights. More than normal limitation, derogation means temporary suspension or restrictions beyond those authorized in normal times. Not mentioned explicitly in the UDHR (but perhaps implied in article 30, below), it is nevertheless a well known phenomenon. At the same time, indispensable from the point of view of governments and lending itself to abuse from the point of view of the citizens, the declaration of a public emergency either threatens the recognized values, or sacrifices them for the higher value.

The UDHR nowhere deals expressly with emergencies justifying departures from the rights, i.e., derogations rather than such limitations as are allowed in normal circumstances. Silence on this point does not have to mean that the issue was not known to authors. Since there is no reference to derogation in a national emergency, Verdoodt[28] concluded that each of the articles of the UDHR remain valid in these extreme situations. This point of view, however, begs the question of how far 'limitations' or measures to

---

[27] See also Verdoodt 1964, p. 271.
[28] Verdoodt 1964, p. 271 with note 23.

defend human rights may go in such situations. The silence of the UDHR is hardly decisive. Governments are not bound to regard the UDHR as more than a desirable standard of achievement, and they will pay less attention to it in an emergency. Article 30 seems, in fact, to give some support to a State's right to resist threats to its existence if its overthrow would destroy human rights. We shall therefore return to the question in that context.

Article 30: The Vicious Circle

Nothing in this Declaration may be interpreted as implying for any State, group or person any right to engage in any activity or to perform any act aimed at the destruction of any of the rights and freedoms set forth herein.

Abuse of human rights provisions is not only conceivable, it probably happens every day, in propaganda, and in oppressive practices. This last article of the UDHR pursues the difficult task of explaining, in the realm of metalegal principles, that rights are not only to be limited, they should not be allowed to be abused. The thought is well known through the slogan "No freedom for the enemies of freedom."

This idea at first sight seems logical and inevitable. But it may also be dangerous; history offers many examples where governments and oppositions are engaged in a struggle leading into a vicious circle of controversial aims and doubtful means. The reference to the State in this article, together with 'group or person', lays the circle bare; the *State* could abuse the enforcement of limitations, aiming at the destruction of, say, a political opposition exercising its rights. On the other side, an opposition group could abuse freedom of expression through violent 'demonstrations' destroying the democratic process. The terrorist is a person who sometimes seeks to justify his unacceptable acts in human rights terms.

Objectively the principle of interpretation stated in article 30 excludes all of these positions. But the legal and political dilemmas of allowing the parties — government or opposition — to be judges in their own cause, are obvious. Only when a third party is entrusted with applying the principle will it become meaningful.

Even then difficult and controversial assessments are called for, as later experience has shown, for instance the prohibition of the Communist Party in the Federal Republic of Germany because of its revolutionary doctrine.[29]

There is no evidence in the background and *travaux préparatoires*[30] that these difficulties were apparent to the drafters of the UDHR — who on this point were mostly concerned with the need to prevent the resurrection of Nazism — or of the European version. The drafters may have entered the article as a common sense 'savings clause' without seeing all its possible implications.

The Daes study[31] goes into the derogation problem, discussing it on the basis of CCPR article 4 and corresponding provisions in other conventions. Emergency derogation could be seen as a kind of extraordinary limitation for a particularly serious situation.

In the binding instruments, States have explicitly reserved to themselves this opportunity not only to impose certain limitations on the rights, but also in emergency situations to suspend them fully or partly "to the extent strictly required by the situation" as some of the relevant provisions say (CCPR article 4, ECHR article 15).

All over the world peoples suffer under gross internal violence or even civil war, often with outside interference. Regimes which have little else in common — both 'good' and 'bad' ones — resort to emergency measures when they face serious crisis. They declare 'states of exception', deploy particular 'security forces' and other 'emergency measures', and exercise 'special powers' to deal with, for instance, revolutionary or secessionist movements caused by political discontent or ethnic conflicts.

Many constitutional orders authorize the exercise of exceptional emergency powers (martial law, states of siege or exception) not only in wartime, but to meet other such threats as well. Besides the use of arms and violence, in practice the most common emergency measures affecting human rights are arrests, searches, internment, summary trials, curfews, censorship and control of organizations

[29] Fawcett 1987, pp. 315-319 points out that the ECHR version of the principle (article 17) presents a problem because it adds "or at their limitation to a greater extent than is provided for in the Convention." Referring to European case law, he describes the position as a dilemma for the combat against terrorism, amounting to 'acquiescence'.

[30] Verdoodt 1964, pp. 272–274.

[31] Daes 1983, Part III, pp. 181–204.

like political parties or trade unions, postponement of elections and other curbs on political activity.

The international instruments, while recognizing as inevitable that a public emergency may justify derogation from some of the rights individuals have in normal times, specify the conditions which must then be present. Moreover, certain rights have to be respected and ensured in all circumstances. The emergency must threaten 'the life of the nation' and be officially proclaimed; and the derogation shall be controlled in relation to the situation, obligations under international law and be non-discriminatory. Derogation must not under any circumstances affect specific rights and shall be notified to other States.

Rules in this area are, as they must be, a compromise between State power and individual freedom. Without such a 'safety valve' it is unlikely that international human rights instruments would have been adopted. They can, however, easily be abused by oppressive regimes. In any event a regime that survives only by emergency powers is a tragic phenomenon, and its claim under the rules may be weak because it is the life of the nation which may be defended, not that of any regime actually in power.

Obviously a derogation, if justified under international human rights law, must mean that rights are neither violated nor terminated. Rather they are suspended, or limited more than otherwise allowed. The legal assessment of these matters, for instance what is 'strictly required', is very difficult, however, and easily influenced by one's sympathies. Some have said that declaring a public emergency and derogating from human rights is an exercise of State sovereignty. True, a nation fighting for its life may be too busy to consider international procedures. Nevertheless, they exist and are available even in times of emergency, as practice has confirmed. Derogation affects the substantive but not the procedural obligations of a State, to report or to answer complaints before international supervisory bodies. Emergency measures may be and have been reviewed by such organs as the European Commission and European Court, for instance, in the cases brought by several States against Greece after the coup of 1967, and by Ireland against the United Kingdom concerning the situation in Northern Ireland after 1971. A government acting in good faith may find it to be in its own interest to defend its action before such a body rather than being condemned by less objective media and opinion.

The position in the Nordic countries is not so dramatic as these illustrations and considerations suggest. Two of them can be mentioned here. In Norway, a doctrine allowing emergency derogations from the normal constitutional order, the 'unwritten law of necessity', was the basis for the exercise of extraordinary powers by the government in exile during the occupation 1940–1945. Against a background of new international tension in 1950 special legislation for emergency situations was enacted. However, throughout these developments it was attempted to draw a distinction between measures derogating from the normal constitutional division of functions between the highest State organs, and measures setting aside the constitutional guarantees for the individual. The former category of derogation took place several times, including the 1940–1945 period, and is authorized on certain conditions by the 1950 legislation; while the latter category, although to some extent accepted by the human rights conventions, was said not to have taken place during the 1940–1945 period[32] and is not foreseen in the 1950 legislation.[33] The history of *Finland* in this respect appears to be more complex. A relevant factor is the power of the Riksdag to derogate from the Constitution in urgent matters by a 5/6 majority. An old State of War Act of 1930, said to be problematic in the light of later human rights developments, is being replaced by new legislation on emergency powers (Bills no. 248/1989 and 249/1989) expected to be adopted in 1991. The new laws are aiming at the harmonization of international and national standards.[34]

---

[32] This view, however, had to admit rather flexible interpretations of some of the constitutional provisions, in particular the prohibition in the Norwegian Constitution article 97 against retroactive law. See the interpretation in relation to the war crimes legislation extending the use of capital punishment and adopted during the wartime and immediately after it, judgment of the Supreme Court of Norway in *Norsk Retstidende* (Norwegian Court Reports) 1946, p. 198.

[33] From the constitutional point of view the permissibility of derogations from entrenched provisions protecting individuals must still depend on the unwritten principles of constitutional emergency law, Andenæs 1990, pp. 545–546. But the Constitution as other Norwegian law should today be understood to conform to international obligations, including the provisions limiting derogation under human rights conventions.

[34] Rosas 1991 (forthcoming).

Conclusion

This concludes our Commentary to the UDHR. After the examination of its articles 29 and 30 as the other side of the coin, we have to admit that its claim to universality could not at once be met in the areas of duties, limitations and derogations. There was not the same need, nor were common standards far enough developed. Instead, it opened a dynamic process of developing a worldwide protection of fundamental rights and freedoms through global, regional and functional instruments. In that process the pioneering and harmonizing role of the UDHR has become more and more obvious.

References

Alston, Philip, "The Universal Declaration at 35: Western and Passé or Alive and Universal", *The ICJ Review*, no. 31, December 1983.

Andenæs, Johs, *Statsforfatningen i Norge*, 7th ed., Oslo: Tano, 1990.

Daes, Irene A., *The Individual's Duties to the Community and the Limitations on Human Rights and Freedoms under Article 29 of the Universal Declaration of Human Rights*, E/CN.4/Sub.2/432/Rev.2, New York: United Nations, 1983.

Fawcett, James E.S., *The Application of the European Convention on Human Rights*, 2nd. ed., Oxford: Oxford University Press, 1987.

Rosas, Allan, "Human Rights at Risk in Situations of Internal Violence and Public Emergency: Towards Common Minimum Standards", in Asbjørn Eide and Jan Helgesen (eds.), *The Future of Human Rights Protection in a Changing World*, Oslo: Norwegian University Press, 1991 (forthcoming).

Sieghart, Paul, *The International Law of Human Rights*, Oxford: Clarendon Press, 1983.

"The Siracusa Principles on the Limitation and Derogation Provisions in the International Covenant on Civil and Political Rights (1984)", *Human Rights Quarterly*, vol. 7, 1985, and *The ICJ Review*, no. 36, June 1986.

Tretter, Hannes, "Human Rights in the Concluding Document of the Vienna Follow-up Meeting of the Conference on Security and Co-operation in Europe of January 15, 1989, An Introduction", *Human Rights Law Journal* 10, 1989.

UNESCO, *Human Rights, Comments and Interpretations*, A Symposium edited by UNESCO, London: Allan Wingate, 1949.

United Nations, *United Nations Action in the Field of Human Rights*, ST/HR/2/Rev.3, New York: United Nations 1988.

Verdoodt, Albert, *Naissance et Signification de la Déclaration Universelle des Droits de l'Homme*, Société d'Etudes Morales, Sociales et Juridiques, Louvain-Paris: Editions Nauwelaerts, 1964.

Wieruszewski, Roman, *Podstawowe obowiazki obywateli PRL* (Duties of the Individual Towards the Community, in Polish), Wroclaw: Polska Akademia Nauk, 1984.

Authors' Biographies

Gudmundur Alfredsson: (1949), Iceland. Secretary of the UN Working Groups on Indigenous Peoples and Minorities, Centre for Human Rights, Geneva. Doctoral Degree in International Law from Harvard Law School (SJD, 1982).

Bård-Anders Andreassen: (1955), Norway. Researcher at the Norwegian Institute of Human Rights, Oslo. Political Science, University of Bergen, Norway.

Pentti Arajärvi: (1948), Finland. Secretary of the Committee for Social Affairs and Health of the Finnish Parliament. Master in Law.

Michael Bogdan: (1946), Sweden. Professor of Private Law, University of Lund. Law degree from the Universities of Prague and Lund. Doctor juris, Prague, 1969; Juris doctor, Lund, 1975.

Hans Danelius: (1934), Sweden. Since 1988, Judge, Supreme Court; since 1982, member of Permanent Court of Arbitration, The Hague; since 1983, member of European Commission of Human Rights, Strasbourg. Bachelor of Law, Stockholm University, 1955; Doctor juris honoris causa, Stockholm University, 1988.

Asbjørn Eide: (1933), Norway. Director, Norwegian Institute of Human Rights, Oslo; member of the UN Sub-Commission on Prevention of Discrimination and Protection of Minorities. Studies in philosophy and law; LL.M., University of Oslo, 1960. Doctor juris honoris causa, Lund University, 1991.

Atle Grahl-Madsen: (1923–1990), Norway. Professor, Doctor juris. Professor of International Law, University of Bergen, Norway.

Lauri Hannikainen: Finland. Doctor of Juridical Science. Research Fellow at the Åbo Akademi Institute for Human Rights.

Maja Kirilova Eriksson: Sweden. Doctor iuris., Professor in International Law at the Law Department in Uppsala, Sweden.

Kent Källström: (1948), Sweden. Lecturer in Private Law at the law faculties in Stockholm and Uppsala; since 1983, Assistant Professor (docent) in Private Law in Uppsala. Jur. kand. 1972 and Juris doctor 1979 at the Faculty of Law, University of Stockholm.

Morten Kjærum: (1957), Denmark. LLM. Since 1991, Director of the Danish Center of Human Rights; Head of asylum department, the Danish Refugee Council from 1985–1991.

Raimo Lahti: (1946), Finland. Professor of Criminal Law, University of Helsinki, since 1979; Head of the Department of Criminal Law and Judicial Procedures since 1989. LL.B. 1966, LL.Lic. 1967, M.Sc. (Pol. Sc.) 1971, LL.D. 1974, all from the University of Helsinki.

Nina M. Lassen: (1957), Denmark. Since 1990, Legal Counsellor at the Danish Refugee Council; Cand. jur., University of Copenhagen, 1987.

Lauri Lehtimaja: (1945), Finland. Legal Adviser, Ministry for Foreign Affairs. Counsellor to Parliamentary Ombudsman (on leave). LL.B., University of Helsinki, 1970; LL.Lic., University of Turku, 1978.

Tore Lindholm: (1941), Norway. Since 1990, Researcher at the Norwegian Institute of Human Rights. From 1963–1973, studied in Oslo and Heidelberg, fields of philosophy of science, and hermeneutics; sociology of science; the theology of Martin Luther.

Jan Mårtenson: (1933), Sweden. UN Under-Secretary-General for Human Rights, is also Director-General of the UN Office at Geneva. Swedish diplomat and a law graduate from the University of Uppsala.

Göran Melander: (1938), Sweden. Director of the Raoul Wallenberg Institute, Lund, Sweden since 1984; since 1974, Assistant Professor (docent) at the University of Lund. Studied law at the University of Lund. Juris doctor at the same university in 1972.

Kristian Myntti: Finland. MSc. Acting Assistant of State Law and International Law at the University of Åbo Akademi, Finland.

Jakob Th. Möller: (1936), Iceland. Since 1971, Chief, Communications Section, Centre for Human Rights. Candidatus juris, University of Iceland, 1967.

Johanna Niemi-Kiesiläinen: (1957), Finland. Assistant in Procedural Law, University of Helsinki. Master of Law, University of Helsinki, 1982; Licenciate of Law, University of Helsinki 1988; specialized in Bankruptcy Law and Refugee Law.

Torkel Opsahl: (1931), Norway. Professor of Law, University of Oslo. Chairman of the Board of the Norwegian Institute of Human Rights since the Institute was established in 1987. Doctor juris, 1965; University of Oslo, Faulty of Law, 1955; postgraduate studies in Salzburg, Moscow and at Columbia University in New York.

Matti Pellonpää: (1950), Finland. Associate Professor of International Law, University of Helsinki; Member of the European Commission of Human Rights. LL.B, LL.Lic., LL.M. and LL.D from the University of Helsinki; LL.M. from the University of Toronto.

Lars Adam Rehof: (1958), Denmark. Since 1991, Associate Professor of Public International Law, University of Copenhagen. Director of the Danish Center for Human Rights, Copenhagen, 1987–1990. LL.M.

Allan Rosas: (1948), Finland. Armfelt Professor of State Law and International Law, Åbo Akademi University; Head of the Åbo Akademi University Department of Law; Director, Åbo Akademi University Institute for Human Rights. LL.B. 1969; LL.M. 1971; LL.D. (Doctor iuris) 1977, all from the University of Turku.

Martin Scheinin: (1954), Finland. Researcher in the Institute of Public Law of the University of Helsinki, participating in a major legal research project "Limits of Law", financed by the Academy of Finland (1986–1992); member of the Human Rights Advisory Board of the Finnish Government. Candidate of Laws, 1982; Licentiate of Laws, 1987, from the University of Turku.

Gunnar G. Schram: (1931), Iceland. Since 1974, Professor of International Law and Constitutional Law, University of Iceland; member of the Constitutional Committee from 1983; legal adviser to the Ministry for the Environment. Law degree, University of Iceland; postgraduate studies in law, University of Heidelberg and Cambridge, 1958–1961.

Sigrun Skogly: (1959), Norway. Since 1989, Honorary Fellow with the Institute of Legal Studies, University of Wisconsin Law School, and Doctoral Candidate, University of Oslo, Norwegian Institute of Human Rights, Law Faculty; since 1990, MacArthur Program Coordinator, Office for International Studies and Programs, University of Wisconsin. LL.M., International Human Rights Law, University of Essex, 1987; College of Europe, Brugge, Belgium, Diplome de Hautes Etudes Européennes, 1984. Cand. mag. degree, University of Oslo, Political Science and Public Law, 1983.